The
Man of Genius

BY

CESARE LOMBROSO

Professor of Legal Medicine at the University of Turin

WITH ILLUSTRATIONS

London
Spradabach Publishing
2022

Spradabach Publishing
BM Box Spradabach
London WC1N 3XX

The Man of Genius
Originally published in Italian as
L'Uomo di genio rapporto alla psichiatria (1888)

First Spradabach published 2022

Interior designed by Alex Kurtagic

ISBN 978-1-999357-39-9

British Library Cataloguing-in-Publication Data:
A catalogue record for this book is available from the British Library.

Table of Contents

PART II
THE CAUSES OF GENIUS

Note on This Edition

The text of the present edition is based on the English-language edition originally published by Water Scott, London, in 1891. The text is reproduced in its entirety, with its original spelling and punctuation, and complete with the original graphs and illustrations.

While the work deals with men of genius, many of whom readers will have at least heard of, a significant proportion of them are either less well known or would be recognised only by readers with specialist knowledge; not all would be considered to have had genius of the first order, or even of the second order (his was noted in a contemporaneous review); and many are mentioned in passing, often as part of a list. For these reasons, biographical footnotes have been added. In a small number of cases, however, it has not been possible to ascertain to whom Lombroso was referring, even from the context of his discussion, due to his reliance on simple surnames and the fact that, particularly given his wide criteria (some would say low threshold), a single surname may be shared by more than one man of genius. In those cases, no footnote has been added, pending more evidence. In the few cases where a positive identification seemed very likely but not completely certain, it has been so indicated in the footnote. In a handful of cases, an individual's name was misspelt in the original text; these have been silently corrected.

The original text came with its own set of footnotes. Among those, the biographical ones have been brought into conformity with the style recommended today by the Modern Language Association. Where the source could not be identified, the footnote has been left as in the original.

Finally, the 1891 index suffered from numerous omissions. A comprehensive new index was prepared for this edition.

Preface

It has never before happened that in the latest edition of a book I have had to disown so much in preceding editions; my first imperfect and spontaneous idea has never before been so modified and transformed, the final form being, perhaps, not even yet altogether attained.

The idea that genius was a special morbid condition had indeed often occurred to me, but I had always repelled it; and besides, without a sure experimental basis, ideas to-day do not count. Like still-born children, they appear but for a moment, to disappear at once. I had been enabled to discover in genius various characters of degeneration which are the foundation and the sign of nearly all forms of congenital mental abnormality, but the exaggerated extension which was at that time given to theories of degeneration, and still more the vague and inexact character of that conception, had repelled me; so that I accepted the facts, but not their ultimate consequences. How, in fact, can one suppress a feeling of horror at the thought of associating with idiots and criminals those individuals who represent the highest manifestations of the human spirit?

But recent teratologic researches, especially those of Gegenbaur,[1] have shown that the phenomena of atavistic retrogression do not always indicate true degradation, but that very often they are simply a compensation for considerable development and progress accomplished in other directions. Reptiles have more ribs than we have; quadrupeds and apes possess more muscles than we do, and an entire organ, the tail, which we lack. It has been in losing these advantages that we have gained our intellectual superiority. When this is seen, the repugnance to the theory of genius as degeneration at once disappears. Just as giants pay a heavy ransom for their stature in sterility and relative muscular and mental weakness, so the giants of thought expiate their intellectual force in degen-

1 Karl Gegenbaur (1826 – 1903) was a German anatomist and professor who demonstrated that the field of comparative anatomy offers important evidence supporting of the theory of evolution. The name appears as 'Gegenbauer' in the original English edition; I have corrected it. —Ed.

eration and psychoses. It is thus that the signs of degeneration are found more frequently in men of genius than even in the insane.

And again, this theory has entered to-day on so certain a path, and agrees so entirely with my studies on genius, that it is impossible for me not to accept it, and not to see in it an indirect confirmation of my own ideas. I find this confirmation in the characters of degeneration recently discovered;[2] and still more in the uncertainty of the theories which were at first advanced to explain the problem of genius. Thus Joly[3] affirms in a too convenient formula that "it is not even necessary to refute the theory of insanity in genius; "for," he says, "strength is not weakness, health is not disease, and for the rest the cases quoted in favour of these hypotheses are only particular cases."[4] But the physician knows that very often, in the delirious and epileptic, strength is precisely an index of

---

2 Valentin Magnan, *Annales Médico-Psychologiques* 6 (1887); Cesare Lombroso, *Tre tribuni studiati da un alienista* (Rome, Turni, Florence: Fratelli Bocca, Librai di S.M., 1887) 3-9, 16-23, 148-150; H. Saury, *Études Cliniques sur la folie héréditaire. (Les dégénerés).* (Paris: Delahaye & Lecrosnier, 1886).

3 Jules-Charles-Henry Joly (1839 – 1925), known as Henry Joly, was a French philosopher and sociologist, who was known in his day for his works in criminology. *The Psychology of the Saints* (1913) seems to be the only work of his available in English. —Ed.

4 Lombroso gives as his source '*Psychologie du Genie*, 1883', but this seems to be an error, and he must have been referring to Joly's *Psychologie des grands hommes* (Paris: Hackette, 1883). —Ed.

disease. As to the second objection, it falls to the ground as facts accumulate. It is certain that there have been men of genius presenting a complete equilibrium of the intellectual faculties; but they have presented defects of affectivity and feeling; though no one may have perceived it, or, rather, recorded it. Up to recent years, historians, being chroniclers rather than psychologists, very careful to transmit to us the adventures and pageantries of princes and peoples, and the wars which have so much importance in the eyes of the multitude, have neglected everything which concerns the psychology of thought. They have very seldom informed us concerning the disorders and degenerative characters which exist in men of genius and their families; while vanity, which is extreme in men of genius, has never allowed them, save in rare instances (such as Cardan,[5] Rousseau,[6] J. S.

5 Gerolamo (or Girolamo, or Geronimo) Cardano (1501 –1576) autobiography, *The Book of My Life*, and presents an unvarnished, cranky, outrageous, and detailed self-portrait.—Ed.

6 Jean-Jacques Rousseau (1712 – 1778)'s biography, titled *Confessions*, was driven by his paranoid delusions and a consequent desire to explain himself fully in the face of real or imagined calumnies by perceived detractors.—Ed.

Mill,[7] Renan[8]), to yield spontaneous revelations of themselves. If Richelieu had not on one single occasion been caught in an epileptic fit,[9] who could ever have guessed it? If it had not been for the recent works of Berti[10] and Mayor,[11] who would have believed that Cavour twice attempted to kill himself? If Taine had not been one of those rare writers who understand what help psychiatry can give

---

7 In his autobiography, John Stuart Mill, FRSE (1806 – 1873) talks mostly about his education and intellectual influences. His father subjected him to a rigorous education, and began teaching him Greek at the age of three. At the same time, Mill *père* neglected his son's emotions, which by his own account left John emotionally sterile and in his 20s sunk him into a deep depression. —Ed.

8 With respect to Joseph Ernest Renan (1823 – 1892)'s autobiography, *Souvenirs d'enfance et de jeunesse* (Paris: Calman Lévy, 1883) a contemporary reviewer wrote 'M. Renan will find freely accused of egotism, of blindness, of an audacious contempt for average opinion, so long as he allows himself to write in teh tone which underlines these strange confessions.' M. A. W., "Renan's Autobiography", *MacMillan's Magazine*, Vol. XLVIII, No. 285 (May 1883 - October 1883) 213 - 227.—Ed.

9 It seems Armand Jean du Plessis, cardinal-duc de Richelieu et de Fronsac (1585 – 1642) did not, in fact, suffer from epilepsy, but rather from psychogenic non-epileptic seizures, manifesting in bouts of tears. There are many conditions that produce paroxysmal attacks or events, which in non-medical, historical literature have been referred to as fits, seizures, or convulsions, but these are not exclusive to epilepsy. —Ed.

10 Domenico Berti, *Il Conde di Cavour Avanti II 1848* (Rome: Voghera Carlo, 1886). —Ed.

11 Edmondo Mayor des Plaches, *Nuove lettere inedite del conte Camillo di Cavour. Con prefazione e note di Edmondo Mayor.* (Turin and Rome: L. Roux & Co., 1895). —Ed.

in the study of history, he would never have been able to surprise those characteristics which make Napoleon's moral insanity manifest to all. Carlyle's wife wrote the narration of her tortures; few wives do as much, and, to tell the truth, few husbands are anxious to publish such narratives.[12] Many persons still regard as an angelic being the celebrated painter Aivożovsky,[13] who succoured hundreds of poor persons and left his own wife and children to die of hunger.

It must be added that moral insanity and epilepsy which are so often found in association with genius are among the forms of mental alienation which are most difficult to verify, so that they are often denied, even during life, although quite evident to the alienist. There are still many estimable

12 After the death of his wife, Jane Welsh, in 1866, and upon reading her diaries and letters, Carlyle (1795 - 1881) was struck by her unhappiness and his own irritability and inconsideration, prompting him to atone by writing a memorial. He then gave this memorial along with a bundle of Jane's papers to his biographer, James Froude, to be published after his death. Froude published the memorial (*Reminiscences*) in 1881, and the letters (*Letters and Memorials of Jane Welsh Carlyle*) in 1883. This proved controversial, but it was, nevertheless, consistent with Carlyle's conviction that the flaws of heroes should be openly discussed, without diminishing their achievements. Carlyle would have preferred no biography were written of him, but, knowing his wishes would not be respected and that several people were waiting for him to die before they published, he appointed Froude one of his literary executors and supplied him with his papers. —Ed.

13 Ivan Konstantinovich Aivazovsky (1817 – 1900), a Russian Romantic painter. —Ed.

persons who doubt the insanity of King Ludwig of Bavaria,[14] and even openly deny it.[15]

There are, also, no individual cases in nature; all particular cases are the expression and effect of a law. And the fact, now unquestioned, that certain great men of genius have been insane, permits us to presume the existence of a lesser degree of psychosis in other men of genius.

But, adds Joly, genius is often precocious; as Raphael at fourteen years of age, Mozart at six, Michelangelo at sixteen; and sometimes it is tardy, with special characteristics, as in Alfieri. This is true; precocious originality is one of the characteristics of genius; but precisely because genius is a neurosis, an accidental circumstance may provoke it even at a comparatively late age, and like every neurosis which depends on irritation of the cerebral cortex it may take on different aspects, according to the spot attacked, while preserving the same nature.

Hailes, in a much praised essay on genius in art, maintains that genius is a continuation of the conditions of ordinary life; thus, as we all write prose we must all have a little genius. But how then does

14 Ludwig II (Ludwig Otto Friedrich Wilhelm), (1845 – 1886), King of Bavaria from 1864 until his death, is said to have been peculiar, eccentric, and irresponsible, but there is no agreement as to clinical insanity. Cf. Ludwig Desing, *Wahnsinn oder Verrat - war König Ludwig II. von Bayern geisteskrank?* (Lechbruck: Verlag Kienberger, 1996). —Ed.

15 Francesco De Renzis, *L'Opera d'un Pazzo* (Rome: Impressioni di viaggio e d'arte, 1887).

it happen, Brunetière[16] rightly objects,[17] that one individual alone becomes a great painter or a great poet? And how is it that so many philosophers affirm, and quite truly, that genius consists in an exaggerated development of one faculty at the expense of others?

The man of genius is a monster, say others. Very well, but even monsters follow well-defined teratologic laws.

Brunetière remarks that there have been men of talent, like Addison and Pope,[18] who were lacking in genius; and men of genius, like Sterne, who were lacking in talent. These two facts, however, are not contradictory; to be lacking in talent, or rather in good sense or common sense, is one of those characters of genius which witness to the presence of neurosis, and indicate that hypertrophy of certain psychic centres is compensated by the partial atrophy of other centres.[19] As to the first

---

16 Ferdinand Brunetière (1849 – 1906), a French writer and critic. —Ed.

17 *Revue des deux mondes* (1886).

18 Joseph Addison (1672 - 1719) co-founded *The Spectator*, along with Richard Steele, for whose *Tatler* he had been a contribor. His best-known work is *Cato, A Tragedy*, which was published with a prologue by Alexander Pope, and which proved influential among figures of the American Revolution. Although he reached position of Secretary of State for the Southern Department, in politics he was of limited ineffectiveness. —Ed.

19 Thus, Laurence Sterne's (1713 - 1768) *The Life and Opinions of Tristram Shandy*, a deliberately frustrating novel that doesn't get much past the subject's birth after six-hundred pages, Lombroso would consider genius because of its originality, but

assertion, it confirms rather than destroys my conclusions. Certainly talent is not genius, just as vice is not crime, but there is a transition from one to the other in virtue of that law of continuity which may be observed in all natural phenomena. *Natura non facit saltus.*[20]

I must confess here that very often in this book I have had to confound genius with talent; not because they are not quite distinct, but because the line that separates them, like that which separates vice from crime, is very difficult to define. A man of scientific genius, lacking in education and opportunities—a Gorini,[21] for example—will appear more sterile than a man of talent, who has been favoured by circumstances from the first.

For the rest—and this is the point which concerns us most—the morbid effects and analogies are the same in both, since the man of talent, even without genius, presents various slight but real abnormalities. A man of even ordinary talent may be so exhausted as to exhibit the pathological central reactions of the most powerful genius, and to leave traces of degeneration in his offspring; and, although it is rare, it is not impossible for the man of talent to descend from the neurotic and insane.

talent-deficient because lacking in good sense. —Ed.

20 Latin: 'nature does not make jumps'. —Ed.

21 Paolo Gorini (1813 - 1881) became known for his work as embalmer and as a pioneer of cremation in Europe. He constructed the cremator at the Woking Crematorium, founded in 1878. Initially he trained as a mathematician. —Ed.

This may easily be explained: talent, like genius, is accompanied by cortical excitation, only in a less degree and in a smaller brain. The true normal man is not the man of letters or of learning, but the man who works and eats—*fruges consumere natus*.[22]

But our nature, it is customary to say, revolts against a conception which tends to lower the most sublime manifestation of humanity to the level of the sorrowfully degenerate, to idiocy and insanity. It is sad, I do not deny, but has not nature caused to grow from similar germs, and on the same clod of earth, the nettle and the jasmine, the aconite and the rose? The botanist cannot be blamed for these coincidences; and since they exist it is not a crime that he should record them as he finds them. Repugnance also is a sentiment, not a reason, and a sentiment, moreover, which has not been shared by the race generally, who long ago reached conclusions—repugnant to the academic world, which sometimes closes its eyes in order not to see—entirely in harmony with the results here presented. We may see this in the most ancient etymologies; in Hebrew as well as in Sanskrit the lunatic is synonymous with the prophet. We may see it, too, in proverbs: "*I matti ed i fanciulli indovinano*;"[23] "*Kinder und Narren sprechen die Wahrheit*;"[24]

22 Latin: Born to consume the fruits of the earth; born only to eat. —Ed.

23 Italian: Fools and children foretell. —Ed.

24 German: Children and fools speak the truth. —Ed.

"*Un fol advise bien un sage*;"[25] "*Sæpe enim est morio valde opportune locutus*."[26] The lunatic, again, among barbarous people is feared and adored by the masses who often confide to him supreme authority.

In modern times the same conviction has been preserved, but in a form, it must be confessed, altogether disadvantageous to genius. Not only is fame (and until recent years even liberty), denied to men of genius during their lives, but even the means of subsistence. After death they receive monuments and rhetoric by way of compensation. And why is this? Neither the jealousy of rivals nor the envy of mediocre men is enough to explain it. The reason is that if we leave out certain great statesmen (though there are exceptions—Bismarck, for example), men of genius are lacking in tact, in moderation, in the sense of practical life, in the virtues which are alone recognized as real by the masses, and which alone are useful in social affairs. "*Le bon sens vaut mieux que le genie*"[27] says an old French adage. And as Mirabeau said, "Good sense is the absence of every strong passion, and only men of strong passions can be great." Good sense travels on the well-worn paths; genius, never. And that is why the crowd, not altogether without reason, is

25 French: A madman advices the sage well. —Ed.

26 Latin: Even a vegetable-grower often speaks very much to the point. Or, as the English proverb goes, 'a gardener has spoken to purpose'. —Ed.

27 French: Good sense is worth more than genius. —Ed.

so ready to treat great men as lunatics, while the lettered crowd cry out when—as I have attempted to do here—this general opinion is attached to a theory.

By some of those persons who have too much good sense—and who do not know that that destroys every great truth, because we reach truth more by remote paths than by smooth and ordinary roads—it has been objected: "Many of these defects that you find in great men may be found also in those who are not men of genius."! This is very true, but it is by the quality and quantity that the abnormal character is marked; and, above all, by the contradiction with the whole of the other characters of their personality, that the abnormality appears. Cooks are vain, but in those matters which refer to their occupation they are not so vain as to believe themselves gods. The nobleman will boast of descent from a mediæval hero, but not of being a sculptor. We are all forgetful sometimes, but not so far forgetful that we cannot recall our own names while at the same time we have an extraordinary memory for our own discoveries. Many have said what Michelangelo said of monks, but they have not afterwards spent large sums in fattening monasteries. In short, it is the doubling and contradiction of personality in genius which reveals the abnormality!

It has again been objected to me that these studies are deficient in utility. To this I might reply with Taine that it is not always necessary that the true should be useful. Yet numerous practical applications arise out of these researches; they furnish us with explanations of those strange religious insanities which become the nucleus of great historical events. The examination of the productions of the insane supply us with new sources of analysis and criticism for the study of genius in art and literature; and, above all, these data bring an important element to the solution of penal questions, for they overthrow for ever that prejudice by virtue of which only those are declared insane, and therefore irresponsible, whose reason has entirely departed, a prejudice which has handed thousands of irresponsible creatures to the executioner. They show us, lastly, that literary madness is not only a curious psychiatric singularity, but a special form of insanity, which hides impulses the more dangerous, because not easy to perceive, a form of insanity, which, like religious insanity, may be transformed into a historical event.

C. LOMBROSO.

PART I

THE CHARACTERISTICS OF GENIUS

CHAPTER I

History of the Problem

Aristotle — Plato — Democritus — Felix Plater — Pascal — Diderot — Modern writers on genius

It is a sad mission to cut through and destroy with the scissors of analysis the delicate and iridescent veils with which our proud mediocrity clothes itself. Very terrible is the religion of truth. The physiologist is not afraid to reduce love to a play of stamens and pistils, and thought to a molecular movement. Even genius, the one human power before which we may bow the knee without shame, has been classed by not a few alienists as on the confines of criminality, one of the teratologic forms of the human mind, a variety of insanity.

This impious profanation is not, however, altogether the work of doctors, nor is it the fruit of modern scepticism. The great Aristotle, once the father, and still the friend, of philosophers, observed that, under the influence of congestion of the head, "many persons become poets, prophets, and sybils, and, like Marcus the Syracusan, are pretty good poets while they are maniacal; but when cured can no longer write verse."[1] And again,

> Men illustrious in poetry, politics, and arts, have often been melancholic and mad, like Ajax, or misanthropic, like Bellerophon. Even in modern times such characters have been noted in Socrates, Empedocles, Plato, and in many others, especially poets.[2]

In the *Phædo*, Plato affirms that

> delirium is by no means an evil, but, on the contrary, when it comes by the gift of the gods, a very great benefit. In delirium, the prophetesses of Delphi and Dodona performed a thousand services for the citizens of Greece; while in cold blood they were of little use, or rather of none. It often happened that, when the gods afflicted men with fatal epidemics, a sacred delirium took possession of some mortal, and inspired him with a remedy for those misfortunes. Another kind of delirium, that inspired by the Muses, when a simple and pure soul is excited to glorify with poetry the deeds of heroes, serves for the instruction of future generations.

---

1 *De Pronost.*, i. p. 7.

2 *Problemata*, sect. xxx.

Democritus was more explicit, and would not believe that there could be a good poet who was not out of his mind:—

> *Excludit sanos Helicone poetas*
> *Deniocritus*[3]

It was, evidently, the observation of these facts, wrongly interpreted and, according to a common habit, transformed into superstitions, which caused ancient nations to venerate the insane as beings inspired from on high. We possess not only the witness of history to this effect, but also that of the words *navi* and *mesugan* in Hebrew and *nigrata* in Sanskrit, in which the ideas of insanity and prophecy are confused and assimilated.

Felix Plater[4] affirmed that he had known persons who, although they excelled in certain arts, were yet mad, and betrayed their infirmity by a curious seeking for praise, and by strange and indecent acts. He had known at Court an architect, a celebrated sculptor, and a distinguished musician, who were mad.[5]

3 Horace, *Ars Poetica*, 296-297

4 Felix Plater (or Platter) (1536 – 1614) was a Swiss physician, professor in Basel, well known for his classification of psychiatric diseases. —Ed.

5 *Observationes in Hominis Affectibus plerisque, Corpori & Animo, Functionum læsione, Dolore, aliave Molestiâ & Vitio infensis*, lib. 10 (Basileæ: Ludovici König, 1641) 305. More singular examples in Italy were collected by F. Gazoni, in the *Hospitale dei folli incurabili*, 1586. [The original edition puts the

Pascal, later on, repeated that extreme intelligence was very near to extreme madness, and himself offered an example of it.[6] Diderot wrote:

> I conjecture that these men of sombre and melancholy temperament only owed that extraordinary and almost Divine penetration which they possessed at intervals, and which led them to ideas, sometimes so mad and sometimes so sublime, to a periodical derangement of the organism. They then believed themselves inspired, and were insane. Their attacks were preceded by a kind of brutish apathy, which they regarded as the natural condition of fallen man. Lifted out of this lethargy by the tumult within

---

publication date as 1620, but that was for the French translation, *L'Hospital des fols incurables, où sont déduites de poinct en poinct toutes les folies et les maladies d'esprit, tant des hommes que des femmes* (Paris: F. Julliot, L. Sevestre, 1620) —Ed.]

6 While still a teenager, Blaise Pascal (1623 – 1662), the French mathematician, physicist, and inventor, began pioneering work on calculating machines; after three years and fifty prototypes, he was one of the first two inventors of the mechanical calculator. He also wrote a significant treatise on the subject of projective geometry at the age of 16. Charles Binet-Sanglé wrote in 1899 that Pascal suffered from 'neurasthenia', and Maurizio Paciaroni, in 'Visual Experiences of Blaise Pascal', in *Neurological Disorders in Famous Artists, Part 3*, edited by Julien Bogousslavsky, M. G. Hennerici, H. Baezner (Basel: Karger, 2010) 160, wrote: 'There is evidence that Pascal suffered from visual migraines with recurrent headaches, episodes of blindness in half of his visual field, zigzag, fortification spectra, and other visual hallucinations. It is believed that the migraine aura experiences might have acted as a source of inspiration for Pascal's philosophical reflections.' —Ed.

> them, they imagined that it was Divinity, which came down to visit and exercise them. . . . Oh! how near are genius and madness! Those whom heaven has branded for evil or for good are more or less subject to these symptoms; they reveal them more or less frequently, more or less violently. Men imprison them and chain them, or raise statues to them.[7]

Many examples of men who were at once mad and highly intelligent were offered by Hécart *in his Stultitiana, ou Petite biographie des fous de la ville de Valenciennes, par un homme en démence* [1823]; by Delepierre,[8] an enthusiastic bibliophile, in his curious *Histoire littéraire des Fous* (1860); by Forgues,[9] in *Revue de Paris* (1826); and by an anonymous writer in *Sketches of Bedlam* (London, 1823).[10]

On the other hand, it was shown in Lélut's *Démon de Socrate* (1836) and *Amulette de Pascal*

7 Diderot, *Dictionnaire Encyclopédique*.

8 Gabriel Antoine Joseph Hécart (1755 – 1838) was, like Joseph Octave Delepierre (1802 – 1879), a bibliophile and antiquarian. —Ed.

9 French literary critic, writer, and translator, Paul-Émile Daurand-Forgues (1813 – 1883), also known by his pseudonyms Old Nick and Tim, did translations of Charlotte Brontë, John Hanning Speke, Nathaniel Hawthorne, and his friend, Wilkie Collins. —Ed.

10 The original has the year of publication as 1873, but the book was published fifty years earlier, so I have corrected it. —Ed.

(1846),[11] in Verga's[12] *Lipemania del Tasso* (1850) and in my own *Pazzia di Cardano* (1856), that there are men of genius who have long been subject to hallucinations, and even to monomania. Other proofs, the more precious because impartial, were supplied by Réveillé-Parise,[13] in his *Physiologie et Hygiene des homines livrés aux travaux de l'esprit* (1856).[14] Moreau (de Tours),[15] who delighted in the least verisimilar aspects of truth, in his solid monograph, *Psychologie Morbide* (1859), and J. A. Schilling,[16] in his *Psychiatrische Briefe* (1863), endeavoured to show, by researches that were very copious although not very strict in method, that genius is always a neurosis, and often a true insanity. Hagen[17] has more recently sought to prove a the-

11 Louis Francisque Lélut (1804–1877) was a French medical doctor and philosopher; in the above-cited works he claimed Socrates and Blaise Pascal were insane. —Ed.

12 Italian psychiatrist and neurologist Andrea Verga (1811 – 1895) is remembered for his pioneer study of the criminally insane, as well as his early research of acrophobia, a condition from which he personally suffered. —Ed.

13 Joseph-Henri Réveillé-Parise (1782-1852), a French doctor. —Ed.

14 The book was first published in 1834. —Ed.

15 Jacques-Joseph Moreau (1804 – 1884), nicknamed 'Moreau de Tours', was a French psychiatrist and member of the Club des Hashischins. He was the first physician to do systematic work on drugs' effects on the central nervous system, and to catalogue, analyse, and record his observations. —Ed.

16 Johann August Schilling (1829 - 1884), a German physician, psychiatrist, and writer. —Ed.

17 Friedrich Wilhelm Hagen, Jr. (1814 – 1888) was a German

sis which is partly the same in his *Verwandtschaft des Genies mit dem Irrsinn* (Berlin, 1877), and, indirectly, Jürgen-Meyer,[18] in his admirable monograph, *Genie und Talent* (from the *Zeitschrift für Volker-psychologie*, 1879). These two writers have tried to explain the physiology of genius, and, singularly, they have reached conclusions which were reached, more by intuition than through close observation, by an Italian Jesuit, now quite forgotten—Bettinelli[19]—in his book, *Dell'entusiasmo nelle belle Arti* (Milan, 1769).

Radestock,[20] in his *Genie und Wahnsinn* (Breslau, 1884), added little to the solution of the problem, as he merely copied, for the most part, from his predecessors, without profiting greatly by their work.

Among recent writers, I note Tarnowski[21] and Tchukinova, who to the Russian translation of my book (St. Petersburg, 1885) have added many new

---

psychiatrist. —Ed.

18 Jürgen Bona Meyer (1829 – 1897), a German philosopher. —Ed.

19 Saverio Bettinelli (1718 – 1808), an Italian Jesuit writer, whose major works are the literary criticisms and observations of culture. —Ed.

20 Paul Radestock, a 19th-century German pedagogue and translator, and one of physician and psychologist Wilhelm Wundt's many disciples. —Ed.

21 A disciple of Lombroso, Pauline Tarnowski (1848 – 1910) was one of the first women criminologists in Europe and an expert on female criminality in turn-of-the-century France. Her major work was *Étude anthropométrique sur les prostituées et les voleuses* (Paris: E. Lecrosnier et Bebé, 1889). —Ed.

documents from the history of Russian literature; Maxime du Camp,[22] who in his curious *Souvenirs Littéraires* (1887), has shown how many modern French writers have concealed within them the sorrowful seed of insanity; Ramos Mejia,[23] who, in his *Neurosis de los Hombres Celebres de la Historia Argentina* (Buenos Aires, 1885), shows how nearly all the great men of the South American republics were inebriate, neurotic, or insane; A. Tebaldi,[24] who, in his book *Ragione e Pazzia* (Milan, 1884), brings fresh documents to the literature of insanity; and, finally, that acute thinker and brilliant writer, Pisani-Dossi,[25] who has given us a curious study,[26] which is a monograph on madness in art; as in my *Tre Tribuni* (1889) I have attempted to do with the insane and semi-insane in their relation to politics.

22 (1822 – 1894), a French writer and photographer. —Ed.

23 José María Ramos Mejía (1849 – 1914) was a politician and historian of Argentina. —Ed.

24 Augusto Tebaldi (1833 – 1895) was an Italian psychiatrist who headed an asylum in Pavia.

25 Carlo Alberto Pisani Dossi (1849 - 1910) was an Italian writer, politician, and diplomat. —Ed.

26 *I Mattoidi e il Monumente a Vittorio Emanuele* (Rome: Sommaruga, 1884). [The original English edition has 1885 as the publication date, but the work was first published the year before. —Ed.]

Chapter II

Genius and Degeneration

The signs of degeneration — Height — Rickets — Pallor — Emaciation — Physiognomy — Cranium and Brain — Stammering — Left-handedness — Sterility — Unlikeness to Parents — Precocity — Delayed development — Misoneism —Vagabondage — Unconsciousness — Instinctiveness — Somnambulism — The Inspiration of Genius Contrast — Intermittence — Double Personality — Stupidity — Hyperæsthesia — Paræsthesia — Amnesia — Originality — Fondness for special words

The paradox that confounds genius with neurosis, however cruel and sad it may seem, is found to be not devoid of solid foundation when examined from various points of view which have escaped even recent observers.

A theory, which has for some years flourished in the psychiatric world, admits that a large proportion of mental and physical affections are the result of degeneration, of the action, that is, of heredity in the children of the inebriate, the syphilitic, the insane, the consumptive, &c.; or of accidental causes, such as lesions of the head or the action of mercury, which profoundly change the tissues, perpetuate neuroses or other diseases in the patient, and, which is worse, aggravate them in his descendants, until the march of degeneration, constantly growing more rapid and fatal, is only stopped by complete idiocy or sterility.

Alienists have noted certain characters which very frequently, though not constantly, accompany these fatal degenerations. Such are, on the moral side, apathy, loss of moral sense, frequent tendencies to impulsiveness or doubt, psychical inequalities owing to the excess of some faculty (memory, æsthetic taste, &c.) or defect of other qualities (calculation, for example), exaggerated mutism or verbosity, morbid vanity, excessive originality, and excessive preoccupation with self, the tendency to put mystical interpretations on the simplest facts, the abuse of symbolism and of special words which are used as an almost exclusive mode of expression. Such, on the physical side, are prominent ears, deficiency of beard, irregularity of teeth, excessive asymmetry of face and head, which may be very large or very small, sexual precocity, smallness or disproportion of the body, left-handedness, stammering, rickets, phthisis, excessive fecundity, neutralized afterwards by abortions or complete sterility, with constant aggravation of abnormalities in the children.[1]

1 Valentin Magnan, *Annales Médico-Psychologiques*, 1887; Jules Dejerine, *L'Hérédité dans les Maladies Mentales* (Paris: Asselin and Houzeau, 1886); William W. Ireland, *The Blot upon the Brain* (Edinburgh: Bell & Bradfute, 1885).

Without doubt many alienists have here fallen into exaggerations, especially when they have sought to deduce degeneration from a single fact. But, taken on the whole, the theory is irrefutable; every day brings fresh applications and confirmations. Among the most curious are those supplied by recent studies on genius. The signs of degeneration in men of genius they show are sometimes more numerous than in the insane. Let us examine them.

Height.—First of all it is necessary to remark the frequency of physical signs of degeneration, only masqued by the vivacity of the countenance and the prestige of reputation, which distracts us from giving them due importance.

The simplest of these, which struck our ancestors and has passed into a proverb, is the smallness of the body.

Famous for short stature as well as for genius were: Horace (*lepidissimum homunculum dicebat Augustus*),[2] Philopœmen, Narses, Alexander (*Magnus Alexander corpore parvus crat*), Aristotle, Plato, Epicurus, Chrysippus,[3] Laërtes, Ar-

2 Latin: 'Charming little man, said Augustus'. Charles Sanders Peirce interjected that Lombroso fails to note the implication that Augustus was himself large. Augustus is said to have been 5 ft 7in in height, when the average Roman was 5 ft to 5 ft 5 tall. He is, nevertheless, also said to have been conscious of his height, to the extent that he wore sandals with thicker soles to make him appear taller. —Ed.

3 Chrysippus (279 BCE – 206 BCE)'s shortness has been disputed. —Ed.

chimedes, Diogenes, Attila, Epictetus, who was accustomed to say, "Who am I? A little man."[4] Among moderns one may name, Erasmus, Socinus, Linnaeus, Lipsius, Gibbon, Spinoza,[5] Hairy, Montaigne, Mézeray, Lalande, Gray, John Hunter (5ft. 2in.), Mozart, Beethoven, Goldsmith, Hogarth, Thomas Moore, Thomas Campbell, Wilberforce, Heine, Meissonnier, Charles Lamb, Beccaria, Maria Edgeworth, Balzac, De Quincey, William Blake (who was scarcely five feet in height), Browning, Ibsen, George Eliot, Thiers, Mrs. Browning, Louis Blanc, Mendelssohn, Swinburne, Van Does (called the Drum, because he was not any taller than a drum), Pieter van Laer (called the Puppet). Lulli, Pomponazzi, Baldini, were very short; so also were Nicholas Piccinini, the philosopher Dati, and Baldo, who replied to the sarcasm of Bartholo, "*Minuit præsentia fama*," with the words, "*Augebit cætera virtus*;"[6] and again, Marsilio Ficino, of whom it was said, "*Vix ad lumbos viri stabat.*"[7] Albertus Magnus was of such small size that the Pope, having allowed him to kiss his foot, commanded him to

4 With this statement, Epictetus (55 – 135 CE) referred to his submission to God, not to his height, about which there is no information. —Ed.

5 'The accounts of the biographers agree that he was of middle height', 'Spinoza', *The Contemporary Review* 29 (1877) 584.

6 Latin: 'Presence weakens fame'; and the retort: 'Virtue will enlarge everything else'. —Ed.

7 Latin: 'Hardly standing at the loins of a man'. —Ed.

stand up, under the impression that he was still kneeling. When the coffin of St. Francis Xavier was opened at Goa in 1890, the body was found to be only four and a half feet in length.

Among great men of tall stature I only know Volta, Goethe, Petrarch, Schiller, D'Azeglio, Helmholtz, Foscolo, Charlemagne, Bismarck, Moltke, Monti, Mirabeau, Dumas *père*, Schopenhauer, Lamartine, Voltaire, Peter the Great, Washington, Dr. Johnson, Sterne, Arago, Flaubert, Carlyle, Tourgueneff, Tennyson, Whitman.[8]

Rickets.—Agesilaus, Tyrtæus, Æsop, Giotto, Aristomenes, Crates, Galba, Brunelleschi, Magliabecchi, Parini, Scarron, Pope,[9] Leopardi, Talleyrand, Scott, Owen, Gibbon, Byron, Dati, Baldini, Moses Mendelssohn, Flaxman, Hooke, were all either rachitic, lame, hunch-backed, or club-footed.

Pallor.—This has been called the colour of great men; "*Pulchrum sublimium virorum florem* (S. Gregory, *Orationes* XIV.). It was ascertained by

8 In his critical review of the present book, Charles Sanders Pierce cited a list of great historical figures, complied using more strict criteria than Lombroso: out of a total of 88 men and one woman, 44 were tall, 19 were of medium height, and 29 were short, suggesting that men of genius have tended to be of slightly above average height. See *Writings of Charles S. Peirce: A Chronological Edition*, Volume 6: 1886-1890 (Bloomington: Indiana University Press, 2009) —Ed.

9 Alexander Pope was also unusually short, standing at 4ft 6in (1.37m). —Ed.

Marro[10] that this is one of the most frequent signs of degeneration in the morally insane.

Emaciation.—The law of the conservation of energy which rules the whole organic world, explains to us other frequent abnormalities, such as precocious greyness and baldness, leanness of the body, and weakness of sexual and muscular activity, which characterize the insane, and are also frequently found among great thinkers. Le-Camus[11] has said that the greatest geniuses have the slenderest bodies. Cæsar feared the lean face of Cassius. Demosthenes, Aristotle, Cicero, Giotto, St. Bernard, Erasmus, Salmasius, Kepler, Sterne, Walter Scott, John Howard, D'Alembert, Fénelon, Boileau, Milton, Pascal, Napoleon, were all extremely thin in the flower of their age.

Others were weak and sickly in childhood; such were Demosthenes, Bacon, Descartes, Newton, Locke, Adam Smith, Boyle, Pope, Flaxman, Nelson, Haller, Körner, Pascal, Wren, Alfieri, Renan.

Ségur wrote of Voltaire that his leanness recalled his labours, and that his slight bent body was only a thin, transparent veil, through which one seemed to see his soul and genius. Lamennais was "a small, almost imperceptible man, or rather a flame chased from one point of the room to the other by the breath of his own restlessness."

10 Antonio Marro, *I caratteri dei delinquenti: Studio antropologico-sociologico* (Turin: Bocca, 1887).

11 Antoine Le-Camus, *Médecine de l'Esprit*, ii (Paris: Ganeau, 1753).

Physiognomy.—Mind, a celebrated painter of cats, had a cretin-like physiognomy. So also had Socrates, Škoda, Rembrandt, Dostoyevsky, Magliabecchi, Pope, Carlyle, Darwin, and, among modern Italians, Schiaparelli, who holds so high a rank in mathematics.

Cranium and Brain.—Lesions of the head and brain are very frequent among men of genius. The celebrated Australian novelist, Marcus Clarke, when a child, received a blow from a horse's hoof which crushed his skull.[12] The same is told of Vico, [13]Gratry, Clement VI., Malebranche, and Cornelius, hence called a *Lapide*. The last three are said to have acquired their genius as a result of the accident, having been unintelligent before. Mention should also be made of the parietal fracture in Fusinieri's skull;[14] of the cranial asymmetry of Pericles, who was on this account surnamed Squillhead (σκινοκέφαλος) by the Greek comic writers;[15] of Romagnosi, of Bichat, of Kant,[16] of

12 *Revue Britannique* (1884).

13 In The Carnevalis of Eusebius Asch (Beverly Hills, CA: Red Heifer Press, 1999) 92, Peter Gimpel writes that as a child, Giambattista Vico (1668 – 1744) 'was known for his extreme dullness of mind—a condition that persisted until he suffered a severe head injury through falling off a stone wall.' —Ed.

14 Giovanni Canestrini, Il cranio di Ambrogio Fusinieri: studio antropologico (Venice: Grimaldo, 1875).

15 Plutarch, *Life of Pericles*, iii.

16 Carl Kupffer, "Der Schädel Immanuel Kant's", *Archiv für Anthropologie* 13, (1881) 359 ff..

Chenevix,[17] of Dante, who presented an abnormal development of the left parietal bone, and two osteomata on the frontal bone; the plagiocephaly of Brunacci and of Machiavelli; the extreme prognathism of Foscolo (68°) and his low cephalic-spinal and cephalic-orbital index;[18] the ultra-dolichocephaly of Fusinieri (index 74), contrasting with the ultra-brachycephaly which is characteristic of the Venetians (82 to 84); the Neanderthaloid skull of Robert the Bruce;[19] of Kay Lye,[20] of San Marsay (index 69), and the ultra-dolichocephaly of O'Connell (index 73), which contrasts with the mesocephaly of the Irish; the median occipital fossa of Scarpa;[21] the transverse occipital suture of Kant, his ultra-brachycephaly (88.5), platycephaly (index of height 71.1), the disproportion between the superior portion of his occipital bone, more developed by half, and the inferior or cerebellar portion. It is the same with the smallness of the frontal arch compared to the parietal.

---

17 Hermann Welcker, *Schillers Schädel und Todtenmaske, nebst Mitteilungen über Schädel und Todtenmaske Kants* (Braunschweg: Vieweg, 1883).

18 Paolo Mantegazza, *Sul Cranio di Foscolo* (Florence: 1880).

19 William Turner, 'The Fossil Skull Controversy', *Quarterly Journal of Science*, vol. 1 (1864) 258.

20 Jean-Louis-Armand de Quatrefages de Bréau and Ernest-Théodore Hamy, *Crania Ethnica*, Part I (Paris: Bailliere et fils, 1879) 30.

21 Giovanni Zoja, "La Testa di Scarpa", *Archivio per l'antropologia e la etnologia* VII (1878) 443-450. [I have changed the original reference from 'Zoja, La Testa di Scarpa, 1880'. —Ed.]

In Volta's skull[22] I have noted several characters which anthropologists consider to belong to the lower races, such as prominence of the styloid apophyses, simplicity of the coronal suture, traces of the median frontal suture, obtuse facial angle (73°), but especially the remarkable cranial sclerosis, which at places attains a thickness of 16 millimetres; hence the great weight of the skull (753 grammes).

The researches of other investigators have shown that Manzoni, Petrarch, and Fusinieri had receding foreheads; in Byron, Massacra (at the age of 32), Humboldt, Meckel, Foscolo, Ximenes, and Donizetti there was solidification of the sutures; submicrocephaly in Rasori, Descartes, Foscolo, Tissot, Guido Reni, Hoffmann, and Schumann; sclerosis in Donizetti and Tiedemann who, moreover, presented a bony crest between the sphenoid and the basilar apophysis; hydrocephalus in Milton, Linnaeus, Cuvier, Gibbon, &c.

The capacity of the skull in men of genius, as is natural, is above the average, by which it approaches what is found in insanity. (De Quatrefages noted that the greatest degree of macrocephaly was found in a lunatic, the next in a man of genius.) There are numerous exceptions in which it descends below the ordinary average.

It is certain that in Italy, Volta (1,860 c.cm.), Petrarch (1,602 c.cm.), Bordoni (1,681 c.cm.), Brun-

22 "Sul Cranio di Volta", *Giornale délia R. Accademia di medicina* (10 September 1878) 195 – 208.

acci (1,701 c.cm.), St. Ambrose (1,792 c.cm.), and Fusinieri (1604 c.cm.), all presented great cranial capacity. The same character is found to a still greater degree in Kant (1,740 c.cm.), Thackeray (1660 c.cm.), Cuvier (1,830 c.cm.), and Tourguen-eff (2,012 c.cm.).

Le Bon studied twenty-six skulls of French men of genius, among whom were Boileau, Descartes, and Jourdan.[23] He found that the most celebrated had an average capacity of 1,732 cubic centimetres; while the ancient Parisians offered only 1,559 c.cm. Among the Parisians of to-day scarcely 12 per cent, exceed 1,700 c.cm., a figure surpassed by 73 per cent, of the celebrated men.

But sub-microcephalic skulls may also be found in men of genius. Wagner and Bischoff,[24] exam-

23 "Sur la capacité du crâne d'un certain nombre d'hommes célèbres", *Bulletins de la Société d'anthropologie de Paris* 2 (1879) 492 – 503. [Here Lombroso gives as his source '*Revue scientifique*, 1882'. An English translation, with the title "On the Capacity of the Skull of a Certain Number of Celebrated Men" is available online. —Ed.]

24 Wagner (Das Hirngewicht, 1877) gives these measurements of scientific men of Gottingen:

Dirichlet	Mathematician	Age 54	1520 g.
Fuchs	Physician	" 52	1499 g.
Gauss	Mathematician	" 78	1492 g.
Hermann	Philologist	" 51	1358 g.
Hausmann	Mineralogist	" 77	1226 g.

[Theodor] Bischoff (*Hirngewichte bei Münchener Gelehrten*)

ining twelve brains of celebrated Germans, found the capacity very great in eight, very small in four. The latter was the case with Liebig, Döllinger, Hausmann, in whose favour advanced age may be advanced as an excuse; but this reason does not exist for Guido Reni, Gambetta, Harless, Foscolo (1426), Dante (1403), Hermann (1358), Lasker

---

gives the following measurements:

Hermann	Geometrician	Age 60	1590 g.
Pfeufer	Physician	" 60	1488 g.
Bischoff	Physician	" 79	1452 g.
Melchior Meyer	Poet	" 61	1415 g.
Arnoldi	Orientalist	" 85	1730 g.
Thackeray	Novelist	" 52	1660 g.
Abercrombie	Physician	" 64	1780 g.
Cuvier	Naturalist	" 63	1829 g.
Doell	Archæologist	" 85	1650 g.
Schiller	Poet	" 46	1580 g.
Huber	Philosopher	" 47	1499 g.
Fallmerayer	Historian	" 74	1349 g.
Liebig	Chemist	" 70	1352 g.
Tiedemann	Physiologist	" 79	1254 g.
Harless	Chemist	" 40	1238 g.
Döllinger	Physiologist	" 71	1207 g.

The measurement of the cerebral area often gives superiority even to those men of genius who present a feeble weight. Fuchs had a cerebral surface of 22,1005 square c. and Gauss of 21,9588; while with the same weight the same surface in an unknown woman was 20,4115 and in a workman 18,7672.

(1300). Shelley's head was remarkably small.

In the face of all these facts I shall not be taxed with temerity if I conclude that, as genius is often expiated by inferiority in some psychic functions, it is often associated with anomalies in that organ which is the source of its glory.

Reference should here be made to the ventricular dropsy in Rousseau's brain,[25] to the meningitis of Grossi, of Donizetti, and of Schumann, to the cerebral œdema of Liebig and of Tiedemann. In the last-named, besides remarkable thickness of the skull, especially at the forehead, Bischoff noted adherence of the *dura mater* to the bone, thickening of the arachnoid and atrophy of the brain. In the physician Fuchs, Wagner found the fissure of Rolando interrupted by a superficial convolution, an anomaly which Giacomini found only once in 356 cases, and Heschl once in 632.[26] Pascal's brain showed grave lesions of the cerebral hemispheres. It has recently been discovered that Cuvier's voluminous brain was affected by dropsy; in Lasker's there was softening of the corpora striata, pachymeningitis, hæmorrhage, and endarteritis deformans of the artery of the fissure of Sylvius.[27]

In eighteen brains of German men of science Bischoff and Rüdinger found congenital anoma-

---

25 *Bulletin de la Societé d'Anthropologie* 2 (1861).

26 Heschl R. "Tiefen-Windungen des menschlichen Grosshirns und die überbrückung der Zentralfurche". *Wien. Med. Wochenzeitschr.* 41 (1877) 987 – 988.

27 Emanuel Mendel, *Neurologisches Centralblatt* 4 (1884).

lies of the cerebral convolutions, especially of the parietal.[28] In the brains of Wülfert and Huber, the third left frontal convolution was greatly developed with numerous meanderings. In Gambetta this exaggeration became a real doubling; and the right quadrilateral lobule is divided into two parts by a furrow which starts from the occipital fissure; of these two parts the inferior is subdivided by an incision with numerous branches, arranged in the form of stars, and the occipital lobe is small, especially on the right.[29]

"The comparative study of these brains," writes Hervé,[30]

> shows that individual variations of the cerebral convolutions are more numerous and more marked in men of genius than in others. This is especially the case in regard to the third frontal convolution which is not only more variable in men of genius, but also more complex, especially on one side, while in ordinary persons it is very simple both on the left and on the right. Without doubt the individual arrangements which may be presented by the brains of men

28 Nikolaus Rüdiger and Jacob Henle, "Ein Beitrag zur Anatomie der Affenspalte und der Interparietalfurche beim Menschen nach Race, Geschlecht und Individualität", *Beiträge zur Anatomie und Embryologie* (1886) 186 – 198.

29 Theophile Chudzinski and Mathias Duval, "Description morphologique du cerveau de Gambetta", *Bulletin de la Societé d'Anthropologie* 3.9 (1886) 135.

30 Georges Hervé, *La Circonvolution de Broca: étude de morphologie cérébrale* (Paris: A. Delahaye & E. Lecrosiner, 1888).

> of remarkable intelligence may also be found in ordinary brains, but only in rare exceptions.

I refer those who wish to form an idea of the development reached by Broca's centre in some of the brains of the Munich collection to Rüdinger's monograph, and to the beautiful plates which accompany it. One remarks especially the enormous size and the numerous superficial folds at the foot of the left convolution in the jurist Wülfert, who was remarkable among other qualities for his great oratorical talent. On the other hand, the convolution is much reduced and very simple on the left, much developed in all its parts on the right, in the brain of the pathologist Buhl,[31] a professor whose speech was clear and facile, but who was left-handed, or at all events ambidextrous. To these facts others may be added, showing the morphological complexity of Broca's convolution in distinguished men; in the brains, for instance, of various men of science, described and figured by R. Wagner. [32]Among these was the illustrious geometrician, Gauss: compared with Gauss's brain that of an artisan called Krebs was much less complicated, and notably narrower in the frontal region. The frontal convolutions were also inferior in development to those of Gauss; and the anterior lobes were vo-

---

31 Ludwig von Buhl (1816 – 1880). —Ed.

32 Rudolph Wagner, *Vorstudien zu einer wissenschaftlichen Morphologie und Physiologie des menschlichen Gehirns als Seelenorgan* (Göttingen: Dietrich, 1860).

luminous in another celebrated mathematician, Professor De Morgan, whose brain is in Bastian's possession.

Stammering.—Men of genius frequently stammer. I will mention: Aristotle, Æsop, Demosthenes, Alcibiades, Cato of Utica, Virgil, Manzoni, Erasmus, Malherbe, C. Lamb, Turenne, Erasmus and Charles Darwin, Moses Mendelssohn, Charles V., Romiti, Cardan, Tartaglia.

Left-handedness.—Many have been left-handed. Such were: Tiberius, Sebastian del Piombo, Michelangelo, Flechier, Nigra, Buhl, Raphael of Montelupo, Bertillon. Leonardo da Vinci sketched rapidly with his left hand any figures which struck him, and only employed the right hand for those which were the mature result of his contemplation; for this reason his friends were persuaded that he only wrote with the left hand.[33] Mancinism or left-sidedness is to-day regarded as a character of atavism and degeneration.[34]

Sterility.—Many great men have remained bachelors; others, although married, have had no children. "The noblest works and foundations," said Bacon,[35] "have proceeded from childless men, which have sought to express the images of their

33 Émile Galichon, "Un dessin de Léonard de Vinci pour le tableau de l'Adoration des mages" *Gazette des Beaux-Arts* XXIII (1867) 530 – 536.

34 Cesare Lombroso, *Sul Mancinismo motorio e sensorio nei sani e negli alienat* (Turin: 1885).

35 Francis Bacon, Essay VII., *Of Parents and Children.*

minds, where those of their bodies have failed. So the care of posterity is most in them that have no posterity." And La Bruyere said, "These men have neither ancestors nor descendants; they themselves form their entire posterity."

Croker, in his edition of Boswell, remarks that all the great English poets had no posterity. He names Shakespeare, Ben Jonson, Milton, Otway, Dryden, Rowe, Addison, Pope, Swift, Gay, Johnson, Goldsmith, Cowper. Hobbes, Camden, and many others, avoided marriage in order to have more time to devote to study. Michelangelo said, "I have more than enough of a wife in my art." Among celibates may be mentioned also: Kant, Newton, Pitt,[36] Fox, Fontenelle, Beethoven, Gas-

36 This would be William Pitt the Younger (1759 – 1806), the self-described 'independent Whig' politician. William Hague wrote in his biography of Pitt, *William Pitt the Younger* (London: Harper Collins, 2004): 'Pitt was happiest among his Cambridge companions or family. He had no social ambitions, and it was rare for him to set out to make a friend. The collaborators of his first 18 months in office—Beresford, Wyvill, and Twining—passed in and out of his mind along with their areas of expertise. Pitt's lack of interest in enlarging his social circle meant that it did not grow to encompass any women outside his own family, a fact that produced a good deal of rumour. From late 1784, a series of satirical verses appeared in *The Morning Herald* drawing attention to Pitt's lack of knowledge of women: "Tis true, indeed, we oft abuse him,/Because he bends to no man;/But slander's self dares not accuse him/Of stiffness to a woman." Others made snide references to Pitt's friendship with Tom Steele, Secretary to the Treasury. At the height of the constitutional crisis in 1784, Sheridan had compared Pitt to James I's favourite, the Duke of Buckingham, a clear reference to homosexuality. Socially, Pitt preferred the

sendi, Galileo, Descartes, Locke, Spinoza, Bayle, Leibnitz, Malebranche, Gray, Dalton, Hume, Gibbon, Macaulay, Lamb, Bentham, Leonardo da Vinci, Copernicus, Reynolds, Handel, Mendelssohn, Meyerbeer, Schopenhauer, Camoens, Voltaire, Chateaubriand, Flaubert, Foscolo, Alfieri, Cavour, Pellico, Mazzini, Aleardi, Guerrazzi. And among women: Florence Nightingale, Catherine Stanley, Gaetana Agnesi (the mathematician), and Luigia Laura Bassi. A very large number of married men of genius have not been happy in marriage:

---

company of young men, and would continue to do so into his thirties and forties. It may be that Pitt had homosexual leanings but suppressed any urge to act on them for the sake of his ambitions. He could be charming to women, but it seems certain that he rejected intimacy whenever it was proffered – and would do so publicly at a later date. In practical terms it appears that Pitt was essentially asexual throughout his life, perhaps one example of how his rapid development as a politician stunted his growth as a man.' At one point Pitt has said to intend marrying Eleanor Eden, but he abandoned the idea, writing to Lord Auckland, 'I am compelled to say that I find the obstacles to it decisive and insurmountable'. —Ed.

Shakespeare,[37] Dante,[38] Marzolo, Byron,[39] Coler-

37 That William Shakespeare (1564 – 1616) was unhappy in marriage is speculation. Among the basis for it is that he, aged 18, had a shotgun marriage to Anne Hathaway, aged 26, precipitated by her pregnancy, and that he left her, in his will, his second-best bed, which could either have been an insult or the matrimonial bed, in which case it was the opposite. However, this provision was squeezed in between lines, apparently as an afterthought, in a document that otherwise makes no mention of his wife. Some have speculated that Shakespeare left for London to escape his unhappy marriage. —Ed.

38 It is assumed that Dante Alighieri (1265 – 1321) would have been happier with his muse, Bice Portinari, and Vittorio Imbriani wrote that Gemma Donati was not a good choice of wife for the poet. According to Boccaccio, the relationship between husband and wife deteriorated irretrievably during Dante's exile, and it seems that from this point on, the couple had no desire to see each other again. After 17 years of marriage, Gemma remained with the children and Dante petitioned for Gemma's dowry to be refunded to her from his patrimony, which the municipality had confiscated. —Ed.

39 Lord Byron (1788 – 1824) married Anne Isabella Milbanke in 1815, having only accepted his marriage proposal after rejecting the first. She was morally righteous, intelligent, mathematically gifted, and an heiress. Byron, however, treated her badly, and Annabella left him within just over a year. Rumours of violence, adultery with actresses, incest with Augusta Leigh, and sodomy were spread by Annabelle's cousin, Lady Catherine Lamb, who was jealous and would later write a popular novel, *Glenarvon*, wherein Byron is portrayed unflatteringly as the rakish character Lord Ruthven. —Ed.

idge,[40] Addison, Landor,[41] Carlyle,[42] Ary Scheffer,

40 Samuel Taylor Coleridge (1772 - 1834) married Sarah Fricker in 1795 purely out of social constraints and grew to detest her, which eventually led to a separation. —Ed.

41 Ernest Dilworth writes in his biography of Landor (New York: Twayne Publishers: 1971): '. . . [Landor] married a pretty girl with no money. The pretty girl, Julia Thuillier, could not keep pace with his noble stride, was uninterested in his mind, and balked at his humors; she pitied herself, became a shrew, and at last made him a cuckold.' —Ed.

42 Thomas Carlyle (1795 – 1881)'s biographer, James Froude, thought his subject's marriage to Jane Welsh remained unconsummated. The couple's affection for each other was spoiled by frequent and angry quarrels. After Jane died, Carlyle was greatly distressed, a feeling that was aggravated upon discovering, in her letters and diaries, the extent of her unhappiness. He wrote a self-critical 'Reminiscences of Jane Welsh', which was published posthumously. —Ed.

Rovani, A. Comte,[43] Haydn,[44] Milton,[45] Sterne,[46] Dickens,[47] &c. St. Paul boasted of his absolute continence; Cavendish altogether lacked the sexual instinct, and had a morbid antipathy to women. Flaubert wrote to George Sand: "The muse, however intractable, gives fewer sorrows than woman. I cannot reconcile one with the other. One must

43 Auguste Comte (1798 - 1857) met his future wife, Caroline Massin, while she was engaging in prostitution. Their marriage was difficult due to their very different personalities and Comte's instability. They separated in 1842. —Ed.

44 Joseph Haydn (1732 – 1809)'s marriage was so completely unhappy that they produced no children and both took up lovers. —Ed.

45 John Milton (1608 – 1674) married three times. His first wife, who was 17 when the poet was 34, apparently prompted him to write *The Doctrine and Discipline of Divorce* when she returned to live with her family after the outbreak of the English Civil War, which has led to the assumption that when she returned to the household in 1645, he wished she had not, but conjugal relations resumed quickly and she bore him four children, dying from complications after the birth of their fourth child. His second wife died four months after the birth of their first child, who also died. His third wife was chosen to him by his doctor, as the poet, by then 55, needed a live-in carer; the young woman, 24 at the time, was poor and her only reward was her inheritance. —Ed.

46 Laurence Sterne's infidelities were a cause of discord in his marriage. His wife, Elizabeth Lumley, at one point had a nervous breakdown and threatened suicide. Both were ill with consumption. —Ed.

47 Charles Dickens (1812 – 1870) found his wife an increasingly incompetent mother and housekeeper and blamed her for the birth of their 10 children, which strained his finances. She eventually left him after he, aged 45, fell in love with Ellen Ternan. —Ed.

choose."[48] Adam Smith said he reserved his gallantry for his books. Chamfort, the misanthrope, wrote: "If men followed the guidance of reason no one would marry; for my own part, I will have nothing to do with it, lest I should have a son like myself." A French poet has said:

> *Les grands esprits, d'ailleurs très-estimables,*
> *Out très peu de talent pour former leurs semblables.*[49]

Unlikeness to Parents.—Nearly all men of genius have differed as much from their fathers as from their mothers (Foscolo, Michelangelo, Giotto, Haydn, &c.). That is one of the marks of degeneration. For this reason one notes physical resemblances between men of genius belonging to very different races and epochs; for example, Julius Cæsar, Napoleon, and Giovanni of the Black Bands; or Casti, Sterne, and Voltaire. They often differ from their national type. They differ by the possession of noble and almost superhuman characters (elevation of the forehead, notable development of the nose and of the head, great vivacity of the eyes); while the cretin, the criminal, and often the lunatic, differ by the possession of ignoble features: Humboldt, Virchow,

48 *Lettres de Gustave Flaubert à Georges Sand* (Paris: Charpentier, 1884). [The original gives the publication date as 1885. —Ed.]

49 Philippe Néricault Destouches, *Le Philosophe Marié* (Paris: Nilsson, 1727).

Bismarck, Helmholtz, and Holtzendorf, do not show a German physiognomy. Byron was English neither in his face nor in his character; Manin did not show the Venetian type; Alfieri and d'Azeglio had neither the Piedmontese character nor face. Carducci's face is not Italian. Nevertheless, one finds very notable and frequent exceptions. Michelangelo, Leonardo da Vinci, Raphael, and Cellini, presented the Italian type.

Precocity.—Another character common to genius and to insanity, especially moral insanity, is precocity. Dante, when nine years of age, wrote a sonnet to Beatrice; Tasso wrote verses at ten. Pascal and Comte were great thinkers at the age of thirteen, Fornier at fifteen, Niebuhr at seven, Jonathan Edwards at twelve, Michelangelo at nineteen, Gassendi, the Little Doctor, at four, Bossuet at twelve, and Voltaire at thirteen. Pico de la Mirandola knew Latin, Greek, Hebrew, Chaldee, and Arabic, in his childhood; Goethe wrote a story in seven languages when he was scarcely ten; Wieland knew Latin at seven, meditated an epic poem at thirteen, and at sixteen published his poem, *Die Vollkommenste Welt*. Lope de Vega composed his first verses at twelve,[50] Calderón at thirteen. Kotzebue was trying to write comedies at seven, and at eighteen his

50 Félix Arturo Lope de Vega y Carpio (1562 – 1635) was also incredibly prolific. Some 3,000 sonnets, 3 novels, 4 novellas, 9 epic poems, and about 1,800 plays are attributed to him. Although he has been criticised for putting quantity ahead of quality, nevertheless at least 80 of his plays are considered masterpieces. —Ed.

first tragedy was acted. Schiller was only nineteen when his epoch-making *Räuber* appeared. Victor Hugo composed *Irtamène* at fifteen, and at twenty had already published *Han d'Islande*, *Bug-Jargal*, and the first volume of *Odes et Ballades*; Lamennais at sixteen dictated the *Paroles d'un Croyant*. Pope wrote his ode to *Solitude* at twelve and his *Pastorals* at sixteen. Byron wrote verses at twelve, and at eighteen published his *Hours of Idleness*. Moore translated *Anacreon* at thirteen. Meyerbeer at five played excellently on the piano. Claude Joseph Vernet drew very well at four, and at twenty was already a celebrated painter. At thirteen Wren invented an astronomical instrument and offered it to his father with a Latin dedication. Ascoli at fifteen published a book on the relation of the dialects of Wallachia and Friuli. Metastasio improvised at ten; Ennius Quirinus Visconti excited the admiration of all at sixteen months, and preached when six years old. At fifteen Fénelon preached at Paris before a select audience; Wetton at five could read and translate Latin, Greek, and Hebrew, and at ten knew Chaldee, Syriac, and Arabic. Mirabeau preached at three and published books at ten. Handel composed a mass at thirteen, at seventeen *Corinda* and *Nero*, and at nineteen was director of the opera at Hamburg. Raphael was famous at fourteen. Rétif de la Bretonne had already read much at four; at eleven he had seduced young girls, and at fourteen had composed a poem on his first twelve mistresses. Eichorn, Mozart, and

Eybler gave concerts at six. At thirteen Beethoven composed three sonatas. Weber was only fourteen when his first opera, *Das Waldmädchen*, was represented. Cherubini at thirteen wrote a mass which filled his fellow-citizens with enthusiasm. Bacon conceived the *Novum Organum* at fifteen. Charles XII. manifested his great designs at the age of eighteen.[51]

This precocity is morbid and atavistic; it may be observed among all savages. The proverb, "A man who has genius at five is mad at fifteen" is often verified in asylums.[52] The children of the insane are often precocious. Savage knew an insane woman whose children could play classical music before the age of six, and other children who at a tender age displayed the passions of grown men. Among the children of the insane are often revealed aptitudes and tastes—chiefly for music, the arts, and mathematics—which are not usually found in other children.

Delayed Development.—Delay in the development of genius may be explained, as Beard remarks, by the absence of circumstances favourable to its blossoming, and by the ignorance of teachers

51 George M. Beard, *American Nervousness* (New York: Putnam's, 1887); Francesco Cancellieri, *Intorno Uomini dotati di gran memoria* (1815); Johann Klefeker, *Bibliotheca eruditorum præcocium* (Hamburg: [n.p.], 1717); Johann Heinrich von Seelen, Adrien Baillet, David Schultetus, Johann Christoph Wolf, *Oratio Solemnis De Præcocibus Eruditis* (Flensburg: Sumtibus Et Operis Vogelianis, 1713).

52 George H. Savage, Moral Insanity (New York: 1886).

and parents who see mental obtusity, or even idiocy, where there is only the distraction or amnesia of genius. Many children who become great men have been regarded at school as bad, wild, or silly; but their intelligence appeared as soon as the occasion offered, or when they found the true path of their genius. It was thus with Thiers, Pestalozzi, Wellington, Du Guesclin, Goldsmith, Burns, Balzac, Fresnel,[53] Dumas *père*, Humboldt, Sheridan, Boccaccio, Pierre Thomas, Linnaeus, Vofta, Alfieri. Thus Newton, meditating on the problems of Kepler, often forgot the orders and commissions given him by his mother; and while he was the last in his class he was very clever in making mechanical playthings. Walter Scott, who also showed badly at school, was a wonderful story-teller. Klaproth, the celebrated Orientalist, when following the courses at Berlin University, was considered a backward student. In examination once a professor said to him: "But you know nothing, sir!" "Excuse me," he replied, "I know Chinese." It was found that he had learnt this difficult language alone, almost in secret. Gustave Flaubert "was the very opposite of a phenomenal child. It was only with extreme difficulty that he succeeded in learning to read. His mind, however, was already working, for he composed little plays which he could not write, but which he represented alone, playing the different

53 Augustin-Jean Fresnel (1788 – 1827) still could not read when he was eight years old. —Ed.

personages, and improvising long dialogues."[54] Domenichino, whom his comrades called the great bullock, when accused of being slow and not learning so fast as the other pupils, replied: "It is because I work in myself."

Sometimes children have only made progress when abandoned to their own impulses. Thus Cabanis, although intelligent, was regarded at school as obstinate and idle, and was sent home. His father then decided to risk an experiment. He allowed his son, at fourteen years of age, to study according to his own taste. The experiment succeeded completely.

Misoneism.—The men who create new worlds are as much enemies of novelty as ordinary persons and children. They display extraordinary energy in rejecting the discoveries of others; whether it is that the saturation, so to say, of their brains prevents any new absorption, or that they have acquired a special sensibility, alert only to their own ideas, and refractory to the ideas of others. Thus Schopenhauer, who was a great rebel in philosophy, has nothing but words of pity and contempt for political revolutionaries; and he bequeathed his fortune to men who had contributed to repress by arms the noble political aspirations of 1848.[55]

54 Guy de Maupassant, "Étude sur Gustave Flaubert", in Gustave Flaubert, *Oeuvres complètes*, Vol. 7, Ed. Henry May (Paris: Conrad, 1885).

55 Arthur Schopenhauer (1788 – 1860) said that he would 'prefer to be ruled by a lion than by a fellow rat', and during the riots

Frederick II., who inaugurated German politics, and wished to foster a national art and literature, did not suspect the worth of Herder, of Klopstock, of Lessing, of Goethe;[56] he disliked changing his coats so much that he had only two or three during his life. The same may be said of Napoleon and his hats. Rossini could never travel by rail; when a friend attempted to accustom him to the train he fell down fainting, remarking afterwards: "If I was not like that I should never have written the *Barbiere*" Napoleon rejected steam, and Richelieu sent Salomon de Caus, its first inventor, to the Bicètre. Bacon laughed at Gilbert and Copernicus; he did not believe in the application of instruments, or even of mathematics, to the exact sciences. Baudelaire and Nodier detested freethinkers.[57] Laplace denied the fall of meteorites, for, he said, with an argument much approved by the Academicians, how can stones fall from the sky when there are none there? Biot denied the undulatory theory. Voltaire denied fossils. Darwin did not believe in the Stone Age nor in hypnotism.[58] Robin laughed at the Darwinian theory.

---

of 1848, he lent his opera glasses to an army officer shooting from a distance at violent rioters. —Ed.

56 *Revue des deux mondes* (1883) 92. [*Revue des deux mondes* was published as a two-volume monthly; Lombroso specifies neither month nor volume. —Ed.]

57 *Revue Blate* (1887) 17.

58 Francis Darwin, *The Life and Letters of Charles Darwin, Including an Autobiographical Chapter* (London: John Murray, 1887).

Vagabondage.—Love of wandering is frequent among men of genius. I will mention only Heine, Alfieri, Byron, Giordano Bruno,[59] Leopardi, Tasso, Goldsmith, Sterne, Gautier, Mussei, Lenau. "My father left me his wandering genius as a heritage," wrote Foscolo. Hölderlin, after his much loved wife had entered a convent, wandered for forty years without settling down anywhere. Everyone knows of the constant journeys of Petrarch, of Paisiello, of Lavoisier, of Cellini, of Cervantes, at a time when travelling was beset by difficulties and dangers. Meyerbeer travelled for thirty years, composing his operas in the train. Wagner travelled on foot from Riga to Paris. One knows that sometimes, at the Universities, professors are seized by the desire of change, and to satisfy it forget all their personal interests.

Unconsciousness and Instinctiveness.—The coincidence of genius and insanity enables us to understand the astonishing unconsciousness, instantaneousness and intermittence of the creations of genius, whence its great resemblance to epilepsy, the importance of which we shall see later, and

59 Giordano Bruno (1548 – 1600) generated a great deal of controversy due to his thinking and taste for forbidden books, which forced him to flee Naples in 1576 and spend seven years wandering in Europe. In 1583 he settled in England for two years, after which he moved to Paris. There, however, his writings put him in ill favour, causing him to spend the next years wandering again, until, in 1592, he was denounced to the Venetian Inquisition, which led to his imprisonment, trial, and execution. —Ed.

whence also a distinction between genius and talent. "Talent," says Jürgen Meyer,[60] "knows itself; it knows how and why it has reached a given theory; it is not so with genius, which is ignorant of the how and the why. Nothing is so involuntary as the conception of genius." "One of the characters of genius," writes Ilagen,

> is irresistible impulsion. As instinct compels the animal to accomplish certain acts, even at the risk of life, so genius, when it is dominated by an idea is incapable of abandoning itself to any other thought. Napoleon and Alexander conquered, not from love of glory, but in obedience to an all-powerful instinct; so scientific genius has no rest; its activity may appear to be the result of a voluntary effort, but it is not so. Genius creates, not because it wishes to, but because it must create.

And Paul Richter writes:

> The man of genius is in many respects a real somnambulist. In his lucid dream he sees farther than when awake, and reaches the heights of truth; when the world of imagination is taken away from him he is suddenly precipitated into reality.[61]

Haydn attributed the conception of the *Crea-*

---

60 Jürgen Bona Meyer, *Genie und Talent: eine psychologische Betrachtung* (1870).

61 Fischer, *Æsthetik*, ii. I, p. 386.

tion to a mysterious grace from on high: "When my work does not advance," he said, "I retire into the oratory with my rosary and say an Arc; immediately ideas come to me." When our Milli produces, almost without knowing it, one of her marvellous poems, she is agitated, cries, sings, takes long walks, and almost becomes the victim of an epileptic attack.

Many men of genius who have studied themselves, and who have spoken of their inspiration, have described it as a sweet and seductive fever, during which their thought has become rapidly and involuntarily fruitful, and has burst forth like the flame of a lighted, torch. Such is the thought that Dante has engraved in three wonderful lines:—

I' mi son un che, quando
Amore spira, noto ed in quel modo
Che detta dentro vo significando.[62]

Napoleon said that the fate of battles was the result of an instant, of a latent thought; the decisive moment appeared; the spark burst forth, and one was victorious. (Moreau.) Kuh's most beautiful poems, wrote Bauer, were dictated in a state between insanity and reason; at the moment when his sublime thoughts came to him he was incapable of simple reasoning. Foscolo tells us in his *Epistolario*, the finest monument of his great

62 "I am one who, when Love inspires, attend, and according as he speaks within me, so I express myself."

soul, that writing depends on a certain amiable fever of the mind, and cannot be had at will: "I write letters, not for my country, nor for fame, but for the secret joy which arises from the exercise of our faculties; they have need of movement, as our legs of walking." Mozart confessed that musical ideas were aroused in him, even apart from his will, like dreams. Hoffmann often said to his friends, "When I compose I sit down to the piano, shut my eyes, and play what I hear."[63] Lamartine often said, "It is not I who think; my ideas think for me."[64] Alfieri, who compared himself to a barometer on account of the continual changes in his poetic power, produced by change of season, had not the strength in September to resist a new, or rather, renewed, impulse which he had felt for several days; he declared himself vanquished, and wrote six comedies. In Alfieri, Goethe, and Ariosto creation was instantaneous, often even being produced on awaking.[65]

---

63 Johann August Schilling, *Psychiatrische Briefe oder die Irren, das Irresein und das Irrenhaus: eine vollständige, systematische Darlegung aller Seelenkrankheiten, in klassischen und naturgetreuen Beispielen für das gebildete Publikum erläutert* (Augsburg: Schlosser, 1863) 486.

64 Benjamin Ball, *Leçons sur les maladies mentales* (Paris: Asselin & Houzeau, 1890). [The latter is the second edition; the original has the reference as 'Ball, *Leçons des maladies mentales*, 1881', but the latter does not appear in any of the bibliographies I was able to examine. —Ed.]

65 Paul Radestock, *Genie und Wahnsinn: Eine psychologische Untersuchung* (Breslau: Eduard Trewendt, 1884) 42.

This domination of genius by the unconscious has been remarked for many centuries. Socrates said that poets create, not by virtue of inventive science, but, thanks to a very certain natural instinct, just as diviners predict, saying beautiful things, but not having consciousness of what they say.[66] "All the manifestations of genius," wrote Voltaire to Diderot,

> are the effects of instinct. All the philosophers of the world put together would not be able to produce Quinault's *Armide*, or the *Animaux malades de la peste*, which La Fontaine wrote without knowing what he did. Corneille composed *Horace* as a bird composes its nest.[67]

Thus the greatest conceptions of thought, prepared, so to say, by former sensations, and by exquisite organic sensibility, suddenly burst forth and develop by unconscious cerebration. Thus also may be explained the profound convictions of prophets, saints, and demoniacs, as well as the impulsive acts of the insane.

Somnambulism.—Bettinelli wrote: "Poetry may almost be called a dream which is accomplished in the presence of reason, which floats above it with open eyes." This definition is the more exact since many poets have composed their poems in a dream or half-dream. Goethe often said that a certain cer-

66 Plato, *Apologia*.

67 Letter of 20 April 1752.

ebral irritation is necessary to the poet; many of his poems were, in fact, composed in a state bordering on somnambulism. Klopstock declared that he had received several inspirations for his poems in dreams. Voltaire conceived during sleep one of the books of his *Henriade*; Sardini, a theory on the flageolet; Seckendorf, his beautiful ode to imagination, which in its harmony reflects its origin. Newton and Cardan resolved mathematical problems in dreams. Nodier composed *Lydia*, together with a complete theory of future destiny, as the result of dreams which "succeeded each other," he wrote, "with such redoubled energy, from night to night, that the idea transformed itself into a conviction." Muratori, many years after he had ceased to write verse, improvised in a dream a Latin pentameter. It is said that La Fontaine composed in a dream his *Deux Pigeons*, and that Condillac completed during sleep a lesson interrupted in his waking hours.[68] Coleridge's *Kubla Khan* was composed, in ill health, during a profound sleep produced by an opiate; he was only able to recall fifty-four lines. Holde's *Phantasie* was composed under somewhat similar conditions.

Genius in Inspiration.—It is very true that nothing so much resembles a person attacked by madness as a man of genius when meditating and moulding his conceptions. *Aut insanit homo ant*

68 Andrea Verga, *Davide Lazzaretti e la pazzia sensioria* (Milan: Reicheidei, 1880).

versus facit.[69] According to Réveillé-Parise, the man of genius exhibits a small contracted pulse, pale, cold skin, a hot, feverish head, brilliant, wild, injected eyes. After the moment of composition it often happens that the author himself no longer understands what he wrote a short time before. Marini, when writing his *Adone*, did not feel a serious burn of the foot. Tasso, during composition, was like a man possessed. Lagrange felt his pulse become irregular while he wrote. Alfieri's sight was troubled. Some, in order to give themselves up to meditation, even put themselves artificially into a state of cerebral semi-congestion. Thus Schiller plunged his feet into ice. Pitt and Fox prepared their speeches after excessive indulgence in porter. Paisiello composed beneath a mountain of coverlets. Descartes buried his head in a sofa. Bonnet retired into a cold room with his head enveloped in hot cloths. Cujas worked lying prone on the carpet. It was said of Leibnitz that he "meditated horizontally," such being the attitude necessary to enable him to give himself up to the labour of thought. Milton composed with his head leaning over his easy-chair.[70] Thomas and Rossini composed in their beds. Rousseau meditated with his

69 Latin: The mad is either insane or composing verses. Horace, Satirae, II. —Ed.

70 Joseph-Henri Réveillé-Parise, *Physiologie et hygiène des hommes livrés aux travaux de l'esprit*, 2 vols. (Paris: G. A. Dentu, 1834) 2: 314. [In the original, Lombroso gives page 285, but he specifies neither the work nor the edition; the page number above is from the first edition. —Ed.]

head in the full glare of the sun.[71] Shelley lay on the hearthrug with his head close to the fire. All these are instinctive methods for augmenting momentarily the cerebral circulation at the expense of the general circulation.

It is known that very often the great conceptions of thinkers have been organized, or at all events have taken their start, in the shock of a special sensation which produced on the intelligence the effect of a drop of salt water on a well-prepared voltaic pile. All great discoveries have been occasioned, according to Moleschott's remark, by a simple sensation.[72] Some frogs which were to furnish a medicinal broth for Galvani's wife were the origin of the discovery of galvanism; the movement of a hanging lamp, the fall of an apple, inspired the great systems of Galileo and Newton. Allied composed or conceived his tragedies while listening to music, or soon after. A celebrated cantata of Mozart's Don *Giovanni* came to him on seeing an orange, which recalled a popular Neapolitan air heard five years before. The sight of a porter suggested to Leonardo da Vinci his celebrated *Giuda*. The movements of his model suggested to Thorwaldsen the attitude

---

71 François Arago, *Œuvres complètes de François Arago*, Ed. Jean-Augustin Barrall, 15 vols. (Paris: Gide, 1851-1862) 2:84. [The original footnote in the 1891 edition gives page iii, but there is no reference to Rousseau there; neither is there a reference to the volume. —Ed.]

72 Jacob Moleschott, *Kreislauf des Lebens: Physiologische Antworten auf Liebig's chemische Briefe* (Mainz: Victor von Zabern, 1855) Brief. xviii.

of his Seated Angel. *Salvator Rosa* owed his first grandiose inspirations to the scenes of Posilipo. Hogarth conceived his grotesque scenes in a Highgate tavern, after his nose had been broken in a dispute with a drunkard. Milton, Bacon, Leonardo da Vinci, liked to hear music before beginning to work. Bourdaloue tried an air on the violin before writing one of his immortal sermons. Reading one of Spenser's odes aroused the poetic vocation in Cowley. A boiling teakettle suggested to Watt the idea of the steam-engine.

In the same way a sensation is the point of departure of the terrible deeds produced by impulsive mania. Humboldt's nursemaid confessed that the sight of the fresh and delicate flesh of his child irresistibly impelled her to bite it. Many persons, at the sight of a hatchet, a flame, a corpse, have been drawn to murder, incendiarism, or the profanation of cemeteries.

It must be added that inspiration is often transformed into a real hallucination; in fact, as Bettinelli well says, the man of genius sees the objects which his imagination presents to him. Dickens and Kleist grieved over the fates of their heroes. Kleist was found in tears just after finishing one of his tragedies: "She is dead," he said. Schiller was as much moved by the adventures of his personages as by real events.[73] T. Grossi told Verga that in

73 "Über die Einbildungskraft der Dichter. (rec.: Goethe, Vorlesungen von Hermann Grimm, 1877)." *Zeitschrift für Völkerpsychologie* 10. (1878) 42-104. [Under the title: "Goethe

describing the apparition of Prina, he saw the figure come before him, and was obliged to relight his lamp to make it disappear. Brièrre de Boismont[74] tells us that the painter Martina really saw the pictures he imagined.[75] One day, someone having come between him and the hallucination, he asked this person to move so that he might go on with his picture.

Contrast, Intermittence, Double Personality.— When the moment of inspiration is over, the man of genius becomes an ordinary man, if he does not descend lower; in the same way personal inequality, or, according to modern terminology, double, or even contrary, personality, is the one of the characters of genius. Our greatest poets, Isaac Disraeli remarked (in *Curiosities of Literature*), Shakespeare and Dryden, are those who have produced the worst lines. It was said of Tintoretto that sometimes he surpassed Tintoretto, and sometimes was inferior to Caracci. Great tragic actors are very cheerful in society, and of melancholy humour at home. The contrary is true

---

und die dichterische Phantasie".].

74 *Des hallucinations, ou Histoire raisonnée des apparitions, des visions, des songes, de l'extase, du magnétisme et du somnambulisme* (Paris, G. Baillière, 1845) 30. Recent investigations in hypnotism show that the hallucination often has the character of real sensation; that, for example, visual suggestions may be modified by lenses. See my *Nuove Studii sull' ipnotismo e sulla credulità* (Stamperia dell'unione tipografico-editrice, 1889).

75 Lazzaretti, *op. cit.*, 1880.

of genuine comedians. *John Gilpin*, that masterpiece of humour, was written by Cowper between two attacks of melancholia. Gaiety was in him the reaction from sadness. It was singular, he remarked, that his most comic verses were written in his saddest moments, without which he would probably never have written them. A patient one day presented himself to Abernethy; after careful examination the celebrated practitioner said, "You need amusement; go and hear Grimaldi; he will make you laugh, and that will be better for you than any drugs." "My God," exclaimed the invalid, "but I am Grimaldi!" Debureau in like manner went to consult an alienist about his melancholy; he was advised to go to Debureau. Klopstock was questioned regarding the meaning of a passage in his poem. He replied, "God and I both knew what it meant once; now God alone knows." Giordano Bruno said of himself: "*In hilantate tristis, in tristitia hilaris*" Ovidio justly remarked concerning the contradictions in Tasso's style, that "when the inspiration was over, he lost his way in his own creations, and could no longer appreciate their beauty or be conscious of it."[76] Renan described himself as "a tissue of contradictions, recalling the classic *hirocerf* with two natures. One of my halves is constantly occupied in demolishing the

76 The original footnote reads '*Studi Critici*, Naples, 1880, p. 95.' However, it seems Lombroso was referring to Francesco d'Ovidio, *Saggi Critici* (Naples: Domenico Morano, 1878). — Ed.

other, like the fabulous animal of Ctesias, who ate his paws without knowing it."[77]

"If there are two such different men in you," said his mistress to Alfred de Musset, "could you not, when the bad one rises, be content to forget the good one?"[78] Musset himself confesses that, with respect to her, he gave way to attacks of brutal anger and contempt, alternating with fits of extravagant affection;

> an exaltation carried to excess made me treat my mistress like an idol, like a divinity. A quarter of an hour after having insulted her I was at her knees; I left off accusing her to ask her pardon; and passed from jesting to tears.

Stupidity.—The doubling of personality, the amnesia and the misoneism so common among men of science, are the key to the innumerable stupidities which intrude into their writings: *quandoque bonus dormitat Homerus.*[79] Flaubert made a very curious collection of these, and called it the "*Dossier de la sottise humaine*"[80] Here are some examples: "The wealth of a country depends on its general prosperity" (Louis Napoleon). "She did

77 *Souvenirs d'enfance et de jeunesse* (Paris: Calmann Lévy, 1883) 73.

78 *La Confession d'un Enfant du Siècle* (Paris: F. Bonnaire, 1836) 218, 251.

79 Latin: 'I become annoyed when the great Homer is being drowsy'. —Ed.

80 French: 'Record of human folly'. —Ed.

not know Latin, but understood it very well" (Victor Hugo, in *Les Misérables*). "Wherever they are, fleas throw themselves against white colours. This instinct has been given them in order that we may catch them more easily. . . . The melon has been divided into slices by nature in order that it may be eaten *en famille*; the pumpkin, being larger, may be eaten with neighbours" (Bernardin de Saint Pierre in *Harmonie de la Nature*). "It is the business of bishops, nobles, and the great officers of the State to be the depositaries and the guardians of the conservative virtues, to teach nations what is good and what is evil, what is true and what is false, in the moral and spiritual world. Others have no right to reason on these matters. They may amuse themselves with the natural sciences. What have they to complain of?" (De Maistre in *Soirées de St. Petersbourg*, 8e *Entretien*, p. 131). "When one has crossed the bounds there are no limits left" (Ponsard). "I have often heard the blindness of the council of Francis I. deplored in repelling Christopher Columbus, when he proposed his expedition to the Indies" (Montesquieu, in *Esprit des Lois*, liv., xxi., chap. xxii. Francis I. ascended the throne in 1515; Columbus died in 1506). "Bonaparte was a great gainer of battles, but beyond that the least general is more skilful than he. . . . It has been believed that he perfected the art of war, and it is certain that he made it retrograde towards the childhood of art" (Chateaubriand, *Les Buonaparte et les Bourbons*). "Voltaire is nowhere as a philosopher, without authority as a critic and historian, out of date as a man of science" (Dupanloup, *Haute éducation intellectuelle*). "Grocery is respectable. It is a branch of commerce. The army is more respectable still, because it is an institution, the aim of which is order. Grocery is useful, the army is necessary" (Jules Noriac in *Les Nouvelles*). Let us recall Pascal, at one time more incredulous than Pyrrho, at another, writing like a Father of the Church; or Voltaire, believing sometimes in destiny, which "causes the growth and the ruin of States";[81] sometimes in fatality which "governs the affairs of the world";[82] sometimes in Providence.[83]

Hyperæsthesia.—If we seek, with the aid of autobiographies, the differences which separate a man of genius from an ordinary man, we find that they consist in very great part in an exquisite, and sometimes perverted, sensibility.

The savage and the idiot feel physical pain very feebly; they have few passions, and they only attend to the sensations which concern more directly the necessities of existence. The higher we rise in the moral scale, the more sensibility increases; it is highest in great minds, and is the source of their misfortunes as well as of their triumphs. They feel and notice more things, and with greater vivacity and tenacity than other men; their recollections are richer and their mental combinations

81 Introduction to *Essai sur les mœurs et l'esprit des nations.*

82 *Siècle de Louis XIV.*, i.

83 *Dictionnaire Philosophique*, art. Climat.

more fruitful. Little things, accidents that ordinary people do not see or notice, are observed by them, brought together in a thousand ways, which we call creations, and which are only binary and quaternary combinations of sensations.

Haller wrote:

> What remains to me except sensibility, that powerful sentiment which results from a temperament vividly moved by the impressions of love and the marvels of science? Even to-day to read of a generous action calls tears from my eyes. This sensibility has certainly given to my poems a passion which is not found elsewhere.[84]

Diderot said: “If nature has ever made a sensitive soul it is mine. Multiply sensitive souls, and you will augment good and evil actions.”[85]

The first time that Alfieri heard music he experienced as it were a dazzling in his eyes and ears. He passed several days in a strange but agreeable melancholy; there was an efflorescence of fantastic ideas; at that moment he could have written poetry if he had known how, and expressed sentiments if he had had any to express. He concludes, with Sterne, Rousseau, and George Sand, that “there is nothing which agitates the soul with such unconquerable force as musical sounds.” Berlioz

84 *Tagebuch seiner Beobachtungen übert Schriftsteller und übert sich selbst* (Bern: Hallerschen Buchhandlung, 1787) ii: 120.

85 *Paradoxe sur le Comédien* (Paris: A. Sautelet, 1830).

has described his emotions on hearing beautiful music: first a sensation of voluptuous ecstasy, immediately followed by general agitation with palpitation, oppression, sobbing, trembling, sometimes terminating with a kind of fainting fit. Malibran, on first hearing Beethoven's symphony in C minor, had a convulsive attack and had to be taken out of the hall. Musset, Goncourt, Flaubert, Carlyle had so delicate a perception of sounds that the noises of the streets and bells were insupportable to them; they were constantly changing their abodes to avoid these sounds, and at last fled in despair to the country.[86] Schopenhauer also hated noise.

86 Noise had become an obsession to Jules de Goncourt, says his brother Edmund, in a note to the former's Lettres: "It seemed to him that he had 'an ear in the pit of his stomach,' and indeed noise had taken, and continued to take as his illness increased, as it were in some f eerie at once absurd and fatal, the character of a persecution of the things and surroundings of his life. . . . During the last years of his life he suffered from noise as from a brutal physical touch. . . . This persecution by noise led my brother to sketch a gloomy story during his nightly insomnia. . . . In this story a man was eternally pursued by noise, and leaves the rooms he had rented, the houses he had bought, the forests in which he had camped, forests like Fontainebleau, from which he is driven by the hunter's horn, the interior of the pyramids, in which he was deafened by the crickets, always seeking silence, and at last killing himself for the sake of the silence of supreme repose, and not finding it then, for the noise of the worms in his grave prevented him from sleeping. Oh, noise, noise, noise! I can no longer bear to hear the birds. I begin to cry to them like Debureau to the nightingale, 'Will you not be still, vile beast?'". Lettres de Jules de Goncourt (Paris: Charpentier, 1885).

Urquiza fainted on breathing the odour of a rose. Baudelaire had a very delicate sense of smell; he perceived the odour of women in dresses; he could not live in Belgium, he said, because the trees had no fragrance.

Guy de Maupassant says of Gustave Flaubert:

> From his early childhood the distinctive features of his nature were a great naïveté and a horror of physical action. All his life he remained *naïf* and sedentary. It exasperated him to see people walking or moving about him, and he declared in his mordant, sonorous, always rather theatrical voice, that it was not philosophic. 'One can only think and write seated,' he said.

Sterne wrote that intuition and sensibility are the only instruments of genius, the source of the delicious impressions which give a more brilliant colour to joy, and which make us weep with happiness. It is known that Alfieri and Foscolo often fell at the feet of women who were very unworthy of them. Alfieri could not eat on the day when his horse did not neigh. Every one knows that the beauty and love of the Fornarina[87] inspired Raphael's palette,

87 La Fornarina ('the baker's daughter'), real name Margarita Luti, was Raphael's mistress and model. His infatuation with her was such that when commissioned by Agostino Chigi to decorate the Villa Farnesina, he was unable to dedicate himself properly to his work until she was allowed to come to live at his side. He also delayed his marriage for long on her account. —Ed.

but very few know that he also composed one hundred sonnets in her honour.[88]

Dante and Alfieri fell in love at nine years of age, Scarron at eight, Rousseau at eleven, Byron at eight. At sixteen Byron, hearing that his beloved was about to marry, almost fell into convulsions; he was almost suffocated and, although he had no idea of sex, he doubted if he ever loved so truly in later years. He had a convulsive attack, Moore tells us, on seeing Kean act. The painter Francia died of joy on seeing one of Raphael's pictures.[89] Ampère

88 Among the fragments that have been preserved some are of great sweetness:—

Quanta fu dolce il giogo e la catena
De' suoi candidi bracci al col mio volle,
Che sciogliendomi io sento mortal pena;
D'altre cose non dico che son molte,
Chè soverchia dolcezza a morte mena.

89 In Matthew Pilkington's *Dictionary of Painters: from the revival of the art to the present period* (J. Johnson; R. Faulder; J. Walker; etc., 1805) 428, there is a different version of this story, and it is suggested that it may be altogether apocryphal. Under Raibolini's entry, it reads: 'In a letter of 1508, edited by Malvasia, Raphael declares that the Madonnas of Francia were inferior in his opinion to none, for beauty, devoutness, and form; he went still further, and addressed to the care, and if he saw occasion to the emendation of Francia, his S. Cecilia destined for the church of S. Gio, in Monte, at Bologna, and this at the summit of his powers, in 1518, the year in which Vasari fixes the death of Raibolini, who, he says, died of grief at the sight of such superior execellence: Vasari is confuted by Malvasia, who proves, that he lived many years after that event . . .' —Ed.

was so sensitive to the beauties of nature that he thought he would die of happiness on seeing the magnificent shores of Genoa. In one of his manuscripts he had left the journal of an unfortunate passion. Newton was so affected on discovering the solution of a problem that he was unable to continue his work. Gay-Lussac and Davy, after making a discovery, danced about in their slippers.

It is this exaggerated sensibility of men of genius, found in less degree in men of talent also, which causes great part of their real or imaginary misfortunes. "This precious gift," writes Mantegazza,

> this rare privilege of genius, brings in its train a morbid reaction to the smallest troubles from without; the slightest breeze, the faintest breath of the dog-days, becomes for these sensitive persons the rumpled rose-petal which will not let the unfortunate sybarite sleep.

La Fontaine perhaps thought of himself when he wrote:—

> *Un souffle, une ombre, tin rien leur donne la fièvre*

Offences which for others are but pin-pricks for them are sharpened daggers. When Foscolo heard a mocking word from one of his friends he became indignant, and said to her: "You wish to see me dead; I will break my skull at your feet"; so saying, he threw himself with great violence and lowered head against the edge of the marble mantelpiece; a charitable bystander promptly seized him by the collar of his coat, and saved his life by throwing him on the ground. Boileau and Chateaubriand could not hear any one praised, even their shoemakers, without a certain annoyance. Hence the manifestations of morbid vanity which often approximate men of genius to ambitious monomaniacs. Schopenhauer was furious and refused to pay his debts to any one who spelled his name with a double "p." Barthez could not sleep with grief because in the printing of his *Génie* the accent on the e was divided into two. Whiston said he ought not to have published his refutation of Newton's chronology, as Newton was capable of killing him. Poushkin was seen one day in the crowded theatre, in a fit of jealousy, to bite the shoulder of the wife of the Governor-General, Countess Z., to whom he was then paying attention.

Any one who has had the rare fortune to live with men of genius is soon struck by the facility with which they misinterpret the acts of others, believe themselves persecuted, and find everywhere profound and infinite reasons for grief and melancholy. Their intellectual superiority contributes to this end, being equally adapted to discover new aspects of truth and to create imaginary ones, confirming their own painful illusions. It is true, also, that their intellectual superiority permits them to acquire and to express, regarding the nature of things, convictions different from those adopted by the majority, and to manifest them with an unshakeable firmness which increases the opposition and contrast.

But the principal cause of their melancholy and their misfortunes is the law of dynamism which rules in the nervous system. To an excessive expenditure and development of nervous force succeeds reaction or enfeeblement. It is permitted to no one to expend more than a certain quantity of force without being severely punished on the other side; that is why men of genius are so unequal in their productions. Melancholy, depression, timidity, egoism, are the prices of the sublime gifts of intellect, just as uterine catarrhs, impotence, and tabes dorsalis[90] are the prices of sexual abuse, and gastritis of abuse of appetite.

Milli, after one of her eloquent improvisations which are worth the whole existence of a minor poet, falls into a state of paralysis which lasts several days. Mahomet after prophesying fell into a state of imbecility. "Three *suras* of the *Koran*" he said one day to Abou-Bekr, "have been enough to whiten my hair."[91] In short, I do not believe there has ever been a great man who, even at the height of his happiness, has not believed and proclaimed, even without cause, that he was unfortunate and persecuted, and who has not at some moment ex-

90 Tabes dorsalis, also known as syphilitic myelopathy, is a slow degeneration of the nerves primarily in the dorsal columns of the spinal cord. —Ed.

91 *Journal des Savans* (1863).

perienced the painful modifications of sensibility which are the foundation of melancholia.

Sometimes this sensibility undergoes perversion; it consumes itself, and is agitated around a single point, remaining indifferent to all others. Certain series of ideas or sensations acquire, little by little, the force of a special stimulant on the brain, and sometimes on the entire organism, so that they seem to survive life itself. Heine, who in his letters declared himself incapable of understanding the simplest things, Heine, blind and paralytic, when advised to turn towards God, replied in his dying agony: "*Dieu me pardonnera; c'est son métier*;"[92] thus crowning with a stroke of supreme irony the most æsthetically cynical life of our time. The last words of Aretino after extreme unction were, it is said, "Keep me from the rats now I am anointed." The dying Rabelais enveloped his head in his domino, and said, "*Beati qui in Domino moriuntur.*" Malherbe, in his last illness, reproached his nurse with the solecisms she committed, and rejected the counsel of his confessor on account of its bad style. The last words of Bouhours the grammarian, were, "*Je vais ou je va mourir: l'un et l'autre se disent.*"

Foscolo confesses that "very active in some directions, he was in others inferior to a man, to a woman, to a child."[93] It is known that Corneille, Descartes, Virgil, Addison, La Fontaine, Dryden,

92 French: God will forgive me; it's his job. —Ed.

93 Ugo Foscolo, *Epistolario* 3: 163.

Manzoni, Newton, were almost incapable of expressing themselves in public. D'Alembert and Ménage, insensible to the sufferings of a surgical operation, wept at a slight critical censure. Luce de Lancival smiled when his legs were amputated, but could not endure Geoffrey's criticisms. Linnaeus, at the age of sixty, rendered paralytic and insensible by an apoplectic stroke, was aroused when carried near to his beloved herbarium.[94] Lagny was stretched out comatose, insensible to the strongest stimulants, when it occurred to someone to ask him the square of twelve, he replied immediately, "One hundred and forty-four." Sebouyah, the Arab grammarian, died of grief because the Khalif Haroun-al-Raschid did not agree with him on some grammatical point.

It should be observed here that men of genius, at all events, if men of science, often present that species of mania which Wechniakoff[95] and Letourneau[96] have called *monotypic*. Such men occupy themselves throughout their whole lives with one single problem, the first which takes possession of their brains, and which henceforth rules them. Otto Beckmann was occupied during the whole of his life with the pathology of the kidneys; Fresnel with light; Meyer with ants. Here is a new and striking point of resemblance with monomaniacs.

94 Felix Vicq d'Azir, *Éloge historique du médecin Girod* (Besançon: Jacques-François Couché, 1785) 209.

95 *Physiologie des Génies* (1875).

96 *Science et Matérialisme* (Paris: Reinwald, 1890) 103.

On account of this exaggerated and concentrated sensibility, it becomes very difficult to persuade or dissuade either men of genius or the insane. In them the roots of error, as well as those of truth, fix themselves more deeply and multiplexly than in other men, for whom opinion is a habit, an affair of fashion, or of circumstance. Hence the slight utility of moral treatment as applied to the insane; hence also the frequent fallibility of genius.

In the same way we can explain why it is that great minds do not seize ideas that the most vulgar intelligence can grasp, while at the same time they discover ideas which would have seemed absurd to others: their greater sensibility is associated with a greater originality of conception. In exalted meditation thought deserts the more simple and easy paths which no longer suit its robust energy. Thus Monge resolved the most difficult problems of a differential calculus, and was embarrassed in seeking an algebraic root of the second degree which a schoolboy might have found. One of Lulli's friends used to say habitually on his behalf: "Pay no attention to him; he has no common sense: he is all genius."

Paræsthesia.—To the exhaustion and excessive concentration of sensibility must be attributed all those strange acts showing apparent or intermittent anæsthesia, and analgesia, which are to be found among men of genius as well as among the insane. Socrates presented a photoparæsthesia which enabled him to gaze at the sun for a considerable time without experiencing any discomfort. The Goncourts, Flaubert, Darwin had a kind of musical daltonism.

Amnesia.—Forgetfulness is another of the characters of genius. It is said that Newton once rammed his niece's finger into his pipe; when he left his room to seek for anything he usually returned without bringing it.[97] Rouelle generally explained his ideas at great length, and when he had finished, he added: "But this is one of my arcana which I tell to no one." Sometimes one of his pupils rose and repeated in his ear what he had just said aloud; then Rouelle believed that the pupil had discovered the arcanum by his own sagacity, and begged him not to divulge what he had himself just told to two hundred persons. One day, when performing an experiment during a lecture, he said to his hearers: "You see, gentlemen, this cauldron over the flame? Well, if I were to leave off stirring it an explosion would at once occur which would make us all jump." While saying these words, he did not fail to forget to stir, and the prediction was accomplished; the explosion took place with a fearful noise: the laboratory windows were all smashed, and the audience fled to the garden.[98] Sir Everard Home relates that he once suddenly lost his memory for half an hour, and was unable to recognise the house and the street in which he

97 Sir David Brewster, *The Life of Isaac Newton* (New York: J. & J. Harper, 1831).

98 *Revue Scientifique* (1888).

lived; he could not recall the name of the street, and seemed to hear it for the first time. It is told of Ampère that when travelling on horseback in the country he became absorbed in a problem; then, dismounting, began to lead his horse, and finally lost it; but he did not discover his misadventure until, on arrival, it attracted the attention of his friends. Babinet hired a country house, and after making the payments returned to town; then he found that he had entirely forgotten both the name of the place and from what station he had started.[99]

One day Buffon, lost in thought, ascended a tower and slid down by the ropes, unconscious of what he was doing, like a somnambulist. Mozart, in carving meat, so often cut his fingers, accustomed only to the piano, that he had to give up this duty to other persons. Of Bishop Minister, it is said that, seeing at the door of his own ante-chamber the announcement: "The master of the house is out," he remained there awaiting his own return.[100] Of Toucherel, it is told by Arago, that he once even forgot his own name. Beethoven, on returning from an excursion in the forest, often left his coat on the grass, and often went out hatless. Once, at Neustadt, he was arrested in this condition, and taken to prison as a vagabond; here he might have remained, as no one would believe that he was Beethoven, if Herzog,

99 Alfred Michiels, *Le monde du comique et du rire* (Paris: Calmann-Lévy, 1886).

100 *Réveillé-Parise, op. cit.*

the conductor of the orchestra, had not arrived to deliver him. Gioia, in the excitement of composition, wrote a chapter on the table of his bureau instead of on paper. The Abbe Beccaria, absorbed in his experiments, said' during mass: "*Ite! experientia facta est*" Saint Dominic, in the midst of a princely repast, suddenly struck the table and exclaimed: "*Conclusum est contra Manicheos*" It is told of Ampère that having written a formula, with which he was preoccupied, on the back of a cab, he started in pursuit as soon as the cab went off.[101] Diderot hired vehicles which he then left at the door and forgot, thus needlessly paying coachmen for whole days. He often forgot the hour, the day, the month, and even the person to whom he was speaking; he would then speak long monologues like a somnambulist.[102] Rossini, conducting the orchestra at the rehearsal of his *Barbiere,* which was a fiasco, did not perceive that the public and even the performers had left him alone in the theatre until he reached the end of an act.

Originality.—Hagen notes that originality is the quality that distinguishes genius from talent. And Jürgen-Meyer:

> The imagination of talent reproduces the stated fact; the inspiration of genius makes it anew. The first disengages or repeats; the second in-

101 Bernard Perez, *L'enfant de trois à sept ans* (Paris: Félix Alcan, 1886).

102 Edmond Scherer, *Diderot* (Paris: Calmann-Lévy, 1880).

> vents or creates. Talent aims at a point which appears difficult to reach; genius aims at a point which no one perceives. The novelty, it must be understood, resides not in the elements, but in their shock.

Novelty and grandeur are the two chief characters which Bettinelli attributes to genius; "for this reason," he says, "poets call themselves *troubadours* or *trouvères*." Cardan conceived the idea of the education of deaf mutes before Harriot;[103] he caught a glimpse of the application of algebra to geometry and geometric constructions before Descartes.[104] Giordano Bruno divined the modern theories of cosmology and of the origin of ideas. Cola di Rienzi conceived Italian unity, with Rome as capital, four hundred years before Cavour and Mazzini. Stoppani admits that the geological theory of Dante, with regard to the formation of seas, is at all points in accordance with the accepted ideas of to-day.

Genius divines facts before completely knowing them; thus Goethe described Italy very well before knowing it; and Schiller, the land and people of Switzerland without having been there. And it is on account of those divinations which all precede common observation, and because genius, occupied

103 Friedrich Wilhelm Hagen junior, "Über die Verwandtschaft des Genies mit dem Irrsinn", *Allgemeine Zeitschrift für Psychiatrie und psychisch-gerichtliche Medicin* 33 (1877).

104 Antonino Bertolotti, *Il Testamenti di Girolamo Cardano medico, filosofo e matematico del secolo* 16 (Milano: Tipografia Bortolotti di Dal Bono & C. 1882).

with lofty researches, does not possess the habits of the many, and because, like the lunatic and unlike the man of talent, he is often disordered, the man of genius is scorned and misunderstood. Ordinary persons do not perceive the steps which have led the man of genius to his creation, but they see the difference between his conclusions and those of others, and the strangeness of his conduct. Rossini's *Barbiere,* and Beethoven's *Fidetio* were received with hisses; Boito's *Mefistofele* and Wagner's *Lohengrin* have been hissed at Milan. How many academicians have smiled compassionately at Marzolo, who has discovered a new philosophic world! Bolyai, for his invention of the fourth dimension in anti-Euclidian geometry, has been called the geometrician of the insane, and compared to a miller who wishes to make flour of sand. Everyone knows the treatment accorded to Fulton and Columbus and Papin, and, in our own days, to Piatti and Praga and Abel, and to Schliemann, who found Ilium, where no one else had dreamed of looking for it, while learned academicians laughed. "There never was a liberal idea," wrote Flaubert,

> which has not been unpopular; never an act of justice which has not caused scandal; never a great man who has not been pelted with potatoes or struck by knives. The history of human intellect is the history of human stupidity, as M. de Voltaire said.[105]

105 Flaubert, *Lettres de Gustave Flaubert à Georges Sand.*

In this persecution, men of genius have no fiercer or more terrible enemies than the men of academies, who possess the weapons of talent, the stimulus of vanity, and the *prestige* by preference accorded to them by the vulgar, and by governments which, in large part, consist of the vulgar. There are, indeed, countries in which the ordinary level of intelligence sinks so low that the inhabitants come to hate not only genius, but even talent.[106]

Originality, though usually of an aimless kind, is observed with some frequency among the insane—as we shall see later on—and especially among those inclined to literature. They sometimes reach the divinations of genius: thus Bernardi, at the Florence Asylum in 1529, wished to show the existence of language among apes.[107]

In exchange for this fatal gift, both the one and the other have the same ignorance of the necessities of practical life which always seems to them less important than their own dreams, and at the same time they possess the disordered habits which renders this ignorance dangerous.

Fondness for Special Words.—This originality causes men of genius, as well as the insane, to create special words, marked with their own imprint,

106 Highly controversial today, and not accepted by mainstream academics, Richard Lynn has done work in this area. See, for example, *The Global Bell Curve* (2008).

107 Octave Delepierre, *Histoire Littéraire des fous* (London: Trübner & Co., 1860).

unintelligible to others, but to which they attach extraordinary significance and importance. Such are the *dignità* of Vico, the individuità of Carrara, the *odio serrato* of Alfieri, the *albero epogonico* of Marzolo, and the *immiarsi*, the *intuarsi*, and the *entomata* of Dante.

CHAPTER III

Latent Forms of Neurosis and Insanity in Genius

Chorea and Epilepsy — Melancholy — Megalomania — Folie du doute — Alcoholism — Hallucinations — Moral Insanity — Longevity

It is now possible to explain the frequency among men of genius, even when not insane, of those forms of neurosis or mental alienation which may be called latent, and which contain the germs and as it were the outlines of these disorders.

Chorea and Epilepsy.—Many men of genius, like the insane, are subject to curious spasmodic and choreic movements. Lenau and Montesquieu left upon the floor of their rooms the signs of the movements by which their feet were convulsively agitated during composition; Buffon, Dr. Johnson, Santeuil, Crébillon, Lombardini, exhibited the most remarkable facial contortions. There was a constant quiver on Thomas Campbell's thin lips. Chateaubriand was long subject to convulsive movements of the arm. Napoleon suffered from habitual spasm of the right shoulder and of the lips; "My anger," he said, one day after an altercation with Lowe, "must have been fearful, for I felt the vibration of my calves, which has not happened to me for a long time." Peter the Great suffered from convulsive movements which horribly distorted his face. Carducci's face at certain moments, writes Mantegazza, is a veritable hurricane; lightnings dart from his eyes and his muscles tremble.[1] Ampère could only express his thoughts while walking, and when his body was in a state of constant movement.[2] Socrates often danced and jumped in the street without reason, as if by a freak.

Julius Cæsar, Dostoyevsky, Petrarch, Molière, Flaubert, Charles V., Saint Paul, and Handel, appear to have been all subject to attacks of epilepsy. Twice upon the field of battle the epileptic vertigo nearly had a serious influence on Cæsar's fate. On another occasion, when the Senate had decreed him extraordinary honours, and had gone out to meet him with the consuls and prætors, Cæsar, who at that moment was seated at the tribune, failed to rise, and received the Senators as though they were ordinary citizens. They retired showing signs of discontent, and Cæsar, suddenly return-

1 Paolo Mantegazza, *Physiognomy and Expression* (London: Walter Scott, n.d.).

2 Arago 2:82.

ing to himself, immediately went home, took off his clothes and uncovering his neck, exclaimed that he was ready to deliver his throat to any one who wished to cut it. He explained his behaviour to the Senate as due to the malady to which he was subject; he said that those who were affected by it were unable to speak standing, in public, that they soon felt shocks in their limbs, giddiness, and at last completely lost consciousness.[3]

Convulsions sometimes hindered Molière from doing any work for a fortnight at a time. Mahomet had visions after an epileptic fit: "An angel appears to me in human form; he speaks to me. Often I hear as it were the sound of cats, of rabbits, of bells: then I suffer much." After these apparitions he was overcome with sadness and howled like a young camel. Peter the Great and his son by Catherine were both epileptics.

It may be noted here that artistic creation presents the intermittence, the instantaneousness, and very often the sudden absences of mind which characterize epilepsy. Paganini, Mozart, Schiller, and Alfieri, suffered from convulsions. Paganini was even subject to catalepsy.[4] Pascal from the age of twenty-four had fits which lasted for whole days. Handel had attacks of furious and epileptic rage. Newton and Swift were subject to vertigo, which is related to epilepsy. Richelieu, in a fit, believed he was a horse, and neighed and jumped; afterwards

3 Plutarch, *Life*, &c.

4 Radestock, *op. cit.*

he knew nothing of what had taken place.[5] Maudsley remarks that epileptics often believe themselves patriarchs and prophets. He thinks that by mistaking their hallucinations for divine revelations they have largely contributed to the foundation of religious beliefs. Ann Lee, who founded the sect of Shakers, was an epileptic: she saw Christ come to her physically and spiritually. The vision which transformed Saint Paul from a persecutor into an apostle seems to have been of the same order. The Siberian Shamans, who profess to have intercourse with spirits, operate in a state of convulsive exaltation, and choose their pupils by preference from among epileptic children.

Melancholy.—The tendency to melancholy is common to the majority of thinkers, and depends on their hyperæsthesia. It is proverbially said that to feel sorrow more than other men constitutes the crown of thorns of genius. Aristotle had remarked that men of genius are of melancholic temperament, and after him Jürgen-Meyer has affirmed the same. "*Tristes philosophi et severi*" said Varro.

Goethe, the impassible Goethe, confesses that "my character passes from extreme joy to extreme melancholy;" and elsewhere that "every increase of knowledge is an increase of sorrow;" he could not recall that in all his life he had passed more than four pleasant weeks. "I am not made for enjoyment," wrote Flaubert.[6] Giusti was affected by

5 Moreau, *op. cit.* 523.

6 Gustave Flaubert, *Correspondance*, 4 vols. (Paris: Biblio-

hypochondria, which reached to delirium; sometimes he thought he had hydrophobia. Corradi has shown[7] that all the misfortunes of Leopardi, as well as his philosophy, owe their origin to an exaggerated sensibility, and a hopeless love which he experienced at the age of eighteen. In fact, his philosophy was more or less sombre according as his health was better or worse, until the tendency was transformed into a habit. "Thought," he wrote, "has long inflicted on me, and still inflicts, such martyrdom as to produce injurious effects, and it will kill me if I do not change my manner of existence."[8] In his poems Leopardi appears the most romantic and philanthropic of men. In his letters, on the other hand, he appears cold, indifferent to his parents, and still more to his native country. From the publications of his host and protector Ranieri[9] may be seen how little grateful he was to his friends, and that he was eccentric to the verge of insanity. Desiring death every moment in verse, he took exaggerated pains to cling to life, exposing himself to the sun for hours together, sometimes eating only peaches, at other times only flesh, always in extremes. No one hated the country more than he, who so often sang its praises. He hardly reached it before he wished to return, and stayed

---

theque-Charpentier, 1887-93) 3:119

7 Alfonso Corradi, *Memorie dell Istiluto Lombardo* (1878).

8 Letter to Giordani, Aug., 1817.

9 Antonio Ranieri, *Sette Anni Di Sodalizio Con Giacomo Leopardi* (Naples: Riccardo Ricciardi Editore, 1919).

with difficulty an entire day. He made day night, and night day. He suspected every one; one day he even suspected that he had been robbed of a box in which he preserved old combs.

The list of great men who have committed suicide is almost endless. It opens with the names of Zeno,[10] Aristotle (?), Hegesippus, Cleanthes,[11] Stilpo,[12] Dionysius of Heraclea,[13] Lucretius,[14] Lu-

10 The story goes that Zeno (336 – 265 BCE) tripped coming out of the school and broke his toe; lying on the ground, he quoted a line from the Niobe of Timotheus, 'I come of my own accord; why call me thus?' and then, interpreting the accident as a sign he should depart from life, strangled himself. —Ed.

11 Cleanthes (330 – 230 BCE), the Stoic philosopher, was apparently compelled to fast due to a dangerous ulcer. Subsequently, he continued his abstinence, saying that, as he was already half-way on the road to death, he would not trouble to retrace his steps. —Ed.

12 Diogenes Laërtius tells that Stilpo died at a great age, taking wine to hasten his end.

13 Dionysius (d. 306 or 305 BCE), tyrant of Heraclea, suffered from extraordinary obesity, which increased to the point that he could take no food; the latter was therefore introduced into his stomach by artificial means. At last, however, he was choked by his own fat. —Ed.

14 Writing four centuries after Lucretius (c. 99 – 55 BCE)'s death, Jerome tells in his Chronicon, 'Titus Lucretius the poet is born. Later he was driven mad by a love potion, and when, during the intervals of his insanity, he had written a number of books, which were later emended by Cicero, he killed himself by his own hand in the 44th year of his life'. —Ed.

can, [15]and reaches to Chatterton,[16] Clive,[17] Creech,[18] Blount,[19] Haydon,[20] David. Domenichino was led to commit suicide by the contempt of a rival; Spagno-

15 Marcus Annaeus Lucanus (39 – 65 CE), the Roman poet, better known in English as Lucan, became involved in the conspiracy of Gaius Calpurnius Piso against Nero. When his treason was discovered, he was obliged to commit suicide by opening a vein, but not before incriminating his mother, among others, in the hopes of a pardon. Lucan bled to death. —Ed.

16 Thomas Chatterton (1752 – 1770) poisoned himself with arsenic, aged 17. —Ed.

17 For a time it was thought that Robert Clive, 1st Baron Clive, KB MP FRS (1725 – 1774) committed suicide, but biographer John Watney concluded that he likely died of an opium overdose: Clive had been suffering from gall-stones, and had been trying to manage the excruciating pain with opium. —Ed.

18 Reasons for his suicide have been subject of speculation, but it is thought that Thomas Creech (1659 - 1700) most likely caused was his suffering from depression. —Ed.

19 Alexander Pope wrote in a footnote to his 'Epilogue to the Satires: Dialogue I' that Charles Blount (1654 - 1693), 'being in love with a near kinswoman of his, and rejected, gave himself a stab in the arm, as pretending to kill himself, of the consequence of which he really died'. —Ed.

20 Benjamin Robert Haydon (1786 - 1846)'s commercial success was damaged by his often tactless dealings with patrons, and by the enormous scale on which he preferred to work. He was troubled by financial problems throughout his life, which led to several periods of imprisonment for debt. The artist's difficulties increased to such an extent that, whilst employed on his last grand effort, Alfred and the Trial by Jury, overcome by debts of over £3,000, disappointment, and ingratitude, he wrote 'Stretch me no longer on this rough world', and shot himself. The bullet failed to kill him, so he finished the job by cutting his throat. —Ed.

letto by the abduction of his daughter;[21] Nourrit by the success of Dupré;[22] Gros could not survive the decadence of his genius.[23] Robert, Chateaubriand, Cowper, Rousseau, Lamartine on several occasions nearly put an end to their lives. Burns wrote in a letter: "My constitution and frame were *ab origine* blasted with a deep incurable taint of melancholia which poisons my existence." Schiller passed through a period of melancholy which caused him to be suspected of insanity. In B. Constant's letters we read: "If I had had my dear opium, it would have been the moment, in honour of ennui, to put an end to an excessive movement of love."[24] Dupuytren thought of suicide even when he had reached the climax of fame. Pariset and Cavour were only saved from suicide by devoted

21 Spanish tenebrist painter José Ribera (1591 - 1652), known as Lo Spagnoletto, was in serious debt at the end of his life, and his daughter had been seduced by Don Juan of Austria, but it seems he died of grief, the story of his suicide being a fiction. —Ed.

22 Adolphe Nourrit (1802 – 1839) suffered from liver disease, and this eventually affected his mental state and memory. On 7 March 1839 he sang at a benefit concert but was disappointed by the quality of his performance and the audience's reaction to it. The following morning, he jumped to his death from the Hotel Barbaia. —Ed.

23 Exasperated by criticism and the consciousness of failure, Antoine-Jean Gros (1771 – 1835) sought refuge in the grosser pleasures of life, until he was found drowned on the shores of the Seine at Meudon, near Sèvres. From a paper found in his hat it became known that he, betrayed by last faculties which rendered life bearable, had resolved to end it. —Ed.

24 Bièrre de Boismont, *op. cit.* 265.

friends. The latter twice attempted to kill himself. Lessmann, the humorous writer, who wrote the *Journal of a Melancholiac*, hanged himself in 1835 during an attack of melancholia. So died, also, the composer of *Masaniello*, Fischer, Romilly, Eult von Burg, Hugh Miller,[25] Gohring, Kuh (the friend of Mendelssohn), Jules Uberti, Tannahill,[26] Prevost-Paradol,[27] Kleist,[28] who died with his mistress, and Majláth, who drowned himself with his daughter.[29]

George Sand, who seems, however, free from all neurosis, declared that whether it was that bile made her melancholy, or that melancholy made her bilious, she had been seized at moments of her life by a desire for eternal repose—for suicide. She

25 Scottish geologist Hugh Miller (1802 – 1856) likely suffered from psychotic depression and feared he would harm his wife and children because of persecutory delusions. He shot himself in the chest with a revolver. —Ed.

26 Following the rejection of some of his work by a publisher, Scottish poet Robert Tannahill (1774 – 1810) drowned himself in a stream. —Ed.

27 French journalist Lucien-Anatole Prévost-Paradol (1829 – 1870), a proponent of moderate liberalism shot himself after political developments went against him, which led to his being attacked. —Ed.

28 Kleist's lover, Henriette Vogel, was suffering from cancer and he was embittered and disheartened. At her bidding, he first killed her and then himself on the shore of Kleiner Wannsee. —Ed.

29 A few years before his death János Majláth, or Count John (1786 – 1855) removed to Munich, where he fell into a state of destitution and extreme despondency. —Ed.

attributed this to an affection of the liver.

> It was an old chronic disorder, experienced and fought with from early youth, forgotten like an old travelling companion whom one believes one has left behind, but who suddenly presents himself. This temptation,

she continues,

> was sometimes so strange that I regarded it as a kind of madness. It took the form of a fixed idea and bordered on monomania. The idea was aroused chiefly by the sight of water, of a precipice, of phials.

George Sand tells us that Gustave Planche was of strangely melancholy character. Edgar Quinet suffered at times from unreasonable melancholy, in this taking after his mother. Rossini experienced, about 1848, keen grief because he had bought a house at a slight loss. He became really insane, and took it into his head that he was reduced to extreme misery, so that he must beg. He believed that he had become an idiot. He could, indeed, neither compose nor even hear music spoken of. The care of Sansone, of Ancona, gradually restored him to fame and to his friends. The great painter Van Leyden believed himself poisoned, and during his latter years never rose from his bed. Mozart was convinced that the Italians wished to poison him. Molière had numerous attacks of melancholia.[30] Voltaire was hypochondriacal. "With respect to my body," he wrote,

> it is moribund. . . . I anticipate dropsy. There is no appearance of it, but you know that there is nothing so dry as a dropsical person. . . . Diseases, more cruel even than kings, are persecuting me. Doctors only are needed to finish me.

"All this" (travels, pleasures, &c.), said Grimm, "did not prevent him from saying that he was dead or dying; he was even very angry when one dared to assure him that he was still full of strength and life." Zimmermann was afraid sometimes of dying of hunger, sometimes of being arrested; he actually died of voluntary starvation, the result of a fixed idea that he had no money to pay for food. The poet Gray, the "melancholy Gray," was of a gloomy and extremely reserved character. Abraham Lincoln was a victim of constitutional melancholy, which assumed a most dangerous form on one or two occasions in his earlier years.

Chopin during the last years of his life was possessed by a melancholy which went as far as insanity. An abandoned convent in Spain filled his imagination with phantoms and terrors. One day G. Sand and her son were late in returning from a walk. Chopin began to imagine, and finally believed, that they were dead; then he saw himself dead, drowned in a lake, and drops of frozen water

30 Hagen, *op cit.*

fell upon his breast. They were real drops of rain falling upon him from the roof of the ruin, but he did not perceive this, even when George Sand pointed it out. Some trifling annoyance affected him more than a great and real misfortune. A crumpled petal, a fly, made him weep.[31]

Cavour from youth believed himself deprived of domestic affections. He saw no friends around; he saw above him no ideal to realise; lie found himself alone.[32] His condition reached such a point that, to avoid greater evils and to leave an insipid life, he wished to kill himself. He hesitated only because he was doubtful about the morality of suicide.

> But, while this doubt exists, it is best for me to imitate Hamlet. I will not kill myself: no, but I will put up earnest prayers to heaven to send me a rapid consumption which may carry me off to the other world.

At a very youthful age he sometimes gave himself up to strange attacks of bad temper. One day, at the Castle of Diluzers, at Balangero, he threw himself into so violent a rage on being asked to study that he wished to kill himself with a knife and throw himself from the window. These attacks were very frequent but of brief duration.[33] When

31 George Sand, *Histoire de ma vie* (Paris: V. Lecou, 1854-1855) v. 9.

32 Domenico Berti, *Il Conde di Cavour Avanti il 1848* (Rome: Voghera Carlo, 1886) 154.

33 *Ibid.*; Mayor, in *Archivo di Psichiatria*, v. IV.

the hopes of war raised by the words of Napoleon III. to Baron Hübner seemed suddenly to give place in the Emperor's mind to thoughts of peace, Cavour was carried away by such agitation that some extreme resolution was apprehended. This is confirmed by Castelli, who went to his house and found him alone in his room. He had burnt various papers, and given orders that no one should be admitted. The danger was plain. He looked fixedly at Castelli, who spoke a few calm words calculated to affect him, and then burst into tears. Cavour rose, embraced him convulsively, took a few steps distractedly about the room, and then said slowly: "Be at rest; we will brave everything, and always together." Castelli ran to reassure his friends, but the danger had been very grave.[34]

Chateaubriand relates, in his *Mémoires d'outre tombe*, that one day as a youth he charged an old musket, which sometimes went off by itself, with three balls, inserted the barrel in his mouth and struck the stock against the ground. The appearance of a passer-by suspended his resolution.

Gerard de Nerval was never so much inspired as in those movements when, according to the saying of Alaxandre Dumas, his melancholy became his muse. "Werther, Rene, Antony," says Dumas, "never uttered more poignant complaints, more sorrowful sighs, tenderer words, or more poetic cries."

34 Mayor, *op. cit.*

J. S. Mill[35] was seized during the autumn of 1826, at the age of twenty, by an attack of insanity which he himself could only describe in these words of Coleridge's:

> A grief without a pang, void, dark, and drear,
> A drowsy, stifled, unimpassioned grief,
> Which finds no natural outlet or relief
> In word, or sigh, or tear.

I quote these lines the more willingly as they show in their extreme energy that Coleridge himself was affected by the same malady. To this state of mind succeeded another in which Mill sought to cultivate the feelings; among other preoccupations he feared the exhaustion of musical combinations:

> The octave consists only of five tones and two semi-tones, which can be put together in only a limited number of ways, of which but a small proportion are beautiful: most of them, it seemed to me, must have been already discovered, and there could not be room for a long succession of Mozarts and Webers to strike out, as these had done, entirely new and surpassingly rich veins of musical beauty. This source of anxiety may, perhaps, be thought to resemble that of the philosophers of Laputa, who feared lest the sun should be burnt out.[36]

35 *Autobiography*.

36 *Autobiography* 145.

Megalomania (Delusions of grandeur).—The delirium of melancholia alternates with that of grandiose monomania.

"The title 'Son of David,'" writes Renan, "was the first which Jesus Christ accepted, probably without taking part in the innocent frauds by which it was sought to make it certain. The family of David had, in fact, long been extinct." Later on he declared himself the son of God. "His Father had given him all power; nature obeyed him; he could forgive sins; he was superior to David, to Abraham, to Solomon, to the prophets. It is evident," Renan continues,

> that the title of Rabbi, with which he was at first contented, no longer satisfied him; even the title of Prophet or Messenger from God no longer corresponded to his conception. The position which he attributed to himself was that of a superhuman being.

He declared that he was come to give sight to the blind, and to blind those who think they see. One day his ill humour with the Temple called forth an imprudent expression: "This Temple, made by human hands," he said, "I could, if I liked, destroy, and in its place build another, not made by human hands. The Queen of Sheba," he added,

> will rise up at the Judgment against the men of to-day and condemn them, because they came from the ends of the earth to hear Solomon's

> wisdom; yet a greater than Solomon is here. The men of Nineveh will rise up at the Judgment against the men of to-day and condemn them, because they repented at the preaching of Jonah; yet a greater than Jonah is here.

Dante's pride, legitimate as it may have been, is proverbial. It is well known that he placed himself "*sesto fra cotanto senno*," and declared himself superior to his contemporaries in style and the favourite of God:—

> *. . . e forse e nato*
> *Chi l'uno e l'altro caccierà di nido. . . .*
> *. . . perchè tanta*
> *Grazia in te luce prima che sei morto. . . .*

At the Institute, Dumas said with truth of Hugo: "Victor Hugo was dominated by a fixed idea: to become the greatest poet and the greatest man of all countries and all ages." It is this, according to Dumas, which explains the entire life and all the changes in Victor Hugo, who began by being a Catholic and monarchist.

> He could not submit to be shut up within a government and a religion where he had not the right to say anything and the chance to be first. The glory of Napoleon long-haunted Victor Hugo. But the day came when he could no longer tolerate that any one should have glory equal to his own. The great captain must give way to the great poet; the giant of action must

> efface himself before the giant of thought. Is not Homer greater than Achilles? Victor Hugo came to believe himself superior to all human beings. He did not say, 'I am Genius,' but he began to believe firmly that the world would say so. His personages do not possess the characters of reality nor the proportions of man; they are always above and beyond humanity, sometimes reversed, not to say upside down; that was because Nature had for him aspects that were seen by no other. His eye enlarged everything; he saw herbs as tall as trees; he saw insects as large as eagles.

Hegel believed in his own divinity. He began a lecture with these words: "I may say with Christ, that not only do I teach truth, but that I am myself truth."[37]

"Man is the vainest of animals, and the poet is the vainest of men," wrote Heine, who knew.[38] And in another letter: "Do not forget that I am a poet, and, as such, convinced that men must forsake all and read my verses."

"Everyone knows," wrote George Sand of her friend Balzac,[39]

> how the consciousness of greatness overflowed in him, how he loved to speak of his works and to narrate them. Genial and ingenuous, he

37 Karl Johann von Seidlitz, *Schopenhauer* (Dorpat: W. Gläser, 1872).

38 *Letters* (1885).

39 *Histoire de ma vie* v:9.

> asked advice from children, but never waited for the answer, or else opposed it with all the obstinacy of his superiority. He never instructed, but always talked very well indeed of himself, of himself alone. One evening, having on a beautiful new dressing-gown, he wished to go out, thus clothed, with a lamp in his hand, to excite the admiration of the public.

Chopin directed in his will that he should be buried in a white tie, small shoes, and short breeches. He abandoned the woman whom he tenderly loved because she offered a chair to someone else before giving the same invitation to himself.[40]

Giordano Bruno declared himself illumined by superior light, a messenger from God, who knew the essence of things, a Titan who would destroy Jupiter: "And what others see far ahead I leave behind."[41] And again:—

> *Nam me Deus alter*
> *Vertentis sæcli melioris non mediocrem*
> *Destinat, haud veluti, media de plebe, magistrum*

The poet Lucilius did not rise when Julius Cæsar entered the college of poets because he believed himself his superior in the art of verse. Ariosto, after receiving the laurel from Charles V., ran like a

40 George Sand, *op. cit.*

41 *De immenso et innumerabilibus.* III.

madman through the streets.[42] The celebrated surgeon Porta would not suffer any medical paper to be read at the Lombard Institute without murmuring and showing his contempt; as soon as a mathematical or philological paper was brought forward he became quiet and attentive. Comte gave out that he was the High Priest of Humanity. Wetzel intitled his works, *Opera Dei Wetzelii*. Rouelle, the founder of chemistry in France, quarrelled with all his disciples who wrote on chemistry. They were, he said, ignorant bunglers, plagiaries; this latter term assumed so odious a significance in his mind that he applied it to the worst criminals; for instance, to express his horror of Damiens he said he was a plagiary.

Many men of genius, while avoiding these excesses, nevertheless believe that they embody in themselves absolute truth; they modify scientific conclusions in their own interests, and in accordance with the part they are themselves able to take. Delacroix, become incapable of drawing beautiful lines, declared, "Colour is everything." Ingres said, "Drawing is honesty, drawing is honour." Chopin charged Schubert and Shakespeare with temerity because in these great men he al-

42 Johann Burchard Mencke, *De charlataneria eruditorum* (Amsterdam: Excudebat Ulricus Christianus Saalbachius, 1747) 154. [Lombroso gives here an inaccurate footnote, which in the original reads 'G. Menke, *De ciarlataneria eruditorum*, 1780'; I have corrected the citation and been able to find the passage to which he refers in an earlier edition, so I have also been able to add the page number. —Ed.]

ways sought a correspondence with his own temperament.[43] The Princess Conti having said to Malherbe, "I wish to show you some of the most beautiful verses in the world, which you have not yet seen," he replied immediately with emotion, "Pardon me, madame, I have seen them; for, since they are the most beautiful in the world, I must have written them myself."

Folie du doute.—Among men of genius we often find the phenomena which characterizes that disorder termed by alienists *folie du doute*, one of the varieties of melancholia. In this form of insanity the subject has every appearance of mental health; he reasons, writes, and speaks like other people; everything goes well until he has to execute a definite action, and in this he finds all sorts of imaginary dangers. Thus I have treated a woman who when she had to get up in the morning, would hesitate for hours beside her bed, with one arm in the sleeve of her chemise, and the other sleeve hanging down, until her husband came to her help. Sometimes the husband was obliged to give her a few slight blows to induce her to take action. If she went for a walk and knocked against a stone, or came across a puddle, she would remain motionless; her husband had then to carry her for a few instants. In conversation she seemed the best and most sensible of mothers, but woe to the unfortunate person who dropped any word she regarded with suspicion, such as "devil," "death," "God"; she

43 *Revue des Deux Mondes* (1883).

immediately seized him and cried out, until he repeated a certain formula, declaring a dozen times that the word had not been uttered to injure her. A peasant, affected by the same disorder, was incapable of attending to his work, unless someone was there to watch over him; for, said he, "I cannot make up my mind whether I ought to dig or to hoe, to go to the field or to the hill, and my uncertainty is so great that I end by doing nothing."

When Johnson walked along the streets of London he was compelled to touch every post he passed; if he omitted one he had to return. He always went in or out of a door or passage in such a way that either his right or his left foot (Boswell was not certain which) should be the first to cross the threshold; when he made any mistake in the movement, he would return, and, having satisfactorily performed the feat, rejoin his companions with the air of a man who had got something off his mind. Napoleon I. could not pass through a street, even at the head of his army, without counting and adding up the rows of windows. Manzoni, in a letter (addressed to Giorgio Briano) which has become famous, declared that he was incapable of giving himself up to politics because he did not know how to decide on anything; he was always in a state of uncertainty before every resolution, even the most trifling. He was afraid of drowning in the smallest puddle, and could never resolve to go out alone; he confessed on various occasions that, from his youth up, he had suffered from melancholy.[44] He passed whole days without being able to apply himself to anything,[45] so that in a month there were five or six useful days during which he worked five hours, and then he became incapable of thinking.[46] Ugo Foscolo said that "very active in regard to some things, he was in regard to others less than a man, less than a woman, less than a child."[47] Tolstoi confesses that philosophic scepticism had led him into a condition approximating to madness; let us add, to *folie du doute*. "I imagined," he said,

> that there existed nothing outside me, either living or dead; that the objects were not objects, but vain appearances; this state reached such a point that sometimes I turned suddenly round, and looked behind me in the hope of seeing *nothing* where I was not.

"The deplorable mania of doubt exhausts me," cried Flaubert, "I doubt about everything, even about my doubts."[48] I am embarrassed and frightened at my own ideas," wrote Maine de Biran,

---

44 *Letters* 62.

45 *Ibid.* 62, 119, 123.

46 Alessandro Manzoni, *Epistolario di Alessandro Manzoni, raccolto e annotato da Giovanni Sforza*, Ed. Giovanni Sforza (Milan: P. Carraca, 1882-1883).

47 *Epistolario* 3:163.

48 *Correspondance* 1:119

> every expression stops me and gives me scruples. I have no confidence in anything that I publish, and am always tempted to withdraw my works when they have scarcely appeared, to substitute others which would certainly be worthless. I always call those happy who are tied down to fixed labour, who are not submitted to the torment of uncertainty, to the indecision which poisons men who are masters of their time. I am always trying my strength; I commence, and recommence again and again. It is my fortune to be useless, to be wanting in measure, never to feel my existence, never to have confidence in my capacity. I am never happy wherever I am, because I carry within my own organism a source of affliction and unrest. I have only sufficient feeling of my own personality to feel my impotence, which is a great torture. I am always ready to do a number of things . . . and I do nothing.[49]

The little miseries of existence were tortures for Carlyle; to have to pack his portmanteau was a grave affair of state; the idea of ordering coats or buying gloves crushed him. "I have long renounced the omnibus," wrote Renan in his *Souvenirs de jeunesse*,

> the conductors refuse to regard me as a serious traveller. At the railway station, unless I have the protection of an inspector, I always obtain the worst place. . . . I see too well that to do a good turn to one, is usually to do a bad one to

49 *Journal de ma vie intime.*

another. The, vision of the unknown person I am injuring stops short my zeal.

Renan, indeed, is a most singular instance of these characteristics in connection with genius, from his earliest years. At mass his childish eye wandered over the roof of the chapel, and he thought of the great men told of in books. It was his dream to write books. "My gentleness," he writes,

> which often arises from indifference, my indulgence, which is very sincere and which depends on a clear perception of the injustice of men to each other, the conscientious habits which are a pleasure to me, the indefinite endurance of ennui which I possess—having, perhaps, been inoculated in my youth—may be explained by my surroundings, and the deep impressions I have received. The paradoxical vow to preserve the clerical virtues without the faith which serves as basis for them, and in a world for which they are not made, produced, so far as I am concerned, the most amusing incidents. If ever a comic writer wishes to amuse the public at my expense, he needs but my collaboration; I could tell him things far more amusing than he could invent.

A layman and a sceptic he preserved, involuntarily, the vow of poverty.

> My dream would be to be housed, fed, clothed, and warmed, without having to think about it, by someone who would take charge of me and

> leave me free. The competence which I possess came late, and in spite of myself. . . . I always thought about writing; it did not occur to me it could bring me any money. What was my astonishment when I saw a gentleman of agreeable and intelligent appearance enter my garret, compliment me on some articles I had published, and offer to collect them in a volume. He brought a stamped paper stipulating conditions I thought astonishingly generous, so that when he asked me to include all my future writings in the same contract, I consented. The idea came to me to make some observations, but I paused at sight of the document; the thought that that beautiful sheet of paper would be lost stopped me. I did well to stop.

The politeness which he wrongly believes he learnt at the seminary is not the raw and cold politeness of the priest, but the special and excessive timidity of genius. He could not, he says, treat even a dog with an air of authority. But authority is the chief characteristic of priests. To imagine as he does that men are always good and deserving could only be, as he himself justly notes, a continual danger.

> Notwithstanding all my efforts to the contrary, I was predestined to be what I am, a romantic protesting against romanticism, an Utopian preaching materialistic politics, an idealist uselessly giving himself much trouble to appear *bourgeois*, a tissue of contradictions. . . . It is as a great observer Challemel-Lacour has ex-

> cellently said, 'He thinks like a man, feels like a woman, and acts like a child.' I do not complain, since this moral constitution has procured me the most vivid intellectual joys that may be tasted.[50]

But the most striking example of this permanent state of doubt is supplied by another philosopher, the author of a journal of his own life, Amiel. He was so tormented by doubt that the strength of his genius was only shown after his death, when in his journal he revealed with absolute exactness the wound which gnawed him. Let us read a few of the most remarkable passages:—

"As life flees," he says,

> I mourn the loss of reality: thought is sad without action, and action is sad without thought: the real is spoilt when the ideal has not added its perfume; but the ideal, when not made one with the real, becomes a poison. I have never learnt the art of writing; it would have been useful to me, but I was ashamed of the useful: on the other hand, I have acquired two opposed intellectual habits: to note immediately passing impressions and to analyse them scientifically. . . . This journal will be useful to no one, and even for me it will serve rather to plan out life than to practice it; it is a pillow of idleness. . . . And even in style I am unequal. Always energetic and correct: that results from my existence: I see before me several expressions and I do not know which I ought to choose. The unique ex-

50 *Souvenirs d'enfance et de jeunesse.*

> pression is an act of courage which implies confidence in oneself. . . . I discovered very early that it is easier to give up a wish than to gratify it. . . . The idea may be modified, but not the action, so I abhor it, for I fear useless remorse: I thrust aside the idea of a family, because every lost joy is the stab of a knife, because every hope is an egg from which may proceed a serpent as well as a dove. . . . Action is my cross because it would be my dream; but to be false to the ideal would soil the conscience and be an unpardonable error. . . . It is my passion to injure my interests. When a thing attracts me I flee from it.[51]

Every one may see the glorious kinship to genius of all these forms of disease. And every one will think of the great poet-alienist who divined insanity in genius, and left of it a monumental portrait in *Hamlet*, the man afflicted by *folie du doute*.

It is scarcely necessary to add that these great disordered minds must not be confused with the poor inmates, without genius, of our asylums. Although, as diseased persons, they belong to the same category, and have some of the same characters, they must not be identified with them. While ordinary lunatics are reduced to inaction, or the agitation of sterile delirium, these disordered men of genius are the more active in the ideal life because the less apt for practical life. Further, when

51 Henri Frédéric Amiel, *Amiel's Journal: The Journal Intime of Henri Frédéric Amiel*, Tr. Mrs Humphry Ward (London; New York: Macmillan & Co., 1889).

we analyse more delicately this form of insanity, or rather of impotence for practical action, so common among men of genius, we see that it is distinct from the other forms. In scientific work these men do not lack precision, or decision, or audacity. But by expending their strength on theoretical problems, they end by ailing with reference to practical things. By carrying their glance above and beyond, these sublimely far-sighted persons become, like astronomers, unable to perceive neighbouring objects. The effects seem partly identical, but the nature of the phenomena and their causes are absolutely different.

In his "Dialogue of Nature," Leopardi, after having shown how the excellence of genius involves a greater intensity of life, and consequently a more vivid sense of individual misfortune, makes Nature address him thus:

> Besides, the delicacy of your own intelligence and the vivacity of your imagination will shut you out, for a great part, from your empire of yourself. The brutes follow easily the ends that they propose to themselves, with all their faculties and all their strength. But men very rarely utilize all their power; they are usually stopped by reason and imagination, which create for them a thousand uncertainties in deliberation, a thousand obstacles in execution. Those who are less apt or less accustomed to consider and balance motions are the most prompt in taking a resolution, the most powerful in action. But those who are like you, the elect souls, contin-

> ually folded on themselves and outrun, as it were, by the greatness of their own faculties, consequently powerless to govern themselves, are most often subjected, either in deliberation or execution, to irresolution, which is one of the greatest penalties which afflict human life. Add to this that the excellence of your aptitudes will enable you to surpass, easily and briefly, all other souls in the most profound sciences and the most difficult researches; but, nevertheless, it will always be impossible or extremely difficult for you to learn or to put in practice a great many things, insignificant in themselves, but absolutely necessary in your relations with other men. And at the same time you will find these things learnt and easily applied by minds, not only inferior to yours, but altogether contemptible.

Alcoholism.—Many men of genius have abused alcoholic drinks. Alexander died, it is said, after having emptied ten times the goblet of Hercules, and it was without doubt in an alcoholic attack, while pursuing naked the infamous Thais, that he killed his dearest friend. Cæsar was often carried home on the shoulders of his soldiers. Neither Socrates, nor Seneca, nor Alcibiades, nor Cato, nor Peter the Great (nor his wife, Catherine, nor his daughter, Elizabeth), were remarkable for their abstinence. One recalls Horace's line:

> *Narratur et prisci Catonis sæpe mero caluisse virtus.*

Tiberius Nero was called by the Romans Biberius Mero. Septimius Severus and Mahomet II. succumbed to drunkenness or *delirium tremens*. Among confirmed drunkards must be counted the Constable de Bourbon and Avicenna, who, it was said, devoted the second half of his life to showing the uselessness of the studies to which he had devoted the first half; so also have been many famous painters, such as the Caracci, Jan Steen, Barbatelli (on this account nicknamed Pocetta), G. Morland, Turner; and many poets and novelists, such as Murger, Gérard de Nerval, Alfred de Musset, Kleist, Poe, Hoffmann, Addison, Steele, Carew, Sheridan, Burns, Charles Lamb, James Thomson, Majláth, Hartley Coleridge. Tasso wrote in a letter: "I do not deny that I am mad, but I believe that my madness is caused by intoxication and love; for I know that I drink too much." Coleridge, on account of his lack of will, and his abuse of alcoholic drinks and opium, never succeeded in executing any of his gigantic projects; in youth he was offered thirty guineas for a poem he had improvised, but he never succeeded in getting it on to paper. His son, Hartley, a distinguished writer, gave himself up to drink so entirely that he died of it. It was said of him that he "wrote like an angel and drank like a fish." Savage, during the last days of his life almost lived on wine and died in a Bristol prison. Helius, a German poet of the sixteenth century, affirmed that it was the greatest of shames to be beaten in drinking. Shenstone said of his comrade in poetry, Somerville, that he was "forced to drink himself into pains of the body, in order to get rid of the pains of the mind." Madame de Staël and De Quincey abused opium; the latter has left a vivid picture of his excesses in the *Confessions of an Opium Eater*. Many musical composers were great drinkers; such were Dussek, Handel, and Glück, who used to say that he loved money, wine, and fame for an excellent reason: the first enabled him to obtain the second, and the second, by inspiring him, procured him fame. But besides wine he liked brandy, and one day he drank so much that he died of it.[52] One may say the same of Rovani and of Praga.

Hallucinations.—We have already seen that hallucinations are so closely connected with artistic and genial creations *that* Brierre de Boismont associated them with the physiology of great men. Everyone knows the celebrated hallucination of Cellini in his cell, those of Brutus, of Cæsar, of Napoleon, of Swedenborg, who believed that he had visited Heaven, conversed with the spirits of the great dead, and seen the Eternal Father in person; Van Helmont declared that he had seen his own soul in the form of a brilliant crystal; Kerner was visited by a spectre. Shelley thought he saw a child rise from the sea and clap its hands. Clare, after having read some historical episode, imagined that he was himself spectator and actor. Blake thought

52 Felix Clement, *Les musiciens célèbres depuis le seizième siècle jusqu' à nos jours* (Paris: Hachette, 1868).

he really perceived the fantastic images reproduced by his pencil. A celebrated professor was often subject to a similar illusion, and he believed himself changed into Confucius, Papirius, and Tamerlane. Hobbes confessed that he could not go in the dark without thinking that he saw visions of the dead.[53] Bunyan heard voices.

When Columbus was cast on the shores of Jamaica he had an hallucination of hearing. He heard a voice reproaching him for giving himself up to grief and for having but a weak faith in God:

> What happens to you to-day is a deserved punishment for having served the masters of the world and not God. All these tribulations are engraved on marble, and are not brought about without reason.

Later, Columbus declared that in him was accomplished an ancient prophecy announcing the end of the world on the day on which the universal diffusion of Christianity would be realized. According to the same prophecy, only 156 years of existence remained for humanity.[54]

Malebranche declared that he had distinctly heard within himself the voice of God. Descartes, after a long seclusion, believed himself haunted by an invisible person who charged him to follow up

53 Washington Irving, *Life and Works of Washington Irving* (New York: Pollard and Moss, 1880).

54 Andrea Verga, *David Lazzaretti e la pazzia sensoria* (Milan: Rechiedei, 1880).

the search for truth.[55] Byron sometimes imagined he was haunted by a spectre; he afterwards explained this himself by the extreme excitability of his brain.[56] Dr. Johnson distinctly heard his mother call him "Samuel!" although she was living in a distant town. Pope, who suffered much from the bowels, one day asked his doctor about an arm which seemed to protrude from the wall. Goethe assures us that he one day saw his own image coming to meet him. When Oliver Cromwell was lying on his bed, kept awake by extreme fatigue, the curtain opened and a woman of gigantic proportions appeared and announced that he would be the greatest man in England.[57]

Moral Insanity.—Complete absence of moral sense and of sympathy is frequently found among men of genius, as well as among the morally insane. It is an old proverb that "*Quo quisque est doctior eo est nequior.*" Aristotle, in reply to the question, "Why the most learned man is of all living beings the most unjust?" replies: "Because he aims always at pleasures which can only be attained by injustice. And, besides, knowledge resembles the stone which is good to sharpen instruments on, but may also serve the murderer's turn." And Philippe de Commines says: "*Doctrina vel meliores reddit homines vel pejores pro cujusque natura.*" And Cardan:

55 Forbes Winslow, *op. cit.* 123.

56 *Ibid.* 126.

57 Dendy, *op. cit.* 41.

> *Sapientes cum calidissimi natura sint, ac humidissimi, nisi philosophia proficiant, pessimi omnium sunt. Adiuvant ad scelera perpetranda industria quam ex studiis acquisuerunt, et melancolia quæ resoluto humore pinguiore gignitur ex superfluis studiis, atque vigiliis,* [&c.]

"The older I grow," wrote George Sand,

> the more I reverence goodness because I see that this is the gift of which God is most avaricious. Where there is no intelligence, that which is called goodness is merely stupidity. Where there is no strength the pretended goodness is apathy. Where there is strength and intelligence, goodness can scarcely be found, because experience and observation have given birth to suspicion and hate. The souls devoted to the noblest principles are often the most rough and bitter, because they have become diseased through deceptions. One esteems them, one admires them still, but one cannot love them. To have been unhappy without ceasing to be intelligent and good implies a very powerful organization, and it is such that I seek and love. . . . I am sick of great men (forgive the expression); I should like to see them all in Plutarch. There they do not make one suffer on the human side. Let them be cut in marble or cast in bronze, and let them be silent. So long as they live they are wicked, persecuting, fantastic, despotic, bitter, suspicious. They confuse in the same proud contempt the goats and the sheep. They are worse to their friends than to their enemies. God protect us

> from them; be good—stupid if you will.[58]

"I regret," said Valerius Maximus,[59] "to speak of the youth of Themistocles, when I see, on the one hand, his father disinheriting him with ignominy, and, on the other, his mother, from shame of such a son, hanging herself with grief." Sallust, who wrote such beautiful tirades on virtue, passed his life in debauchery. Speusippus, the disciple of Plato, was killed in the act of adultery. Democritus [60]is said to have blinded himself because he could not look at a woman without desiring her. Aristippus, under the mask of austerity, abandoned himself to debauchery. Anaxagoras denied a deposit confided in him by strangers; Aristotle basely flattered Alexander. Theognis wrote moral maxims, particularly on a happy death, and bequeathed his patrimony to a prostitute (?), leaving his own family destitute. Euripides, Juvenal, and Aretino remarked that women of letters were nearly always licentious. Thus Sappho, Philena, and Elephantina were prostitutes, as was Leontion, philosopher and priestess, who gave herself to all the philosophers; and Demophila who told little love stories, and put them in practice. At the Renaissance, Veronica Franco, Tullia of Aragon, and other prostitutes, were as well known for their licentiousness as for

58 *Correspondance*, vol. II, letter 9.

59 *De Factis Dictisque Memorabilibus*, Lib. vi. Cap. 9.

60 Tertullian, *Apologeticum*, c. XLVI. But see *Auli Gellii Noctes Atticæ*, X:17.

their poetry. Voigt considers that immorality was a characteristic feature of the Renaissance period.[61]

In my *Uomo Delinquente* I have considered criminal genius. Sallust, Seneca, and Bacon were accused of peculation; Cremani was a forger, Demme a poisoner. One may also refer to Casanova, who was declared to have forfeited his nobility for a crime the nature of which is not known, and Avicenna, an epileptic, who in old age plunged into debauchery, and took opium in excess, so that it was said of him that philosophy had not enabled him to live honestly, or medicine to live healthily.

Among poets and artists criminality is, unfortunately, well marked. Many among them are dominated by passion which becomes the most powerful spur of their activity; they are not protected by the logical criticism and judgment with which men of science are armed. This is why we must count among criminals Bonfadio, Rousseau, Aretino, Ceresa, Brunetto Latini, Franco, Foscolo, possibly Byron. Observe that I leave out of the question ancient times and barbarous countries among which brigandage and poetry went hand in hand.

More criminal still seem to have been Albergati, a comic writer belonging to the highest aristocracy, who killed his wife through jealousy;[62] Muret,

61 *Wiederbelebung des Classischen Alterthums*, 2 vols. (Berlin: G. Reimer, 1882).

62 Ernesto Masi, *La vita, i tempi, gli amici di Francesco Albergati, commediografo del secolo XVIII* (Bologna: Presso Nicolà Zanichelli, 1878). [The original gives an edition date of 1882,

the humanist, condemned in France for sodomy; and Casanova, so highly gifted for mathematical science and finance, who stained his line genius by a life of swindling and turpitude, giving us in his *Mémoires* a complete and cynical picture of it. Villon belonged to an honourable family; he received the name by which he is known (*villon*, rascal, robber), when he became famous in scoundrelism, to which he was led, by his own confession, by gaming and women. He began by stealing objects of little value to give a good dinner to his mistresses and companions in idleness; it was their wine that he stole. His chief robbery was inspired by hunger when the woman, at whose expense he lived, turned him out of doors at night in winter. It is to this woman whom, in his *Petit testament* he bequeaths his heart. He is supposed to have joined a band of armed robbers, who attacked travellers on the Rueil road, and being arrested a second time he with difficulty escaped the halter.

It has been said of the man of genius, as of the madman, that he is born and dies in isolation, cold and insensible to family affection and social conventions. Men of letters, it is true, make much of the powerful cries of pain in artists and writers who have lost, or been abandoned by, a loved person. But often, as in Petrarch's case, this is only a pretext, an opportunity for literary labours.[63] Very

but I have only been able to find two editions from around this period, one from 1878 and another from 1888. —Ed.]

63 Laura had eleven children and Petrarch himself two when he

often such cries were sincere (or could they have been so powerful and effective?) but they were then intermittent explosions, in opposition to the habitual state of these men, or else temporary reactions against their ordinary apathy, from which they were only drawn by personal vanity, and the passion of æsthetic and scientific researches.

Bulwer-Lytton, from the first days of his marriage illtreated his wife by biting and insulting her, so that the courier who accompanied them on the honeymoon refused to proceed to the end. Later he confessed to the wrong he had done her, but wrote to her that a common life was insupportable, and that he must live in liberty.

It is curious to observe that the writers who have been most chaste in their lives are least so in their writings, and *vice versa*. Flaubert wrote in one of his letters, "Poor Bouilhet used to say to me, 'There never was so moral a man who loved immorality so much as you.' There is truth in that. Is it a result of my pride, or of a certain perversity?"[64] George Sand and Sallust offer the opposite phenomenon.

It is not known whether Comte ever forgave an injury. He certainly always preserved the rancour and the recollection of injuries, and pursued, even to the grave, the memory of his unfaithful wife.

---

dedicated to her 294 sonnets. In politics he turned from Cola di Rienzi to his enemy Colonna and from Robert to Charles IV. (*Famil*, xix. 1. p. 32). He was too much occupied with himself, says Perrens, to be occupied with his country.

64 *Lettres à George Sand* (1885).

The amorous worship which he dedicated to Clotilde de Vaux was so little sincere that he determined beforehand the month, day, and hour when he should shed tears over her memory.[65]

Bacon employed all his eloquence for the condemnation of the greatest of his benefactors, Essex;[66] by cowardly complaisance to the king, he introduced for the first time into the court of justice an odious abuse, and submitted Peacham to torture so as to be able to condemn him; he sold justice at a price, and, as Macaulay concludes, he was one of those of whom we may say, *scientiis tanquam angeli, cupiditatibus tunquam serpentes*.

"Bridget," confesses A. de Musset, "calumniated, exposed (by her love) to the insults of the world, had to endure all the disdain and injury which an angry and cruel libertine can heap on the girl whom he pays. . . . The days passed on and my fits of ill-hu-

65 *Revue Philosophique* (1887) 69.

66 In 1591, Francis Bacon became acquainted with Queen Elizabeth's favourite, Robert Devereux, 2nd Earl of Essex. The latter subsequently used his influence in an attempt to secure for Bacon the Attorney-Generalship, but this was given to Sir Edward Coke. The lesser office of Solicitor General also went to another, Thomas Fleming. As consolation for these disappointments, Lord Essex presented Bacon with a property at Twickenham, which he later sold for £1800. In 1596 Bacon became Queen's Counsel. Though his finances remained exiguous, to the point of being, at one point, arrested for debt, his standing with the Queen improved, especially after severing all ties with Lord Essex, and he was later appointed to investigate charges against his former benefactor. The latter was executed for treason in 1601. —Ed.

mour and sarcasm took on a sombre and obstinate character."[67]

Byron's intimate friend, Hobhouse, wrote of him that he was possessed by a diseased egoism. Even when he loved his wife he refused to dine with her, so as not to give up his old habits. He afterwards treated her so badly that, in good faith, and perhaps with reason, she consulted specialists as to his mental condition.

Napoleon's conduct towards his wife, his brothers, and towards those who trusted in him was that of a man without moral sense. Taine sums up the diagnosis in one word: he was a *condottiere*.

"A man's genius is no sinecure," said Carlyle's wife, a most intelligent and cultivated woman, who, though capable of becoming (as she had hoped and been assured) her husband's fellow-worker, was compelled to be his servant. The idea of travelling in a carriage with his wife seemed to him out of the question; he must have his brother with him; he neglected her for other women, and pretended that she was indifferent. Her chief duty was to preserve him from the most remote noises; the second was to make his bread, for he detested that of the bakers; he obliged her to travel for miles on horseback as his messenger, only saw her at meal-time, and for weeks together never addressed a word to her, although his prolonged silence caused her agony. It was only after her death, accelerated by his conduct, that, in a literary form, he showed his re-

67 *Confessions d'un enfant du siècle* 250, 251.

pentance, and narrated her history in affecting language, but, as his biographer adds, if she had been still alive he would have tormented her afresh.

Frederick II. said, like Lacenaire, that vengeance is the pleasure of the gods, and that he would die happy if he could inflict on his enemies more evils than he had suffered from them. He experienced real delight in morally tormenting his friends, sometimes beating them; if a courtier liked to pomade himself, he soaked his clothes in oil; he bargained with Voltaire over sugar and chocolate, and deprived him of his money.

Donizetti treated his family brutally; it was after a fit of savage anger, in which he had beaten his wife, that he composed, sobbing, the celebrated air, *Tu che a Dio spiegasti l'ali*;[68] a remarkable instance of the double nature of personality in men of genius, and at the same time of their moral insensibility.

Houssaye narrates a similar scene, in which A. Dumas was so carried away during a quarrel, as to tear out his wife's hair. She, in despair, wished to retire to a convent; yet after some minutes he gaily wrote a comic scene, and said to his friends: "If tears were pearls, I would make myself a necklace of them."

Byron used to beat the Guiccioli, and also his Venetian mistress, the gondolier's wife, who, however, gave him as good.

68 Guillaume Cottrau, *Lettres d'un mélomane* (Naples: A. Morano, 1885).

Fontenelle, seeing his companion at table struck by apoplexy, was not disconcerted; he simply took advantage of the incident to change the sauce for the asparagus to vinegar; out of deference to his friend's taste he had previously ordered butter.

It is sufficient to be present at any academy, university, faculty, or gathering of men who, without genius, possess at least erudition, to perceive at once that their dominant thought is always disdain and hate of the man who possesses, almost or entirely, the quality of genius. The man of genius, in his turn, has nothing but contempt for others. He believes he has all the more right to laugh at others, from being himself sensitive to the slightest criticism; he is even offended at praise given to another as blame directed to himself. That is why at academical gatherings the greatest men only agree in praising the most ignorant person. We have seen that Chateaubriand was offended when his shoemaker was praised. Lisfranc called his colleague, Dupuytren, a brigand, and Roux and Velpeau forgers.

I have been able to observe men of genius when they had scarcely reached the age of puberty: they did not manifest the deep aversions of moral insanity, but I have noted among all a strange apathy for everything which does not concern them; as though plunged in the hypnotic condition, they did not perceive the troubles of others, or even the most pressing needs of those who were dearest to them; if they observed them, they grew tender, and even at once hastened to attend to them; but it was a fire of straw, soon extinguished, and it gave place to indifference and weariness.

Genius, said Schopenhauer, is solitary. Genius, wrote Goethe, is only related to its time by its defects.

This emotional anæsthesia may be found even in philanthropists, who possess the genius of sentiment, and have made goodness and pity for the poor the pivot of their actions. It is difficult to explain otherwise some pages in the Gospel. "You think, perhaps," said Jesus,

> that I have come to bring peace to the earth? No, I have come to throw down a sword there. . . . In a household of five persons, three will be against two, and two against three. I have come to bring division between father and son, between mother and daughter, between daughter-in-law and mother-in-law. From this time a man's enemies will be of his own household.[69]

"I have come to bring fire on to the earth: if it burns already, so much the better!"[70] "I declare to you," he added," whoever leaves house, wife, brothers, and parents, will receive a hundredfold in this world, and in the world to come everlasting life."[71] "If any one comes to me and does not hate his father, mother, wife, children, brothers, sisters,

69 Matthew x. 34-36; Luke xii. 51-53.

70 Luke xii. 49. See the Greek text.

71 Luke xviii. 29-30.

and even his own life, he cannot be my disciple."[72] "He who loves his father and his mother more than me is not worthy of me; he who loves his son or his daughter more than me, is not worthy of me." [73]Jesus said to a man, "Follow me." "Lord;" this man replied, "let me first go and bury my father." Jesus answered: "The dead may bury their dead: go, you, and preach the kingdom of God."[74]

Dante, Goethe, Leopardi, Byron, and Heine were reproached with hating their country. Tolstoi disapproves of patriotism. Schopenhauer said, "In the face of death I confess that I despise the Germans for their unspeakable bestiality, and am ashamed to belong to them."

Longevity.—This diseased apathy, this diminution of affection, which furnishes genius with a breastplate against so many assaults, and which rapidly destroys fibres at once so delicate and so strong, explains the remarkable longevity of men of genius, in spite of their hyperæsthesia in other directions. I have noted this character in 134 cases out of 143.

Sophocles, Humboldt, Fontenelle, Brougham, Xenophon, Cato the Elder, Michelangelo, Petrarch, Bettinelli, died at 90; Passeroni, Auber, Manzoni, Xavier de Maistre at 89; Hobbes at 92; Dandolo at 97; Titian at 99; Cassiodorus and Mile. Scudéry at 94; Viennet and Diogenes at 91; Voltaire, Frank-

72 Luke xiv. 26.

73 Matthew x. 37, xvi. 24; Luke v. 23.

74 Matthew viii. 21; Luke v. 23.

lin, Watt, John of Bologna, Vincent de Paul, Baroccio, Young, Talleyrand, Raspail, Grimm, Herschel, Metastasio at 84; Victor Hugo, Donatello, Goethe, Wellington at 83; Zingarelli, Metternich, Theodore de Beza, Lamarck, Halley at 86; Bentham, Newton, St. Bernard de Menthon, Bodmer, Luini, Scarpa, Bonpland, Chiabrera, Carafa, Goldoni at 85; Thiers, Kant, Maffei, Amyot, Villemain, Wieland, Littré at 80; Anacreon, Mercatori, Viviani, Buffon, Palmerston, Casti, J. Bernouilli, Pinel at 81; Galileo, Euler, Schlegel, Béranger, Louis XIV., Corneille, Cesarotti at 78; Herodotus, Rossini, Cardan, Michelet, Boileau, Garibaldi, Archimedes, Paisiello, Saint Augustine, at 75; Tacitus and B. Disraeli at 76; Pericles at 70; Thucydides at 69; Hippocrates, at 103; and Saint Anthony at 105.

According to Beard the average life of 500 men of genius is 54, and that of 100 modern men of genius is 70. The average duration of life of 35 men of musical genius was 63 years, and 8 months.[75] But this fact does not exclude degeneration when, as among persons with moral insanity, it is united with an apathy which renders temperaments otherwise mobile, insensible to the strongest griefs, and I have shown in another book[76] that instinctive criminals, living out of prison, enjoy great longevity. It should be added that longevity is not always found in genius; many great men of genius, such as Raphael, Pascal, Burns, Keats, Byron, Mo-

75 Florentino, *La Musica* (Rome: 1884).

76 *Il Uomo Delinquente*, 2 vols., 4th ed. (Turin: Bocca, 1889).

zart, Felix Mendelssohn, Bellini, Bichat, Pico de la Mirandola died before the age of forty.

Chapter IV

Genius and Insanity

Resemblance between genius and insanity — Men and women of genius who have been insane — Montanus — Harrington — Haller — Schumann Gérard de Nerval — Baudelaire — Concato — Mainländer — Comte — Codazzi — Bolyai — Cardan — Tasso — Swift — Newton — Rousseau —Lenau — Széchényi — Hoffmann — Foderà — Schopenhauer — Gogol.

The resemblance between insanity and genius, although it does not show that these two should be confounded, proves at all events that one does not exclude the other in the same subject.

In fact, without speaking of the numerous men of genius who at some period of their lives were subject to hallucinations or insanity, or of those who, like Vico, terminated a great career in dementia, how many great thinkers have shown themselves all their lives subject to monomania or hallucinations!

In recent times insanity has shown itself in Farini, Brougham, Southey, Govone, Gounod,

Gutzkow, Monge, Fourcroy, Cowper, Rocchia, Ricci, Fenicia,[1] Engel, Pergolèse,[2] Batjusckoff, Mürger, William Collins, Techner, Hölderlin,[3] Von der West, Gallo, Spedalieri, Bellingeri, Salieri, Johannes Müller, Lenz, Barbara, Fuseli, Petermann, the caricaturist Cham,[4] Hamilton, Poe, Uhlrich.

In France, remarks Martini, many young and orginal poets have died insane.[5] Such also seems to have been the fate of Briffault, and of Laurent attacked by a veritable mania of calumny.[6] Among women Günderrode, Stieglitz (who both committed suicide with great deliberation),[7] Brachmann, L. E. Landon lived and died insane.[8]

---

1 Mastriani, *Sul Genio e la Follia* (Naples: 1881).

2 This is the French spelling for Giovanni Battista Pergolesi (1710 – 1736). —Ed.

3 The text has it as 'Holderlen' here, but Lombroso was referring to Hölderlin, whose name is spelt correctly elsewhere. —Ed.

4 Real name: Charles Amédée de Noé (1818 – 1879).

5 Ferdinando Martini, *Fra un sigaro e l'altro: chiacchiere di Fantasio* (Milano: G. Brigola, 1876) 194. [I have put down the first edition, which is more or less contemporary, but the original footnote does not specify the edition and Martini's book went through many up until 1930. —Ed.]

6 Maxime du Camp, *Souvenirs littéraires*, 2 vols. (Paris: Hachette, 1882-1883). [The original gives 1884 as the publication date. —Ed.]

7 Karoline Friederike Louise Maximiliane von Günderrode (1780 – 1806), the German Romantic poet, killed herself with a dagger. Charlotte Stieglitz (1806 – 1834), the writer, stabbed herself in the heart. —Ed.

8 Johann August Schilling, *Psychiatrische Briefe* (Augsburg: J. A. Schlosser, 1863) 488.

Montanus, a victim to solitude and a disordered imagination, was convinced that he had become a grain of wheat. He refused to move for fear of being swallowed by birds.[9] Harrington is said to have imagined that diseases took the form of bees and flies, and for this reason he retired to a cabin armed with a broom to disperse them.[10] Haller believed that he was persecuted by men and damned by God on account of the vileness of his soul and his heretical works. He could only soothe his excessive terror by enormous doses of opium and by converse with priests.[11] Ampère burnt a treatise on the future of chemistry believing he had written it by Satanic suggestion. The great Dutch artist, Van Gogh, thought he was possessed. Carlo Dolci, a prey to religious monomania, vowed only to paint religious pictures. He devoted his pencil to Madonnas, though his Madonna, indeed, is the portrait of

9 Johann Georg Zimmermann, *La Solitude* (Paris: Leroy, 1791).

10 If Lombroso is referring to James Harrington (1611 – 1677), the English political theorist of classical republicanism best known for *The Commonwealth of Oceana* (1656), the story is told by John Aubrey that, while imprisoned at the Tower of London, Harrington thought his sweat was creating bees and flies. Harrington was badly treated during his imprisonment, and after his release, his health quickly deteriorated, due to ingesting, on medical advice, the addictive druge guaiacum, which affected his mind and caused him to have intermittend delusions. One observer judged him 'simply mad'. —Ed.

11 *Tagebuch seiner Beobachtungen über Schriftsteller und über sich selbst: zur Karakteristik der Philosophie und Religion dieses Mannes*, 2 vols. (Bern: Hallersche Buchhandlung, 1787).

Balduini. On his wedding-day he alone was missing; after some hours he was found prostrated before the altar of the Annunciation. Nathaniel Lee, the dramatist, composed thirteen tragedies during the course of his disease; one day a feeble dramatic colleague told him that it was easy to write like a madman. "It is not easy to write like a madman," he replied, "but it is very easy to write like a fool." Thomas Lloyd, who wrote excellent verse, was a strange mixture of malice, pride, genius, and insanity.[12] If he was not satisfied with his verses he put them in his glass to polish them, as he said. Everything that he came across, even coal, paper, and tobacco, he was accustomed to mix with his food for hygienic reasons; the carbon purified it, stone imparted mineral virtues, &c. Charles Lamb in early life had an attack of insanity which was hereditary in his family; writing of this to Coleridge, he said:

> At some future time I will amuse you with an account, as full as my memory will permit, of the strange turns my frenzy took. I look back upon it at times with a gloomy kind of envy, for, while it lasted, I had many, many hours of pure happiness. Dream not, Coleridge, of having tasted all the grandeur and wildness of fancy till you have gone mad. All now seems to me vapid, or comparatively so.

12 Anonymous, *Sketches of Bedlam* (London: Sherwood, Jones and Co., 1823) 27-38.

Robert Schumann (1810 – 1856), the precursor of the music of the future, was the youngest son of a well-to-do bookseller in Zwickau, and met with no obstacles in the pursuit of his cherished art. When a law student he met Clara Wieck, the celebrated pianist, and in her found an excellent and lovable companion; but at the age of twenty-three he became subject to melancholia; at forty-six he was pursued by turning-tables which knew everything; he heard sounds which developed into concords and even whole compositions. For several years he was afraid of being sent to a lunatic asylum; Beethoven and Mendelssohn dictated musical combinations to him from their tombs. In 1854 he threw himself into the Rhine; he was saved, and died two years later in a private asylum at Bonn.[13] The autopsy revealed osteophytes, thickening of the cranial membranes and atrophy of the brain.[14]

Gérard de Nerval was subject to *folie circulaire*, with alternate periods of exaltation and depression, each of which lasted six months. In his moments of calm he was a spiritualist; he heard the spirits of Adam, Moses, and Joshua in a piece of furniture; and practised cabalistic exorcisms, executing the dance of the Babylonians. During his stay at an asylum he imagined that it was the superintendent who was a victim to insanity. "He believes,"

13 He was interned at his own request; he had previously warned Clara that he feared he would do her harm. —Ed.

14 Wilhelm Joseph von Wasielewski, *Robert Schumann: Eine Biographie* (Dresden: Kunze, 1858).

he said, "that he is superintending an asylum, but he is himself the madman and we feign madness in order to humour him." With the honey of flowers he traced on paper symbols which radiated round a fantastic giantess who united the characters of Diana, Saint Rosalie, and of an actress named Colon with whom he believed he was in love. In reality he adored her from a great distance, sending her large bouquets, and buying enormous opera-glasses in order to see her, and superb canes with which to applaud her; so that it was said of him that he ruined himself in orgies of opera-glasses and debaucheries of canes. He had discovered a mediæval bed which was to serve for his *amours*, and in order to set it in suitable surroundings he obtained an apartment and luxurious furniture. In days of poverty the furniture was sold, leaving the bed alone in the room, then in a barn, and at last it also disappeared, and its proprietor passed his nights in taverns and low lodging-houses, or writing beneath trees and porches. Later, when he had ceased to see Colon, she became for him a kind of idol with which he lived and who in his mystic ideas became confounded partly with the saints and partly with the stars; one day he declared that she was an incarnation of Saint Theresa. When he heard that she had declared she had never loved him and only seen him once, which was true, he said: "What good if she had loved me?" and he added, quoting a verse of Heine, "He who loves for the second time without hope is a madman. I am that madman. The sky, the sun, the stars laugh at it; I also laugh at it, laugh at it and die of it."

One day, at sunset, he was on the balcony of a house. He suddenly saw a phantom and heard a voice calling him. He ran forward, fell, and was nearly killed. That was his first attack, characterised by hallucinations of sight and hearing.

Towards the end of his life, at the age of forty-six, *folie des grandeurs* developed in him; he spoke of his *châteaux* at Ermenonville, of his physical beauty which was astonishing, he said, to his attendants; he bought up coins of Nerva, not wishing that the name of his ancestors should circulate as money, yet Nerval was only a pseudonym. Sometimes he gave out that he was a descendant of Folobello de Nerva whose history he wished to write, and all whose male descendants presented, according to him, a supernatural sign, the tetragramma of Solomon, on their breasts. Timid and cautious in his days of calm, he became bold and noisy when the attack came on, and even threatened his friends with weapons. In spite of the low temperature he refused to leave off his summer clothes. "Cold," he declared, "is a tonic and the Lapps are never ill." A few days after, he hanged himself.[15]

Baudelaire appears before us, in the portrait placed at the beginning of his posthumous works, as the type of the lunatic possessed by the *délire des grandeurs*.[16] He was descended from a family of in-

15 Maxime du Camp, *Souvenirs littéraires* (1887).

16 Ferdinand Brunetière, "Charles Baudelaire", *Revue des Deux*

sane and eccentric persons. It was not necessary to be an alienist to detect his insanity. In childhood he was subject to hallucinations; and from that period, as he himself confessed, he experienced opposing sentiments; the horror and the ecstasy of life; he was hyperæsthetic and at the same time apathetic; he felt the necessity of freeing himself from "an oasis of horror in a desert of *ennui.*" Before falling into dementia he committed impulsive acts; for instance, he threw pots from his house against shop windows for the pleasure of hearing them break. He changed his lodgings every month; asked the hospitality of a friend in order to complete work he was engaged on, and wasted his time in reading which had no relation to it whatever. Having lost his father, he quarrelled with his mother's second husband, and one day, in the presence of friends, attempted to strangle him. Sent out to India, in order, it is said, to be put to business, he lost everything and only brought back from his voyage a negress to whom he dedicated exotic poems. He desired to be original at all costs; gave himself to excess in wine before high personages, dyed his hair green, wore winter garments in summer, and vice versa. He experienced morbid passions in love. He loved ugly and horrible women, negresses, dwarfs, giantesses; to a very beautiful woman he expressed a desire that he might see her suspended by the hands to the ceiling

---

Mondes LXXXI (1 June 1887) 695-706. Paul Desjardins, "Poètes contemporains: Charles Baudelaire", *Revue Bleue: Revue Politique et Littéraire* 14.1 (2 July, 1887).

that he might kiss her feet; and kissing the naked foot appears in one of his poems as the equivalent of the sexual act.

BAUDELAIRE

He was constantly dreaming of work, calculating the hours and the lines necessary to pay his debts: two months or more. But that was all, and the work was never begun.[17]

Proud, misanthropic, and apathetic, he said of himself:

17 Maxime du Camp, *Souvenirs littéraires*.

> Discontented with others and discontented with myself, I desire to redeem myself, to regard myself with a little pride in the silence and solitude of the night. Souls of those I have loved, souls of those I have sung, strengthen me, sustain me, remove from me the lies and the corrupting vapours of the world; and thou, O Lord my God, grant me grace to produce some fine lines which will prove to myself that I am not the last of men, that I am not inferior to those whom I contemn.[18]

And he had need of it, for he called Gustave Planche imbecile, Dumas a *farceur*, Sue stupid, Féval an idiot, George Sand a Veuillot without delicacy. What he attacked in all these writers was the fame he wished to possess; that is why he made fun of Molière and Voltaire.

With the progress of insanity he used to invert words, saying "shut" when he meant to say "open," &c. He died of progressive general paralysis of the insane, of which his excessive ambition was already a fore-running symptom.

Concato was the son of a poor tailor, the victim of grave cerebral affections. He himself presented certain characters of degeneration, such as pallor and large cheek bones; during many years he was subject to various forms of insanity. At the age of seventeen he was seized by the terror of sudden death, and provided himself with nitre to prevent

18 "A une Heure du Matin," in *Petits poèmes en prose, Œuvres complètes de Charles Baudelaire* (Paris: Michel Lévy frères, 1869).

future cerebral crises. At twenty he resolved to become a monk, although in childhood he had been so little devout that he had fabricated false notes of confession. Afterwards he quarrelled with an Austrian officer, and then became afraid of all sentinels and soldiers. He would never allow an officer to enter his house with his sword by his side; and even in old age trembled at the sight of one of the city guards. One night he dreamt he had committed a homicide, and for many days he was a prey to strange terrors. He suffered from claustrophobia: woe to whomsoever tried to lock him up in a carriage or a room! There were some days during which he considered himself the lowest of men. He was so irascible that he used to say that, to be in good health, one must be angry at least once a day. Yet he was one of the greatest of European physicians.[19]

Mainländer had a grandfather who, after the death of a son, carried religious mysticism to the extent of insanity, and died of inflammation of the brain at the age of thirty-three. A brother, also insane, wished to embrace Buddhism. As a youth, looking at the sea at Sorrento, he felt impelled to throw himself in, merely attracted by the purity of the water. He educated himself and wrote his celebrated book, *Die Philosophie der Erlösung*, but to realize his theories entirely, he adopted a rule of absolute chastity, and on the day on which his

19 Luigi Bufalini, *Sulla vita e sulla mente di Luigi Concato* (Milano: Bortolotti, 1883).

book was published hanged himself, the better to confirm a passage which said: "In order that man may be redeemed it is necessary that he should recognize the value of not-being, and desire intensely not to be."[20]

The great Auguste Comte, the initiator of the positivist philosophy, was for ten years under the care of Esquirol, the famous alienist; he recovered, but only to repudiate, without any cause, the wife who had saved him; later, he—who had wished to abolish all priest-craft—believed himself the priest and apostle of a materialistic religion. In his works, amidst stupendous elucubrations, genuinely maniacal ideas may be found, as, for example, the prophecy that one day women will be fecundated without the help of the male.[21]

It is said that mathematicians are exempt from psychical derangements, but this is not true; it is sufficient to recall not only Newton and Enfantin, of whom I will speak at length, but the two famous distractions of Archimedes, the hallucination of Pascal, and the vagaries of the mathematician Co-

20 Lucien Arréat, "La Philosophie de la Rédemption d'après un pessimiste", *Revue philosophique de la France et de l'étranger* 19 (1885) 619-651. [The footnote in the 1891 edition is imprecise, reading only 'Revue Philosophique, 1886'; the above seems the most likely source. There is also an English language profile of Philipp Mainländer in T. Whittaker, "P. Mainländer, *Die Philosophie der Erlösung*," Mind. A quarterly review of *Psychology and Philosophy* XI (1886) 419-425. —Ed.]

21 Émile Littré, *Auguste Comte et la Philosophie Positive* (Paris: Hachette, 1863).

dazzi (not to be confounded with Codazza). Codazzi was sub-microcephalic, oxycephalic, alcoholic, sordidly avaricious; to affective insensibility he added vanity so great that while still young he set apart a sum for his own funeral monument, and refused the least help to his starving parents; he admitted no discussion of his judgment even if it only concerned the cut of a coat; and he had taken it into his head that he could compose melodic music with the help of the calculus.

All mathematicians admire the great geometer Bolyai, whose eccentricities were of an insane character; thus he provoked thirteen officials to duels and fought with them, and between each duel he played the violin, the only piece of furniture in his house; when pensioned he printed his own funeral card with a blank date, and constructed his own coffin—a vagary which I have found in two other mathematicians who died in recent years. Six years later he had a similar funeral card printed, to substitute for the other which he had not been able to use. He imposed on his heir the obligation to plant on his grave an apple-tree, in remembrance of Eve, of Paris, and of Newton.[22] Such was the great reformer of Euclid.

Cardan, called by his contemporaries the greatest of men and the most foolish of children—Cardan, who first dared to criticise Galen, to exclude fire from the number of the elements, and to

22 Wilfrid de Fonvielle, *Comment se font les miracles en dehors de l'Église* (Paris: Maurice Dreyfous 1879).

call witches and saints insane—this great Cardan was the son, cousin, and father of lunatics, and himself a lunatic all his life. “A stammerer, impotent, with little memory or knowledge,” he himself wrote, “I have suffered since childhood from hypno-fantastic hallucinations.” Sometimes it was a cock which spoke to him in a human voice; sometimes Tartarus, full of bones, which displayed itself before him. Whatever he imagined, he could see before him as a real object. From the age of nineteen to that of twenty-six, a genius, similar to one which already protected his father, gave him advice and revealed the future. When he had reached the age of twenty-six he was not altogether deprived of supernatural aid; a recipe which was not quite right forgot one day the laws of gravity, and rose to his table to warn him of the error he was about to commit.[23]

He was hypochondriacal, and imagined he had contracted all the diseases that he read of: palpitation, sitophobia, diarrhœa, enuresis, podagra, hernia—all these diseases vanished without treatment, or with a prayer to the Virgin. Sometimes his flesh smelled of sulphur, of extinguished wax; sometimes he saw flames and phantoms appear in the midst of violent earthquakes, while his friends perceived nothing. Persecuted by every government, surrounded by a forest of enemies, whom he

23 “*Libri quo tempore à me conscripti, cur quinam editi*” (Ch. XLV), Girolamo Cardano (Hyeronimi Cardani), *De Vita Propria* (Amsterdam: Apud Joannem Ravesteinium, 1654).

knew neither by name nor by sight, but who, as he believed, in order to afflict and dishonour him, had condemned his much-loved son, he ended by believing himself poisoned by the professors of the University of Pavia, who had invited him for this purpose. If he escapes from their hands, he owes it to the help of St. Martin and of the Virgin. Yet such a man in theology had audaciously anticipated Dupuis and Renan!

He declares himself inclined to all vices—wine, gaming, lying, licentiousness, envy, cunning, deception, calumny, inconstancy; he observes that four times during the full moon he found himself in a state of real mental alienation. His sensibility was so perverted, that he never felt comfortable except under the stimulus of some physical pain; and in the absence of natural pain, he procured it by artificial means, biting his lips or arms until he fetched blood. "I sought causes of pain to enjoy the pleasure of the cessation of pain, and because I perceived that when I did not suffer I fell into so grave and troublesome a condition, that it was worse than any pain." This fact helps us to understand many strange tortures which madmen have voluptuously imposed on themselves.[24] He had so blind a faith in the revelations of dreams, that he printed a strange work, *De Somniis*, conducted his medical consultations, concluded his marriage,

24 Byron said, also, that intermittent fevers came at last to be agreeable to him, on account of the pleasant sensation that followed the cessation of pain.

and began his works (for example, that on the *Varietà delle Cose* and *Sulle Febbri*) in accordance with dreams.[25]

He was impotent up to the age of thirty-four. Virility was given to him in a dream, and to this gift was added, not altogether happily, the cause of his troubles—his future wife, a brigand's daughter, whom, before this dream, as he asserts, he had never even seen. His unhappy mania even led him to regulate his medical consultations according to his dreams, as he himself boasts of doing in the case of Borromeo's son. It is possible to cite other examples, sometimes comic, sometimes strange or terrible. I will quote one which unites all these characters: his dream of the jewel.

It was in May, 1560, when Cardan was fifty-two years of age. His son had just been publicly condemned for poisoning. No misfortune could wound more deeply Cardan's already sensitive soul. He loved his son with all a father's tenderness, as is witnessed by his fine verses, *De Morte*

---

25 "One day I thought I heard very sweet harmonies in a dream. I awoke, and I found I had resolved the question of fevers: why some are lethal and others not a question which had troubled me for twenty-five years" (*De Somniis*, c. iv.). [A modern translation into Italian, with commentary, exists: Girolamo Cardano, *De Somniis: Sui sogni e sul sognare*, Tr. Silvia Montiglio (Genova: Masilio, 1989).]

"In a dream there came to me the suggestion to write this book, divided into exactly twenty-one parts; and I experienced such pleasure in my condition and in the subtlety of these reasonings as I had never experienced before" (*De subtilitate*, lib. xviii, p. 915).

Filii, in which there is the imprint of real passion. He hoped also for a grandson who should resemble himself. Drawn more and more into insane ideas by grief, he saw in this condemnation the hands of persecutors.

> Thus overwhelmed, I sought distraction in vain in study or in play. In vain I bit myself and struck my arms and legs. It was my third night of sleeplessness, about two hours before dawn. I saw that there was nothing else for me but to die or go mad. Therefore I prayed God to snatch me entirely away from life. And then, against my expectation, sleep took possession of me, and at the same time I heard a person approaching me, whose form I could not see, but who said, 'Why grieve about your son? Put into your mouth the precious stone which you bear suspended from your neck, and as long as you carry it there you will not think of your son.' On waking up, I asked myself what connection there could be between forgetfulness and an emerald; but as I had no other resource, I recalled the sacred words, '*Credidit et reputatum ei est ad justitiam*'; I put the emerald into my mouth, and then, against all expectation, everything that recalled my son vanished from my memory. It was so for a year and a half. It was only during my meals, and at my public lectures, when I was unable to keep the precious stone in my mouth, that I fell back into my old grief.

This singular cure had its pretext in the double sense of the Italian word *gioia*, which means at once "joy" and "jewel." Cardan had, however, no need of the revelation of a genius, for in his own works he had already recognized a consoling virtue in precious stones, due to the bond of this absurd etymology.[26]

A megalomaniac, he called himself "the seventh physician since the creation of the world;" he claimed to know the things which are before and above us, and those which shall come after.[27]

Like Rousseau and like Haller, Cardan, during the last days of his tormented existence, wrote his own life; he also foretold the exact date of his death, which he looked for, and perhaps himself brought about, in order that his horoscope should not be made to lie.[28]

What shall we say of Tasso? For those who do not know Verga's monograph (*Lipemania del Tasso*), it will be enough to quote the following letter:

> So great is my grief, that I am considered by others and by myself as mad, when, powerless to keep my sorrowful thoughts hidden, I give myself up to long conversations with myself. My troubles are at once human and diabolical; the human are cries of men, and especially of

26 "Jewels in sleep are symbolical of sons, of unexpected things, of joy also; because in Italian gioire means 'to enjoy' (*De Somniis*, cap. 21; *De Subtilitate*, p. 338).

27 Francesco Buttrini, *Saggio psico-biografico su Gerolamo Cardano* (Savona: Ricci, 1884).

28 [Antonio] Bertolotti, ("I testamenti di Girolamo Cardano medico filosofo e matematico del secolo XVI", *Archivio storico lombardo* 9 (1882) 615-660.) has shown that this legend has no foundation.

> women, and also the laughter of beasts; the diabolical are songs, &c. When I take into my hands a book to give myself up to study, I hear voices sounding in my ear, and distinguish the name of Paul Fulvius.

In his *Messaggiero*, which became with him, later on, a real hallucination, he had already made the often-repeated confession of his madness, which he attributed to wine and to women. I am thus inclined to believe that he described himself in the character of Thyrsis, in that admirable stanza of the *Aminta*, which another monomaniac, Rousseau, loved so much:—

> *Vivrò fra i miei tormenti e fra le cure,*
> *Mie giuste furie, forsennato, errante;*
> *Paventerò l'ombre solinghe e scure*
> *Che il primo error mi recheranno avante;*
> *E del sol che scoprì le mie sventure*
> *A schivo ed in orror avrò it sembiante:*
> *Temerò me medesmo, e da me stesso*
> *Sempre fuggendo, avrò me sempre appresso*[29]

One day, certainly under the influence of some hallucination, or in a maniacal attack, he drew a knife, and was about to attack a serving-man who

29 "I shall live in the midst of my torments, and among the cares that are my just furies, wild and wandering; I shall fear dark and solitary shades, which will bring before me my first fault; and I shall have in horror and disgust the face of the sun which discovered my misfortunes; I shall fear myself, and, for ever fleeing from myself, I shall never escape."

entered the ducal chamber; he was imprisoned, says the Tuscan Ambassador, more to cure him than to punish him.

The unfortunate poet went from one country to another, but sorrowful visions everywhere threatened him; and with them came ceaseless remorse, suspicions of poison, and the terrors of hell for the heresies of which he accused himself in three letters to the "too-indulgent" inquisitor.

"I am always troubled by sad and wearisome thoughts," he confesses to the physician Cavallaro, "by figures and phantoms; also by a great weakness of memory, therefore I beg of your lordship to think to strengthen my memory in the pills that you order for me." "I am frenzied," he wrote to Gonzaga,

> and I am surprised that they have not written to you of all the things that I say in talking to myself: honours, the good graces of emperors and kings which I dream of, forming and reforming them according to my fancy.

This curious letter shows us how sombre and sorrowful images alternated in him with others that were joyous, like subjective colours in the retina.

Some days later he wrote to Cattaneo:

> I have here much more need of the exorcist than of the physician, for my trouble is caused by magic art. I will tell you about my goblin. The little thief has robbed me of many crowns; he puts all my books upside down, opens my chests, hides my keys, so that I do not know how to pro-

> tect myself against him. I am always unhappy, but especially at night, and I do not know if my trouble should be attributed to frenzy.

In another letter:

> When I am awake I seem to see lights sparkling in the air; sometimes my eyes are inflamed so that I fear I may lose my sight. At other times I hear horrible noises, hissings, and tinklings, the sound of bells, and, as it were, clocks all striking the hour at the same time. When I am asleep I seem to see a horseman throwing himself on me and casting me to the earth, or else I imagine that I am covered by filthy beasts. All my joints feel it; my head becomes heavy, and in the midst of so many pains and terrors sometimes there appears to me the image of the Virgin, beautiful and young, with her Son, and crowned with a rainbow.

Later he told Cattaneo how a goblin carried away letters in which he was mentioned,

> and that is one of the miracles which I saw myself at the hospital. Thus I possess the certainty that these wonders must be attributed to a magician. I have numerous proofs of it. One day a loaf was taken from me, beneath my eyes, towards three o'clock.

When ill with acute fever he was cured, thanks to an apparition of the Virgin, to whom he testified his gratitude in a sonnet. He wrote and spoke to, almost touched, his genius, who often resembled his former *Messaggiero*, and suggested to him ideas which he had not conceived before.

Swift, the inventor of irony and humour, predicted even in youth that he would die insane, as had been the case with a paternal uncle. He was walking one day in a garden when he saw an elm almost completely deprived of foliage at the top. "Like that tree," he said, "I shall die at the top." Proud almost to monomania with the great, he yet led a wild and vicious life, and was known as the "Mad Parson." Though a clergyman, he wrote irreligious books, and it was said that before making him a bishop it would be desirable to baptise him. His giddiness began, as he himself tells us, at the age of twenty-three, so that his brain disease lasted for over fifty years. *Vertiginosus, inops, surdus, male gratus amicis*, as he defined himself, he almost succumbed to the grief caused by the death of his beloved Stella, and at the same time he wrote his burlesque *Directions to Servants*. Some months later he lost his memory and only preserved his mordant loquacity; he remained for a whole year without speaking or reading or recognising any one; he would walk for ten hours a day, eating his meals standing, or refusing food, and giving way to attacks of rage when any one entered his room. With the development of some boils his condition seemed to improve; he was heard to say several times: "I am a fool;" but the interval of lucidity was short. He fell back into the stupor of dementia, although his irony seemed to survive reason, and even, as it were, life itself. He died in 1745 in a state of complete dementia, leaving by a will made some years previously a sum of nearly £11,000 to a lunatic asylum. A post-mortem examination showed softening of the brain and extreme effusion; his skull (examined in 1855) showed great irregularities from thickening and roughening, signs of enlarged and diseased arteries, and an extremely small cerebellar region. In an epitaph which he had written for himself he summed up the cruel tortures of his soul now at rest, "*ubi sæva indignatio ulterius cor lacerare nequit*".

Newton, of whom it was truly said that his mind conquered the human race, was in old age afflicted by mental disorder, though of a less serious character than that of which we have just read. It was probably during this illness that he wrote his *Chronology*, his *Apocalypse*, and the *Letters to Bentley*, so inferior in value to the work of his earlier years. In 1693, after his house had been burnt a second time, and after excess in study, he is reported to have talked so strangely and incoherently to the arch-bishop that his friends were seriously alarmed. At this time he wrote two letters which, in their confused and obscure form, seem to show that he had been suffering from delusions of persecution. He wrote to Locke (1693):

> Being of opinion that you endeavoured to embroil me with women, and by other means, I

> was so much affected with it, as that when one told me you were sickly and would not live, I answered, 'twere better if you were dead. I desire you to forgive me this uncharitableness; for I am now satisfied that what you have done is just, and I beg your pardon for my having hard thoughts of you for it, and for representing that you struck at the root of morality, in a principle you laid in your book of ideas, and designed to pursue in another book, and that I took you for a Hobbist. I beg your pardon also for saying or thinking that there was a design to sell me an office or to embroil me. I am your most humble and unfortunate servant, Is. Newton.[30]

Locke replied kindly, and a month later Newton again wrote to him:

> The last winter, by sleeping too often by my fire, I got an ill habit of sleeping; and a distemper, which this summer has been epidemical, put me further out of order, so that when I wrote to you I had not slept an hour a night for a fortnight together, and for five days together not a wink. I remember I wrote to you, but what I said of your book I remember not.

And in a letter to Pepys he says that he has "neither ate nor slept this twelvemonth, nor have my former consistency of mind."[31]

---

30 David Brewster, *Memoirs of the Life, Writings, and Discoveries of Sir Isaac Newton*, 2 vols. (Edinburgh: Thomas Constable & Co., 1855) 2:100.

31 David Brewster, *Memoirs of the Life, Writings, and Discover-*

Those who, without frequenting a lunatic asylum, wish to form a fairly complete idea of the mental tortures of a monomaniac, have only to look through Rousseau's works, especially his later writings, such as the *Confessions*, the *Dialogues*, and the *Rêveries*. "I have very ardent passions," he writes in his *Confessions*,

> and while under their influence, my impetuosity knows no bounds; I think only of the object which occupies me; the entire universe besides is nothing to me; but this only lasts a moment, and the moment which follows throws me into a state of prostration. A single sheet of fine paper tempts me more than the money to buy a ream of it. I see the thing and am tempted; if I only see the means of acquiring it I am not tempted. Even now, if I see anything that tempts me, I prefer taking it to asking for it.

This is the distinction between the kleptomaniac and the thief: the former steals by instinct, to steal; the latter steals by interest, to acquire: the first is led away by anything that strikes him; the second is attracted by the value of the object.

Dominated by his senses, Rousseau never knew how to resist them. The most insignificant pleasure, he says, so long as it was present, fascinated him more than all the joys of Paradise. In fact, a monk's dinner (Father Pontierre) led him to apos-

---

ies of Sir Isaac Newton, 2 vols. (Edinburgh: Thomas Constable & Co., 1855) 2:94.

tasy, and a feeling of repulsion caused him to abandon cruelly an epileptic friend on the road.

It was not only his passions that were morbid and violent; his intelligence also was affected from his earliest days, as he shows in his *Confessions*:

> My imagination has never been so cheerful as when I have been suffering. My mind cannot beautify the really pleasant things that happen to me, only the imaginary ones. If I wish to describe spring well, it must be in winter.

Real evils had little hold on Rousseau, he tells us; imaginary evils touched him more nearly. "I can adapt myself to what I experience, but not to what I fear." It is thus that people kill themselves through fear of death.

On first reading medical books Rousseau imagined that he had the diseases which he found described, and was astonished, not to find himself healthy, but to find himself alive. He came to the conclusion that he had a polypus at the heart. It was, as he himself confesses, a strange notion, the overflow of an idle and exaggerated sensibility which had no better channel. "There are times," he says,

> in which I am so little like myself that I might be taken for a man of quite different character. In repose I am indolence and timidity itself, and do not know how to express myself; but if I become excited I immediately know what to say.

This unfortunate man went through a long series of occupations from the noblest to the most degrading; he was an apostate for money, a watchmaker, a charlatan, a music-master, an engraver, a painter, a servant, an embryo diplomatic secretary; in literature and science he took up medicine, music, botany, theology, teaching.

The abuse of intellectual work, especially dangerous in a thinker whose ideas were developed slowly and with difficulty, joined to the ever-increasing stimulus of ambition, gradually transformed the hypochondriac into a melancholiac, and finally into a maniac. "My agitations and anger," he wrote, "affected me so much that I passed ten years in delirium, and am only calm to-day." Calm! When disease, now become chronic, no longer permitted him to distinguish what was real, what was imaginary in his troubles. In fact, he bade farewell to the world of society, in which he had never felt at home, and retired into solitude; but even in the country, people from the town zealously pursued him, and the tumult of the world and notions of *amour-propre* veiled the freshness of nature. It is in vain for him to hide himself in the woods, he writes in his *Rêveries*; the crowd attaches itself to him and follows him. We think once more of Tasso's lines:—

e da me stesso
Sempre fuggendo, avrò me sempre appresso.

Rousseau doubtless alluded to these lines when he

wrote to Corancez that Tasso had been his prophet. He wrote later that he believed that Prussia, England, France, the King, women, priests, men, irritated by some passages in his works, were waging a terrible war against him, with effects by which he explained the internal troubles from which he suffered.

In the refinement of their cruelty, he says in the *Rêveries*, his enemies only forgot one thing—to graduate their torments, so that they could always renew them. But the chief artifice of his enemies was to torture him by overwhelming him with benefits and with praise. "They even went so far as to corrupt the greengrocers, so that they sold him better and cheaper vegetables. Without doubt his enemies thus wished to prove his baseness and their generosity."[32] During his stay in London his melancholia was changed into a real attack of mania. He imagined that Choiseul was seeking to arrest him, abandoned his luggage and his money at his hotel, and fled to the coast, paying the innkeepers with pieces of silver spoons. He found the winds contrary, and in this saw another indication of the plot against him. In his exasperation he harangued the crowd in bad English from the top of a hill; they listened stupefied, and he believed he had affected them. But on returning to France his invisible enemies were not appeased. They spied and misinterpreted all his acts; if he read a news-

32 "Premier dialogue", Jean-Jacques Rousseau, *Rousseau juge de Jean-Jacques: Dialogues* (London: [s.n.], 1782).

paper, they said he was conspiring; if he smelled the perfume of a rose, they suspected he was concocting a poison. Everything was a crime: they stationed a picture-dealer at his door; they prevented the door from shutting; no visitor came whom they had not prejudiced against him. They corrupted his coffee-merchant, his hairdresser, his landlord; the shoeblack had no more blacking when Rousseau needed him; the boatman had no boats when this unfortunate man wished to cross the Seine. He demanded to be put in prison—and even that was refused him.

In order to take from him the one weapon which he possessed, the press, a publisher, *whom he did not know*, was arrested and thrown into the Bastille. The custom of burning a cardboard figure at the micareme had been abolished. It is re-established, certainly to make fun of him and to burn him in effigy; in fact, the clothes placed on it resembled his.[33] In the country he meets a child who smiles at him; he turns to respond, and suddenly sees a man whom, by his mournful face (note the method of recognition), he sees to be a spy placed by his enemies.

Under the constant impression of this monomania of persecution he wrote his *Dialogues sur Rousseau jugé par Rousseau*, in which, in order to appease his innumerable enemies he presented a faithful and minute portrait of his halluci-

33 "Second dialogue", Jean-Jacques Rousseau, *Rousseau juge de Jean-Jacques: Dialogues* (London: [s.n.], 1782).

nations. He began to distribute his defence, in a truly insane manner, by presenting a copy to any passer-by whose face did not appear prejudiced against him by his enemies. It was dedicated: "*A tous les Français aimant encore la justice et la verité.*" In spite of this title, or, perhaps, because of it, he found no one who accepted it with pleasure; several even refused it.

No longer able to put trust in any mortal he turned, like Pascal, to God, to whom he addressed a very tender and familiar letter; then in order to ensure the arrival of his letter at its destination, he placed it together with the manuscript of the *Dialogues* on the altar of Nôtre-Dame at Paris. Then, having found the railing closed, he suspected a conspiracy of Heaven against him.

Dussaulx, who saw him often in the last years of his life, writes that he even distrusted his dog, finding a mystery in his frequent caresses.[34] The *délire des grandeurs* was never absent; it may be seen continually in the *Confessions*, in which he defies the human race to show a better being than himself.

After all this testimony, it does not seem to me that Voltaire and Corancez were altogether wrong in affirming that Rousseau had been mad, and that he confessed it himself. Numerous passages

34 Alfred Bugeault, *Étude sur l'état mental de Rousseau et sa mort à Ermenonville* (Paris: E. Plon, 1883) 123. [The 1891 edition of Man of Genius gives 1876 as the publication year; the page number given for the source is correct, however. —Ed.]

in the *Confessions* and in Grimm's letters allude to other affections such as paralysis of the bladder and spermatorrhœa, which probably originated in the spinal cord, and which certainly aggravated his melancholia. It must also be remembered that from childhood, Rousseau, like so many other subjects of degeneration, showed sexual precocity and perversion; it appears that he had no pleasure in his relations with women unless they beat him naked, like a child, or threatened to do so.[35]

Nicolaus Lenau, one of the greatest lyric poets of times, ended, forty years ago, in the asylum of Döbling at Vienna, a life which from childhood shows a mingling of genius and insanity.

He was born in 1802 in Hungary, the son of a proud and vicious aristocrat, and of a melancholy, sensitive, and ascetic mother. At an early age he manifested tendencies to sadness, to music, and to mysticism. He studied medicine, law, agriculture, and especially music. In 1831 Kerner remarked in him strange fits of sadness and melancholy, and noted that at other times he would spend whole nights in the garden playing his favourite violin. "I feel myself," he wrote to his sister, "gravitating towards misfortune; the demon of insanity riots in my heart; I am *mad*. To you, sister, I say it, for you will love me all the same." This demon induced him to go, almost aimlessly, to America. He returned to find himself fêted and received with gladness by all; but hypochondria, in his own words, had

35 *Revue Philosophique* (1883).

planted its teeth deep in his heart, and everything was useless.[36] And, in fact, this unhappy heart had an attack of pericarditis, from which it recovered only imperfectly. From that time sleep, once the only medicine for his troubles, ceased to visit him; every night he is surrounded by terrible visions. "One would say," he wrote, in a truly insane fashion, "that the devil is hunting in my belly. I hear there a perpetual barking of dogs and a funereal echo of hell. Without joking, it is enough to make one despair."

That misanthropy which we have already noted in Haller and Swift and Cardan and Rousseau took possession of Lenau in 1840 with all the accompaniments of mania. He is afraid and ashamed of men, disgusted with them. Germany was preparing bouquets and triumphal arches in his honour, but he fled, and without any cause went to and fro from one country to another; he was causelessly angry and impatient, and felt himself incapable of work; *non est firmum sinciput*, it seemed, as he himself said; at the same time his appetite became as insane as his brain. He returned with a strange taste to the mysticism of his childhood, wished to study the Gnostics, and read over again the stories of sorcerers which he had found so attractive in his youth, while he drank coffee enor-

36 Anton Schurz, *Lenau's leben: Grossentheils aus des dichters eigenen briefen*, 2 vols. (Stuttgard and Augsburg, 1855) 1:275. [Here the original footnote in the 1891 edition gave the title as *Lenaus Werke*. —Ed.]

mously and smoked excessively. It was incredible, he observed, how in moving his body, in lighting or changing a cigar, new ideas arose within him. He wrote during entire nights, wandered, journeyed, meditated a marriage, projected great works, and executed none.

It was the last flickering of a great spirit; in 1844 Lenau complained more and more of headache, of constant perspiration, of extreme weakness. His left hand and the muscles of the eyes and cheeks were paralysed, and he began to write with orthographic errors and quibbles, as *Wie gut es mir gut* for *mir geht*; or "I am not delirious, but lyrical." Suddenly, on the 12th of October, he had a violent attack of suicidal mania. He was restrained, and furiously struck and broke everything, burning his manuscripts. Gradually he became composed and intelligent again, and even analyzed his attack minutely in that terrible, chaotic poem the *Traumgewalten*. It was a ray of sunlight in the dark night; it was, as Schilling well said, genius for the last time dominating insanity. In fact, his condition was constantly getting worse; another suicidal attack was followed by that fatal comfort, that pleasant excitement which marks the commencement of general paralysis. "I enjoy life," he said; "I am glad that the terrible visions of old have been succeeded by pleasant and delightful visions." He imagined that he was in Walhalla with Goethe, and that he had become King of Hungary and was victorious in battle; he made puns on his family name, Niembsch. In 1845 he lost his sense of smell, which had previously been very delicate, and ceased to care for violets, his favourite flowers. He no longer recognised his old friends. Notwithstanding this sad condition, he was still able to write a lyric marked by extravagant mysticism, but not without the old beauty. One day when conducted to Plato's bust, he said: "There is the man who invented stupid love." Another time, hearing some one say, "Here lives the great Lenau," the unfortunate man replied: "Now Lenau has become very, very small," and he wept for a long time. "Lenau is unhappy" were his last words. He died on the 21st of August, 1850. The autopsy only revealed a little serum in the ventricles and traces of progressive pericarditis.

In this same asylum at Döbling died some years later another great man, Széchenyi,[37] the creator of Danubian navigation, the founder of the Magyar Academy, the promoter of the revolution of 1848. At the very apogee of the revolution, when Széchenyi was a minister, he was heard one day begging Kossuth, one of his colleagues in the Ministry, not to let him be hanged. It was looked upon as a joke, but it was not so. He foresaw the misfortunes which would fall on his country, and wrongly judged himself responsible. The monomania of

37 Aurél Kecskeméthy, *Graf Stephan Széchenyi's staatsmännische Laufbahn, seine letzen Lebensjahre in der döblinger Irrenanstalt und sein Tod* (Pest: Hornyánszky & Hummel, 1866).

persecution took possession of him, and threatened to lead him to suicide. He gradually became calm, but exhibited a morbid loquacity, strange in a diplomatist and conspirator, and all day long he would stop the lunatics and idiots, and, what was worse, the enemies of his country whom he met in prison, and narrate to them the long confession of his imaginary sins. In 1850 an old passion for chess awoke in him, and took an insane character. It became necessary to pay a poor student to play with him for ten or twelve hours at a time. The unfortunate student went mad, but Széchenyi slowly became sane. At the same time he began to lose an aversion for contact with human beings which had taken possession of him, and which made it impossible for him even to see his relations. There only remained of his morbid habits a certain repugnance to the bright country light, and a great objection to leave his room. On certain days of the month he consented to receive his much-loved children; with a gesture he led them tenderly to his table, and read what he had written; but it required much diplomacy to bring him out into the park. His intelligence remained clear; it was even more robust than ever. He kept himself acquainted with the whole German and Magyar literary movement, and he watched for the smallest sign of better fortune to come to his country. When he saw an Austrian intrigue hindering the completion of the eastern railway to which he had devoted himself so vigorously he wrote a letter to Zichy, in which he shows all his old power, as may be seen from the following passages:

> What has existed once often reappears in the world under another form and different conditions. A broken bottle cannot be put together, yet those poor fragments of glass are not lost; they may be thrown into the furnace and become a vessel for Tokay, the king of wines, to sparkle in, while the broken bottle may have held but a very inferior wine. . . . The greatest praise that can be given to a Hungarian is to tell him that he has stood firm. You know, my friend, our old proverb: 'Stand firm, even in the mire.' Let us apply that motto; distrust the reproaches even of our brothers to serve the common cause. To remain at one's post, in spite of the mud that fanatical or frivolous patriots throw in the faces of their brothers and companions in arms, to remain obstinately there, even when insult strikes one in the face—that should be the *mot d'ordre* of the present time.

In 1858, when the Austrian Ministry exerted pressure on the Hungarian Academy to abolish the articles of its statutes which constituted the culture of the Magyar language, its fundamental task, Széchenyi wrote another letter, which describes his mental condition:

> Can I be silent when I see that noble seed crushed? Can I forget the services which that powerful benefactor has rendered us? I ask—I,

> whose misfortune lies, not in a vague confusion of ideas, but, on the contrary, in the fatal gift of seeing too clearly, too distinctly, to make any illusion possible. Ought I not to raise a cry of alarm, seeing our dynasty possessed by I know not what evil influence, fighting against the most energetic of its peoples, against that for whom the future reserves the highest destiny, and not only contemning it but stifling it, depriving it of its proper character, shaking to its roots the secular tree of the empire. Founder of this Academy, it is my duty to-day to speak. So long as my head is on my shoulders, so long as my brain is not entirely obscured, so long as the light of my eyes remains unveiled by eternal night, I shall retain my right to decide concerning the rules. Our Emperor will sooner or later understand that the assimilation of the races of the empire is merely the Utopia of his ministers; the day will come when all will detach themselves. Hungary alone, which has no racial affinity with the other European nations, will seek to accomplish its own destiny beneath the ægis of the royal dynasty.

That was in 1858. In 1859, even before the outbreak of war, he prophesied defeat, and showed its results: "There are crises," he said, "which lead to cure when the sick person is not incurable." He published at London a book in which, in a strange and humorous, but at the same time terrible way, he traced the history of Hungary's sufferings under Bach's iron rule, sketched the future of his country, and counselled a policy of concord, parallel but not servile to that of Austria. "In truth," he wrote himself,

> this book is miserable; but do you know how the Margaret Island was formed? According to an old legend, the Danube once occupied its site; some carrion once, no one knows how, settled on to a sand-bank and became attached there. Whatever the river swept down, froth, leaves, branches, trees, all were piled up there, and at last a magnificent island arose. My work is something like that carrion. Who knows what may arise out of it at last?

A few months later Hübner succeeded Bach, and the Liberal system was inaugurated. Széchenyi was wild with joy; from his humble room he encouraged the minister, sent him plans of reform, inspired or wrote papers on the renewal of Austria, not forgetting Hungary. The dream was soon dissipated; Hübner was succeeded by Thierry, a bad disciple of Bach, armed with the old and superannuated systems of Austria; all reform was abandoned. The unfortunate Széchényi resisted sorrowfully; he called Rechberg, begged him to inform the Emperor of his mistake while there was still time, and submitted programmes for an Austrian constitution and a Hungarian constitution, internal affairs to be treated separately, and external affairs conjointly. Rechberg, far less foreseeing than this inspired madman, said, shaking his head: "One can easily see that this project comes from a lunatic asylum." Worse still, Thierry, suspecting a vulgar conspirator in the great Magyar, sent a troop of police to visit the asylum, threatened to imprison him, and deprived him of his papers.

The unhappy man, whose madness was merely an irresistible need to serve his country at all costs, had only one remorse; he feared he had not sufficiently served his country, and henceforth all hopes were closed. He sought in vain to stifle his poignant grief by playing desperately at chess. At last he shot himself with a revolver. That was on the 8th of April, 1860. In 1867, Francis Joseph was crowned King of Hungary, thus realizing the dreams of the Dobling lunatic; and Rechberg, who had laughed at them, was called upon to put them in practice.

E. T. A. Hoffmann, that strange poet, artist, and musician, whose drawings ended in caricature, his tales in extravagance, and his music in a mere medley of sound, but who was, nevertheless, the real creator of fantastic poetry, was a drunkard. Many years before his death he wrote in his journal: "How is it that, awake or asleep, my thoughts are always running, in spite of myself, on this miserable theme of madness? Disorderly ideas seem to rise out of my mind like blood from opened veins." He was so sensitive to atmospheric variations that he constructed a meteorological scale out of his subjective emotions. For many years he was subject to a real monomania of persecution, with hallucinations in which the fantasies of his stories were converted into realities.

The famous Sicilian physiologist Foderà often declared that he could furnish bread for 200,000 men with a single oven of very simple construction, and that, with forty soldiers he could overcome any army, even 1,000,000 strong. When about fifty years of age he fell violently in love with a young girl who lived opposite him. One fine day, being in the street, he gazed up rapturously at the charming maiden, who, to free herself from her wearisome adorer, emptied a vessel of dirty water on his head. Foderà, however, regarded this act as a manifestation of love, and returned home full of joy. In the courtyard he saw a fowl, which, as he declared, had an extraordinary resemblance to the beloved maiden; he immediately bought it, covered it with kisses, allowed the precious creature to do anything, to soil his books, and his clothes, and even to perch on his bed.[38]

The most complete type of madness in genius is presented to us by Schopenhauer.[39] He himself considered that he inherited his intelligence from his mother, a literary woman full of vivacity, but heartless; while his character came from his father, a banker, who was misanthropic and eccentric to monomania. From childhood his hearing was de-

38 Gaetano Costanzo, *Sulla follia anomala* (Palermo: G. Lorsnaider, 1876).

39 Wilhelm von Gwinner, *Schopenhauer's Leben* (Leipzig : F. A. Brockhaus, 1878); Théodule Ribot, *La philosophie de Schopenhauer* (Paris: Alcan, 1885); Carl von Seidlitz, *Dr. Arthur Schopenhauer vom medizinischen Standpunkt betrachtet* (Dorpat: Glaser, 1872).

fective, and he believed and it is probably true—that he inherited his deafness, his very large head, and his brilliant eyes, from his father. He lived for some time in England under the care of a clergyman. He learnt to know the English language and literature, and also learnt to despise the bigotry of his hosts. Notwithstanding constant change of scene involved in his travels, he was never cheerful, and gave free course to his discontent with himself and his surroundings. "From my youth," he says,

> I have always been melancholy. Once, when I was perhaps eighteen, I thought to myself, in spite of ray youth, that the world could not be the work of a God, but rather of a devil. During my education I certainly had to suffer too much from my father's temperament.

He was frightened by imaginary diseases. In Switzerland the Alps aroused in him sadness rather than admiration. His mother, like all those who came in contact with him, experienced the unhappy effects of his character, for when, in 1807, he wished, at the age of nineteen, to come and see her at Weimar, she wrote to him,

SCHOPENHAUER

I have always told you that it would be very difficult for me to live with you; the more nearly I observe you, the more this difficulty increases, so far at least as I am concerned. I do not hide from you that, so long as you remain what you are now, I would support any sacrifice rather than submit to it. I do not misunderstand the foundation of goodness in you; what separates me from you is not your heart, not your inner, but your outer, self, your views, your judgments, your manner of behaving; in short, I cannot harmonize with you in anything that concerns your external self. Even your ill-humour, your lamentations over the inevitable, your sombre face, your extravagant opinions, which you give forth like oracles, and tolerate no opposition to,

> oppress me, shock my serenity, and are no use to yourself. Your disagreeable discussions, your lamentations over the stupidity of the world and human misery, give me wretched nights and bad dreams.[40]

He became more and more estranged from his mother, alleging that she had not respected his father's memory, that she had dissipated the common fortune by her extravagance, and had thus reduced him to the necessity of working for his living. This effort was entirely repugnant to his nature. In this he yielded to a feeling of anguish, which, by his own confession, bordered on madness. "If there is nothing to cause me misery, I am tormented by the thought that there must be something hidden from me. *Misera conditio nostra.*"[41]

In 1814 Schopenhauer left Weimar to complete his great work. He was convinced that he could and mast open a new and only way to lead men of mind and heart to truth; he felt in himself something more than mere science, something demoniacal (*dämonisches*).

In 1813 he had already said:

> Beneath my hand, and still more in my head, a work, a philosophy, is ripening, which will be at once an ethic and a metaphysic, hitherto so unreasonably separated, just as man has been divided into body and soul. The work grows,

40 Gwinner 26.

41 *Memorabilien* 2:332.

> and gradually becomes concrete, like the foetus in its mother's womb. I do not know what will appear at last. I recognize a member, an organ, one part after another. I write without seeking for results, for I know that it all stands on the same foundation, and will thus compose a vital and organic whole. I do not understand the system of the work, just as a mother does not understand the fœtus that develops in her bowels, but she feels it tremble within her. My mind draws its food from the world by the medium of intelligence and thought; this nourishment gives body to my work; and yet I do not know why it should happen in me and not in others who receive the same food. O Chance! sovereign of this world, let me live in peace for a few years yet, for I love my work as a mother loves her child. When it is ripe and brought to the light, then exercise your rights, and claim interest for the delay. But if, in this iron century, I succumb before that hour, may these unripened principles and studies be received by the world as they are, until perhaps some related mind appears who will collect and unite the members.

All the characteristic symptoms of the various steps that lead up to insanity, the rapid passage from profound grief to excessive joy, may be found in Schopenhauer. In a moment of tranquil reflection on himself, in 1814, after having found that men were "a soup of bread dipped in water with a little arsenic," and after having declared that "their egoism is like that which binds the dog to his master," he wrote: "And now do not except yourself;

examine your loves and your friendships; observe if your objective judgments are not in great part subjective and impure." And in another page: "Just as the most beautiful body contains within it fæcal and mephitic gases, so the noblest character offers traits of badness, and the greatest genius presents traces of pettiness and excessive pride."

The same alternations may be found throughout his life; sometimes, a keen and contemptuous critic, he shows haughty presumption; at other times he descends to the lowest literary platitudes; sometimes he wandered about the delightful suburbs of Dresden lost in the contemplation of nature; at other times he wallowed in prosaic love adventures, from which distinguished friends were obliged to save him, and this while he was elaborating his great work, *Die Welt als Wille und Vorstellung*, which was to astonish the world. "He thus," remarks Von Sedlitz, "gave the example of a *mania puerperii spiritualis*, such as sometimes takes possession of pregnant women." Schopenhauer himself told Frauenstädt that at the time when he was writing his great work he must have been very strange in his person and behaviour, as people took him for a madman. One day when he was walking in a conservatory at Dresden, and, while contemplating the plants, talked aloud to himself and gesticulated, an attendant came up and asked him who he was. "If you can tell me who I am," replied Schopenhauer, "I shall be very much obliged to you." And he walked away leaving the astonished attendant fully persuaded that he was a lunatic. With such a disposition it is not surprising that Schopenhauer, like many prophets, believed that he was impelled by a demon or spirit.

> When my intelligence had touched its apogee, and was, under favourable conditions, at its point of greatest tension, it was capable of embracing anything; it could suddenly bring forth revelations and give birth to chains of thought well worthy of preservation.[42]

In 1816 he wrote: "It happens to me among men as to Jesus of Nazareth when he had to awake his disciples always asleep." Even in old age he spoke of his great work in such a way as to exclude all doubt as to the inspiration which had produced it, such a work only being possible under the influence of inspiration. At that age he gazed with astonishment at his work, especially at the fourth book, as at a work written by some other person. It is worth while recalling here the doubling of personality so common in men of genius.

After he had handed his book over to the publisher he set out for Italy, without awaiting its publication, with the proud faith that he had given a revelation to the world. His *délire des grandeurs* at this period increased, and the mental disturbance he underwent revealed itself later. He wrote: "In enchanting Venice, Love's arms held me

---

42 *Parerga* 2:38.

long enfettered, until an inner voice bade me break free and lead my steps elsewhere." And again: "If I could only satisfy my desire to look upon this race of toads and vipers as my equals, it would be a consolation to me." While oscillating between mental exaltation and depression he heard of the collapse of his banking-house. It is easy to understand the grief which this news caused him; he was reduced to the necessity of living by philosophy, instead of for philosophy, as he had desired to do. He twice sought to become a *Privatdozent* in Berlin, but he was unsuccessful in these attempts. His violent attacks on his contemporaries displeased his hearers, and his passionate disputations, and his tenacity in holding strange opinions, which he gave forth as oracles, rendered precarious his relations with friends and men of learning.

The invasion of cholera, at the beginning of 1831, completed his troubles. On the last night of 1830 he had already had a dream, which he looked upon as a prophecy, foretelling his death in the new year. "This dream," he wrote in his *Cogitata*,

> influenced me in my departure from Berlin immediately the cholera began in 1831. I had scarcely reached Frankfort-on-the-Main, when I had a very distinct vision of spirits. They were, as I think, my ancestors, and they announced to me that I should survive my mother, at that time still living. My father, who was dead, carried a light in his hand.

That this hallucination was accompanied by real brain affection is proved by the fact that at that time he "fell into deep melancholy, not speaking to any one for weeks together." The doctors were alarmed, and induced him to go to Mannheim for change of scene. More than a year later he returned to Frankfurt, when the acute period of his illness had apparently passed. Signs of it remained, however, in his peculiar bearing, his habit of gesticulating and talking aloud to himself as he walked through the streets of the city, or sat at table in the restaurant, and in his fury against "such philosophasters as Hegel, Schleiermacher, and similar charlatans, who shine like so many stars in the firmament of philosophy, and rule the philosophic market." He accused them of depriving him of the praise and fame he deserved, by deliberately keeping silence concerning his work. This was a fixed idea with him, like the idea of his own infallibility, even after he seemed to return to a relatively normal condition, thanks to the fame which, after a delay of thirty years, at length crowned his name and his works.

His *délire des grandeurs*, his melancholy accompanied by morbid rage, born of the idea of persecution, had really shown themselves in him from childhood. At six years of age he believed that his parents wished to abandon him. As a student he was always morose. One of the things which caused him most trouble was noise, especially when produced by the whips of drivers. "To be sensitive to noise," he wrote, u is one of the numerous misfortunes which discount the privilege of genius." "*Qui non habet indignationem*" he wrote, "*non habet ingenium*" But his indignation was excessive, a morbid rage. One day when his landlady was chattering in the anteroom he came out and shook her so violently that he broke her arm, and was fined for damages. He was genuinely hypochondriacal. He was driven from Naples by the fear of smallpox, from Verona by the idea that he had been poisoned by snuff, from Berlin by the dread of cholera, and previously by the conscription. In 1831, he had a fresh attack of restlessness; at the least sound in the street he put his hand to his sword; his fear became real suffering; he could not open a letter without suspecting some great misfortune; he would not shave his beard, but burnt it; he hated women and Jews and philosophers, especially philosophers, and loved dogs, remembering them in his will. He reasoned about everything, however unimportant; about his great appetite, about the moonlight, which suggested quite illogical ideas to him, &c. He believed in table-turning, and that magnetism could heal his dog's paws and restore his own hearing. One night the servant dreamt that she had to wipe some ink stains; in the morning he spilt some, and the great philosopher deduced that "everything happens necessarily."

He was contradiction personified. He placed annihilation, *nirvana*, as the final aim of life, and predicted (which means that he desired), one hundred years of life. He preached sexual abstinence as a duty, but did not himself practise it. He who had suffered so much from the intolerance of others, insulted Moleschott and Büchner, and rejoiced when the Government deprived them of their professorial chairs.

He lived on the first storey, in case of fire; would not trust himself to his hairdresser; hid gold in the ink-pot, and letters of change beneath the bedclothes. "When I have no troubles," he said (like Rousseau), "it is then that I am most afraid." He feared to touch a razor; a glass that was not his own might communicate some disease; he wrote business documents in Greek or Latin or Sanskrit, and disseminated them in books to prevent unforeseen and impossible curiosity, which would have been much easier avoided by a simple lock and key. Though he regarded himself as the victim of a vast conspiracy of professors of philosophy, concerted at Gotha, to preserve silence concerning his books, he yet dreaded lest they should speak of them; "I would rather that worms should gnaw my body than that professors should gnaw my philosophy." Lacking all affection, he even insulted his mother, and drew from her example conclusions against the whole female sex, "long of hair and short of sense." Yet, while despising monogamy, he recommended tetragamy, to which he saw but one objection—the four mothers-in-law. The same lack of affection made him despise patriotism, "the passion of fools, and the most foolish of passions;"

he took part with the soldiers against the people, and to the former and to his dog he left his property. He was always preoccupied with himself, not only with the self that was the creator of a new system, but in hundreds of his letters he speaks with strange complaisance of his photograph, of his portrait in oils and of a person who had bought it "in order to place it in a kind of chapel, like the image of a saint."

No one has, for the rest, maintained more openly than Schopenhauer, the relationship of genius to insanity. "People of genius," he wrote, "are not only unpleasant in practical life, but weak in moral sense and wicked." And elsewhere:

> Such men can have but few friends; solitude reigns on the summits. . . . Genius is closer to madness than to ordinary intelligence. . . . The lives of men of genius show how often, like lunatics, they are in a state of continual agitation.

Nicolaï Vasilyevitch Gogol (born 1809), after suffering from an unhappy love affair, gave himself up for many years to unrestrained onanism, and became eventually a great novelist. Having known Poushkin he was attracted to the short story, then he fell under the influence of the Moscow school, and become a humourist of the highest order. In his *Dead Souls* he satirises the Russian bureaucracy with so much *vis comica* as to show the need of putting an end to a form of government which is a martyrdom both for the victims and the executioners.

On the publication of his historical Cossack romance, *Taras Bulba,* he reached the summit of his fame. His admirers compared him to Homer; even the Government patronized him. Then a new idea began to dominate him; he thought that he painted his country with so much crudity and realism that the picture might incite to a revolution which would not be kept within reasonable limits, and might overturn society, religion, and the family, leaving him the remorse of having provoked it. This idea took possession of his mind and dominated it, as it had formerly been dominated by love, by the drama, and by the novel. He then sought by his writings to combat western liberalism, but the antidote attracted fewer readers than the poison. Then he abandoned work, shut himself up in his house, giving himself up to prayer to the saints, and supplicating them to obtain God's pardon for his revolutionary sins. He accomplished a pilgrimage to Jerusalem, from which he returned somewhat consoled, when the revolution of 1848 broke out, and his remorse was again aroused. He was constantly pursued by visions of the triumph of Nihilism, and in his alarm he called on Holy Russia to overthrow the pagan West, and to found on its ruins the orthodox Panslavist empire. In 1852, the great novelist was found dead at Moscow of exhaustion, or rather of tabes dorsalis, in front of the shrine before which he was accustomed to lie for days in silent prayer.

PART II

THE CHARACTERISTICS OF GENIUS

CHAPTER I

Meteorological Influences on Genius

The influence of weather on the insane — Sensitiveness of men of genius to barometrical conditions — Sensitiveness to thermometrical conditions.

The Influence of Weather on the Insane.—A series of clinical researches, which I carried on for six consecutive years, has shown me with certainty that the mental condition of the insane is modified in a constant manner by barometrical and thermometrical influences.[1] When the temperature rose above 25°, 30°, and 32° C., especially if the rise was sudden, the number of maniacal attacks increased from 29° to 50°. On the days on which the barometer showed sudden variations, especially of elevation—and more particularly two or three

1 *Pensiero e meteore; studii di un alienista in Biblioteca scientifica internazionale*, v. 16 (Milano: Dumolard, 1878); *Azione degli astri e delle meteore sulla mente umana* (Milan: Raedelli, 1871).

days before and after the variation—the number of maniacal attacks rapidly increased from 34° to 46°. This meteoric sensibility, as I term it, increased in an inverse ratio to the integrity of the nervous tissues, being very great in idiots and slightest in monomaniacs. The study of 23,602 lunatics has shown me that the development of insanity generally coincides with the increase of monthly temperature and with the great barometrical perturbations in September and March; the onset of heat, acts more efficaciously, however, than the intense heat which follows; and the heat which has become habitual in August acts much less harmfully. The minimum number of outbreaks of insanity is found in the coldest months. (*See* Plate.)

This coincidence is seen best in the French lunatics studied by Esquirol.[2] The French figures present with most clearness the effect of thermometrical influences, because in France the entry of lunatics into asylums, being little impeded by red-tapeism, follows closely on the outbreak.

Month	INSANE[3]		Temperature
	Italy	France	
January	1,476	42	1° 63 C
February	1,420	40	5° 73 C

2 Adolphe Quetelet, *Physique sociale*, 2 vols. (Paris: C. Muquardt, 1869) Book 4, Ch. 1.

3 This table appears with the rows out of sequence in the original English version. It has been re-arranged using the month as the key. —Ed.

March	1,829	49	6° 60 C
April	2,237	50	16° 12 C
May	2,642	58	16° 75 C
June	2,704	55	21° 29 C
July	2,614	58	23° 75 C
August	2,261	45	21° 92 C
September	1,604	48	19° 00 C
October	1,637	44	12° 77 C
November	1,452	47	7° 17 C
December	1,529	35	1° 01 C

Now, a similar influence may be noted in those to whom nature, benevolently or malevolently, has conceded the power of intellect more generously than to others. There are few among these who do not confess that their inspiration is strangely subject to the influence of weather. Those who associate with them, or who read their correspondence, know that they suffer so greatly from this cause that they often complain to every one, and struggle, with the help of various artifices, against the malignant influences which impede the free flight of their thought.

Sensitiveness to Barometrical Conditions.—Montaigne wrote: "*Si la santé me sied et la clarté d'un beau jour, me voilà honnête homme.*"[4] Diderot wrote, "*Il me semble que j'ai l'esprit fou dans les grands vents.*"[5] Giordani foretold storms two

4 French: If my health allows and in the light of a fine day, here I am, an honest man. —Ed.

5 French: It seems to me that my soul goes crazy in high wind.

days beforehand.[6] Maine de Biran, a very spiritualistic philosopher, wrote, in his *Journal de ma vie intime*, "I do not know how it is that in bad weather I feel my intelligence and will so unlike what they are in fine weather;" and again,

> There are days in which my thought seems to break through the veils which surround it. In some conditions of the weather I feel delight in good, and adore virtue; at other times I am indifferent to everything, even to my duties. Are our sentiments, our affections, our principles, related to the physical condition of our organs?[7]

The study of his *Journal* shows us the justice of his doubts. Let us take 1818. In April we find two periods of good inspiration and four of bad, although the weather was fine; in May he was constantly sad, and in November only cheerful during ten days.

> 1815, *May.*—I am suffering from the nervous disposition which I experience in spring; and though wishing to do too much, I do nothing. . . .
>
> 23 *May.*—I am happy because of the air that I breathe and the birds that are singing; but inspiration passes away through the senses. Each season has not merely special forms of sensation, but a certain way of understanding life

—Ed.

6 Mantegazza, *op. cit.*

7 Ernest Naville, *Maine de Biran, sa vie et ses pensées* (Paris: J. Cherbuliez, 1854) 129.

which is peculiar to it. . . .

17 *May.*—Irresistible pleasure of thought: inspiration. . . .

4, 16, 17 *October.*—Empty of ideas; sad. . . .

1816, 25 *January.*—Sad and idle. My life is useless. . . .

24 *April.*—I am another man. Every day seems a feast day. At this time of the year something seems to lift the soul to another region, and to give it strength to surmount all impediments. . . .

1817, 13 *April.*—Excited. . . .

7 *May.*—Working on Condillac. . . .

10, 18 *July.*—Marvellous activity. . . .

12 *October.*—Am transformed; thought turns to commonplace triviality. . . .

22, 23, 28 *November.*—Sterile agitation. Alteration of all my mental faculties. . . .

1818, 1 *April.*—Northerly wind. Am weary, sad, suffering, stolid. . . .

1820, 31 *March.*—At this time of the year it always happens to me that body and mind are alike heavy; I have the consciousness of my degradation. . . .

1821, *May.*—All this month I am sad, and yield to external causes like a marionette. . . .

21 *October.*—I feel myself newborn. I was returning to work, but the weather has changed; the wind has turned to the south; it is strong, and I am another man. I feel inert, with a distaste for work, and inclined to those sad and melancholy fantasies which are always so fatal to me. . . .

Alfieri wrote,

> I compare myself to a barometer. I have always experienced more or less facility in writing, according to the weight of the air; absolute stupidity in the great solstitial and equinoxial winds, infinitely less perspicacity in the evening than in the morning, and a much greater aptness for creation in the middle of the winter or of summer than in the intermediate seasons. This has made me humble, as I am convinced that at these times I have had no power to do otherwise.

Monod says that the phases of Michelet's intellectual life followed the course of the seasons.[8] Poushkin's poetic inspiration was greatest during dark and stormy nights.

We catch a glimpse in these facts of an appreciable influence of barometrical conditions upon men of genius as upon the insane.

Heat.—Thermometrical influence is much clearer and more evident. Napoleon, who defined man as "a product of the physical atmosphere and the moral atmosphere," and who suffered from the faintest wind, loved heat so much that he would have fires even in July. Voltaire and Buffon had their studies warmed throughout the year. Rousseau said that the action of the sun in the dog-days aided him to compose, and he allowed the rays of the mid-day sun to fall on his head. Byron said that he feared cold as much as a gazelle. Heine wrote in one of his letters, "It snows; I have little fire in the

8 *Revue Bleue* 9 (1888).

room, and my letter is cold." Spallanzani, in the Ionian Islands, found himself able to study for three times as many hours as in misty Pavia.[9] Leopardi confesses in his letters, "My temperament is inimical to cold. I wait and invoke the reign of Ormuzd." Giusti wrote in the spring, "Inspiration is becoming favourable. . . . If spring aids me as in all other things . . ." Paisiello could only compose beneath six quilts in the summer and nine in the winter. Similar facts are told of Varillas, Méry, and Arnaud. Sylvester tells how, when on board the *Invicta*, beneath the vivifying rays of a powerful sun, the method of resolving a multiple equation occurred to him, and he succeeded, without pen or pencil.[10] Lesage, in his old age, became animated as the sun advanced in the meridian, gradually gaining his imaginative power, together with his cheerfulness; as the day declined, his mental activity gradually diminished, until he fell into a lethargy, which lasted to the following day.[11]

Giordani could only compose in the sun, or in the presence of abundant light and great heat.[12] Foscolo wrote in November: "I keep near the fire; my friends laugh at me, but I am seeking to give my members heat which my heart will concen-

9 *Viaggio Alle Due Sicilie E In Alcune Parti Dell' Appennino* (Pavia: Comini, 1792) Vol. VII.

10 *Nature* (Nov. 1883).

11 Joseph Henri Réveille-Parise, *Physiologie des hommes livres aux travaux de l'esprit* (Paris: Dentu, 1834).

12 Giussani, *Vita*, &c. 188.

trate and sublime within."[13] And in December he writes: "My natural infirmity, the fear of cold, has constrained me to live near the fire, and the fire has inflamed my eyelids." Milton confessed in his Latin elegies that in winter his muse was sterile; he could only write from the spring equinox to that of autumn. In a letter he complains of the cold of 1678, and fears that, if it lasts, it will hinder the free development of his imagination. Dr. Johnson, who tells us this in his *Life of Milton*, may be believed on this point, for imagination never smiled upon him, only the cold and tranquil intelligence of criticism, and he adds the commentary that all this must be the result of eccentricity of character, he, Johnson, never having experienced any effects from the variations of the weather. Poushkin often said that he found himself most disposed to composition in autumn; the brilliant spring sunshine produced on him an impression of melancholy. Salvator Rosa laughed in youth, as Lady Morgan tells us in her *Life*, at the pretended influence of the weather on works of genius; but in old age he became incapable of painting or thinking, almost of living, except in the heat of spring. In reading Schiller's correspondence with Goethe one is struck by the singular influence which the gentle and imaginative poet attributed to the weather. In November, 1817, he wrote: "In these sad days, beneath this leaden sky, I have need of all my elasticity to feel alive, and do not yet feel capable of

13 *Epistolario* 395.

serious work." And in December: "I am going back to work, but the weather is so dull that it is impossible to preserve the lucidity of the soul." In July, 1818: "Thanks to the fine weather I am better; the lyric inspiration, which obeys the will less than any other, does not delay." In December he complains that the necessity of completing Wallenstein unfortunately coincides with an unfavourable period of the year, "so that," he writes, "I am obliged to use all my strength to preserve mental clearness." And in May, 1799: "I hope to make progress in my work if the weather continues fine."

All these examples allow us to suspect, with some probability, that heat, with rare exceptions, aids in the productions of genius, as it aids in vegetation, and also aids, unfortunately, in the stimulation of mania.

If historians, who have squandered so much time and so many volumes in detailing minutely to us the most shameless exploits of kings, had sought with as much care the memorable epoch in which a great discovery or a masterpiece of art was conceived, they would no doubt have found that the hottest months and days have always been most fruitful for genius, as for nature generally.

Let us endeavour to find more precise proofs of this little-suspected influence.

Dante wrote his first sonnet on the 15th of June, 1282; in the spring of 1300 he wrote the *Vita Nuova*; on the 3rd of April he began his great poem.[14]

14 Lebin, *Sur l'epoque de la composition de la Vita Nuova*, p. 28.

Darwin had the earliest ideas of his great work first in March, then in June.[15] Petrarch conceived the *Africa* in March, 1338. Michelangelo's great cartoon, the work which so competent a judge as Cellini considered his most wonderful masterpiece, was imagined and executed between April and July, 1506. Manzoni wrote his *5 Maggio* in summer. Milton's great poem was conceived in the spring. Galileo discovered Saturn's ring in April, 1611. Balzac wrote *La cousine bette* in August and September, *Père Goriot* in September, *La recherche de l'absolu* in June to September. Sterne began *Tristram Shandy* in January, the first of his sermons in April, the famous one on errors of conscience in May.[16] Giordano Bruno composed his *Candelajo* in July; and in his witty dedication he attributed it to the heat of the dog-days. Voltaire wrote *Tancred* in August. Byron wrote the fourth canto of *Childe Harold* in September, his *Prophecy of Dante* in June, his *Prisoner of Chillon* during the summer in Switzerland. Giusti wrote of *Gingillino* and *Pero*: "Here are the only leaves that April has drawn out of my head after fourteen months of idleness." Schiller, it appears from his letters to Goethe, conceived *Don Carlos and Wallenstein* in the autumn, as well as

15 Francis Darwin, *The life and letters of Charles Darwin, including an autobiographical chapter* (London: John Murray, 1887) 1:51.

16 Paul Stapfer, *Laurence Sterne: sa personne et ses ouvrages. Étude précédé d'un fragment inédit de Sterne* (Paris: Thornin, 1870). [The footnote in the 1891 edition reads Stopfer, *Vie de Sterne*, Paris, 1870. —Ed.]

Fiesco and *Wilhelm Tell*; *Wallensteins Lager* and *Letters on Æsthetics* in September; *Kabale und Liebe* in winter; the *Magician*, the *Glove*, the *Ring of Polycrates*, the *Cranes of Ibycus*, and *Nadowessir's Song* in June; the *Jungfrau von Orleans* in July. Goethe wrote *Werther* in autumn; *Mignon* and other lyric poems in May; *Cellini*, *Alexis*, *Euphrosyne*, *Metamorphosis of Plants*, and *Parnass* in June and July; the *Xenien*, *Hermann und Dorothea*, *Westöstlichen Divan*, and *Natürliche Tochter* in winter. In the first days of March, 1788, which, he wrote, were worth more to him than a whole month, he dictated, besides other poems, the beginning of *Faust*.[17] Salomo's *Hymn to Liberty* was written in May. Rossini composed the *Semiramide* almost entirely in February, and in November the last part of the *Stabat Mater*.[18] Mozart composed the *Mitridate* in October; Beethoven his ninth symphony in February.[19] Donizetti composed *Lucia di Lammermoor*, perhaps entirely, in September; in any case, the famous *Tu che a Dio spiegasti l'ale* belongs to that date; the *Figlia del Reggimento* was also composed in autumn; *Linda de Chamoumix* in spring; *Rita* in summer; *Don Pasquale* and the *Miserere*

17 Johann-Wolfgang von Goethe, *Aus meinem Leben. Dichtung und Wahrheit*, 3 vols. (Tübingen: Cotta 1811, 1812, 1814).

18 Antonio Zanolini, *Biografia di Gioachino Rossini* (Bologna: N. Zanichelli, 1875).

19 Félix Clément, *Les musiciens célèbres depuis le seizième siècle jusqu'à nos jours* (Paris: Hachette et Cie., 1878).

in winter.[20] Wagner composed *Der Fliegende Holländer* in the spring of 1841. Canova modelled his first work, *Orpheus and Eurydice*, in October.[21] Michelangelo conceived his *Pietà* between September and October, 1498,[22] the design of the *Libreria* in December, the model in wood of the tomb of Pope Julius in August.[23] Leonardo da Vinci conceived the equestrian statue of the Sforza and began his book *Delia luce e delle Ombre* in April; for we find in his autograph manuscript these words: "On April the 23rd, 1492, I commenced this book and recommenced the horse." On the 2nd of July, 1491, he designed the pavilion of the Duchess's Bath; on the 3rd of March, 1509, St. Christopher's Canal. The first idea of the discovery of America came to Columbus between May and June, in 1474, in the form of a search for the western passage to India.[24] Gal-

20 Federico Alborghetti and Michelangelo Galli, *Gaetano Donizetti e G. Simone Mayr. Notizie e documenti* (Bergamo: Gaffuri e Gatti, 1875).

21 Antonio D'Este, *Memorie di Antonio Canova* (Florence: Felice Le Monnier, 1864).

22 Aurelio Gotti, *Vita di Michelangelo Buonarroti, narrate con l'aiuto di nuovi documenti*, 2 vols. (Florence: Tipografia della Gazzetta d'Italia, 1875).

23 Gaetano Milanesi, *Le lettere di Michelangelo Buonarroti: pubblicate coi ricordi ed i contratti artistici* (Florence: Coi tipi dei successori le Monnier, 1875).

24 Washington Irving, *History of the Life and Voyages of Christopher Columbus*, 3 vols. (New York: G. & C. Carvill, 1828) 1:42. [The original 1891 edition gives the source as page 819 of volume 1, without specifying the edition; the first volume in the American first edition, which comprises three volumes,

ileo discovered the sun's spots contemporaneously with, or before, Scheiner in April, 1611;[25] in December, 1610, and even in September (since he speaks of his observation having been made three months previously), he discovered the analogy between the phases of Venus and those of the moon; in May, 1609, he invented the telescope;[26] in July, 1610, he discovered two stars, afterwards found to be the most luminous points of Saturn's ring, a discovery which, according to his custom, he expressed in verse:—

Altissimum planetam tergeminuni observavi

In January he found Jupiter's satellites; in November, 1602, the isochronism of the oscillations of the pendulum.[27]

Kepler discovered the law which bears his name in May, 1618; the discovery of Zucchi regarding Jupiter took place in May; that of Tycho Brahe in

---

was less than 450 pages long. I have therefore located the passage Lombroso must have been referring to, which is at the beginning of Chapter VI in the 1828 American edition. —Ed.]; Roselly de Lorgues, *Christophe Colomb; histoire de sa vie et de ses voyages, d'aprè des documents authentiques tirés d'Espagne et d'Italie* (Paris, Didier et cie., 1856).

25 According to [Angelo] Secchi [*Le Soleil* (Paris: Gauthier-Villars, 1875-1877)], Scheiner preceded Galileo, and was himself preceded by Fabricio, though the discovery of this last was not known until a later date.

26 Galilei, *Opere* 1:69. [No edition specified. —Ed.]

27 François Arago, *Œuvres complètes de François Arago*, Ed. Jean-Augustin Barrall, 15 vols. (Paris: Gide, 1851-1862).

November. Fabricius discovered the first changing star in August, 1546. Cassini discovered the spots which indicate the rotation of Venus in October and April (1666-67), and in October, December, and March (1671, 1672, 1684) four satellites of Saturn. Herschel discovered two in March, 1789. In June, 1631, Hevelius conceived the first ideas of selenography.[28] A satellite of Saturn was discovered by Huygens on the 25th of March, 1665; another by Dawes and Bond on the night of the 19th of September, 1848. Two satellites of Uranus were discovered by Herschel in 1787; one of them, considered as doubtful by Herschel, was again discovered by Struve and Lassel in October, 1847; the last, Ariel, was discovered by Lassel on the I4th of September, 1847; on the 8th of July in the same year he had also seen Neptune's satellite for the first time.[29] Uranus was discovered by Herschel in March, 1781. The same astronomer observed the moon's volcanoes in April. Bradley discovered in September (1728) the aberration of light, Enke's and Vico's fine observations on Saturn took place in March and April (1735-38). Of the comets discovered by Gambart, three were in July, two in March and in May, one in January, April, June,

28 Hœfer, *op. cit.* [No work by this author is referred to earlier in the text, but a few footnotes down the following source is given: Jean Chrétien Ferdinand Hœfer, *Histoire de la chimie*, 2 vols. (Paris: Didot, 1869). —Ed.]

29 John F. W. Herschel, *Outlines of Astronomy* (Shanghai: 1874).

August, October, December.[30] The last three comets discovered in 1877 were perceived in October, February, and September; in August Hall observed the satellites of Mars. Schiaparelli's discovery on falling stars dates from August, 1866.

We read in Malpighi's journal that in July he made his great discoveries in the suprarenal glands. It is curious to observe how some one month predominates in certain years: for example, January in 1788 and 1790, and June in 1771, during which he made thirteen discoveries.[31]

The first idea of the barometer came to Torricelli in May, 1645, as may be seen by his letters to Ricci; in March, 1644, he had made the discovery, of great moment at that time, of the best way of making glasses for spectacles. The first experiments of Pascal on the equilibrium of fluids were made in September, 1645.[32] In March, 1752, Franklin began his experiments with lightning conductors, and concluded them in September.

Goethe declared that it was in May that his original ideas on the theory of colours arose, and in June that he made his fine observations on the

---

30 François Arago, *Notices biographiques* (Paris: Gide, 1855).

31 Gaetano Atti, *Notizie edite ed inedite della vita e delle opere di Marcello Malpighi e di Lorenzo Bellini* (Bologna: tip. governativa alla Volpe, 1847). [In the 1891 edition of *Man of Genius*, 1774 is given as the publication date for this source, but Gaetano Atti, its author, lived between 1809 and 1879, so clearly this was an error. —Ed.]

32 Jean Chrétien Ferdinand Hœfer, *Histoire de la chimie*, 2 vols. (Paris: Didot, 1869).

metamorphoses of plants. Hamilton discovered the calculus of Quaternions on the 16th of October, 1843.

Volta invented the electric pile in the beginning of winter, 1799-1800. In the spring of 1775 he invented the electrophore. In the first days of November, 1784, he discovered the production of hydrogen in organic fermentations. His invention of the eudiometer took place in the spring, about May. In April of the same year (1777) Volta wrote to Barletta the famous letter in which he divined the electric telegraph. In the spring of 1788 he constructed his great conductor.

Luigi Brugnatelli found out galvanoplasty in November, 1806, as is shown by a letter which the advocate Zanino Volta found in the correspondence of his grandfather. Nicholson discovered the oxydation of metals by means of the Voltaic pile, in the summer of 1800.

From the examination of Galvani's manuscripts it appears that his studies on intestinal gases began in December, 1713. His first studies on the action of atmospheric electricity on the nerves of cold-blooded animals were undertaken, as he himself writes, "at the 20th hour of the 26th of April, 1776." In September, 1786, he began his experiments on the contractions of frogs, whence the origin of galvanism. In November, 1780, he stated his experiments on the contractions of frogs by artificial electricity.[33]

33 Silvestro Gherardi, *Rapporto sui manoscritti del celebre nos-*

We see by Lagrange's manuscripts, published by Boncompagni, that he had the first idea of the Calculus of Variations on the 12th of June, 1755; on the 19th of May (1756) he conceived the idea of the *Mécanique analitique*; in November, 1759, he found a solution of the problem of vibrating cords.[34]

From the manuscripts of Spallanzani, which I have been able to examine in the Communal Library at Reggio, it appears that his observations on moulds began on the 26th of September, 1770. On the 8th of May, 1780, Spallanzani started, to use his own words, "the study of animals which are torpid through the action of cold;" in April and May, 1776, he discovered the parthenogenesis of certain animals. The 2nd of April, 1780, was the richest day in experiments, or rather deductions, on the subject of ovulation. "It becomes clear," he wrote on this same day, after having made forty-three observations,

> that the ova are not fecundated in the womb; that the sperm cells after emission remain apt for fecundation for a certain time, that the vesicular fluid fecundates as well as the seminal, that wine and vinegar are opposed to fecundation.

---

tro Fisico, il Galvani (1839).

34 Boncompagni Baldassarre and Giovanni V. Schiaparelli, *Intorno alcune lettere inedite di Lagrange ad Eulero / recentemente pubblicate da S. E. il principe Baldassarre Boncompagni ; cenni del M. E. prof. G. V. Schiapparelli, letti nell'adunanza del 15 marzo 1877* (Milan: Tip. Bernar-doni, 1877).

"Impatience," adds this curious manuscript, which enables us to assist at the incubation of these wonderful experiments, "will not allow me to draw any more corollaries." On the 7th of May, 1780, he discovered that an infinitely small amount of semen sufficed for fecundation. A letter to Bonnet shows that Spallanzani had, during the spring of 1771, the idea of studying the action of the heart on the circulation. In March, 1773, he undertook his studies on rotifera, and in his manuscripts for May, 1781, may be found a plan of 161 new experiments on the artificial fecundation of frogs.

Géoffroy Saint-Hilaire had his first ideas on the homologies of organisms in February. Davy discovered iodine in December. Humboldt made his first observations on the magnetic needle in November, 1796; in March, 1793, he observed the irritability of organic fibres.[35] The prolegomena of the *Cosmos* was dictated in October.[36] In July, 1801, Gay-Lussac discovered fluoric acid in fishbones; he completed the analysis of alum in July.[37] In September, 1846, Morton used sulphuric ether as an anæsthetic in surgery. In October, 1840, Armstrong invented the first hydro-electric machine.[38]

---

35 Alexander von Humboldt, *Correspondence* (Paris: 1868).

36 Alexander von Humboldt, *Letters of Alexander von Humboldt to Varnhagen von Ense, tr. Friedrich Kapp* (New York: Rudd & Carleton; [etc., etc.], 1860).

37 François Arago, *Notices Biographiques* (Paris: Gide, 1855).

38 William Whewell, *History of the Inductive Sciences* (London: John W. Parker, 1857)

Matteucci made his experiments with the galvanoscope in July, 1830; on torpedoes in the spring of 1836; on electro-motor muscles in July, 1837; on the decomposition of acids in May, 1835; he determined in May, 1837, the influence of electricity on the weather; in June, 1833, he concluded his experiments on heat and magnetism.[39]

The reader who has had the patience to follow this wearisome catalogue to the end, may convince himself that many men of genius have, as it were, a specific chronology; that is to say, a tendency to make their most numerous observations, to accomplish their finest discoveries, or their best æsthetic productions, at a special season or in one month rather than another: Spallanzani in the spring, Giusti and Arcangeli in March, Lanvartine in August, Carcano, Byron, and Alfieri in September, Malpighi and Schiller in June and July, Hugo in May, Béranger in January, Belli in November, Melli in April, Volta in November and December, Galvani in April, Gambart in July, Peters in August, Luther in March and April, Watson in September.

A more general kind of specific chronology, a sort of intellectual calendar, is presented when we sum up various intellectual creations—poetry, music, sculpture, natural discoveries—of which the date of conception can be precisely fixed. This may be seen from the following table:—

39 Nicomede Bianchi, *Carlo Matteucci e l'Italia del suo Tempo* (Rome, Turin, Florence: F.lli Bocca librai, 1874).

Month	Literary and Artistic Works	Astronomical Discoveries[40]	Physical, Chemical, and Mathematical Discoveries	Total
January	101	37	-	138
February	82	21	1	104
March	104	45	5	154
April	135	52	5	192
May	149	35	6	193
June	125	24	5	154
July	105	52	5	162
August	113	42	-	155
September	138	47	5	190
October	83	45	4	132
November	103	42	5	150
December	86	27	2	115

40 The catalogue of small planets has been drawn from the *Annuaire du Bureau des Longitudes* (Paris, 1877-8). The list of comets has been taken from Carl's *Repertorium der Cometen Astronomie* (Munich, 1864). It begins with the comet discovered by Hevelius in 1672, and ends with that found by Donati on the 23rd of July, 1864; Gambart's comets, already separately enumerated, have been excluded. To keep the conditions analogous to those of the small planets, all the comets to which Carl does not assign a discoverer, have been omitted; this includes such as were expected from previous calculations or perceived with the naked eye by the general population. All those that were discovered simultaneously by several observers, unknown to one another, have, however, been included, for it is not a question of priority, but of the psychological moment of the discovery. Three comets discovered in the months of February, May, and December, were found in the southern hemisphere; they must, therefore, with reference to season be registered as for August, November, and June, and have so been counted.

One observes at once that the most favourable month for æsthetic creations is May; then come September and April; the minimum is presented by the months of February, October, and December. The same may be observed partially with astronomical discoveries; but here April and July predominate, while for physical discoveries as well as for æsthetic creations, the months of May, April, and September stand first. Thus the advantage belongs to the months of early heat more than to the months of great heat, as with insanity also; in the same way the months of greatest barometric variation have an advantage over very hot and very cold months.

If we now group these data according to seasons, which will allow us to include other data in which the exact month cannot be stated, we shall find that the maximum of artistic and literary creation falls in spring, 388; then comes summer, with 347; then autumn, 335; and lastly, winter, with 280.

The majority of great physical, chemical, and mathematical discoveries took place in spring, 22; then autumn, 15; very few in summer, 10; and only five in winter. I have separated astronomical discoveries from physical, and other discoveries, because their precise dates are less doubtful and therefore more important. We find 135 in autumn; 131 in spring; 120 in summer; and only 83 in winter. Taking these 1,871 great discoveries altogether, we find spring coming first, with 541; then autumn, with 485; with 477 in summer; and 368 in winter.

It is evident, then, that the first warm months distinctly predominate in the creations of genius, as well as in organic nature generally, although the question cannot be absolutely resolved on account of the scarcity of data, as regards both quantity and quality. It was, however, in the spring that the discovery of America was conceived, as well as galvanism, the barometer, the telescope, and the lightning conductor; in the spring, Michelangelo had the idea of his great cartoon, Dante of his *Divina Commedia*, Leonardo of his book on light, Goethe of his *Faust*; it was in the spring that Kepler discovered his law, that Milton conceived his great poem, Darwin his great theory, and Wagner the *Fliegende Holländer*, the first of his great music dramas.

It may be added that in the few cases in which we may follow, day by day, the traces of the works of great men, we usually find that their activity increases in the warm months and decreases in the cold months. Thus in Spallanzani's journals, and especially during the years 1777-78 and 1780-81, in which he was undertaking his investigations into moulds, digestion, and fecundation, I found 50 days of observation in March, 65 in April, 143 in May, 41 in June, 33 in August, 24 in September; while there were only 17 in December, 10 in November, 18 in January, 17 in July, and 2 in February.

If we examine the curious journal of his own observations, which Malpighi kept day by day for thirty-four years, we find, grouping the observations according to months, July coming first with 71 days, followed by June with 66, May 42, October 40, January 36, September 34, April 33, March 31, August 28, November 20, December 13.[41] Out of over four hundred observations less than a fifth took place in the winter months.

It appears from Galvani's manuscripts, as examined by Gherardi, that between the years 1772 and 1781 his investigations on irritability, muscular movement, the structure of the ear, the tympanic bone, and the organ of hearing, all belong to the month of April, while his work on cataract belongs to March, and that on the hygiene of sight to January. There seems, therefore, to be here a remarkable predominance for April, though there is less certainty than in the preceding cases.

I imagine the objections that may be made against these conclusions; the scarcity of data, their doubtfulness, the boldness of bringing within the narrow circle of statistics those sublime phenomena of intellectual creation which seem the least susceptible of calculation. Such objections may have weight with those who believe that statistics can only deal with large numbers—perhaps more remarkable for quantity than for quality—

41 Gaetano Atti, *Notizie edite ed inedite della vita e delle opere di Marcello Malpighi e di Lorenzo Bellini* (Bologna: tip. governativa alla Volpe, 1847).

and who thrust aside *a priori* all reasoning on the data, as though figures were not facts, subject like all other facts to synthesis, and had not their true value as materials for the thinker. The facts I have brought forward, though not large, are at all events to be preferred to mere hypotheses, or to the isolated statements of authors, the more so as they are in harmony with these latter, and may at least serve as an encouragement to a new series of fruitful psychometeoric researches.

It may be said also that the creations of genius cannot furnish great columns of figures.

It is very true, however, that in regard to many of them the chronological coincidence is connected with accidental circumstances entirely, independent of the psychic condition. Thus naturalists have greater facilities for observation and experiment in warm months; thus, also, the length and equability of equinoctial nights, the difficulty of making examinations on foggy days, the weariness and discomfort experienced on days that are very hot or very cold, largely account for the predominance of discoveries in spring and autumn.

Yet these are not the only determining circumstances. In the case of anatomists, for example, bodies may be had at all seasons, and principally in winter; and, again, the long and clear winter nights, in which the influence of refraction is less, ought to be as favourable to the astronomers of temperate climates as the warm summer nights of northern climates which give us, however, a greater number of astronomical discoveries.

It is well known, also, that accidental circumstances influence even the phenomena of death, birth, murder, when closely considered statistically. If, however, all these phenomena conduce to the same result, we are led to infer a similar cause common to all, and this can only be found in meteorological influences.

I have grouped together æsthetic creations and scientific discoveries because they are associated by that moment of psychic excitation and extreme sensibility which brings together the most remote facts, the fecundating moment which has rightly been called generative, a moment at which poets and men of science are nearer than is generally supposed. Was there not an audacious imagination in Spallanzani's experiments, in Herschel's first attempts, in the great discoveries of Leverrier and Schiaparelli, born of hypothesis, which calculation and observation transformed into axioms? Littrow, speaking of the discovery of Vesta, observes that it was not the result of chance nor of genius alone, but of genius favoured by chance. The star discovered by Piazzi had glimmered in Zach's eyes, but he, with less genius than Piazzi, or in a moment of less perspicacity, attached no importance to it. The discovery of the solar spots only needed time, patience, and good fortune, remarked Secchi; but it needed genius to discover their true theory. How many learned natural philosophers, observes Arago, in going down a river must have observed the fluttering of the vane at the mast-head, without discovering, like Bradley, the law of aberration. And how many artists, one might add, must have seen hideous heads of porters, without conceiving Leonardo's *Judas*, or oranges without creating the cavatina of Mozart's *Don Giovanni*.

There is, however, one last objection which seems more serious. Nearly all great intellectual creations, and all discoveries of modern physics, are the results of the slow and continuous meditations of men of science and their predecessors; so that they form a kind of compilation, the chronology of which is not easy to define, because the date at which we are arrested indicates the moment of birth rather than of conception. This objection, however, may be applied to nearly all human phenomena, even the most sudden. Thus, fecundation is a phenomenon which depends on the good nutrition of the organism, and on heredity; insanity, death itself, though apparently produced by sudden, even casual, circumstances, are yet related on one side to the weather and on the other to organic conditions; so that often, one may say, the precise date is fixed at birth.

CHAPTER II

Climatic Influences on Genius

Influence of great centres — Race and hot climate — The distribution of great masters — Orographic influences — Influence of healthy race — Parallelism of high stature and genius — Explanations.

Buckle thought that most artists, unlike men of science, were produced in volcanic countries.[1] Jacoby, in an excellent monograph,[2] finds the greatest number of superior intelligences where the urban population is densest. It seems impossible to deny that race (the Latin and Greek races, for example, abound in great men), political and scientific struggles, wealth, literary centres have a great influence on the appearance of men

1 Henry Thomas Buckle, *Introduction to the History of Civilization in England*, 2 vols. (London: J. W. Parker & Son: 1857, 1861).

2 Paul Jacoby, *Étude sur la sélection dans ses rapports avec l'hérédité chez l'homme* (Paris: Germer-Baillière, 1881).

of genius. Who would maintain that the political struggles and great liberty of Athens, Siena, and Florence have not contributed to produce in ancient times a more powerful display of genius than at other epochs and in other countries?

But when we recall the preponderating influence of meteorological phenomena on works of genius it becomes clear that a still more important place must be reserved for atmospheric and climatic conditions.

The Influence of Great Centres, of Race, and of Hot Climates.—It is worth while to study the distribution of great artists in Europe, and especially in Italy.

For musicians I have used the works of Fétis[3] and Clement[4] for painters and sculptors I have referred to Ticozzi's two dictionaries.[5] Here are the results:

---

3 François-Joseph Fétis, *Biographie universelle des musiciens et bibliographie générale de la musique* (Paris: Firmin Didot frères, fils et cie, 1869-76).

4 Félix Clément, *Les musiciens célèbres depuis le seizième siècle jusqu'à nos jours* (Paris: Hachette et Cie., 1878).

5 Stefano Ticozzi, *Dizionario dei Pittori, dal rinnovamento delle Belle Arti fino al 1800*, 2 vols. (Milan: Tipografia Vincenzo Ferrario, 1858). [I was unable to find any records of this edition, but there is one from 1818. —Ed.]

MUSICIANS IN EUROPE

Country	*No.*	*Per 1m inhabitants*
Italy	1210	40.7
Belgium	98	16.7
Germany	650	13.8
France	405	10.7
Holland	31	7.7
Greece	15	7.5
Switzerland	20	7.0
Denmark	14	6.6
Austria	239	6.5
England	149	4.6
Portugal	17	3.6
Spain	62	3.5
Ireland	7	1.4
Russia	34	0.4
Sweden	9	0.2

The countries which have furnished the greatest number of musicians after Italy are Belgium, Germany, and France, the countries which have the greatest density of population; the poorest in musicians are Ireland, Russia, and Sweden, with a very slight density, especially the two last. The influence of volcanic soil and of Latin race does not clearly appear, when one notes the feeble proportions given by Spain and Greece compared to Germany.

If, however, we study the distribution of musicians in the various regions of Italy, we see immediately that the hot and non-insular districts stand first; then Emilia and Venetia; Piedmont, the Marches and Umbria stand low, and Sardinia is completely absent. We do not, however, obtain a sufficiently clear view of the orographic influences until we take the provinces separately.[6]

We then see in a remarkable manner how the most populous centres come to the front, including nearly all the provinces containing large towns, except Piedmont, Sardinia, and Sicily. It is sufficient to mention Naples, Rome, Venice, Milan, Bologna, Florence, Lucca, Parma, and Genoa. Here, evi-

---

6

Naples	216	Padua	15	Forli	3
Rome	127	Pisa	13	Messina	3
Venice	124	Reggio	12	Rovigo	3
Milan	95	Piacenza	11	Chieti	3
Bologna	91	Siena	10	Foggia	3
Florence	70	Ravenna	10	Cuneo	2
Lucca	37	Vicenza	10	Pavia	2
Parma	34	Perugia	9	Massa	2
Genoa	30	Pesaro	9	Teramo	2
Turin	27	Alessandria	8	Siracusa	2
Verona	24	Treviso	8	Ascoli	2
Brescia	22	Catania	7	Campobasso	2
Mantua	19	Arezzo	6	Belluno	1
Modena	19	Lecce	6	Catanzaro	1
Cremona	17	Como	5	Avellino	1
Palermo	17	Ancona	5	Potenza	1
Novara	17	Udine	5	Caltanisetta	1
Bergano	16	Macerata	5	Reggio-Calabria	1
Bari	16	Caserta	4		
Ferrara	15	Livorno	3		

dently, we see the influence of healthy, warm, maritime, and, above all, elevated regions; often this influence even struggles against that of civilization and of great centres. Large cities prevail in the proportion of 7 out of 9. In the second line we see other important towns emerge, or great maritime centres, especially if volcanic: Palermo, Bari, Catania, and especially mountainous countries, Bergamo, Brescia, Verona, Vicenza, Perugia, Siena. The racial influence is not clear here; the Berber and Semitic races do not, however, seem to favour art, especially in hot regions, and we may thus explain the paucity of musicians among the Sardinians, Calabrians, and Sicilians. The Greco-Roman and Etruscan races seem better endowed on the other hand, whence the predominance of Naples, Rome, Lucca, and Bologna. The action of earthquakes, which, according to Buckle, has a large part in artistic creation, is not very apparent. If Naples and Aversa are placed in the first rank (which could be explained by race and climate), it is not so with Calabria, where earthquakes are so numerous.

The Distribution of Great Masters.—It must be remarked that quantity does not always correspond to quality; it is sufficient to see that the regions that produced a Bellini and a Rossini appear to be the most sterile centres. Yet the appearance of a single great genius is more than equivalent to the birth of a hundred mediocrities.

If we take account of the proportion of great composers, we see that the most favoured regions are hot and maritime, especially Naples, closely followed by Rome, Parma, Milan, and Cremona. Here the influences of density and of the school come in the third line, after that of climate.

Thus, in searching Clément's book, and Florimo's,[7] we find that out of 118 great composers, 44, or more than a third, belong to Italy; and that among these last, 27, or more than half, are supplied by Sicily (Scarlatti, Pacini, Bellini), and by Naples and neighbouring places, especially Aversa (Jomelli, Stradella, Piccinni, Leo, Feo, Vinci, Fenaroli, the inventor of *opéra-bouffe*, Speranza, Contumaci, Sala, Caffaro, Duni, Sacchini, Carafa, Paisiello, Cimarosa, Zingarelli, Mercadante, Durante, the two Ricci and Petrella), no doubt owing to the influence of Greek race and warm climate. Of the other 17, a few belong to Upper Italy: Donizetti, Verdi, Allegri, Frescobaldi, the two Monteverdi, Salieri, Marcello, Paganini (these last three to the sea-coast); and all the others to Central Italy; Palestrina and Clementi to Rome, and Spontini, Lulli, and Pergolèse, to Perugia and Florence.[8]

If we compare the regions which have produced the greatest composers and relatively few minor masters, we find that Pesaro, Catania, Arezzo, and

7 Francesco Florimo, *La scuola musicale di Napoli e i suoi conservatorii, con uno sguardo sulla storia della musica in Italia* (Naples: Stabilimento tip. V. Morano, 1880-82 [1883]).

8 See my *Pensiero e Meteore* (Milan: Dumolard, 1872), and *Archivio di psichiatria, antropologia criminale e scienze penali per servire allo studio dell'uomo alienato e delinquente* 1 (1880) 157.

Alessandria come first. The coincidence of musical geniuses and mediocrities, both in large numbers, is found at Naples, Rome, Parma, Florence, Milan, Cremona, and Venice, with an evident influence here also of warm maritime climate, of the Greco-Etruscan race and of great centres (5 out of 7).

In painting we find that the large towns predominate both for number and celebrity, with the exception of Sardinia and Sicily. Bologna, Florence, Venice, and Milan come first as regards number; Florence, and in the second line Verona, Naples, Rome, and Venice, both for number and celebrity; and we still find that, after large towns, mountainous countries give the highest figures as regards number. It is sufficient to name Perugia, Arezzo, Siena, Udine, Verona, Vicenza, Parma, Brescia.[9]

9

Bologna	262	Padua	40	Ancona	16
Florence	252	Parma	39	Alessandria	15
Venice	138	Vicenza	39	Belluno	13
Milan	127	Lucca	38	Macerata	13
Rome	100	Bergamo	37	Piacenza	6
Genoa	100	Udine	36	Caserta	6
Naples	95	Arezzo	33	Rovigo	5
Ferrara	85	Ravenna	30	Palermo	4
Verona	83	Reggio	29	Salermo	3
Siena	73	Pisa	29	Lecce	3
Perugia	68	Treviso	24	Cueno	3
Cremona	65	Ascoli	23	Massa	3
Modena	61	Novara	22	Catania	2
Pesaro	61	Pavia	20	Livorno	1
Brescia	50	Mantua	19	Aquila	1

Almost the same relations are observed in regard to sculptors and architects. We see the great centres of civilization and hilly regions in the first rank; Florence especially, then Milan, Venice, Naples, Como, Siena, Verona, Massa, and in the third line Arezzo, Perugia, Vicenza, Bergamo, Macerata, Catania, and Palermo.[10]

To summarize: We see that the chief part is played by warm climate, great centres of civilization, mountainous and maritime regions; some influence must also be attributed to the influence of the Greek and Etruscan races. There is no constant relation between the regions which have produced great geniuses and those which have yielded second-rate geniuses, with the exception of Naples and Florence. For the last city we must bear in mind the influence of its commune, which excited and nourished individual energies, and to this chief cause we must add artistic disposition, race, and beauty of climate, as with Athens. Certainly, Florence enjoyed unquestioned supremacy in painting and sculpture; it is enough to recall the names of Donatello, Michelangelo, Verrochio, Baldinelli, Coccini, Cellini, Giotto, Masaccio, Andrea del Sarto, Salviati, Allori, Bronzino, Pollaiolo, Fra Angelico.

Turin	46	Forli	19	Siracusa	1
Messina	43	Como	17		

10 The difference with weakness of Udine and reference to painters is caused the superiority of Catania and by the numerical Palermo.

Orographic influence.—After the influence of heat and of great centres, comes that of the slighter pressure of the air in hilly but not too mountainous regions.

This climatic influence alone can explain why we find so many poets, and especially *improvvisatori*, even women, among the shepherds and peasants of the Tuscan hills, especially about Pistoja, Buti, Valdontani. It is enough to recall the shepherdess mentioned by Giuliani in his book *Sulla Lingua parlata in Toscana*, and that singular Frediani family with a father, grandfathers, and sons, who were poets; one of them is still alive and composes verses worthy of the poets of ancient Tuscany. Yet peasants of the same race, inhabiting the plain, so far as I know, offer nothing similar.

All flat countries—Belgium, Holland, Egypt—are deficient in men of genius; so also with those, like Switzerland and Savoy, which, being enclosed between very high mountains, are endemically afflicted with cretinism and *goître*; marshy countries are still poorer in genius. The few men of genius possessed by Switzerland were born when the race had conquered the goitrous influence through admixture of French and Italian immigrants—Bonnet, Rousseau, Tronchin, Tissot, De Candolle, Burlamaqui, Pestalozzi, Sismondi. Urbino Pesaro, Forli, Como, Parma, have produced men of genius in greater number and of greater fame than Pisa, Padua, and Pavia, three of the most ancient and important university towns of Italy; it is enough to name Raphael, Bramante, Rossini, Morgagni, Spallanzani, Muratori, Falloppio, Volta.

But, to come to more definite examples, we find that Florence, enjoying a mild temperature and in special degree a city of the hills, has furnished Italy with her most splendid cohort of great men: Dante, Giotto, Machiavelli, Lulli, Leonardo, Brunellesco, Guicciardini, Cellini, Fra Angelico, Andrea del Sarto, Nicolini, Capponi, Vespucci, Viviani, Lippi, Boccaccio, Alberti, Dati, Alamanni, Rucellai, Ghirlandajo, Donati; Pisa, on the other hand, with scientific conditions at least as favourable as Florence, being the seat of a flourishing university, only offers us—if we except a few soldiers and statesmen of no great number and worth who were unable, even with powerful allies, to prevent her fall—Pisa only offers us Nicola Pisano, Giunta, and Galileo who, although born there, was of Florentine parentage. Now Pisa only differs from Florence by being situated on a plain.

In Lombardy, the regions of mountain and lake, like Bergamo, Brescia, and Como, have produced mere great men than the flat regions. I will mention Bernardo Tasso, Mascheroni, Donizetti, Tartaglia, Ugoni, Volta, Parini, Appiani, Mai, Cagnola; while Lower Lombardy can only bring forward Alciato, Beccaria, Oriani, Cavalleri, Aselli, and Boccaccini. Verona, a town of the hills, has produced Maffei, Paolo Veronese, Catullus, Pliny, Fracastoro, Bianchini, Sammicheli, Cagnola, Tiraboschi, Brusasorsi, Lorgna, Pindemonte; and not to speak of artists, economists, and thinkers of the first order (it is enough to name Trezza), I note that, in a very accurate document,[11] it appears that in 1881, there were 160 poets at Verona, many rising considerably above mediocrity. On the other hand, the wealthy and learned Padua has only given to Italy Livy , Cesarotti, Pietro d'Abano, and a few others.

Genoa and Naples, which unite the advantages of a climate at once warm, maritime, and hilly, have produced men of genius at least as remarkable as those yielded by Florence, if not in such great number; such are Columbus, Doria, Mazzini, Paganini, Vico, Caracciolo, Pergolese, Genovesi, Cirillo, Filangeri.

In Spain, the influence of a warm climate is evident. The whole of Catalonia, including Barcelona, though inhabited by a serious race, has not produced artists, having yielded only a single poet, an imitator of Petrarch. Seville, on the contrary, has produced Cervantes, Velasquez and Murillo; Cordova has yielded many men of genius, such as Seneca, Lucan, Morales, Mina, Góngora and Céspedes, at once painter, sculptor, and poet.

In the United States, Beard remarks,[12] the influence of a dry and changeable climate favours in the North a remarkable spirit of progress, the love of knowledge, the agitation of public life and a great desire for novelty; while in the South, the moist

11 *Il Censimento dei Poeti Veronesi* (Dec. 31, 1881).

12 George Miller Beard, *American Nervousness, Its Causes and Consequences* (New York: Putnam, 1881).

and but slightly varying climate develops eminently conservative tendencies, so that manufacturers in Georgia have great difficulty in finding a market there for new stuffs or machines; these are refused, not because they are not good or useful, but because they are new.

In Germany it has been observed that regions enjoying a mild and healthy climate, by reason of protecting mountains, have produced the greatest poets and in greatest number. The regions of the Main and the Neckar are renowned for their mild climate, luxuriant vegetation, and fertility, and the greatest German poets come from these regions. The Main gave us the greatest of German poets, Goethe, and many other *dii minorum gentium*, genial and noteworthy poets, although beneath that giant, men such as Klinger, Börne, Rückert, Bettina von Arnim (*née* Brentano), &c. In the favoured region of the Neckar were born Schiller and Victor von Scheffel, and throughout the Swabian land, we meet with many other great poets and thinkers, such as Wieland, Uhland, Justinus Kerner, Hauff, Schubart, Morike, G. Schwab, Schelling, Müller, Hölderlin, and others. That hilly regions are richer than others in poets is shown in Germany by Hanover (Klopstock, Stolberg, Iffland, Burger, Leisewitz, Bodenstedt, Hoffmann von Fallersleben, the two Schlegels, &c.); by the Rhine province (Heine, Jacobi, J. Müller, Brentano); Saxony, one of the districts possessing a mild climate, which has yielded the largest number of poets (Körner, Gellert, Kästner, Rabener, and, above all, Lessing); and Thuringia (Kotzebue, Rückert, G. Freytag, Heinse, Musaus, Gotter). On the other hand, the flat regions of Germany or those with a severe climate, have produced few poets.[13] As exceptions must be mentioned, Herder (Mohrungen in East Prussia), M. von Schenkendorf (Tilsit), E. M. Arndt (Rugen), Luther (Eisleben), Paul Gerhardt (Grafenhainichen), the two Humboldts, Paul Heyse, Tieck, Gutzkow (Berlin), Immermann (Magdeburg), Wilhelm Müller, Max Müller, Moses Mendelssohn (Dessau). Westphalia, again, is mountainous, but poor in poets.

The Influence of Healthy Race and High Stature.—The regions which have furnished few artists, or none, are those which suffer from malaria or *goître*: Calabria, Sassari, Grosseto, Aosta, Sondrio, Avellino, Caltanisetta, Chieti, Syracuse, Lecce. If we compare the distribution of great artists in Italy with the distribution of high stature, we find a singular coincidence of maximum and minimum points. The stature is very low in the regions I have just mentioned, and very tall at Florence, Lucca, Rome, Venice, Naples, Siena, and Arezzo, not because there is any direct correspondence of intelligence to stature, but because, as I have elsewhere shown,[14] although stature re-

13 See George M. Sternberg, *Archivio di psichiatria, antropologia criminale e scienze penali per servire allo studio dell'uomo alienato e delinquente* 10 (1889) 389.

14 *Statura degli Italiani* (1874); *Della Influenza crografica nella*

veals ethnic influences, it is also the surest index of public health, while mortality statistics have no exact relation to health, because they do not sufficiently show the results of morbid influences, such as *goître* and cretinism, which, although they arrest the physical and mental growth, do not increase the mortality.

If we examine the results furnished by the conscription in Italy, we find that those regions which, from the excellence of their climate, and apart from ethnic influences, yield the greatest number of individuals of high stature, and the smallest number of rejected individuals, are the most fruitful in men of genius; such are Tuscany, Liguria, and Romagna. On the other hand, the regions which are poorest in men of high stature and men fit for military service—Sardinia, Basilicata, and the valley of Aosta—yield a smaller number of men of genius. It is necessary to except Calabria and Valtellina where many are found, notwithstanding shortness of stature, but they appear in parts of the country which, from their exposed or elevated position, escape miasmatic influences and are proofs of the rule rather than exceptions to it.

This influence can be very well shown in France if we compare the list of men of genius produced in the eighteenth century (as brought together by Jacoby) with the statistics of stature given by Bro-

---

Statura (1878).

ca and Topinard,[15] and with the mortality of each province as furnished by Bertillon.[16]

We observe at once an evident parallelism between genius and height, with only n exceptions out of 85, and some of these 11 may be explained by the agglomerated population of great capitals (Seine, Rhône, Bouches-du-Rhône) which favour the development, or rather the manifestation, of genius, as we have already seen to be the case in Italy; thus the exceptions in Var, Herault, Bouches-du-Rhône may be explained by relatively great density of population, and by the southern climate, which favours genius in spite of miasmatic influences. At the same time, if we may agree with Jacoby concerning the favourable influence of great urban agglomerations, such as Paris, Lyons, Marseilles, it must be added that it does not appear so clearly in other centres; thus Nord, Haut-Rhin, Pas-de-Calais, Loire, although possessing a dense population, do not yield a corresponding number of men of genius, standing only in the third rank, the Loire, indeed, only in the fourth.[17]

15 Paul Topinard, *Étude sur la Taille* (Paris Ernest Leroux, 1876).

16 Louis-Adolphe Bertillon, *Demographie figuree de la France* (Paris: G. Masson, 1874). [The original footnote gives 1878 as the date of publication; it could be a reprint or another edition, but I was unable to find records. —Ed.]

17 Inhabitants to the square kilometre:—

Seine	3636.56	Manche	100.20
Rhône	224.40	Bouches-du-Rhône	92.27

If we compare the geographical distribution of men of genius with that of mortality, we note more numerous failures of correspondence (27) with the height; this is because the statistics of mortality do not indicate the influence of cretinism which exists in Ariege, the Basses and Hautes-Alpes, Puy-de-Dôme, the Pyrenees, and the Ardennes, clearly showing itself in short stature and military exemption for *goître*, and, as in Valtellina in Italy, accompanied by a scarcity of intellect. At the same time, all the regions showing high mortality, especially such as are malarious—the Landes, Sologne, Morbihan, Corrèze—offer a feebler proportion of men of genius, with the exception of the great centres; the contrary is found in more healthy districts.

Orographic conditions appear to have great influence. The sunny and fertile land of Languedoc, all mountainous regions not too much affected by *goître*—Doubs, Cote-d'Or, Ardennes—or those in which it has not succeeded in depressing the stature, that is to say, has been unable to produce endemic cretinism (Jura) give us, when we have put aside all influence of density, race, and temperature, a most notable proportion of men of genius. This may be clearly seen in the table on the following page in which the high figures of *goître*, stammering, and deaf-mutism, correspond with low

---

Nord	213.40	Landes	33.80
Naut-Rhin	123.00	Lozère	27.39
Pas-de-Calais	108.60	Hautes-Alpes	23.40
Loire	106.38	Basses-Alpes	21.90

stature in Corrèze, Puy-de-Dôme, Ardèche, Ariège, the Basses-Alpes, and the Pyrenées.

We have seen in Var, Vaucluse, and Herault that a southern climate, perhaps on account of its greater fertility, produces a great number of men of genius; but countries that are cold, but at the same time healthy and mountainous—Jura, Doubs, Meurthe—give still higher figures, and the same isothermal line passes through the Seine-Inferieure and the Seine-et-Oise, both rich in men of genius; and the Vosges, in which they are almost entirely absent, the same line, again, passes through Calvados and Ain, which are very rich in genius, and Saone-et-Loire and Cher, which are deficient in genius.

MOUNTAINOUS DEPARTMENTS	Stature 1831 - 1860 Progressive degree of exemptions	Progressive degree of great talent among 1,000 inhabitants	Goitrous among 1,000 inhabitants	Cretins among 1,000 inhabitants	Deaf-mutes among 1,000 inhabitants	Stammerers among 1,000 inhabitants
Haute-Vienne	86	54	17	2.0	0.61	2.23
Hautes-Alpes	81	49	111	2.2	2.2	2.8
Corrèze	85	50	17	4.3	1.5	2.4
Puy-de-Dôme	84	41	44	3.6	1.2	1.9
Ardèche	80	58	29	6.8	1.3	3.9
Arlège	60	79	82	4.5	0.7	4.1
Lozère	74	76	29	6.8	2.1	3.4
Basses-Alpes	71	33	76	6.3	0.6	7.5
Aveyron	65	44	17	4.9	1.5	2.0
Basses-Pyrénées	51	61	21	3.2	0.6	2.9
Pyrénées-Orientales	50	57	24	3.5	1.8	2.0
Hautes-Pyrénées	37	72	62	6.2	0.7	4.0
Vosges	25	46	56	3.9	1.1	2.5
Ardennes	8	30	17	0.5	0.8	5.2
Jura	3	10	58	2.0	0.6	3.0
Côte-d'Or	2	5	11	3.1	0.8	1.7
Doubs	1	2	22	2.9	0.6	1.0

The nature of the soil has no influence whatever in the production of genius, for we find the highest figures in the Cote-d'Or, the Meuse, and the Moselle, where the soil is calcareous, and the lowest figures in the Nord and Deux-Sèvres, where the soil is of the same character; other high figures are the Doubs, the Jura, and the Meurthe, where the soil is Jurassic, while the same soil offers very low figures in the Hautes-Alpes, the Charente, and the Saône-et-Loire.

The influence of race is also very slight; the descendants of the Burgundians produced numerous men of genius in the Jura and the Doubs, very few in the Saône-et-Loire. The Haute-Garonne, with the same race, produces ten times as many men of genius as Ariège, twice as many as Gers, five times as many as the Landes. In Guienne, the Gironde gives twice as many as Lot, and in Languedoc, Herault gives seven times more than Lozère.

Explanation.—The relation that we have found between genius and climate has been caught sight of long since by the people and the learned, who agree in admitting a frequency of genius in regions which, being hilly, offer mild temperature. The Tuscan proverb says, "Mountaineers, great boots, and keen heads." Vegetius wrote that climate influences not only the strength of the body, but also that of the mind. "*Plaga cæli non solum ad robur corporum sed etiam animorum facit*" (lib. i. cap. 2).[18] Athens, the same author remarks, was chosen by Minerva for its subtle air which produces men of sagacity. Cicero said repeatedly that the keen air of Athens gave birth to wise men; the thick air of Thebes only to torpid natures; and Petrarch, in his *Epistolarium*, which is a kind of summary of his life, remarks with great emphasis that all his chief works were composed, or at all events meditated,

18 Latin: Climate contributes not only to the strength of the body, but also to that of the mind. —Ed.

among the mild hills of Vaucluse. Michelangelo said to Vasari: "Giorgio, if anything good has come out of my brain, I owe it to the subtle air of your Arezzo." Zingarelli, when asked how he had composed the melody of *Giulietta e Romeo*, replied: "Look at that sky, and tell me if you do not feel capable of doing as much." Muratori, in a letter to an inhabitant of Siena, wrote: "Your *air* is admirable, really producing fruitful minds." Macaulay remarks that Scotland, though one of the poorest countries in Europe, stands in the first rank for richness in men of genius; it is sufficient to name Michael Scot, Napier, the inventor of logarithms, Buchanan, Ben Jonson, and, one may perhaps add, Newton. On plains, on the other hand, men of genius are rare. Of ancient Egypt, a country of plains, Kenan writes:

> No revolutionary, no reformer no great poet, no artist, no man of science, no philosopher, not even a great minister, can be met in the history of Egypt. . . . In this sad valley of eternal slavery, for thousands of years they cultivated the fields, carried stones on their backs, and were good officials, living well without glory. There was the same level of moral and intellectual mediocrity everywhere.[19]

And the same may be said in our days.

At first it seems surprising to see a condition of degeneration, such as genius may be called, devel-

19 Ernest Kenan, "Les Antiquités Egyptiennes", in *Revue des Deux Mondes* April (1865).

oping at spots of maximum salubrity. But if there are anærobic microbes, some are ærobic; many forms of degeneration, such as *goître*, malaria, and leprosy, have a special habitat. It is evident that we have to reckon with the dynamogenic influence of light, with the stimulating action of the ozonized air of the hills, and of a warm temperature. We may understand this the better since we have already seen that heat augments the creative power of men of genius, and the need of the brain for oxydated blood in order to work is well known. This is confirmed by the fact that in mountains above an elevation of three thousand metres, no man of genius has ever been produced. The great Mexican and Peruvian civilizations flourished on the high tablelands, but, as Nibbi has well shown, they were not born there;[20] in fact, the Mexican civilization is owing to the Toltecas, who came from the east, and the pretended great men of Mexico, including its sixty presidents, were not born on the tableland. The same may be said of many men who were not quite justly termed illustrious, such as Echeverría in painting, Moizzos and Cervantes in botany, and Ixtlihcochitl.[21] Some men of true genius, as Garcilaso de la Vega and Alvares de Vera, were born

20 *Archivio di psichiatria, antropologia criminale e scienze penali per servire allo studio dell'uomo alienato e delinquente* 8.3 (1887).

21 Guillaume Libri, *Histoire des sciences mathématiques en Italie de la Renaissance au XVIIe siècle*, 4 vols. (Paris: Jules Renouard et Cie., 1838-1841) vol 3.

something below three thousand metres at Quito and Bogota.[22]

There is here again a parallelism between genius and insanity. Those who live in mountainous regions are more liable to insanity than the inhabitants of the plains, a fact which has long been embodied in proverbs concerning the air of Monte Baldo, and the madmen of Collio and Tellio. We may recall also the epidemics of Monte Atniata (Lazzaretti), of Busca and Montenero, of Verzegnis; and we may remember, too, that the hills of Judea and of Scotland have produced prophets and half-insane persons gifted with second sight.

22 Alphonse Pyramus de Candolle, *Histoire des Sciences et des Savants depuis deux Siècles* (Geneva: H. Georg, 1873).

Chapter III

Influence of Race and Heredity on Genius and Insanity

Race — Insanity — The influence of sex — The heredity of genius — Criminal and insane parentage and descent of genius — Age of parents — Conception.

R*ace.*—We have seen that in Italy the Greek and the Etruscan racial elements combine with the temperate and mountainous climate to produce men of genius; the influence of race calling forth genius even where the climate is not happy. We cannot otherwise explain the genius produced at Modena, Mantua, and Lucca, which possess the Etruscan origin, although not the delicious climate, of Florence. The Jews, again, offer us an eloquent example.

I have elsewhere shown (*Uomo Bianco e l'Uomo di Colore* and *Pensiero e Meteore*) how, owing to the bloody selection of mediæval persecutions, and owing also to the influence of temperate climate, the Jews of Europe have risen above those of Africa and the East, and have often surpassed the Aryans. It is not only a difference in general culture, but we find more precocious and extended mental work applied to different sciences. It is certainly thus in music, the drama, satirical and humorous literature, journalism, and in various branches of science. This has been statistically proved by various writers, as by Jacobs in a very careful study on the ability of the Jews in Western Europe and of Jews in general.[1]

In 100,000 celebrities—

	Europeans	Jews
Actors	21	34
Agriculture	2	-
Antiquaries	23	26
Architects	6	6
Artists	40	34
Authors	316	223
Divines	130	105
Engineers	13	9
Engravers	3	-
Lawyers	44	40
Medicals	31	49

1 Joseph Jacobs, "The Comparative Distribution of Jewish Ability," *Journal of Anthropological Institute of Great Britain* (1886) 351-379.

Merchants	12	43
Military	56	6
Miscellaneous	4	3
Metaphysics	2	18
Musicians	11	71
Natural Science	22	25
Naval	12	-
Philologists	13	123
Poets	20	36
Political Economy	20	26
Science	51	52
Sculptors	10	12
Sovereigns	21	-
Statesmen	125	83
Travellers	25	12

The two lists are approximately equal in antiquaries, architects, artists, lawyers, natural science, political economy, science, sculptors. Jews seem to have superiority as actors, chess-players, doctors, merchants (chiefly financiers), in metaphysics, music, poetry, and philology. . . . Of course, Jews have no Darwin. It took England 180 years after Newton before she could produce a Darwin, and as Britishers are five times the number of Jews, even including those of Russia, it would take, on the same showing, 900 years before they produce another Spinoza, or, even supposing the double superiority to be true, 450 years would be needed.

Jews have given to the world musicians like Meyerbeer, Halèvy, Gutzkow, Mendelssohn, Offenbach, Rubinstein, Joachim, Benedict, Moscheles, Cowen, Sullivan, Goldmark, Strauss; poets, novelists, humourists, &c., like Heine, Saphir, Camerini, Revere, Jung, Weill, Fortis, Gozlan, Moritz Hartmann, Auerbach, Börne, Ratisbonne, Kompert, Grace Aguilar, Franzos, Massarani, Lindau, Catulle Mendès; linguists like Ascoli, Benfey, Munk, Fiorentino, Luzzato, Oppert, Bernhardi, Friedland, Weil, Lazarus, Steinthal; physicians like Valentin, Hermann, Haidenhain, Schiff, Casper, Stilling, Gluge, Traube, Fraenkel, Kuhn, Cohnheim, Hirsch, Liebreich, Bernstein, Remak, Weigert, Meynert, Hitzig, Westphal, Mendel, Leidesdorf, Benedikt; philosophers like Spinoza, Maimon, Sommerhausen, Moses Mendelssohn; naturalists like Cohn; economists like Ricardo, Lassalle, Karl Marx; jurists and statesmen like Stahl, Gans, Beaconsfield, Crémieux. Even in sciences in which the Semite formerly showed no ability, such as mathematics and astronomy, we find such men as Goldschmidt, Beer, Sylvester, Kronecker, and Jacobi.

It must be observed that a very large proportion of these men of genius have been radically creative; revolutionary in politics, and in religion, and in science. Jews, indeed, initiated Nihilism and Socialism on the one hand, Mosaism and Christianity on the other. Commerce owes to them the bill of exchange, philosophy owes to them Positivism, literature the Neo-humourism.

Jacobs shows that this abundance of Jewish men of genius of the first order is allied with a deficiency in men of the second order of intellect. He explains the superiority by the higher level of education among the Jews, their devotion to family life, the almost complete absence of priests and dogmas, the facilities which the study of Hebrew offers for investigations in philosophy and for that kind of music which forms part of their religious ceremonies. It is difficult, however, to find a relationship between this rhythmical caterwauling and the sublime notes of Meyerbeer and Mendelssohn; and Jews possess more than enough of priests and dogmas. I would add that if the Jews have not yet produced men like Newton, Darwin, and Michelangelo, it is because they have not yet accomplished their ethnic evolution, as they show by the obstinacy with which they cling to their ancient beliefs.

It is strange that among the factors of Jewish superiority in genius Jacobs does not mention the neurotic tendency, the existence of which, as we shall see, he has himself shown. This would also well explain the deficiency of Jews in intellect of medium quality in which the morbid element is always less marked.

Insanity.—It is curious to note that the Jewish elements in the population furnish four and even six times as many lunatics as the rest of the population. Jacobs, who, as we have seen, does not suspect the correlation between genius and insanity, gives a remarkable proof of it by pointing out that while Englishmen have 3,050 per million afflicted with mental disease, Scotchmen have 3,400, and Jews 3,900, the proportion of insanity in the three races being related to the proportion of genius. And while, according to Galton, there are 256,000 of the mediocre class among a million Englishmen, Jacobs reckons that there are only 239,000 among Scotchmen, and 222,000 among Jews.

Servi found 1 lunatic to 391 Jews in Italy, nearly four times as many as among Catholics.[2] This fact has been made still clearer by Verga[3] who in 1870 found the proportions of lunatics among Catholics to be 1 in 1775, as against 1 in 384 among Jews. Mayr (in 1871)[4] gives the proportion of lunatics in Germany as follows:—

	Per 100,000 Christians	Per 100,000 Jews
Prussia	8.7	14.1
Bavaria	9.8	25.2
All Germany	8.6	16.1

2 Flaminio Servi, *Gli Israeliti d'Europa nella civiltà: memorie storiche, biografiche, e statistiche dal 1789 al 1870* (Turin: Foa, 1871).

3 Andrea Verga, "Censimento dei pazzi che trovavansi ricoverati nei manicomi ed ospitali d'Italia nel 1877", *Archivio di Statistica* 5 (1880) 235-265.

4 G. Mayer, *Die Verbreitung der Blindheit &c. in Bayern* (1877).

This is a singular proportion or disproportion in a population among which the aged who supply so large a number of cases of senile dementia are numerous, but where alcoholism is rare. This fatal privilege has not attracted the attention of the leaders of that anti-Semitic movement which is one of the shames of contemporary Germany.[5] They would be less irritated at the success of this race if they had thought of all the sorrows that are the price of it, even at our epoch; for if the tragedies of the past were more bloody, the victims are not now less unhappy, struck at the source of their glory, and because of it, deprived even of the consolation of being able, as formerly, to contribute to the most noble among the selections of species.

This is not true of the Jews alone. Beard, in his *American Nervousness*, remarks that the neurotic tendency which dominates North America makes of that country a land of great orators.

The influence of race is as visible in genius as in insanity. Education counts for little, heredity for much. "By education," said Helvetius, "you can make bears dance, but never create a man of genius."[6]

---

5 Renan in his *Souvenirs de jeunesse* remarks that since Germany has given herself up to militarism she would have no men of genius, if it were not for the Jews, to whom she should be at least grateful. But he forgets Haeckel, Virchow, and Wagner.

6 One case is known in which parents zealously sought to educate and favour by every means poetic genius in their son. The outcome of their fervent efforts was Chapelain, the too famous singer of the Pucelle.

Influence of Sex.—In the history of genius women have but a small place. Women of genius are rare exceptions in the world. It is an old observation that while thousands of women apply themselves to music for every hundred men, there has not been a single great woman composer. Yet the sexual difference here offers no obstacle. Out of six hundred women doctors in North America not one has made any discovery of importance; and with few exceptions the same may be said of the Russians. In physical science, it is true, Mary Somerville emerges; and in literature we have George Eliot, George Sand, Daniel Stern, and Madame de Staël; in the fine arts, Rosa Bonheur, Lebrun, Maraini; Sappho and Mrs. Browning opened new paths for poetry; Eleonora d'Arborea, it is said (but the assertion is contested), initiated at the beginning of the fifteenth century legal reforms of almost modern character; Catherine of Siena influenced the politics and religion of her time; Sarah Martin, a poor dressmaker, influenced prison reform; Mrs. Beecher Stowe played a large part in the abolition of slavery in the United States. But of all these, none touch the summits reached by Michelangelo, or Newton, or Balzac. Even J. S. Mill, who was very partial to the cause of women, confessed that they lacked originality. They are, above all, conservators. Even the few who emerge have, on near examination, something virile about them. As Goncourt said, there are no women of genius; the women of genius, are men.

Pulcheria, Marie de' Medici, Louise, mother of Francis I., Maria Christina, Maria Theresa, Catherine II., Elizabeth, displayed eminent political ability as rulers; as in the field of democracy Madame Roland, Fonseca, G. Sand, Madame Adam; Mill affirms that when an Indian state is ruled with vigour and vigilance, three times out of four the ruler is a woman. At the same time it is noted that when women rule, men command, just as when men rule, women command. In any case their number is too limited to compare them with masculine rulers. As in politics, so admirable examples of valour were given by Caterina Sforza and Joan of Arc, Anita Garibaldi, Enrichetta Castiglioni, and many others.

These facts become more notable because unexpected and exceptional. It may be said that the disparity would be much less if the predominance of men, depriving women of the vote in politics and of action in war, had not taken away from women the opportunity of manifesting their capacities. But if there had been in women a really great ability in politics, science, &c., it would have shown itself in overcoming the difficulties opposed to it; nor would arms have been lacking, nor allies in the enemy's camp. In revolutions (except in religion) women have always been in a small minority, not being found, for example, in the English Revolution, or in that of the Low Countries, or of the United States. They never created a new religion, nor were they ever at the head of great political, artistic, or scientific movements.

On the contrary, women have often stood in the way of progressive movements. Like children, they are notoriously misoneistic; they preserve ancient habits and customs and religions. In America there are tribes in which women keep alive ancient languages which the men have lost; in Sardinia, Sicily, and some remote valleys of Umbria, many ancient prejudices and pagan rites, perhaps of a prehistoric character—superstitious cures, for instance are preserved by women. As Goncourt remarks, they only see persons in everything; they are, as Spencer observes, more merciful than just.

The Heredity of Genius.—According to Galton[7] and Ribot, genius is often hereditary, especially in the musical art which furnishes so large a contingent to insanity. Thus Palestrina, Benda, Dussek, Hiller, Eichhorn, had sons who were very distinguished in music. Andrea Amati was the most illustrious of a family of violinists at Cremona; Beethoven's father was a tenor at the Elector of Cologne's chapel, and his grandfather had been a singer and then *maestro* at the same chapel; Bellini was the son and nephew of musicians; Haydn had a brother who was an excellent organist and composer of religious music; in Mendelssohn's family there were several musical amateurs; Mozart was the son of a *maestro* of the chapel of the Prince Archbishop of Salzburg; Palestrina had sons who

7 Francis Galton, *Hereditary Genius* (London: Macmillan, 1869).

died young but who left praiseworthy compositions preserved among their father's works.

The Bach family perhaps presents the finest example of mental heredity. It began in 1550, and passed through eight generations, the last known member being Wilhelm Friedrich Ernst, Kapellmeister to the Queen of Prussia, who died in 1845. During two centuries this family produced a crowd of musicians of high rank. The founder of the family was Veit Bach, a Presburg baker, who amused himself with singing and playing. He had two sons who were followed by an uninterrupted succession of musicians who inundated Thuringia, Saxony, and Franconia during two centuries. They were all organists or church singers. When they became too numerous to live together and had to disperse, they agreed to reunite on a fixed day once a year. This custom was preserved up to the middle of the eighteenth century, and sometimes one hundred and twenty persons of the name of Bach met at the same spot. Fétis counts among them twenty-nine musicians of eminence.[8]

Among musicians may be named the Adams, the Coustons, the Sangallos; among painters, the Van der Weldes, the Coypels, the Van Eycks, the Murillos, the Veroneses, the Bellinis, the Caraccis, the Correggios, the Mieris, the Bassanos, the Tintorettos, the Caliaris, the Vanloos, the Teniers, the

8 François-Joseph Fétis, *Biographie universelle des musiciens et bibliographie générale de la musique* (Paris: Firmin Didot frères, fils et cie, 1869-76).

Vernets, and especially the Titians who produced a race of painters, as shown in the following genealogy taken from Ribot's excellent book:—

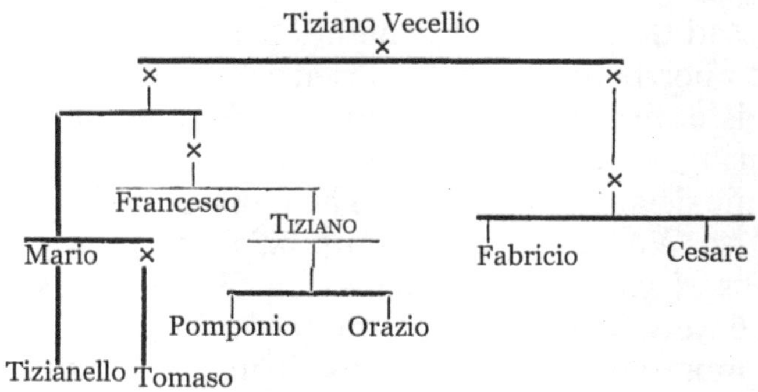

Among poets may be noted Bacchylides, the nephew of Simonides and uncle of Æschylus who again had sons and nephews who were poets; Manzoni, the nephew of Beccaria; Lucan, the nephew of Seneca; Tasso, the son of Bernardo; Ariosto, with a brother and nephew poets; Aristophanes, with two sons who wrote comedies; Corneille, Racine, Sophocles, Coleridge, who had sons and nephews who were poets; the Dumas, father and son; the brothers Joseph and André Chénier, Alphonse and Ernest Daudet.

In the natural sciences we find the two Plinies, uncle and nephew, the families of Darwin, Euler, De Candolle, Hooker, Herschel, Jussieu, Saussure, Geoffrey St. Hilaire. Among philosophers we find the Scaligers, the Vossius, the Fichtes, and the brothers Humboldt, Schlegel and Grimm; among statesmen the Pitts, Foxes, Cannings, Walpoles, Peels, and Disraelis; among archæologists, the Viscontis. Aristotle, himself the son of a scientific physician, had sons and nephews who were men of science. Cassini, an astronomer, had a son, who was a celebrated astronomer, a grandson who was a member of the Academy of Sciences at the age of twenty-two, and a more remote relation who was a distinguished naturalist and philologist.

Here is the genealogical tree of the Bernouilli family:—

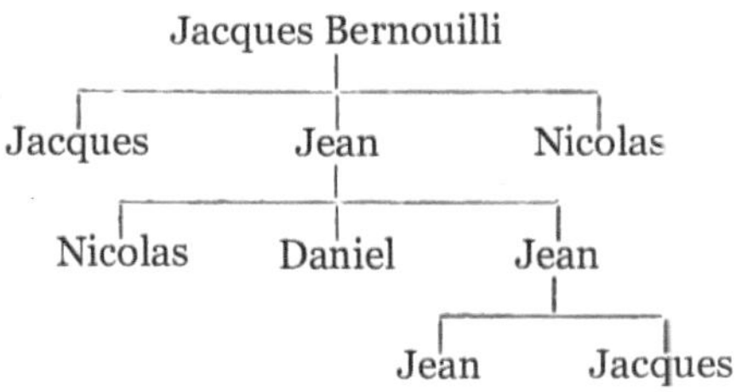

All the members of this family were distinguished in some science; at the beginning of this century there was a Bernouilli who was a chemist of some distinction; and in 1863 there still lived at Bale Christophe Bernouilli, a professor of the natural sciences.

Galton, in a work of great value, but in which he often commits the mistake (from which I also cannot free myself) of confusing talent with genius, calculates a proportion of 425 men of ability to a million among the male population over fifty years of age, and the more select part of them as 250 to a million. Dealing with 300 families, containing 1000 eminent men, he concludes that the percentage of eminent kinsmen in these families would be as follows:—

48 sons	18 uncles
41 brothers	13 cousins
31 fathers	17 grandfathers
14 grandsons	3 great-grandfathers
22 nephews	5 great-uncles

The probabilities of kinsmen of illustrious men rising to eminence are—15½ to 100 in the case of fathers; 13½ to 100 in the case of brothers; 24 to 100 in the case of sons.

Galton remarks that these figures vary, according as we are concerned with artists, diplomatists, soldiers, &c.

I am not, however, inclined to believe that this immense accumulation of fact authorizes us to accept a hereditary influence in genius as complete as in insanity. In the first place, in insanity the hereditary influence is exercised in a more intense and decisive manner, as 48 to 80; and then if Galton's law applies to judges and statesmen, among whom adulation and the fetishistic adoration of a party or a caste can raise the son or grandson of a great man far above his merits, it is quite otherwise with artists and poets, who present an exaggerated hereditary action in brothers and sons and especially nephews, but very little in grandparents and uncles. And while in the heredity of genius the masculine sex prevails over the feminine in the proportion of 70 to 30, in the heredity of insanity there is scarcely any difference between the two sexes.[9]

Many men of genius have been thought to inherit from their mothers: such are Cicero, Condorcet, Cuvier, Buffon, Goethe, Sydney Smith, Cowper, Napoleon, Cromwell, Chateaubriand, Scott, Byron, Lamartine, Saint Augustine, Gray, Swift, Fontenelle, Ballanche, Manzoni, Kant, Wellington, Foscolo. On the other hand, Bacon, Raphael, Weber, Schiller, Milton, Alberti, Tasso, are said to inherit from their fathers. Yet, it may be asked, what was the celebrity of these fathers and mothers that one can feel assured they transmitted any genius to their children? Among most men of genius, also, there can be no heredity because of the predominance of sterility and of degeneration, of which the aristocracy furnishes us with a remarkable proof.[10]

---

9 Ribot in his *L'hérédité Psychologique* refers to French statistics of 1861 according to which in 1000 lunatics of each sex, there was hereditary influence in 264 men and in 266 women.

10 Galton himself remarks that of 31 great families of lawyers raised to the peerage before the end of the reign of George IV., twelve are extinct, especially those which contracted alliances with heiresses. Out of 487 families admitted to citizenship at Berne from 1583 to 1654 only 168 remained in 1783. "When a grandee of Spain is announced we expect to see an abortion" (Ribot, *De L'hérédité*, p. 820). The French and Italian nobility to-day has become for the most part an inert instrument in the hands of the clergy. And how many of the sovereigns of Europe

With a few exceptions, then, such as the Danvins, the Cassinis, the Bernouillis, the Saint Hilaires, the Herschels, men of genius only transmit to their descendants a slight tendency magnified in our eyes by the *prestige* of a great name:—

> *Rare voile risurge per li rami*
> *L'umana probitate*[11]

Who thinks of Tizianello beside Titian, of Nicomachus beside Aristotle, of Orazio Ariosto beside his great uncle; or of the worthy professor Christophe beside his great ancestor Jacques Bernouilli?

Insanity, on the other hand, is often completely transmitted, or even with greater intensity, to succeeding generations. Cases of hereditary insanity in children and grandchildren, the form of insanity often being the same as in the ancestor, are very numerous. All the descendants of a Hamburg noble, whom history registers as a great soldier, were struck by insanity at the age of forty.[12] At Connect-

---

yet preserve those ancestral virtues to the presumed transmission of which they owe in large part their throne and prestige?

11 Dante, *Purgatorio*, canto vii.

12 Prosper Lucas, *Traité philosophique et physiologique de l'hérédité naturelle dans les états de santé et de maladie du système nerveux, avec l'application méthodique des lois de la procréation au traitement général des affections dont elle est le principe. Ouvrage où la question est considérée dans ses rapports avec les lois primordiales, les théories de la génération, les causes déterminantes de la sexualité, les modifications acquises de la nature originelle des êtres, et les diverses formes de névropathie et d'aliénation mentale,* 2 vols. (Paris:

icut Asylum eleven members of the same family have arrived in succession.[13]

A watchmaker, having recovered from an attack of insanity caused by the revolution of 1789, finally poisoned himself: later on his daughter became insane, and fell into a state of dementia; one of his brothers struck a knife into his own abdomen; another became a drunkard and died on the roadside; a third refused food and perished from starvation; his sister, who was of good health, had a son who was an epileptic lunatic, a daughter who became insane after her confinement and rejected food, an infant who refused to be suckled, and two others who died of cerebral diseases.

In a family studied by Berti, in four generations of about eighty individuals descended from an insane melancholiac we find ten subject to insanity, nearly always melancholia, nineteen who were neurotic, three who had special ability and three with criminal tendencies. The disorder was aggravated in the later generations and developed at an earlier age. In the third and fourth branches, the insane and neurotic appeared in every generation; in the others, the hereditary influence passed over one generation in the men and two in the women.

The history of the so-called "Jukes" family[14] shows that such an influence may be still more

---

J. B. Ballière, 1847-1850).

13 Ribot, *L'hérédité psychologique.*

14 Richard L. Dugdale, *The Jukes; a study in crime, pauperism, disease, and heredity* (New York: G. P. Putnam's Sons, 1877).

powerfully developed, especially in association with alcoholism. From the head of the family, Max Jukes, a great drunkard, descended, in 75 years, 200 thieves and murderers, 280 invalids attacked by blindness, idiocy, or consumption, 90 prostitutes and 300 children who died prematurely. The various members of this family cost the state more than a million dollars.

These are not isolated facts. But in what families can we find genius so fatally and progressively fruitful?

Flemming and Demaux, again, have shown that not only do drunkards transmit to their descendants, tendencies to insanity and crime, but that even habitually sober parents, who at the moment of conception are in a temporary state of drunkenness, beget children who are epileptic or paralytic, idiotic or insane, very often microcephalic, or with remarkable weakness of mind which at the first favourable occasion is transformed into insanity. Thus a single embrace, given in a moment of drunkenness, may be fatal to an entire generation.

What analogy can we find here with the rare and nearly always incomplete heredity of genius?

The Criminal and Insane Parentage and Descent of Genius.—The parallelism of genius to insanity is, however, still present. We find that many lunatics have parents of genius, and that many men of genius have parents or sons who were epileptic, mad, or, above all, criminal. It is sufficient to study the history of the Cæsars, of Charles V., of Peter the Great. We see a progressive degeneration in crime and insanity in relations or children, rather than any conservation or increase of genius. This fact confirms a posteriori the degenerative character of genius; and at the same time reveals the relationship which it generally has with moral insanity.[15] Commodus, son of the virtuous Marcus Aurelius, was a monster of cruelty. The son of Scipio Africanus was an imbecile, the son of Cicero a drunkard. Luther's son was insubordinate and violent; William Penn's was a debauched scoundrel. Themistocles, Aristides, Pericles, Thucydides were unhappy in their children.

Cardan had two sons who were criminals; one, of great ability, was condemned to death for poisoning; the other, given up to gaming, drinking, and thieving, was successively imprisoned at Pavia, Milan, Cremona, Bologna, Piacenza, Naples. When arrested he would promise reformation, but as soon as he was free he at once returned to his old habits, and even calumniated his father and attempted to get him imprisoned.[16] Cardan's father

15 *Academie des Sciences* (1871). Five cases of epilepsy, and of insanity, two of general paralysis, one of idiocy and several of microcephaly were observed under these circumstances. The microcephalic condition which so often appears among the hereditary results of alcoholism may be understood when we recall the atrophies, the cerebral scleroses (a kind of histologic microcephaly) which are so constantly found in the drunkard himself.

16 Antonio Bertolotti, "I testamenti di Girolamo Cardano medico filosofo e matematico del secolo XVI", *Archivio storico lom-*

was eccentric and stammered; he did not dress like other people, and pursued various strange studies; he had lost some part of his skull in consequence of a wound received in youth, and he believed that he was guided by a spirit. His mother was irascible; when pregnant with him she attempted to abort.[17]

It appears that Aretino's mother was a prostitute. Petrarch had a lazy and vicious son, "the most refractory to letters that man of letters ever had;" he died at the age of twenty-four.[18] Rembrandt brought up his son Titus, with great care, to be an artist; but in spite of all efforts he could make nothing of him. Walter Scott's son, a cavalry officer, was ashamed of his father's literary celebrity, and boasted that he had never read one of his novels. Mozart's son, when asked by Bianchini if he liked music, replied by throwing a handful of gold on the table: "That is the only music I like!" Sophocles' son tried to represent his old father as imbecile. Frederick the Great's father was morally insane and a drunkard; Peter the Great had a son who was a drunkard and maniacal; Richelieu's sister imagined that her back was made of crystal; his brother thought he was God the Father; Niccolini's sister thought she was damned because of her brother's heresy, and attempted to kill him; Hegel's sister was insane, as also was Diderot's; Lamb's sister killed her mother during a maniacal

bardo 9 (1882) 615-660.

17 Cardano, *De Vita Propria*.

18 *Famil* XIII. 2, XXIII. 12.

attack. Gray's father was a worthless scoundrel, who used to beat his wife, by whose exertions the children were supported. Thomas Campbell's only son was hopelessly imbecile.

Charles V.'s mother suffered from melancholia; his grandchildren and great-grandchildren were also insane: Don Carlos, brutal, cruel, and turbulent; Philip III., subject to convulsions; Charles II., an imbecile epileptic, with whom the race was extinguished; and Alexander Farnese, a bastard grandson of eccentric genius.[19]

The drunkenness of Beethoven's father was notorious. Byron's mother was half-mad; his father, known as "mad Jack Byron," was dissolute and eccentric, and is said to have committed suicide. It has been said of Byron that if ever there was a case in which hereditary influence could justify eccentricity of character it was his, for he was descended from individuals in whom everything seemed calculated to destroy harmony of character and domestic peace. Alexander had a dissolute and perverse mother, a drunken father. Plutarch's grandfather was much given to wine, of which he delighted to celebrate the virtues; and Cimon's was a drunkard and debauched. Kerner had a maternal uncle who was mad; his sister was melancholic and had two children, of whom one was insane,

19 William W. Ireland, *The Blot upon the Brain* (London: Bell and Bradfute, 1885) 147; Joseph J. Déjerine, *L'hérédité dans les maladies du système nerveux* (Paris: Asselin-Houzeau, 1886).

the other a somnambulist.[20] The sons of Tacitus, Carlini, Bernardin de Saint-Pierre, Mercadante, Donizetti, Volta, Manzoni, a daughter of Victor Hugo, the father and brothers of Villemain, the sister of Kant, the brothers of Zimmermann, Perticari, and Puccinotti were all insane. D'Azeglio, who had a grandfather and a brother more than eccentric, records a saying current at Turin: "*I Taparei a l'an nen le grumele a port*"[21]

The origins of Kenan's neurosis, of which I have already spoken, he has himself indicated in speaking of his religious and prematurely sacerdotal education, that education of the seminary which when it once takes hold of a man never more leaves him, and which is so productive of insanity. The alienist will find other sources of neurosis and atavism in the little town of Treguier in which Renan was born. On account of the frequency of consanguineous marriages and of the preponderance of the ecclesiastical element, the place swarmed with the insane and semi-insane. "These inoffensive lunatics," he writes, "were a sort of institution, a municipal affair. We said, 'our lunatics,' as at Venice they say '*nostre carampane*.' One met them nearly everywhere; they saluted you, greeted you with some nauseous pleasantry, which yet raised

20 Justinus Kerner, *Das Bilderbuch aus meiner Knabenzeit. Erinnerungen aus den Jahren 1786-1804* (1837; Braunschweig: Viehweg & Sohn, 1819).

21 *Memorie* 341. *I.e.*, "The heads of the Taparelli are not in the right place." Taparelli was a family name of D'Azeglio.

a smile. They were liked, and they were useful. I shall always remember the good lunatic Brian, who imagined that he was a priest, and passed part of the day in church, imitating the ceremonies of the mass; all the afternoon the cathedral was filled with a nasal murmur; it was the poor lunatic's prayer, well worth any other."[22] A still greater influence on Kenan's psychosis must be attributed to the insanity in his own family. His paternal uncle, semi-insane, passed his days and nights at inns telling stories and legends to the peasants with whom he was a great favourite; one night he was found dead on the roadside. His grandfather, an ardent and honest patriot, lost his reason in 1815, through grief, and used to walk about with an enormous tricoloured cockade, exclaiming: "I should like to know who would dare to snatch from me this cockade!" He himself, a seven-months' child, remained for a long time small and weak, and for this reason was the more easily disturbed by a sacerdotal education, which inflames, like a hot iron, even the most tranquil spirits.

In Schopenhauer, also, the insane and neurotic hereditary tendency was well marked. On his father's side he was descended from an old family of Danzig merchants; his great-grandfather was a man of very strong and energetic character; his grandfather, a man of quiet business habits, seems to have brought the property into the family, but

22 *Souvenirs d'enfance et de jeunesse* (Paris: Calmann Lévy, 1883) 20.

the grandmother had an aunt and a grandmother who were insane. Schopenhauer's father seems to have been a skilled man of business; a republican, he possessed the native arrogance of a democratic patrician; inclined to deafness from childhood, he had attacks of rage from which even the domestic dog and cat fled terrified. With the increase of his deafness he became more irritable, and suffered, if not from actual insanity, at least from morbid fears. It was suspected that he committed suicide. He presented various characters of degeneration: large ears, very prominent eyes, thick lips, a short, up-turned nose; he was, however, of considerable height. Schopenhauer's mother, married at the age of nineteen, was witty and ambitious, and, as he himself said, very frivolous. His brother was imbecile from childhood.

This influence of insane heredity can to-day be controlled by statistics. The Prussian statistics for 1877 show that among 10,676 lunatics, morbid heredity may be traced in 6,369.[23] They are divided as follows:—

23 Meynert, *Jahresber. für Psychiatr.*, Vienna, 1880. [I was not able to find records for this publication except in one source. Meynert edited the *Wiener Jahrbuches für Psychiatrie* and he also published the *Vierteljahrsschrift für Pyschiatrie*, but the latter was based in Neuwied and Leipzig. The citation occurs in N. Neergaard's *Tilskueren* (Copenhagen: P. G. Philipsens Forlag, 1890) 70, but the author also mentions Lombroso's *Man of Genius* in another footnote in page 64, suggesting that was his source. —Ed.]

	Father or Mother, per cent	Grand-parents, or uncles, per cent	Sisters or brothers, per cent
Insanity	89.0	86.0	76.1
Serious Neurosis	12.4	6.7	13.1
Crime	1.0	0.1	0.1
Alcoholism	18.0	3.1	3.3
Suicide	1.7	2.7	2.3

This seems to show that a considerable number of lunatics are descended from men of ability. The number of brothers and sisters of lunatics endowed with ability, surpassing that of suicidal, alcoholistic, or criminal brothers confirms the influence. In twenty-two cases of hereditary insanity Aubonel and Thoré observed two cases of sons of ability.[24]

These facts were not unknown to old observers. Tassoni, a very original writer, in his *Pensieri Diversi* (1621) discusses the question: "How it happens to wise fathers to have very foolish children, and to very foolish fathers to have very wise children." Among the former he mentions the sons of Scipio Africanus, Anthony, Cicero, Agrippa Posthumus, Claudius the son of Drusus, Caligula, of Germanicus, Commodus, of Marcus Aurelius, Lamprocles, of Socrates, Arrhidaeus, of Philip. Among many opinions, more or less extravagant,

24 Théodule Ribot, *L'hérédité psychologique* (Paris: Ballière, 1873) 171.

of learned men of his time, he reports one to the effect that "in great men the vital spirits assemble at the brain to fortify and give vigour to the powers of the intelligence; it happens in consequence that the blood and sperm remain cold and languid, and the children of such men, especially the males, are inclined to stupidity."

Age of Parents.—This is one of the hereditary influences which often escape from view, and are at present not clearly seen. Marro has shown the great influence of the advanced age of the parents on the intelligence or the insanity of the children. Very great is the number of men of genius, and even of talent, issued from aged fathers: Frederick II., Napoleon I., Sciacci, Bizzozzero, Rochefort, Dumas *père*, A. Jussieu, Balzac, J. Cassini, C. Vernet, Beaconsfield, Horace Walpole, William Pitt, Racine, Adler, Auriac, Beclard, Schopenhauer. From young fathers I have, on the other hand, only found Victor Hugo, De Girardin, Arneth, Barral, Bertillon, Ségur. This influence may explain the longevity of men of genius.

Conception.—De Candolle speaks of the influence which strong passion on the part of the parents at conception may have on the offspring, and recalls the considerable number of bastards of genius. Erasmus boasted that he was not the fruit of wearisome conjugal duty. Isaac Disraeli wrote in his "Memoirs of Toland" that birth outside marriage creates strong and resolute characters. Among illegitimate sons were: Themistocles,

Charles Martel, William the Conqueror, the Duke of Berwick whom Montesquieu called the perfect man, Leonardo da Vinci, Boccaccio, A. Dumas, Cardan, D'Alembert, Savage, Prior, De Girardin, La Harpe, Alexander Farnese, Dupanloup.[25] Newton was conceived after his parents had spent two years of forced continence. It will be seen from these and other facts how far we are yet from having exhausted the numerous sources of hereditary genius.

Those who recall how many men of genius have been born of consumptive and drunken parents, and who know how these two forms of degeneration are often transformed in the children into moral insanity, will perceive that there can be other hereditary causes of genius which escape ordinary observers, and are, therefore, little known.

---

25 The same kind of influence may be traced among the insane and degenerate. A son of Louis XIV. and Madame de Montespan, conceived during a crisis of remorse and grief, at the epoch of the Jubilee, was called "*l'enfant du jubilé*" on account of his condition of permanent melancholy. A man of talent, subject to attacks of mental exaltation, had several children, of whom two, conceived during these attacks, were insane. Joseph J. Déjerine, *L'hérédité dans les maladies du système nerveux* (Paris: Asselin-Houzeau, 1886).

CHAPTER IV

The Influence of Disease on Genius

Spinal diseases — Fevers —
Injuries to the head and their relation to genius.

Gérard de Nerval in his book, *Le rêve et la vie*, after having confessed that he often wrote in a state of morbid exaltation, adds that the old saying *Mens sana in corpore sano* is false, for many powerful minds have been allied to weak and diseased bodies.

Conolly treated a man whose intelligence was aroused by the use of blisters, and another whose ability was called forth during the initial period of phthisis and gout. Cabanis, Tissot, and Pomme observe that certain febrile conditions provoke extraordinary mental activity. Sylvester remarks that during the nocturnal fever of what he describes as a fortunate attack of bronchitis he was enabled to reach the solution of a mathematical problem.[1]

A man of genius, Maine de Biran, who was always ill, well expresses the influence of infirmities on genius, "The feeling of existence," he writes,

> is not found among the majority of men because with them it is continuous; when a man does not suffer he does not think of himself; disease alone and the habit of reflection enable us to distinguish ourselves.

It has frequently happened that injuries to the head and acute diseases, those frequent causes of insanity, have changed a very ordinary individual into a man of genius. Vico, when a child, fell from a high staircase and fractured his right parietal bone. Gratry, a mediocre singer, became a

1 *Nature* XXIX (n.d. November 1883). [While *Nature* contained four references to James Joseph Sylvester in the entire volume, which comprises weekly issues spanning from November 1883 to April 1884, they concern (1) his appointment to succeed Henry Smith in the Savilian Chair of Geometry at Oxford (157); (2) his resignation from John Hopkins University and subsequent appointment as Professor Emeritus (183); (3) his departure from America and appointment as Foreign Member of the Royal Academy of Sciences of Göttingen (271); and (4) a report of his departure from America (365). I was unable to find any articles by Sylvester in any of the November 1883 issues. Sylverster's biographer, Karen Hunger Parshall (in *James Joseph Sylvester: Jewish Mathematician in a Victorian World* (Baltimore, MD: John Hopkins University Press, 2006)) records him suffering attacks of bronchitis, but does not mention any of these bringing a solution to a mathematical problem. —Ed.]

great master, after a beam had fractured his skull. Mabillon, almost an idiot from childhood, fell down a stone staircase at the age of twenty-six, and so badly injured his skull that it had to be trepanned; from that time he displayed the characteristics of genius. Gall, who narrates this fact, knew a Dane who had been half idiotic, and who became intelligent at the age of thirteen, after having rolled head foremost down a staircase.[2] Wallenstein was looked upon as a fool until one day he fell out of a window, and henceforward began to show remarkable ability. Some years ago, a cretin of Savoy, having being bitten by a mad dog, became very intelligent during the last days of his life. Cases have been recorded in which ordinary persons have displayed extraordinary intelligence after diseases of the spinal cord.[3] "It is possible that my disease [of the spinal cord] may have given a morbid character to my later compositions," wrote with true divination the unfortunate Heine. And the remark does not apply to his later writings only. "My mental excitement," he wrote, some months before his condition had become aggravated,

2 Franz Joseph Gall, *Anatomie et Physiologie du Système nerveux en général et du cerveau en particulier avec des observations sur la possibilité de reconnaître plusieurs dispositions intellectuelles et morales de l'homme et des animaux par la configuration de leur têtes* (Paris: Schoell, 1810) 21. [No edition specified in the original. —Ed.]

3 *Journal of Mental Science* 18 (1872).

> is the effect of disease rather than of genius. I have written verses to appease my suffering a little. . . . In this horrible night of senseless pain my poor head is flung backwards and forwards, shaking with pitiless gaiety the bells on my jester's cap.[4]

Béclard turned from mere theories to experiment, after a stroke of apoplexy. Pasteur's greatest discoveries were made after a stroke of apoplexy. [5]Bichat and Schroeder van der Kolk have observed that men with anchylosis of the neck possess remarkably bright intelligence. It is a common saying that the hump-backed are keen and malicious. Rokitansky sought to explain this by the resulting curve of the aorta, after giving origin to the vessels which supply the brain, the volume of the heart and the arterial pressure in the head being thus augmented.

---

4 Henri Heine, *Correspondence inédite. Avec une preface et des notes* (Paris: Calmann-Lévy, 1877).

5 *Revue Scientifique* 41 (April 1888).

CHAPTER V

The Influence of Civilization and of Opportunity

Large Towns — Large Schools — Accidents — Misery — Power — Education

However clearly such laws as we have examined may seem to be ascertained, the conclusions deduced from them must be accepted with a certain reserve; since there exists a series of factors, almost impossible to seize, which intercept and confound all these influences, not excepting even the orographic.

We have already seen how great agglomerations of individuals, whatever the climate and race, are sufficient to increase the number of artists and of talents. But might not this be a purely factitious effect, as, for instance, when individuals who have left their birthplace for some great capital (as often happens in the case of infants and invalids), are looked upon as natives of the latter? This becomes certain, if we remember the pernicious influence of great towns, and consider with Smiles, that the life of large towns is not favourable to intellectual work, that men who have had a great influence on their age have been brought up in solitude, and that all the great men of England, and even of London, were born in the country, though this fact is often ignored on account of their having fixed their residence in the capital. Carlyle says that a man born in London seems but the fraction of a man. We read, in the *Lives of the Engineers*,[1] that all great English engineers have been country-bred.

The establishment of a school of painting, even when it is the result of an importation, makes an artistic centre of a place which was not so previously, and, if the establishment goes back to a very distant time, the number of artists becomes very large. Let us look, for example, at Piedmont, where, assuredly, a military education reinforced by climate and race, and, to a still greater degree, by clerical influence, retarded for a long time the development of the fine arts, and especially of music. Up to 1460, celebrated painters were not numerous in Piedmont, and the only ones to be found there were of foreign origin, such as Bono and Bondiforte. But Bondiforte, who had been sent for from Milan, was immediately followed by Sodoma, Martini, Giovannone, Vercellese. Ferro

1 Samuel Smiles, *Lives of the Engineers*, 5 vols. (London: John Murray, 1862).

di Valduggia was followed by Lanini, and Tansi by Valduggia, in the same way as Viotti's example attracted thither, within a short time, five celebrated violinists.

Scarcely had a few distinguished painters—such as Macrino and Gaudenzio Ferrari, shown themselves at Novara, at Alba, and at Vercelli, than others were immediately seen to appear; and, in our own day, wherever military influence has been entirely superseded by social, this province has furnished, in proportion to its size, as many artists as the rest, or even more, and those of quite equal standing—*e.g.*, Gastaldi, Mosso, Pittara, &c.

Had any one undertaken, 300 years ago, to draw up the statistics of Scotch thought, he would scarcely have found a single name to include in his list. Yet Scotland, delivered from the leaden mantle of religious intolerance, has become, as we have seen, one of the richest centres in Europe for bold and original thinkers.

On the other hand, Greece, placed in ancient times by race and nature in the first rank, as regards intellectual creation, no longer shows any trace of her superiority. Nature and the race have not changed, but slavery, political struggles, and hard living have exhausted all her strength; for a nation does not afford itself the luxury of art and high thinking till its existence is assured and easy.

Thus the influences of agglomeration might often have been disguised by the influence of national well-being.

Not that the action of race and climate disappears, but its manifestations remain latent. The mighty intellect due to the Tuscan race and climate reveals itself at the present day—after the enervating influence of the Medici, the priests, and the linguistic pedants, has done its work—in the improvisations of Pistoian peasant women, and the subtle epigrams of the Florentine populace. Genius (such as that of Pacini, Carrara, Betti, Giusti, Guerrazzi, Carducci) is no longer endemic, but occurs sporadically.

It appears to me that, in many cases, social influences are more apparent than real—analogous rather to the peck of the chicken which cracks the eggshell than to the spermatozoid which generates the embryo.

We see that Florence, like Athens, supplied at the epoch of republican agitations the *maximum* of Italian genius. But similar agitations in South America and in France (1789) did not yield as many great men; but simply a number of men who, being useful in the emergency of the time, passed for great.[2] One might even be inclined to suspect that the numerous great men who appeared at Florence were themselves the cause of her revolutions.[3]

The same assertion holds good of opportunity. Opportunity appears, sometimes, to have assisted the development of genius. Thus Mutius Scaevola,

2 Hyppolite Taine, *Les origines de la France* Contemporaine (Paris: Hachette, 1885).

3 *Atlantic Monthly* (1881).

having been reproached by Servius Sulpicius with ignorance of his country's laws became a great jurisconsult.

It has often happened that stonecutters in the quarries of Florence, in the old Republican times, have become celebrated sculptors, like Mino da Fiesole, Desiderio da Settignano, and Cronaca. Canova and Vincenzo Vela were also quarrymen, and Hugh Miller, from working as a mason, became a highly-esteemed geologist.

Andrea del Castagno, a shepherd of Mugello, one day, when overtaken by a storm, took refuge in an oratory, where a house-painter was daubing a picture of the Virgin. From thenceforth he felt an irresistible desire to imitate him, and practised drawing figures in charcoal whenever he could; so much so, that his fame soon spread among the peasants, and, afterwards, by the assistance of Bernadino de' Medici, who enabled him to study, he became a celebrated painter.

Vespasiano de' Bisticci, a Florentine paper-maker, whose profession involved the handling of many books, and contact with a great number of literary and learned men, took to literature himself.

More frequently, however, opportunity is only the last drop which makes the vessel run over. This is so true that the cases in which genius has manifested itself in spite of adverse circumstances and even violent opposition, are innumerable. It is sufficient to recall Boccaccio, Goldoni, Muratori, Leopardi, Ascoli, Cellini, Cavour, Petrarch,

Metastasio, and, finally, Socrates, who was obliged to cut and carve stones. All our recent great musicians—Wagner, Rossini, Verdi—were misunderstood in their youth.

Long ago, it was said, "He to whom Nature would not tell it, would not be told by a thousand Athens and a thousand Romes."[4]

Circumstances, then, and a certain degree of civilization gain acceptance and toleration for genius and its discoveries which, under other conditions, would have either passed unnoticed, or met with ridicule, and even persecution.

History shows that great discoveries are rarely absolute novelties, and that they have long existed as toys or curiosities. "Steam," says Fournier, "was a plaything for children in the time of Hero of Alexandria, and Anthemius of Tralles. The human mind and the needs of our race have to work by experience, a million times over, before deducing all the consequences of a fact."[5]

In 1765, Spedding offered portable gas, prepared and ready for use, to the corporation of Whitehaven, and was refused. At a later date came Chaussier, Minkelers, Lebon, and Windsor, who had no other merit than that of appropriating his discovery.

---

4 *A cui natura non lo voile dire*
Nol dirian mille Atene e mille Rome.

5 Edouard Fournier, *Le vieux-neuf, histoire ancienne des inventions et découvertes modernes*, 2d ed., 3 vols. (Paris: E. Plon, Nourrit, 1887).

Coal had been known ever since the fifteenth century; in 1543 Blasco de Garay appears to have propelled a vessel by steam and paddles in the port of Barcelona; the screw-steamer was invented before 1790. When Papin experimented with steam navigation, he met with nothing but derision, and was treated as a charlatan. When the screw was at last applied, Sauvage, who had invented it, never saw it in action, except from the prison where he was confined for debt.

Daguerreotypy was guessed at in Russia during the sixteenth century, and again, in Italy, by Fabricius, in 1566. It was afterwards discovered anew by Tiphaigne de la Roche. Galvanism was also discovered by Cotugno and by Duverney.

The theory of Natural Selection itself does not belong exclusively to Darwin. Existing species, it was already said by Lucretius, have only been able to maintain themselves by their cunning, strength, or swiftness; others have succumbed. And Plutarch, remarking that horses which have been pursued by wolves are swifter than others, gives this reason—that, the slower ones of the band having been overtaken and devoured, only the more agile survived.

Newton's law of attraction was already foreshadowed in works of the sixteenth century—more particularly in those of Copernicus and Kepler—and was nearly completed by Hooke.

It has been the same with magnetism, chemistry, and even criminal anthropology. Civilization, therefore, does not *produce* men of genius, and discoveries; but it assists their development, or, more correctly speaking, determines their acceptance.

It may therefore be admitted that genius can exist in any age and any country; but, as in the struggle for existence the greater number of beings are only born to become the prey of others, so many men of genius, if they do not meet with the favourable moment, either remain unknown or are misunderstood.

While there are some civilizations which assist the development of genius, others are injurious to it. In those parts of Italy, for instance, where civilization is most ancient, and where it has been frequently renewed, becoming stronger at each renewal, though the temper of the people is more open, the formation of genius is of rare occurrence. In general, when the average culture of a nation is of earlier date, novelties are less eagerly received. On the contrary, in countries where civilization is recent, as in Russia, new ideas are accepted with the greatest favour.

When the repetition of the same observation renders a new truth less difficult to accept, then genius is not only recognized as useful and even necessary, but received with acclamations. The public, perceiving the coincidence between a given civilization and the manifestation of genius, thinks that the two are connected, confusing the slight influence which determines the hatching of the chicks with the act of fecundation—which, on the contrary, depends on race, atmospheric influences, nutrition, &c.

This, too, is what takes place in our own day. Hypnotism exists to prove how many times, even under our very eyes, a scientific notion may be renewed, and each time taken for a new discovery. Every age is not equally ripe for inventions without precedents, or with too few; and those which are not ripe, are incapable of perceiving their inaptitude for adopting them. In Italy, for twenty years, the man who had discovered pellagrozeine was looked upon by the authorities as a madman. At the present day the academic world, always composed of intelligent mediocrities, laughs at criminal anthropology, is mildly sarcastic towards hypnotism, and looks on homœopathy as a joke. Perhaps even my friends and myself, in laughing at spiritualism, are misled by the misoneism latent in us all, and, like hypnotised persons, are utterly unable even to perceive that such is the case.

Misery is often the stimulus of genius. It was necessity rather than natural inclination which drove Dryden to become an author. Goldsmith, when he had knocked at every door in vain, took to writing. And so again and again.

It is true also that extreme misery frequently ruins genius. It placed immense difficulties in the way of Columbus. George Stephenson's steam engine would have been an abortion, if he had not been enabled at great sacrifice to educate his son.

Meyerbeer, who produced so laboriously, and whose genius cannot be explained apart from his Italian journeys and life, would have been in a deplorable condition without wealth.

Many men of genius, on the other hand, have been spoilt by wealth and power. Jacoby has shown that unlimited power hastens degeneration, and tends to produce megalomania and dementia in those who possess it.

The influence of education has been investigated less than it deserves. Without the school, many believe there would be no genius. What, it is said, would have become of Metastasio, if he had not been picked up and educated? Giotto would merely have amazed the shepherds of his native valleys by daubing the walls of some chapel. Paganini would have been unheard of. Pitre, in his admirable book, *Usi e costumi della Sicilia*, writes at length of certain wonderful poetasters, who narrate fantastic lays of knighthood to the people of Palermo, yet they can neither read nor write. Who knows what they would do if they were educated?

Those who have been among the mountains know the works produced by certain shepherds. They are made with coarse instruments, yet they reveal marvellous taste and delicacy. Such men give us the impression of so many aborted Michelangelos; they are men of genius who have lacked the opportunity of manifesting themselves.

But these facts do not neutralize others which show the pernicious influence of the school on genius. Hazlitt well said that whoever has passed through all the grades of classical instruction without having become a fool, may consider himself to have escaped by miracle. Darwin feared to send his sons to school. Who can describe the martyrdom of the child of genius compelled to spend his brains over a quagmire of things in which he will succeed the less the more he is attracted in other directions? He rebels, and then begins a fierce struggle between the pupil of genius and the professor of mediocrity, who cannot understand his fury and his instincts, and who represses and punishes them. Balzac, who proved this, and was driven away from school after school, has minutely analyzed this bitterness of the college in his wonderful study, *Louis Lambert.* One shudders on thinking of the youth of such lofty and serene intelligence, treated with contempt as stupid and idle, and his discourse on will which had cost him so much labour destroyed unread by an ignorant master. And so, also, it was with Valles. Verdi was unanimously rejected at the Conservatorio of Milan in 1832, even as a paying pupil. Rossini was regarded as an idiot by his fellow pupils, and by his teacher, as also was Wagner. Coleridge has written with bitterness of his schooldays, when, he says, his nature was always repressed. Howard was considered so stupid at school that he was sent to a druggist's. Pestalozzi was looked upon as a silly and incapable boy, whose spelling and writing were incorrigibly bad. Crebillon as a youth was regarded as roguish and lazy, and when he left the university he was labelled: *Puer ingeniosus, sed insignis nebulo*. Cabanis as a boy showed very early signs of uncommon intelligence, but the severe discipline of school only served to make him a dissembler, and he was finally expelled. Diderot was regarded as the shame of his house. Verdi, Rossini, Howard, Cabanis, would not allow themselves to be defeated, but how many, discouraged, have lost faith in themselves! It is useless to say that this struggle for existence results in the survival of the fittest; for even the weakest men of genius are worth more than mediocrities, and it is a sin to lose a single one. We are not here dealing with a phenomenon like that presented by the struggle of lower organisms. The case is even opposed, since their great sensibility renders men of genius more fragile. The persecutions of the school, tormenting these beings when they are in their first youth and most sensitive, cause us to lose those who, being more fragile, are better. Here, therefore, the struggle for existence suppresses the strongest, or at all events the greatest. The worst of this is that there is no remedy. Teachers are not men of genius, and in any case they cannot, and should not, look to anything but the manufacture of mediocrity. At all events, let no obstacles be put in the way of genius.

PART III

GENIUS IN THE INSANE

CHAPTER I

Insane Genius in Literature

Periodicals published in lunatic asylums — Synthesis — Passion — Atavism — Conclusion

The connection which, as we have seen, exists between genius and insanity is confirmed by the over-excitement of the intelligence, and the temporary appearance of real genius frequently observed among the insane.

"It seems," writes Charles Nodier,

> as if the divergent and scattered rays of the diseased intellect were suddenly concentrated, like those of the sun in a lens, and then lent to the speech of the poor madman so much brilliancy that one may be permitted to doubt whether he had ever been more learned, clear, or persua-

sive while in full possession of his reason.[1]

"Madness," writes Théophile Gautier,

> which creates such enormous gaps, does not always suspend all the faculties. Poems written during complete dementia often observe the rules of quantity extremely well. Domenico Theotocopuli, the Greek painter, whose master-pieces are admired in the Spanish churches, was insane. We have seen in England, scenes of lions and stallions fighting, the work of an insane patient, done on a board with a red-hot iron, which looked like some of Géricault's sketches rubbed in with bitumen.[2]

Under the influence of insanity,

> an ignorant peasant will make Latin verses; another will suddenly speak in an idiom which he has never learnt, and of which he will not know a word after his recovery. A woman will sing Latin hymns and poems entirely unknown to her; a child, wounded in the head, constructs syllogisms in German, and is unable, when no

1 Charles Nodier, "Jean-François les Bas-Bleus", *Contes de la veillée* (Paris: Charpentier: 1853). [The original footnote gives page 217 of an edition from seven years earlier, but the only edition from that year seems to be *Contes de Charles Nodier* (Paris: Hetzel, 1846) and that includes only "Trilby", "Le songe d'or", "Baptiste Montauban", "La fée aux miettes", "La combe de l'homme mort", "Inès de la Sierras", "Smarra", "La neuvaine de la Chandeleur", "La légende de la soeur Béatrix". —Ed.]

2 *Voyage en Italie* (Paris: G. Charpentier, 1879).

> longer ill; to utter a single expression in that language.[3]

Winslow knew a gentleman, incapable in his normal condition of doing a simple addition sum, who became an excellent mathematician during his attacks of mania. In the same way, a woman who wrote poetry while in the asylum, after her cure became once more a peaceable and prosaic housekeeper.

A monomaniac at the Bicètre lamented his detention in the following striking verse:—

> *Ah! le poète de Florence*
> *N'avait pas, dans son chant sacré*
> *Rêvé l'abîme de souffrance*
> *De tes murs, Bicêtre exécré.*[4]

Esquirol gives an account of a maniac who invented, during the acute period of his malady, a new kind of cannon which was afterwards adopted.

Morel had under his care a madman, subject to intermittent states in which all his faculties were more or less blunted, if not actually lost, who, during his lucid intervals, composed fine comedies.

3 Ulysse Trélat, *Recherches historiques sur la folie* (Paris: J.-B. Ballière, 1839).

4 J. Moreau de Tours, *La Psychologie morbide dans ses rapports avec la philosophie de l'histoire ou de l'influence des névropathies sur le dynamisme intellectual* (Paris: Masson, 1859).

John Clare, who wrote nonsense as soon as he began to express himself in prose, in some of his tender and melancholy elegies rose to a rare perfection of style and the choicest ideas.

Leuret says, in speaking of mania,

> It has happened to me more than once to form too favourable an idea of the intellectual capacity of some persons, when I could only judge of it by what they said or did during an attack of mania. A patient whose conversation and flashes of wit had struck me, sometimes turned out, after his recovery, to be a very ordinary man, far inferior to the opinion I had conceived of him.[5]

Marcé has recorded the case of a young married woman of cultivated mind, but merely ordinary intelligence, who, during the course of an attack of mania, in which ideas of jealousy predominated,

> wrote to her husband letters which, for their eloquence and the passionate energy of their style, might easily be placed beside the most fervent passages of the *Nouvelle Héloise*. When the attack was over her letters became simple and modest, and no one, on comparing them with the others, would have believed that the two sets came from the same pen.[6]

---

5 François Leuret, *Fragments psychologiques sur la folie* (Paris: Crochard, 1834).

6 *Annales médico-psychologiques* (1864) 3:93.

Excessive activity of the intellect, writes Dagonet, is also sometimes observed in the depressive forms of mental aberration, but much less frequently than in the expansive forms. As a proof of this, it is sufficient to cite the following letter, written by a patient affected with melancholic delusion, to her husband, a country schoolmaster. The letter was full of mistakes in spelling; the woman who wrote it had no education, and in her normal condition, no eloquence; but disease had transformed her by developing her intellectual faculties:—

> Why did not the Master of the universe open the tomb to me in my brilliant youth? Why, at the same time, did He not remove me from you, since you do not love me, and I am making you unhappy?
>
> Why did I become a mother? To be unhappy—more than unhappy—to leave the children who are so dear to me. . . . Why do you hate me? Though I stood with my feet in boiling oil, I should still say, I love you! . . .
>
> Why did you not let me die? You would be happy,—and I—my troubles would be over. . . . My dear children would come and play by my grave. I should still be near them—I should still, in the darkness of the grave, hear them say, 'There is our mother!'[7]

---

7 *Annales médico-psychologiques* (1850) 48; Jean-Baptiste-Maximien Parchappe, "Symptomatologie de la folie", *Annales médico-psychologiques* (1851) 1:1-54.

If this woman had fed her mind on the works of Chateaubriand she could not have expressed herself with more poetry or imagination.

"It has been known," says Tissot,

> that a young man, whose tutor had never been able to teach him anything, and who, as the saying is, could not put a noun and an adjective together, spoke Latin fluently, after some days of malignant fever, and developed ideas which till then had not struck him.[8]

Among other examples of what Le Camus[9] calls learned frenzies, he cites Mademoiselle Antheman who, during her delirium, was of

> smiling countenance and agreeable humour. Having lost the use of her right hand through paralysis, she painted and embroidered with her left, with incredible dexterity; and the productions of her mind were no less surprising than those of her hands. She recited verses which showed the greatest possible vivacity and delicacy, though they were the first she had ever composed.[10]

---

8 André David Tissot, *Des nerfs et de leurs maladies* (Paris: Théophil Barrois, 1779) 316. [The original footnote gives page 133, but the edition was not specified; I was able to find the quoted passage in the one above. —Ed.]

9 Changed Lecamus to Le Camus, based on the footnote that follows. —Ed.

10 Antoine Le Camus, *La Médecine de l'esprit. Où l'on cherche: 1° le méchanisme du corps qui influe sur les fonctions de l'âme; 2° les causes physiques qui rendent ce mécanisme ou*

"I am going to try," says Gerard de Nerval, in his book entitled *Le rêvé et la vie*,

> to transcribe the impressions of a long illness which ran its course entirely in the mysteries of my mind. I do not know why I make use of the term illness, for never—as far as I am concerned—did I feel better. Sometimes I thought my strength and activity were doubled; it seemed that I knew and understood everything; imagination gave me infinite delight. In recovering what men called reason, shall I have to regret the loss of this?

What mental practitioner has not heard similar words over and over again from the mouth of unhappy patients who, after recovering their reason, regretted their past state, that new life, that *vita nuova*, which Gerard defines as "*L'epanchement du songe dans la vie réelle!*"

Increase of intellectual activity, says Dr. Parchappe, is frequently met with in insanity; it is even one of the most salient characteristics of this disease in its acute period. The annals of science—adds the same author—contain a certain number of well-authenticated facts, which have contributed to confirm the superstition of a, supernatural heightening of the intellectual faculties, and which explain, up to a certain point, how the love of the

défectueux ou plus parfait; 3° les moyens qui peuvent l'entretenir dans son état libre, ou le rectifier lorsqu'il est gêné (Paris: Ganeau, 1753; 2d ed. 1769) 2:32. [The original footnote does not specify the edition. —Ed.]

marvellous, in credulous observers, by exaggerating and distorting analogous facts, has been able to gain credit for the wonderful tales which abound in the history of religious sects at all epochs, and more especially in the history of diabolical possessions in the Middle Ages.[11]

Van Swieten (Comment., 1121) relates that he had seen a woman who, during her attacks of mania, only spoke in verse, which she composed with admirable facility, although in health she had never shown the least poetic talent.

Lorry cites the case of a lady of rank, of very ordinary intellect, who was subject to attacks of melancholy, during which her intelligence was so far developed as to enable her to discuss the most difficult questions with eloquence.

A young girl of the people, aged fourteen, attacked with insanity in consequence of a religious revival, talked on theological subjects as if she had devoted herself to this study; she spoke like a preacher, of God and of Christian duties, and gave sagacious answers to the objections which were made.[12]

"I have had occasion," writes Morel,[13]

> to remark, in some hypochondriac, hysteric, and epileptic patients, an extraordinary intel-

---

11 *Symptomatalogie de la folie.*

12 J. Frank, *Traité de pathologie interne*, 3 vols. (Brussels: société encyclographique, 1837-1842); Manie fantastique.

13 B. A. Morel, *Traité des maladies mentales* (Paris: Victor Masson, 1858).

lectual activity at the critical periods of the disease. It is not rarely observed that the attacks of exacerbation to which they are subject are preceded by an abnormal manifestation of the intellectual forces. A young hypochondriacal patient, confided to my care, often astonished those who saw him by the facility of his elocution, and the brilliancy with which he expressed his ideas. At certain times he would compose, in the course of a single night, a piece of music or a play which possessed remarkable traits, and some beauties of the first order. But, knowing the patient, I was never mistaken in my prognostications from this state of things. I knew that, after three or four days of excitement, this young man would fall into a dull stupor and become a prey to a torpid apathy which prevented him from feeling the instinct of his greatest natural necessities. The case ended in complete dementia.

In the case of a hysterical patient, with a predominance of exalted religious ideas, I have also observed remarkable phenomena of intellectual reminiscence. She had heard a great number of sermons, and read still more. I have heard her repeat word for word what she had read or what had been delivered in her presence. We were able to follow her, book in hand, when, under the influence of a nervous excitement which quickened her memory, she recited sermons by well-known Christian orators. She was quite unable to repeat this phenomenon in her ordinary condition; but, as in the preceding case, we knew what view to take of a fact of this nature—not to mention that it resembled a large number of other cases, by means of which, at different times, the public credulity has been exploited. In this woman the phenomenon always preceded a crisis of exacerbation followed by stupor.

Let us now pass to the extreme concentration of the attention in a hypochondriacal patient relating her own sensations. The following extracts are from a diary left to me by the patient in question. It summarizes all that is experienced by this class of patients.

September 6, 1852, 9 p.m. This evening, on going to bed, sharp pain in the sacral regions and in the thighs. Tearing pains in the left ear and eye while falling asleep. I was overpowered by the feeling of fear. I seemed to be rolling into bottomless abysses, and to have, as it were, an iron hook fixed in my skull and heart, and dragging them out.

September 7, 1852, 7 a.m. Lancinating pain in the eyes, acute suffering in the eyelids. Pressure on the temples, principally on the left, eyes constantly watering, larynx contracted; a horrible, never-ceasing devouring hunger, which seems to make me start. I am seized by an anger which makes me seem mad in the eyes of others. If I could still cry out, that would relieve me; I am boiling over with anger, and I look wild. It is as though I had a little saw inside my head. Always this motion of sawing—of a wheel which keeps turning and carries me with it. My bones feel to me like dead wood which burns like logwood.

September 8, 1852. The whole day without having been able to do anything. My forehead seemed encircled with a tight iron band. I went to bed with a feeling of deep depression. Fear

> overpowers me sometimes a feeling of hatred—a very little excusable jealousy of those who can act freely and work. I have in my back something like little strings pulling in all directions, making music like an accordion. It is torturing. The strop man would fall dead with terror, if he could see the reality of a person in my state of health. . . . And they laugh at me. . . . The doctors refuse to believe in my sufferings.
>
> There are moments when all that I have ever seen in my life is before my eyes at once. I feel myself lifted into the air or up to the roofs; I feel a horror of myself. It is like an old painting by Rembrandt etched in *aqua fortis*.
>
> *Dreams.*—Dead horses, headless, dismembered—horrors of all kinds. . . . Then there are members of my family who appear to me; but everything I see is distorted and reduced in size; there is, as it were, a *camera obscura* in me, and the reflector shows me everything in miniature. I admit that I may be insane—but you, too, must admit at least that I am very ill," &c.

It is known, says Paulhan,[14] that with some dementia patients, certain faculties remain intact; they can, for instance, play at cards or draughts, though their mind in general may be quite disorganized. The same is found to be the case with idiots. Griesinger saw, in the Earlswood Asylum, a young man who had made, all by himself, a remarkable model of a man-of-war. This individual's intelligence was very limited; he had no idea whatever of numbers. "It more frequently happens,"

14 *Revue Philosophique* 26 (1888).

adds the author, "that complete idiots execute fairly good work in drawing or painting. In such cases, it is, of course, only a mechanical talent."

Esquirol reports the case of a general suffering from mania, whose

> delusions persist throughout the summer, with some lucid intervals, during which the patient writes comedies and vaudevilles which betray the incoherence of his ideas. . . . In spite of the confusion of his mind, the general conceives an idea for the perfecting of a certain weapon, draws designs, and manifests the desire of getting a model constructed.

One day, he went to the foundry, and, on his return, was seized with agitation and delirium. A while later, he paid a second visit to the foundry, and

> the model having been executed, gave an order for fifty thousand. This order was the only act which gave the founder reason to suspect the general's malady. His invention was afterwards officially adopted.

Thus, in the midst of general incoherence, an important series of ideas was maintained and carried out to the end.

A writer not practised in mental disease, Esquiros, whom we have already had occasion to quote, mentions the following facts, which are very significant:—

"Dr. Leuret," he says,

related to us the history of a patient in the Bicètre who, during his malady, had shown a remarkable talent for writing, though when in good health he would have been quite incapable of doing as much. 'I am not quite cured,' he said to the physician, who thought him convalescent. 'I am still too clever for that. When I am well, I take a week to write a letter. In my natural condition I am stupid; wait till I become so again.'

The same observer also cites the case of a merchant whose affairs were in danger. During his illness, this man found means to re-establish them; the result of each of his attacks was the perfecting of some mechanism, or the invention of some means for facilitating his industry; and at the end of this invaluable insanity, he was found to have recovered both his reason and his fortune.

We have been shown at Montmartre, in Dr. Blanche's establishment, traces of charcoal-drawings on a wall. These half-effaced figures, one of which represented the Queen of Sheba, and the other some king, were the work of a distinguished young author, who has since recovered his reason. This illness had developed a new talent, which was non-existent, or at least played a most insignificant part, while he was in health.

It is said that Marion Delorme met, in a madhouse, with the first man who conceived the idea of applying the forces of steam to the needs of industry, Salomon de Caus. Talents created

> by disease forsake the individual, for the most part, at the same time as the disease itself.[15]

I had under treatment at Pavia, a peasant lad, aged twelve, who composed extremely original musical melodies, and bestowed on his companions in misfortune nicknames which fitted so well that they always kept them. With him was a little old man afflicted with rickets and *pellagra* who, when asked whether he was happy, replied, like a philosopher of ancient Greece, "All *men* are happy, even the rich, if they are only willing."

Many of my pupils still remember B——, by turns musician, servant, porter, keeper of a cookshop, tinman, soldier, public letter-writer, but always unfortunate. He left us an autobiography, which, apart from a few orthographical mistakes in spelling, would be quite worth printing; and he asked me for his discharge in terms which, for an uneducated working man, were wanting neither in beauty nor in originality.

Not long ago I heard a poor hawker of sponges, when insane, thus conjecture and sum up the cardinal idea of the circulation of life:

---

15 *Paris au dix-neuvième siècle—Les maisons de fous*, tome II, p. 163. [This footnote seems to mix two works by Alphonse Esquiros. "Les maisons de fous" appeared in the November 1843 issue of La Revue de Paris, pp. 5-24, 102-128, 243-265; the other work seems to be *Paris: ou Les sciences, les institutions, et les mœurs au XIXe siècle* (Paris: Comon et cie., 1847). — Ed.]

> We do not die. When the soul is worn out it melts, and is turned into another shape. In fact, when my father had buried a dead mule, we afterwards saw mushrooms growing in great numbers on the same spot, and the potatoes in the same place, which were formerly very small, grew to twice their usual size.

Thus a vulgar mind, enlightened by the energy of mania, stumbles on theories which the greatest thinkers arrive at with difficulty.

G. B., a maniac, nephew of a celebrated author, said to me one day, when I hesitated before permitting him to ride a somewhat skittish horse, "No fear, doctor—*similia similibus.*"[16]

M. G., a merchant, suffering from melancholia, said to some one who had called him "Count" by mistake, "What count? I have kept plenty of *accounts*—I know no others!"

"Why will you not shake hands with me?" I asked Madame M——, a sufferer from moral insanity, one morning, "Are you angry with me?" "*Pallida virgo cupit, rubiconda recusat*"[17] she replied. Another time I asked her, "Do you hope to leave this establishment soon?" She answered, "I shall leave it when those outside have recovered their reason."

V——, a thief, and insane, made his escape during a walk which had been permitted him. When overtaken and reproached with having betrayed

16 Latin: 'Likes are cured by likes'. —Ed.

17 Latin: The pale virgin desires, the red blush refuses. —Ed.

the confidence reposed in him, he replied, "I only wanted to try whether my knees were stiff or not."

B. B., a maniac woman, over seventy years of age, who had lost all her teeth, made obscene remarks. When remonstrated with for using expressions so unbecoming to her age, she said, "Old! old! Why, do you not see that I have not yet cut my teeth?"

N. B., who became a poet through insanity, writes with much subtlety, but his verses do not scan. His companion, G. R., once told us that he lengthened the feet on purpose, so that, being well *planted*, they should not be able to escape his memory.[18]

Synthesis.—The most original and general characteristic of the poets who are the product of insanity is precisely the forcing of the mind to a state so at variance with previous conditions of life and culture. In many, it is true, the only result of this effect is a continuous flow of epigrams, plays upon words, and assonances—puns, in short, such as are praised in society as evidences of wit; though it is no wonder that they should abound in lunatic asylums, being, as they are, the very negative of truth and logic. This tendency, or, at least, the tendency to alliteration and rhyme, is evident in all their works, even those written in prose. Yet, on the

18 See Appendix. I regret that in the English edition of my work it has not been found possible to give a more copious selection from the poems by the insane which I have at my disposal. I must refer the reader to the original Italian or to the French.

other hand, we not rarely meet with improvised philosophers, who in their utterances reproduce parts of the systems of the Positivists, of Epicurus and Comte; the brain, quickened by insanity, being able to seize upon those salient points of truth from which the systems named took their rise, and that because these men have less hatred of novelty, and more originality, than normal people.

Their most salient characteristic—originality heightened to the point of absurdity—is due to the overflowing of the imagination which can no longer be restrained within the bounds of logic and common sense. It is natural that the mind which has been most injured, or is by nature the most deficient, should exceed most in this respect. We need only refer now to the pretended metamorphosis and journeyings of the soul of P—— of Siena, and the writings of M—— of Pesaro, who had carried his passion for the Greek language so far as to invent a new idiom, in which gravel was called *lithiasis*, the sea, *equor*, convictions, *agonies*, the world, *a vase*.[19]

Their more rapid association of ideas, and livelier imagination, often enable them to solve problems which more cultivated, but normal, intellects can scarcely attack with success.

Another peculiarity characteristic of them, but which, be it noted, is often found also in the writings of criminals, is the tendency to speak of themselves or their companions, and to write autobiog-

19 See my *L'Uomo Delinquente.*

raphies, abandoning themselves without restraint to the torrent of ambition or love. But with insane persons the form of expression is much less artificial than that used by criminals, in whose writings one finds more coherence but less creative power and originality.

The use of assonances in place of reasoning is entirely peculiar to the insane, as also the use of special words, or words used in a peculiar sense, and the exaggerated importance attributed to the most trifling things.

> *C'est le travail des fous d'épuiser leurs cervelles*
> *Sur des riens fatigants, sur quelques bagatelles,*

said Hécart in his *Gualana*, which, by the way, is only the work of a mattoid.

Many of them, though fewer than among the mattoids, mingle drawing with poetry, as though neither art by itself were sufficient for the impetus of their ideas. Their style lacks the polish which comes of much elaboration, but abounds in incisive and vigorous sentences, so that it often equals, and even surpasses, the productions of calmer and more refined art.

Passion.—This should not cause surprise any more than the tendency to versification in individuals who, before losing their reason, were ignorant of prosody, when it is remembered that poetry—as Byron well said and demonstrated in his own person—is the expression of passion under excitement, and grows in vigour and effectiveness as the excitement increases.

That rhythm can relieve and express abnormal psychic excitement much better than prose can be deduced from the poetic inspirations of drunkards, as well as from the spontaneous affirmations of insane poets.

Je vous-écris en vers, n'en soyez point choqué,
En prose je ne sais exprimer ma pensée,

an insane criminal wrote to Arboux, clearly explaining this tendency.[20]

A lunatic at Pesaro gave this reason for some of his verses: "Poetry is a spontaneous emanation from the mind—poetry is the cry of the soul pierced by a thousand griefs."[21]

Atavism.—Vico had already guessed, and Buckle, at a later date, has admirably explained that, among primitive peoples, all thinkers and sages were poets. In fact, the earliest histories were put into a fixed form and handed down by the bards of Gaul, or by the Toolkolos of Tibet; likewise in

20 Jules Arboux, *Les prisons de Paris* (Paris: Imprimerie et Librairie Centrales des Chemins de Fer A. Chaix et Cie., 1881).

21 *Diario del Manicomio di Pesaro* (1879). [The full name of the institution was Manicomio Provinciale San Benedetto di Pesaro. —Ed.]

America,[22] the Deccan,[23] Africa,[24] and Oceania.[25] Ellis writes that the Polynesians have recourse to their ballads as to historical documents when any question arises regarding the deeds of their ancestors. And as in ancient India, so also in mediæval Europe, the sciences were explained in verse. Montucla speaks of a mathematical treatise of the thirteenth century written in verse; an Englishman versified the Institutes of Justinian, and a Pole wrote a rhyming work on heraldry.

History, properly so called, though written in prose was in the Middle Ages no less fabulous and full of fantastic absurdities and puns than poetry. Troyes was derived from Troy, Nuremberg from Nero, the Saracens from Sara; Mahomet was a cardinal; Naples was built on a foundation of eggs; after certain victories of the Turks there were children born with 22 or 23 instead of 32 teeth. Turpin, the Macaulay of those times, relates in his chronicle that the walls of Pampeluna fell as soon as the followers of Charlemagne had begun to pray. Ferrante was 20 cubits in height, and had a

22 William H. Prescott, *History of the Conquest of Peru*, 2 vols. (Paris: Baudry's European Library, 1847) vol. 1.

23 Mark Wilks, *Historical Sketch of the South of India in an Attempt to Trace the History of Mysore*, 2 vols. (London: Longman, Hurst, Rees, Orme, and Brown, 1810-1817).

24 Mungo Park, *Travels of the Interior Disctricts of Africa*, 2 vols. (London: John Murray, 1816) vol. 1.

25 William Ellis, *Polynesian Researches during a residence of nearly six years in the Society and Sandwich Islands*, 4 vols. (London: Fisher, Son, & Jackson, 1834) 4:462.

face a cubit in length. In short, the history of those days was the same as the fairy tales still told at rustic firesides, from which we can gather nothing but the uniform quality of human imbecility which becomes more fantastic the more ignorant it is.

A tendency to revert to ancestral conditions appears even in the prose of the mattoid or insane. Thus Tanzi and Riva,[26] speaking of some works by monomaniacs write as follows:—

> For the demonomaniacs of a hundred years ago —belated representatives of mediæval mysticism, who typify the ancient form of *paranoia*—are now substituted the modern paranoiacs; new alchemists who, with their pseudo-scientific delusions, and their vainglorious phrases, revive in our day the style and thoughts of Trithemius, Agrippa, Paracelsus, and other men of the sixteenth century who were strange, but learned and venerated students of occult science and magic. Paranoia follows the path of humanity through the centuries, undergoing, with a certain delay, all its changes, though often separated from it only by a slight interval. As an example of this latter kind we may take the following passage from an extremely long autobiography, written by a paranoiac, in which the acute and accurate account of his own adventures is found in company with insane statements like the following:—
>
>> It ought to be known that the aristocracy, or persons descended from them, secrete a certain, as yet

26 Eugenio Tanzi and Gaetano Riva, *La Paranoia* (Reggio Emilia: S. Calderini e figlio, 1886).

> undefined, substance which produces electricity. In this way it is easy to understand how there can be communication between one nobly-born person and another if one thinks for a moment of the telegraph and its electric batteries. In this manner two nobles, being placed in communication, act upon each other as electric batteries, transmitting every movement and thought by means of a thread, as if the idea and way of thinking were so many strokes on the part of the manipulator of the telegraphic instrument. The system, as may be understood, is infinitesimal, for thought, transmitted from one side, forms on the other as many infinitesimal points as there are atoms forming the idea.

MM. Riva and Tanzi observe that many of the ancient alchemists expressed themselves in precisely the same way.

"So," they continue,

> nothing could be easier than to recognize a born paranoiac in the King of Bavaria,[27] misanthropic, vain, ambitious, mystical, romantic, voluble, subject to hallucinations, eccentric in his acts, his habits, his judgment and his conduct, perverted in his æsthetic tastes, in love, in the ethical sentiments, exaggerated and unbalanced in everything. He was so profoundly impressed with the stamp of mediæval atavism that political journalism—hitting the mark with unconsciously scientific correctness designated—him as a Sir Percival come to life again.

The pathologic and atavistic origin of many of the literary productions of the insane explains the frequent inequalities of the style, which is as fee-

27 Ludwig II. —Ed.

ble and slovenly when the excitement ceases, as it was at first splendid and vigorous, and the abrupt transition from stanzas worthy of a classic author to the scribbling of an idiot. This origin also accounts for the extreme contradictions to be found in the writings of one and the same author as is seen in Farina and Lazzaretti —their fondness for aphorisms and detached periods, the abrupt and disconnected character of their style which is both primitive and childish—and the monotonous repetition of certain words or phrases, recalling the verses of the Bible or the suras of the Koran. It also explains their propensity for continually dwelling on the same subject, nearly always connected with matters out of the line of their own studies, and (what is more important) of no advantage to themselves or others. Their works are nearly always autobiographical.

Conclusion.—Summing up what has been said, there is a special organization in all the writings of madmen, even the absurdist—a true finality, as Paulhan calls it.

"I understand by this," he says,

> that, as soon as one psychic element exists, it tends to call forth others. It is not the totality of the mind—if it is not itself co-ordinated—which determines the appearance of phenomena, but the elements. That is to say, what is already systematized in the mind tends to acquire a more complete systematization. If it is a sensation, it will tend to awaken particular, precise, and ap-

propriate ideas or acts; if it is a general tendency—a pre-established mental organization—it will tend to make the mind interpret in such or such a manner the sensations which reach it.

As every psychic element is systematic, and as, when finality is not to be found in the totality of a psychic organism, or of a series of actions, or a theory, or an argument, or a passion (and in this case all these facts are not really psychic elements), it exists in the elements. This tendency on the part of the elements to systematic association, exercising itself without higher control, without general direction, ends in producing numerous discords in the totality of psychic operations. The result is somewhat as though all the musicians in an orchestra were to play different tunes in as many different keys.

When, in the constitution of society, an association is dissolved, a law of finality is broken and the elements (the human beings who formed the association) are restored to individual life. They then enter upon new forms of social activity. If, for example, a factory is closed, the men and women who worked there and were united by a systematic association, go to work again, each on his or her own account, either separately, or in new associations, in which some of them may chance to meet again. The same thing takes place with the psychic elements, wherever, from one cause or another, the bond which united them is broken; they enter into new associations where they work, each on its own account, at the risk of producing nothing but incoherence. This isolated activity of the elements is met with in a striking manner in mental disease.

The pun is a form of this disorder. On analyzing it, we find that it consists essentially in this: A sound employed in a particular complexus (consisting of the sound, the ideas, and the systematized images constituting the signification of the sound), itself forming part of a more complex system, separates itself at least partially from these two systems, and becomes associated with other systems of ideas and images. The association through a resemblance between certain parts of the words—for example, by means of rhyme—is an essentially analogous fact. Here it is a sound which, systematically associated with other sounds, allies itself at the same time with different sounds, in order to form simultaneously, or at short intervals, systems which do not harmonise together. Among the latter class may be reckoned the greater number of lapsus linguce and *lapsus calami*.

Examples of this abound. M. Regnard has cited several pieces of verse written by madmen, which show in a high degree the mode of elementary systematic association. Sometimes one observes a remnant of intellectual co-ordination, as in the following lines, in which, however, incoherence is also abundantly manifested:—

J'aime le feu de la fougère
Ne durant pas, mais pétillant;
La fumée est âcre de goût.
Mais, des cendres de: là Fou j'erre
On peut tirer en s'amusant
Deux sous d'un sel qui lave tout,
De soude, un sel qui lave tout.[28]

28 Paul Regnard, *Les maladies épidémiques de l'esprit: sorcellerie, magnétisme, morphinisme, délire des grandeurs*

At other times sense disappears altogether, as in these lines, also quoted by M. Regnard, and composed by a patient whose mania was that of self-conceit, and who had been insane for twenty-five years:—

Magnan! à mon souhait, médecin Magnanime,
Adore de mon sort la force qui . . . t'anime.

. . .
. . .

Admirant son beau crâne . . . autre remord de Phèdre,
Nargue Legrand du Saulle et sois un Grand du Cèdre.[29]

A good example of this phenomenon is afforded by the patient, observed by Trousseau, who wrote down more than five hundred pages of words connected with one another by assonance or sense: *Chat, chapeau, peau, mauchon, main, manches, robe, rose, jupon, pompon, bouquet, bouquetière, cimetière, bièire, &c.*[30]

One need not be either insane or imbecile to make puns and associate words together on account of superficial resemblances. In this case, instead of being a permanent dissociation of the more complex systems, it is a momentary dissociation which gives rise to the phenomenon. Nothing is more natural—when one feels the

(Paris: E. Plon, 1887) 370.

29 *Ibid.*, 390.

30 Quoted by Jules-Bernard Luys, *Études de physiologie et de pathologie cérébrales. De actions réflexes du cerveau dans les conditions normales et morbides de leurs manifestations* (Paris: J.-B. Ballière et fils, 1874) 170.

> need of unbending one's mind—than to restore to themselves the psychic elements retained in complex systems not necessary to life, and to allow them a liberty which they sometimes abuse. To continue the above comparison—which may be carried a long way—the workmen in the factory are not always at work; they have their moments of rest and recreation, and then usually occupy themselves with less complex systems.[31]

Those most prone to these rhythmic manifestations are, in my opinion (which is borne out by Adriani and Toselli), chronic maniacs, alcoholic maniacs, and paralytics in the early stage—in whom, however, there is apt to be more rhyme than verse, and more verse than sense. Melancholy patients would take the next place, owing to the small number of these found in asylums; they seem to find in versification a relief from their habitual silence, or a defence against imaginary persecutions. This is a much more important fact than would appear at first sight, when connected with another, already well known, *viz.*, that all great thinkers and poets are constitutionally inclined to melancholy.

31 *Revue Philosophique* 8 (1888)

CHAPTER II

Art in the Insane

Geographical distribution — Profession —
Influence of the special form of alienation — Originality —
Eccentricity — Symbolism — Obscenity — Criminality
and moral insanity — Uselessness — Insanity as a subject —
Absurdity — Uniformity — Summary —
Music among the insane

Though the artistic tendency is very pronounced, and might almost be called a general characteristic, in some varieties of insanity, few authors have paid sufficient attention to it.

The only exceptions are Tardieu, who, in his *Études médico-légales sur la folie*, remarks that the drawings of the insane are of great importance from the point of view of forensic medicine; Simon,[1] who, in speaking of drawing among megalomaniacs, observes that the imagination appears

1 Max Simon, "L'imagination dans la follie: étude sur les dessins, plans, descriptions et costumes des aliénés", *Annales Medico-Psychologiques* 16 (1876) 358-390.

in them in inverse proportion to the intellect; and Frigerio, who some time later gave a survey of the subject in an excellent essay, published in the *Diario del Manicomio di Pesaro*.[2] Since then I have been able to make a completer examination of this subject, thanks to the curious documents supplied to me by MM. Riva, Toselli, Lolli, Frigerio, Tamburini, Maragliano, and Maxime du Camp.

By comparing their observations with my own, I find a total of 108 mental patients with artistic tendencies, of which:—46 were towards painting, 10 sculpture, 11 engraving, 8 music, 5 architecture, 28 poetry.

The prevailing psychopathic forms in these 108 cases, were:—In 25, sensorial monomania and that of persecution; 21 dementia, 16 megalomania, 14 acute or intermittent mania, 8 melancholia, 8 general paralysis, 5 moral insanity, 2 epilepsy.

It is evident that those which predominate are the congenital and least readily curable forms (monomania and moral insanity), together with dementia, and those forms which it accompanies, or in which it is latent (megalomania and paralysis).

Let us now consider the special characteristics of these insane artists.

Geographical distribution.—In the districts where the artistic tendency is more marked among

2 Regnard has also touched upon the subject, but without going into it deeply, in his *Les maladies épidémiques de l'esprit: sorcellerie, magnétisme, morphinisme, délire des grandeurs* (Paris: E. Plon, 1887).

the sane, the number of insane artists is also higher. In fact, I have found very few of the latter at Turin, Pavia, or Reggio, while at Perugia, Lucca, and Siena they abound.

Profession.—Only in a few cases could the tendency be explained by profession or habits acquired before the appearance of the disease. We find among the insane artists mentioned above—8 expainters or sculptors, 10 exarchitects, carpenters, or cabinet makers; 10 former schoolmasters or priests, 1 telegraphist, 2 students, 6 sailors, soldiers, or officers of engineers.

Among modern painters affected with insanity, we may note Gill, Cham, Chirico, Mancini, and others.

In some cases, former tendencies were accentuated by insanity. Thus, a mechanician made drawings of machines, two sailors constructed models of ships, a major-domo traced, on the floor, pictures of tables prepared for a banquet, with pyramids of fruit. At Reggio, a cabinet-maker carved some very fine foliage and ornaments; a naval officer at Genoa at first carved models of ships, and afterwards was continually occupied in depicting—though he had never learnt to paint—scenes at sea which, he said, consoled him for being debarred from his favourite element.

Sometimes these men were inspired by insanity with a strange energy in their work, "just as if," as MM. de Paoli and Adriani wrote to me, "they had been paid for it. They cover the walls, the tables, and even the floor, with painting." One of them, a painter, who had formerly only reached mediocrity, attained such perfection through his malady, that a copy of one of Raphael's Madonnas, executed by him during one of his attacks, gained a prize medal at the Exhibition.

Mignoni, the celebrated painter of Reggio, who became an inmate of the asylum at that town on account of dementia and megalomania, remained idle there for fourteen years. At last, at the suggestion of Dr. Zani, he resumed his brush, and covered the walls of the asylum with excellent frescoes. One of them represented the story of Count Ugolino so vividly, that one of the patients began to throw meat at it, so that the father and children might not die of hunger, and the grease spots are still to be seen.[3]

Of eight painters, whose history Adriani has related to me, four kept their former skill while under the influence of acute or intermittent mania; in two others, it was so far weakened that one of them, after his recovery, sincerely deplored the work done during his illness.

Influence of the special form of Insanity.—In many cases, the choice of subject is inspired by the malady. A melancholiac was continually carving a figure of a man with a skull in his hand. A woman affected with megalomania was always working the word DIO (God) into her embroidery. Most monomaniacs habitually allude to their imaginary misfortunes by means of special emblems.

3 *Gazzetta del Manicomio di Reggio* (1867).

A monomaniac, who laboured under the delusion that he was being persecuted, drew his enemies pursuing him on one side of the picture and Justice defending him on the other.

Alcoholic maniacs often make an excessive use of yellow in their pictures. One painter, in whom alcohol had completely destroyed the sense of colour, became very skilful in the rendering of white, and, between his drunken fits, became the best painter of snow-scenes in France.

An artist of note, C——, when affected with general paralysis, lost his sense of proportion, *e.g.*, he began to sketch a tree which, if drawn in its entirety, would have reached beyond the frame of the picture. He collected the poorest oleographs and admired them, and coloured everything green.

It is more usual, however, for insanity to transform into painters persons who have never been accustomed to handle a brush, than for it to improve skilled artists. Sometimes the disease, while suppressing some qualities of value to art, causes the appearance of others which did not previously exist, and gives to all a peculiar character.

Insanity changed Luke Clennell from a painter to a poet,[4] while Melmour, a physician who fell into a state of dementia after the loss of his wife, who died on their wedding-day, took to literature and lost his previous aptitudes.

"Exaggeration pushed to its extreme—to the im-

4 Octave Delepierre, *Histoire littéraire des fous* (London: Trübner & Co., 1860).

probable, or even the impossible," says Regnard, "is one characteristic of paralytics. One of these madmen painted a man touching the stars with his head and the earth with his feet."[5]

Daudet, in *Jack*, speaks of insane artists whose pictures seemed to represent earthquakes or the inside of a ship during a storm.

Individuals, who previously had not the remotest idea of art, are impelled by disease to paint, especially at the periods of strongest excitement. B——, a mason, became a painter while in the Pesaro asylum. His attacks of mania were always announced by an outbreak of his tendency to draw caricatures of the hospital staff, whom he condemned, in effigy, to the strangest punishments. For instance, he painted the cook, a stout and ruddy man, in the attitude of an *Ecce Homo*, behind a grating which prevented him from touching the most appetising viands. This was the penalty for having refused B—— one of his favourite dishes.

The grotesque apotheosis of himself, painted by the pederast and megalomaniac, R——, in which he excretes and fecundates eggs which symbolise worlds, is characteristic of the boundless vanity and unbridled imagination of megalomaniacs and paralytics.

5 Regnard, *op. cit.*

Among the pictures executed by the patients at San Servolo, the most curious is one by a lunatic who, in his lucid intervals, paints fairly well, though with excessive minuteness of detail; but during his attacks this minuteness is so far exaggerated as to become grotesque.

Nothing but an intense religious monomania could have inspired the singular self-crucifixion of the Venetian shoe-maker, Matteo Lovat. I have been able to procure an authentic picture of this strange performance which is reproduced below.

Shortly afterwards Lovat died in an asylum.[6]

One patient, G——, was a poor peasant woman, utterly uneducated, in whose family *pellagra* and insanity were both hereditary. In the long isolation required by her state, she developed great skill (quite unknown before her illness) in embroidering on linen, with coloured threads pulled from her clothing, an extraordinary number of figures, which were faithful representations of her delusions. Her autobiography is, so to speak, traced in this embroidery; in every piece of work she has represented herself, sometimes struggling with the nurses or the nuns, sometimes herding cows, or occupied with other rustic work. Elsewhere she would depict tables spread for meals, with an infinite variety of accessories. But the most singular thing is that the outlines are drawn with a clearness which would be the envy of a professional caricaturist; no shading whatever, four stitches, representing nose, eyes, and mouth, were arranged with so much artistic judgment as to show clearly the individual expression of each face.

Another artist in the same line, though of less striking gifts, is a certain I——, suffering from moral insanity, who shows numerous degenerative symptoms. She, too, embroiders figures of men and women with considerable skill, but always in harmony with her perverted sexual tendencies.[7]

---

6 Cesar Ruggieri, *Histoire du crucifiement opéré sur sa propre personne par Mathieu Lovat* (Venice: 1806).

7 Luigi Frigerio, Letter of November 2, 1887.

Originality.—Disease often develops (as we have already seen in the case of insane authors) an originality of invention which may also be observed in mattoids, because their imagination, freed from all restraint, allows of creations from which a more calculating mind would shrink, for fear of absurdity, and because intensity of conviction supports and perfects the work.

At Pesaro there was a woman who drew, or embroidered, by a method peculiar to herself, unravelling cloth, and fastening the threads on paper by means of saliva.

Another embroideress, formerly given to drink, executed butterflies which seemed to be alive. She had applied to white embroidery the methods of coloured work, and was able to produce marvellous effects of light and shade.

At Macerata a patient, with a number of pipe-stems, constructed a model of the front of the asylum; another had the idea of representing a song in sculpture. At Genoa, a dementia patient carved pipes out of coal.

One Zanini, at Reggio, constructed a boot which was unique of its kind, so that, as he said, no one else should be able to put it on. This exceptional foot-gear was open on one side, and tied up with string, its edges were ornamental, and worked with hieroglyphics.

M. L—— of Pesaro was constantly making requests to leave the asylum. When told that there was no means of transporting him to his home, he set about constructing one for himself. This was a four-wheeled cart, with an upright pole, at the top of which was a pulley with a rope running through it. One end of the rope was fastened to the axle of the fore-wheels, the other to that of the hind-wheels. An elastic cord was attached to the rope for a distance of four or five centimetres, and by pulling this, first at one end and then at the other, a person standing on the cart was able to make the wheels go round.[8]

In many arabesques drawn by a megalomaniac, one can trace, carefully hidden among the curves, sometimes a ship, sometimes an animal, a human head, or a railway train, or even landscapes and towns; though the essential character of arabesques is the absence of the human figure.

The best asylums of Italy have sent to the exhibitions of Siena and Voghera, models in relief of their respective buildings, admirably executed by some of the patients. That of the asylum at Reggio could be taken to pieces, and showed the inside arrangements, staircases, rooms, with their furniture, &c., all carefully finished. Even the trees, I am told, were copied accurately from nature.

A canon, who had no technical knowledge of architecture, began, after an attack of melancholia, to construct with cardboard and papier-maché, models of temples and amphitheatres, which excited great admiration.

Dr. Virgilio has made me a present of some portraits of Italian specialists, nearly all of them

8 *Diario del Manicomio di Pesaro* (1879).

exceedingly lifelike, the work of a melancholia patient. The note of originality only comes out in some accessory introduced into each picture, such as a fly, or a butterfly, repeated persistently in every copy, or in the way in which the artist's name is worked into the painting, in vertical lines so as to form some sort of decorative ornament.

A work of extreme though useless skill and originality is the self-crucifixion of Lovat, already mentioned.

> The monomaniac, King Louis of Bavaria, was the first who entirely understood Wagner. His prodigality in spending money, and the creation of the theatre at Bayreuth one of his most original conceptions have been known for years, but the greatest manifestation of his genius is known only to a few. Three castles, three palaces of splendid and indescribable beauty, rose from the earth, as if by enchantment. He superintended even the minutest details himself. King Louis's madness was a dream with his eyes open. By himself, in the space of ten years, he accomplished more than any twenty sovereigns, aided by the artistic genius of the best ages. Certainly no one, at the present day, could produce another such hall, 75 metres in length (without counting the two rooms at either end, which would bring the length up to 100 metres), a gallery illuminated by 17 great windows, 33 rock-crystal chandeliers, 44 candelabra, and who knows what else![9]

9 De Renzis, "L'opera d'un pazzo", *Nuova Antologia di Scienze, Lettere ed Arti*, 3d s., XCV.12 (1887) 5-15.

Eccentricity.—But even originality ends by degenerating, in all, or nearly all, into mere eccentricity, which only seems logical when one enters into the idea of the delusion.

Simon remarks that, in manias of persecution, and in paralytic megalomania, the greater the mental disturbance the livelier the imagination, and the more grotesque the fancies engendered by it. He mentions the case of a painter, who declared that he could see the interior of the earth, filled with houses of crystal, illuminated by electric light, and pervaded by sweet odours. He described the city of Emma, whose inhabitants have two noses and two mouths—one for ordinary food, the other for sweet things—a silver chin, golden hair, three or four arms, and only one leg resting on a little wheel.[10]

These bizarre creations arise in great part from the strange hallucinations to which the patients are subject. We may see an example of this in the four-legged and seven-headed beasts painted by Lazzaretti on his banners. A melancholiac made himself a cuirass of stones, to defend himself against his enemies. Another would continue all day drawing the map of the stains left by damp on the walls of his room. Later on it was discovered that he believed those lines to represent the topography of the regions which God had given him to rule over on earth.

This is one of the reasons why, sometimes, greater excellence in art is found in cases of de-

10 Max Simon, *op. cit.*

mentia, than in those of mania or melancholia.

Symbolism.—Another characteristic trait of art in the insane is the mingling of inscriptions and drawings, and, in the latter, the abundance of symbols and hieroglyphics. All this closely recalls Japanese and Indian pictures, and the ancient wall-paintings of Egypt, and is due in part to the same cause at work in these—the need of helping out speech or picture, each powerless by itself to express a given idea with the requisite energy.

This cause is very evident in a case communicated to me by Dr. Monti, in which an architectural design, though well and accurately drawn, was rendered incomprehensible by the numerous inscriptions, often in rhyme, which had been crowded into it by its author, an aphasiac, who had suffered from dementia for fifteen years.

In some megalomaniacs this happens through the fancy they have for expressing their ideas in a language different from that of ordinary human beings. Such was the case of the master of the world, fully treated of elsewhere, by M. Toselli and myself.[11]

The patient in question was a peasant named G—— L——, 63 years of age, with an easy and confident bearing, prominent cheek-bones, spacious forehead, and expressive and penetrating look. Cranial capacity 1544, index 82, temperature, 37° 6'.

11 *Archivio di psichiatria, antropologia criminale e scienze penali per servire allo studio dell'uomo alienato e delinquente* 1 (1880).

In the autumn of 1871 he became noted for vagrancy and excessive loquacity; he stopped the most notable persons of the village in public places, complaining of injustice which he alleged himself to have suffered; he destroyed the vines, devastated the fields, and rushed about the streets, threatening terrible vengeance.

Gradually he began to identify himself with the Deity, and believe himself ruler of the universe, and preached in the Cathedral of Alba on his lofty destiny. In the asylum he remained calm as long as he was able to believe that his power was recognized by every one, but at the first show of opposition he threatened—in the character of ruler and personification of the elements, calling himself sometimes the son, sometimes the brother, or at others the father of the sun—to convulse the world with earthquakes, overthrow kingdoms and empires, and erect his throne on the ruins. He was tired, he said, of keeping up so many armies, and providing for so many idle persons; it would be but just if the authorities and the rich were at least to send him a large sum of money, to redeem themselves from what he called "the debts of death." In return for this payment he would allow them to live for ever. The poor ought all to die, as useless persons, and it was preposterous that he had to support so many madmen in his own palace. He therefore suggested to the doctor that it would be well to cut their heads off; yet he waited on them with the greatest unselfishness when they were ill, an inconsistency which is among the characteristics of paranoia.

He usually bestowed his scanty earnings on some rogue whom he entrusted with letters and commissions for the other world, addressed to the sun, the stars, the weather, Death, the lightning, and other powers, whose help he was in the habit of invoking, and with whom he held confidential conversations at night. He was quite pleased when some calamity had desolated the country, this being the beginning of the judgments threatened by him, and a sign that the weather, the sun, or the lightning, had obeyed him.

He kept in a trunk some roughly-fashioned crowns which, he said, were the true royal and imperial crowns of Italy, France, and other states. Those worn by the actual sovereigns of these states were no longer of any value, having been usurped by wretched men, doomed to speedy destruction, unless they paid him their *debts of death*, in letters of exchange to the amount of several hundred millions.

But his most characteristic eccentricities were the writings in which his delusion was manifested. Although able to read and write, he scorned the use of the ordinary kind of writing, and, in a character of his own, scrawled letters, orders, and cheques, to the Sun, to Death, or to the civil and military authorities. He always had his pockets full of these documents. His writing consisted mainly of large capital letters, mixed, at intervals, with signs and figures indicating objects or persons. The words are usually separated by one or two large dots, and he only wrote some of the letters of each word (nearly always the consonants) without any respect for the laws of syllabation. In some of his writings, the alphabet almost entirely disappears.

For instance, in order to demonstrate his effective power, he sketched a series of rough figures representing the elements and powers which were his familiar spirits,—the army ready, at a sign from him, to make war on all terrestrial powers contending with him for the dominion of the world. These are—1. The Eternal Father. 2. The Holy Spirit. 3. St. Martin. 4. Death. 5. Time. 6. Thunder. 7. Lightning. 8. Earthquake. 9. The Sun. 10. The Moon. 11. Fire (his minister of war). 12. A very powerful man who has lived ever since the beginning of the world, and is G. L.'s brother. 13. The Lion of Hell. 14. Bread. 15. Wine. The whole is followed of his usual signature a two-headed eagle. Each of these powers is also indicated by letters placed beneath the figures, thus, the 1st=P. D. E.; the 2nd=L. S. P. S., &c.

This mixture of letters, hieroglyphics, and figurative signs, constitutes a kind of writing recalling the phonetico-ideographic stage through which primitive peoples (the Mexicans and Chinese certainly) passed, before the discovery of alphabetic writing.

Among the savages of America and Australia, writing consists in a more or less rough kind of painting; *e.g.*, to indicate, "would that I had the swiftness of a bird," they depict a man with wings instead of arms.[12] These characters are not so much writing as aids to memory still further connected together and vivified by traditional songs or stories.

Some tribes, however, have attained to a somewhat less imperfect mode, which resembles our *rebus*; for instance, the Maya of America, to signify a physician, painted a man with a herb in his hand and wings to his feet; an evident allusion to the rapidity with which he is obliged to hasten to those who require him. Rain is represented by a bucket.[13]

The ancient Chinese represented *malice* by means of three women, light by the sun and moon, and the verb *to listen* by an ear between two doors.

This primitive writing shows us that the rhetorical tropes and figures of which our pedants are so proud, are expressions of poverty rather than wealth on the part of the intellect. In fact, they are frequently found in the speech of idiots and of educated deaf-mutes.

After having used this system for a considerable time, some more civilised races, such as the

12 Hermann Steinthal, *Entwicklung der Schrift* (Berlin: Ferd. Dümmler's Verlagsbuchhandlung, 1852).

13 William Bollaert, "Introduction to the Palæography of America: or, Observations on Ancient Picture and Figurative Writing in the New World; on the Fictitious Writing in North America; on the Quipu of the Peruvians, and Examination of Spurious Quipus", *Memoirs Read Before the Anthropological Society of London*, 3 vols. (London: Trübner and Co. 1865) 1:169-194.

Chinese and Mexicans, took another step forward. They classified the more or less picturesque figures referred to above, and succeeded in forming ingenious combinations which, without directly representing the idea, indirectly suggested a reminiscence of it, as in our charades. Besides this, to prevent any uncertainty on the reader's part, they placed either before or after these signs a sketch of the object to be expressed—a scanty remnant of the actual picture-writing of a previous age. This certainly took place at a time when—the language once being fixed—it was observed how some people, in writing down a given sign, recalled the sound of the words which it suggested. Thus Itzicoatl, the name of a Mexican king, was written by drawing a serpent (Coatl, in Mexican) and a lance (Itzli); thus, too, in Chinese, the character *tschen* represents *boat, lance, and table.*[14]

Our megalomaniac, by reviving this custom, affords one more proof that, in the visible manifestation of their thoughts, the insane frequently revert (as also do criminals) to the prehistoric stage of civilization. In the present case, it is quite easy to understand by what mental process G—— came to use this mode of writing. Under the megalomaniac delusion, believing himself lord of the elements, superior to all known or imaginable forces, he could not make himself properly understood

14 Cesare Lombroso, *L'uomo bianco e l'uomo di colore, letture sull' origine e le varietà delle razze umane* (Padova: F. Sachetto, 1871).

with the common words of ignorant and incredulous men; neither could ordinary writing suffice to express ideas so new and marvellous. The lion's claws, the eagle's beak, the serpent's tongue, the lightning-flash, the sun's rays, the arms of the savage, were much worthier of him, and more calculated to inspire men with fear and respect for his person.

Nor is this an isolated case. One quite analogous to it is described by Raggi in his excellent study of the writings of the insane. Prof. Morselli has furnished me with another and still more interesting instance.

"The patient A. T——" he writes,

> was a joiner and cabinet-maker; he had a certain skill in wood-carving, and his furniture was much sought after.[15] About seven years ago he was attacked with mental disease, apparently melancholia, and tried to commit suicide by throwing himself from the roof of the town hall. He is now subject to attacks of excitement with systematized delusions. His predominant ideas are political—republican and anarchist—on a certain groundwork of ambition. He fancies himself changed into some great criminal; sometimes he is Gasperone, sometimes *Il Passatore*, at others Passanante. He is always drawing or carving, and his work generally takes the form of trophies or allegorical figures.

15 *Archivio di psichiatria, antropologia criminale e scienze penali per servire allo studio dell'uomo alienato e delinquent* 2.3 (1881).

The most curious of all these is a piece of carving which represents a man dressed as a soldier, provided with wings, and standing on an inlaid pedestal covered with allegorical inscriptions. This figure has a trophy on its head, and other objects are carved on or around it, each of which expresses emblematically some one of T——'s delusions. For instance, the wings recall the fact that, when his first attack came on, he was in the square at Porto Recanati, selling his carvings, among which were several figures of angels, at a soldo a-piece. The 'Medal of the order of the Pig' is a token of contempt, wherewith he would like to decorate all the rich and powerful of the earth. The helmet, with a lantern hanging to the vizor (a reminiscence of Offenbach's *Brigands*), symbolises the gendarmes who escorted him to the asylum. The cigar placed crosswise (note the position) represents his disdain for kings and tyrants; and the position of the leg recalls a fracture of that limb sustained by him in his attempt at suicide.

The inscriptions on the pedestal are scraps of verse or extracts from newspapers which T—— is always quoting, and to which he attaches some mysterious significance. They always, however, refer to the state of slavery to which he is reduced (*i.e.*, his detention in the asylum), and the vengeance he will one day wreak on his captors.

The most remarkable thing, however, is the trophy resting on the head of the figure, which is the graphic expression, so to speak, of a song[16] either written by him or adapted from

16 "*Un veleno ho preparato*
Due pugnali tengo in seno:

other popular poetry. Each phrase of the song has its symbol in the trophy. Thus the word *poison* in the first verse is represented by the cup; the *two daggers* are likewise present; the *end of life* and the *tomb* are figured by a kind of sarcophagus or closed chest; *love* by two sprays of flowers. The *bell* of the second stanza is easily recognisable; the *funereal music* are the two trumpets crossed, lower down. The *cross* of the third stanza, and the *priest* (represented by a

---

Questo viver disgraziato
Finirà una volta almeno
T'amerò fino alla tomba
E anche morto t'amerò.

La campana lamentosa
Sonerà la morte mia,
Ed allor tu udrai curiosa
Quella funebre armonia.
T'amerà, ecc. ecc.

Una lunga e mesta croce
Nella via vedrai passar;
Ed un prete sulla forca
Miserere recitar.
T'amerà, ecc. ecc."

"I have prepared a poison / I have two daggers in my bosom: / this unhappy life / at least shall end one day. / I will love thee to my grave / and even when dead, I will love thee still.

The mournful bell shall / sound for my death, / and thou shall listen wonderingly / to that funereal harmony. / I will love thee, &c.

A long and sad cross [*i.e.*, procession] / thou shalt see passing along the road; / and a priest standing by the gallows / reciting the Miserere. / I will love thee, &c."

> clerical hat) are not forgotten. It is curious that the *gallows* should be wanting to complete this trophy. The *spoon* and *fork*, by the by, are T——'s favourite implements. They denote that he eats and drinks in slavery, or, as he says, in a convictprison; and for this reason, he always wears a set, carved in wood by himself, in the button-hole of his coat, or in his cap.

We may once more remind the reader that savages hand down their history by associating picture-signs with poetry.

A most interesting example of elaborate symbolic faculty in a monomaniac, combined with higher artistic power than is usually found among the insane, has been recorded with very full illustrations by Dr. William Noyes.[17] This patient studied art at Paris under Gérome and returned to America to become an illustrator of books and magazines. He developed systematic religious delusions, and frequently worked them out in very beautiful and artistic shapes, nine of which, all executed in the asylum at which he was confined, are here reproduced. The circular design is one of a series of twelve charts (one for each of the tribes of Israel) illustrating the progress of the Holy Spirit. They were all delicately coloured in water colours, the fine shading making it very difficult to give in black and white an adequate idea of the beauty of the original.

17 "Paranoia: A Study of the Evolution of Systematized Delusions of Grandeur," in *American Journal of Psychology* (May, 1888) and (May, 1889).

In the centre is the dove representing the Holy Spirit, and surrounding it are seven different crosses [St. Andrew, St. Colomba, St. George, St. Michael, The Prophet, St. Evangeli Royal Priesthood], and a close study will show the seven crosses, most ingeniously worked together. It is probable that in looking at the design closely for the first time one will suddenly see a new cross take shape before his eyes, and this indeed is what the patient says occurs with him. In describing the crosses he will say, for example, that in drawing the cross of St. Andrew the lines suddenly took a new shape and he found he had also made a cross of St. Michael. This to him is a matter of deep significance, and he feels that his work is directly controlled by a higher power, and that the work of his fancy is really inspired.

Outside these central crosses are the names of three ancient deities who were each characterized by some special attribute, and under these the parts of the body that the artist conceives these deities especially to have represented, and then comes the name of the Biblical personage in whom these elements were finally exemplified and embodied. To the left of the dove is Venus, representing Blood, exemplified in Moses; above is Osiris, representing Flesh, embodied in Adam; and to the right Psyche, representing Water, typified in Noah. These three are but the gross and material parts of Man, representing indeed necessary steps in his progress through life, but secondary and subordinate to the higher part of his nature represented by Truth and the Spirit—which receive their ultimate embodiment in *Christ*.

The Lion denotes Might, and the Eagle signifies Emulation; but it is uncertain just what symbolism is connected with the serpent twining round the cross, and the open book crossed by a sword and pen, unless indeed this last may mean the Bible with the emblems of peace and war lying quietly within it, and it seems not unlikely that the serpent is emblematic of the Betrayal. For the rest of the design, however, we need make no inferences, as it corresponds closely with his description.

Outside of the circle enclosing the crosses are the seals, sealing the Holy Spirit. In the large light triangles, or rather rays of the sun, are given the names of the twelve apostles, forming the Seal of the Prophet. Above these, in the same space, are the signs of the zodiac in the extreme points of the triangle, with the names of the parts of the body underneath, that these signs correspond to in the ancient mythology; this forms the Seal of the Zodiac. Between these large light coloured triangles are the twelve holy stones, represented as ovals, and with their names plainly distinguished in the cut, making the Seal of the Holy Stones. In the small triangles directly above the Holy Stones are given the names of the twelve tribes of Israel, but the colour of these in the chart (vermilion) is such that the lettering does not comes out in the photographic negative. This gives the Seal of the Twelve Tribes. Directly beneath the Holy Stones, filling in the space between the bottom of each large triangle, is the Seal of the Germ, coloured dark green, and running down on each side of the top of these large triangles are small triangles, coloured dark red and forming the Seal of the Aceldama or Bloody Seal. On the circumference are the names of the constellations of the zodiac, and directly under these the names of the corresponding months of the year, and under these again are the mythological representations of the constellations, Leo (July) being at the top, and then in order to the right come Virgo (August), Libra (September), Scorpio (October), Sagittarius (November), Capricornus (December), Aquarius (January), Pisces (February), Aries (March), Taurus (April), Gemini (May), Cancer (June). This gives the last sealing of the Seed, the Seal of the Sun.

> It will be seen that beginning at the circumference at any point and going toward the centre there is a complete astronomical representation of the season of the year, first the name of the constellation, then in succession the month, the constellation depicted pictorially, the sign of the zodiac and the part of the human body corresponding in the old astronomy to this sign of the zodiac.

Of the four designs reproduced together, the first, the Shechinah, or Light of Love, represents that miraculous light or visible glory which was to the Jews a symbol of the Divine presence; the second represents the angel Sandalphon with the Holy Grail at the side and the letters Alpha and Omega at top (the design must be inverted to make out the Omega); the third, Sub Rosa, and the fourth, Imp and Frogs, are graceful fancies which sufficiently explain themselves, as does the Witch.

While working on these sketches, he made at the same time the design for a book-plate, representing Cupid learning the alphabet, and the entire design, he says, is full of symbolism—a favourite word with him. Cupid has his finger on *Alpha*, signifying the beginning of his education; above the book is Cupid's target, with a heart for the centre, that he has pierced with an arrow, while the full quiver stands to the right. The curious fish under the *Veritas* represents the ΙΧΘΥΣ of the early Christians, while three crosses, symbolic of the Christian religion, are in the upper left-hand corner,

brought out by heavy shading of the cross lines. On the book of knowledge is parched the dove, emblematic of purity, while the olive branch at the left of the book and the palm under the Fool's Bauble give still other religious symbols. The lamp of knowledge is burning brightly in front of Cupid, while at his feet are the square, compass, triangle, and pencils, symbolizing the designer's profession.

Minuteness of Detail.—In some insane artists, especially monomaniacs, we find an opposite characteristic—the exaggeration of particular details—the general effect being lost in obscurity through their excessive efforts after verisimilitude. Thus, in a landscape exhibited among those rejected from the Turin *salon*, not only was a general view of the country given, but every separate blade of grass could be distinguished. In another picture, intended to be very imposing, the strokes of the brush produced the effect of pencil shading.

Atavism.—Both minuteness and symbolism are themselves atavistic phenomena; but, in addition to them, there may be noted (in a large number of cases) a total absence of perspective, while the rest of the execution shows clearly enough that the author is not wanting in artistic sense. One would take him to be a true artist, but one brought up in China or ancient Egypt. Here we have evidently a kind of atavism explicable by arrested development of some one organ, and a corresponding backwardness in the products of that organ. A French captain, suffering from paralysis, drew figures stiff as Egyptian profiles. A megalomaniac of Reggio executed a coloured bas-relief, in which the disproportionate size of the feet and hands, the extreme smallness of the faces, and the stiffness of the limbs, completely recall the work of the thirteenth century. Another patient, at Genoa, carved bas-reliefs on pipes and on vases, exactly similar to those of the Neolithic Age.

Raggi has sent me some flints carved by a monomaniac entirely ignorant of archæology, which, in the choice of figures and emblems, recall the style of Egyptian and Phœnician amulets. In these instances we see the influence of similar psychical conditions at work.

Arabesques.—In some few patients, M. Toselli has called my attention to a singular predilection for arabesques and ornaments which tend to assume a purely geometric form, without loss of elegance. This is the case with monomaniacs; in cases of dementia and acute mania there prevails a chaotic confusion, which, however, does not always imply absence of taste. I have seen an instance of

this in a kind of ship, the work of a dementia patient, composed of an enormous number of little slips of wood, brilliantly coloured, very thin, and intertwined in an infinite variety of ways, the general effect being very graceful.

Obscenity.—In some work done by erotomaniacs, paralytics, and demented patients, the salient characteristic, both of the drawings and of the verses, is the most shameless indecency. Thus a cabinet-maker would carve virile members at every corner of a piece of furniture, or at the summits of trees. This, too, recalls many works of savages and of ancient races, in which the organs of sex are everywhere prominent. A captain at Genoa was fond of drawing scenes in a brothel. In many the obscene character is marked by the most singular pretexts, as though it were demanded by artistic requirements. A monomaniac priest used to sketch his figures nude, and then artfully drape them by means of lines which revealed the generative organs. He defended himself against criticism by saying that his figures could only appear indecent to those who were in search of evil.

M—— illustrated his strange and often beautiful verses with innumerable daubs, representing animals of monstrous forms struggling with men and women, or monks and nuns, naked, in the most shameless attitudes.

In others the indecency is, if possible, still more evident, especially in cases of paralytic dementia. I remember an old man who used to draw a vulva on the address of his letters to his wife, surrounding it with obscene couplets in dialect.

It is a curious coincidence that two artists—one at Turin and the other at Reggio—who were both megalomaniacs, should both have had sodomitic instincts, which they combined with the delusion of being deities, and lords of the world, which they had created and emitted from their bodies. One of them (who, nevertheless, had a real artistic sense) painted a full-length picture of himself, naked, among women, ejecting worlds, and surrounded by all the symbols of power. This repeats, and at the same time explains, the Ithyphallic divinity of the Egyptians.

Criminality and Moral Insanity.—In this connection it is important to notice that the greater number of these artists show, in addition to their other forms of mania, a marked tendency to moral insanity, especially in the form of unnatural vice. The painter who produced the picture of "Delirium" was a pederast. The man who constructed the marvellous model of the Reggio Asylum, already alluded to, was neither draughtsman, sculptor, nor engineer. He was a madman, and, in addition, a thief, with unnatural tendencies. This man, whenever the fancy took him, escaped from the asylum, wandered about for some days, began to steal when he had exhausted the small amount of money he had about him, and when imprisoned declared himself a lunatic, and so got acquitted and sent back to Reggio, when, after a short interval, he would repeat the same line of conduct.

Dr. Tamburini told me that he, too, had been struck by the co-existence of artistic faculty and moral insanity in these patients.

Uselessness.—A characteristic common to many is the complete uselessness of the work to which they devote themselves; and here I recall once more Hécart's dictum:—

> *C'est le travail des fous d'épuiser leurs cervelles*
> *Sur des riens fatigants, sur quelques bagatelles.*[18]

A Genevan, affected by persecutory monomania, spent years in embroidering on egg-shells and lemons. Though her work was most beautiful, it could be of no advantage to her, for she kept it jealously concealed; and I myself, though she was very fond of me, never saw any of it till after her death.

Here we have, as in the case of artists of genius, the love of truth and beauty for their own sake alone, only that the aim is reversed.

Sometimes the work done, though very useful in itself, is of no advantage to the artist, and has no connection with his profession. Thus a captain, who had become insane, presented me with the model of a bed for violent patients, which, I believe, would be extremely useful in practice. Two other patients, together, made, out of a piece of beef-bone, some very neat match-boxes, ornamented with carvings in relief, which could be of no profit to themselves, since they refused to part with them for money.

18 Hécart, *op. cit.*

There are, however, some exceptions. A melancholiac patient, with homicidal and suicidal tendencies, manufactured himself a very serviceable knife, fork, and spoon—metal ones not being allowed him—out of the bones which remained over from his dinner. A cafe-keeper at Colligno, a megalomaniac, compounded excellent liqueurs out of the scraps left over from meals, though of the most different kinds of food. A criminal lunatic constructed himself a key out of a number of small pieces of wood joined together. I do not count among these examples those who have prepared themselves real cuirasses of iron and stone—a piece of work in relation to the special delusion of persecutions, and implying an amount of labour out of proportion to the advantage obtained.

Insanity as a subject.—Many choose insanity as the subject of their paintings. Professor Virgilio has furnished me with a very curious portrait of an insane patient at the moment of attack—the eyes rolling, the hair on end, the arms extended. Under his feet is the epigraph: "*Delira*" ("He is raving"). This is the work of an alcoholic pederast.

I think that a sane artist would have some difficulty in painting a closer likeness of delirium. This reminds me how frequently I have found, among the poets of asylums, the tendency to describe insanity; and it has been a favourite theme with great poets who have suffered from ill-health—Tasso, Lenau, Barbara, Musset. Mancini, immediately after his recovery, painted a woman offering for sale the picture executed by a madman; and Gill, in the hospital of Sainte-Anne, painted a raving maniac with terrible truth to nature.[19]

DELIRIUM

Absurdity.—One of the most salient characteristics of insane art is, as might be expected, absurdity, either in drawing or colouring. This is especially noteworthy in some maniacs, owing to the

19 Magnan.

exaggerated association of ideas, through which the connecting links (which would serve to explain the author's conception) are totally lost. Thus, an artist painted a "Marriage at Cana," with all the figures of the apostles exceedingly well drawn; but in place of the figure of Christ was a large bunch of flowers.

Paralytic patients draw objects without any sense of proportion; their hens are the size of horses, and their cherries of melons; or, while striving after perfection in the design, the execution is merely childish. One, who believed himself a second Horace Vernet, drew horses by means of four straight strokes and a tail.[20] Another drew all his figures upside down. Other dementia patients, owing to the same amnesia which is apparent in their speech, leave out the most essential points of their conception, like M—— at Pesaro, who made an excellent drawing of a general, seated, but forgot the chair. (Frigerio.)

Imitation.—There are some who are very successful in imitation, but can produce nothing original; they will, for instance, copy the façade of the asylum, or heads of animals, with the minute accuracy of detail which characterizes primitive art. In this branch I have seen successful work done by cretins and idiots, the latter drawing in exactly the same manner as primitive man.

Uniformity.—Many continually repeat the same idea; thus one, mentioned by Frigerio, filled sheets

20 Simon.

of paper with a bee gnawing the head of an ant; another, who believed that he had been shot, would paint nothing but fire-arms; a third confined himself to arabesques.

Summary.—These traits explain the instances of partial perfection to be found in dementia patients; for a repetition of the same movement tends to bring it nearer and nearer to perfection. At other times, as we have seen in the extempore poets and authors of the asylum, it is the tenacity and energy of the hallucinations which makes a painter of a man who was never one before. Blake was able to picture to himself, as living and present, persons already dead, angels, &c. This was the case, also, with the strange insane poet, John Clare, who believed himself a spectator of the Battle of the Nile, and the death of Nelson; and was firmly convinced that he had been present at the death of Charles I. In fact, he described these events with such remarkable fidelity and accuracy, that it is scarcely probable he could have done it so well had he been in full possession of his reason—the more so, as he was entirely without culture.[21] This explains why insane painters and poets are so numerous. It is easy to reproduce clearly what one sees clearly. Moreover, the imagination is most unrestrained when reason is least dominant; for the latter, by repressing hallucinations and illusions, deprives the average man of a true source of artistic and literary inspiration.

21 Delepierre.

For the same reason, too, art itself, may, in its turn, encourage the development of mental disease. Vasari relates that one Spinelli, a painter of Arezzo, having attempted to paint the deformity of Lucifer, the latter appeared to him in a dream and reproached him with having made him so ugly. The painter was so affected by this apparition as to fall seriously ill; and it continued to haunt him for years.[22]

Music in the Insane.—Musical ability is often diminished in those who, previous to their illness, cultivated this art with passion. Dr. Adriani observed that musicians, under his care for insanity, almost entirely lost their powers. They could still play any piece, but it was done quite mechanically and without expression. Other dementia patients would play the same piece, sometimes even a few phrases, over and over again.

Donizetti, in the last stage of dementia, no longer recognized his favourite melodies. His last works show traces of that fatal influence which critics have also observed in Schumann's symphony of the "Bride of Messina," composed during his attacks of insanity.[23]

These facts, however, do not contradict our assertion that insanity awakens new artistic qualities

---

22 Giorgio Vasari, *Le Vite de' più eccellenti pittori, scultori, e architettori da Cimabue insino a' tempi nostril* (Florence: Lorenzo Torrentino, 1550; Florence: Giunti, 1558).

23 Félix Clément, *Les musiciens célèbres depuis le seizième siècle jusqu'à nos jours* (Paris: Hachette et Cie., 1878).

in persons not previously gifted in that way; they only show that (as we have seen in the case of professional painters) it can give no additional power or skill to those who already possessed them when attacked by disease.

A megalomaniac—formerly a syphilitic patient—under the care of Dr. Tamburini, sang beautiful airs when under excitement, at the same time, instead of playing an accompaniment, she improvised, on the pianoforte, two distinct motives which had no connection with each other or the air she was singing. This fact confirms the observations of Luys as to the independent action of the cerebral hemispheres.

A young man attacked by *pellagra*, who recovered in my hospital, composed expressive and original melodies.

M. Raggi told me that he had had under his care a melancholic patient who, during her attacks, played without enthusiasm, and even with repugnance, but, when the fit passed off, would spend whole days at the piano, and execute the most difficult *partitions* with a truly artistic enthusiasm. In the same way, a paralytic showed, through the whole course of his illness, a genuine musical mania, during which he imitated all instruments, and agitated himself, in frantic enthusiasm, at the *piano* passages.

Raggi also observed a paralytic dementia patient who, after breaking his thigh-bone by a leap from a window, rendered every bandage which could be devised useless by singing, for days together, motives from *Il Trovatore* at the top of his voice, and accompanying his singing with abrupt rhythmical movements of the pelvis. A fancy for monotonous chanting also showed itself in another paralytic, who believed himself to be a great admiral.

In maniacs, acute and joyous notes predominate, and, still more, the repetition of the rhythm.

Every one who has paid even a short visit to an asylum has noticed the frequency of singing and shouting and "high and thin voices, and with them a sound of hands."[24] Nor is it hard to understand this, if we remember how Spencer and Ardigo have shown that the law of rhythm is the most general form under which, in the whole of nature, energy is manifested, from the crystal to the star, or to the animal organism. Man, therefore, only follows a general organic law in giving way to this impulse, which he does the more readily the less he is controlled by reason. This explains the number of poets of the new school who are found in asylums. This is the reason why savage nations have a natural inclination for music; and a missionary told Spencer that many to whom he taught the Psalms, with music, in the evening, could repeat them by heart on the following day.

Savages, in speaking, make use of a sort of monotonous chant analogous to our recitative. Primitive poetry was always sung, whence all the different words connected with singing applied to

---

24 "Voci alte e fioche e siton di man con elle" (Dante, *Inf.* iii. 27.)

poetry and poets. The mysterious magic formulas and recipes of the ancients[25] were also sung, or chanted, whence the word "enchantment." Even at the present day, in the neighbourhood of Novi and Oulx, I have heard peasant-women, in making inquiries of one another, modulate their voices in true musical rhythm. Modern *Improvvisatori* do not seem able to produce their verses except when singing, and agitating all their muscles.

It must be remembered that, according to the observations of Herbert Spencer,

> the act of singing employs and exaggerates the signs of the natural language of passion. Mental excitement is transformed into muscular energy. An infant will laugh and bound in its nurse's arms at the sight of a brilliant colour, or the hearing of a new sound.[26]

Strong sensations or painful emotions cause us to gesticulate; in short, they excite the muscular system, which is acted upon in proportion to the intensity of the sensations. Slight pain calls forth a groan, greater pain a cry: the pitch of the voice varies with the force of the emotion, so that, in the strongest emotions, it rises to the octave, or high-

25 Columella, *De Re Rustica*. [The original footnote attributes this work to Cato, but Cato the Elder wrote *De Agri Cultura*. —Ed.]

26 Herbert Spencer, "On the Origins and Function of Music", *Essays: Political, Scientific, and Speculative*, 3 vols (London: Williams and Norgate, 1891) 2:401.

er; and singing is always involuntarily accompanied by tremors and agitations of the muscles.

What could be more natural than that, in the conditions in which the emotions are most energetic, and so frequently atavistic, as is the case in insanity, these tendencies should be reproduced on a larger scale?

This, too, explains why so many morbid men of genius should be musicians: Mozart, Schumann, Beethoven, Donizetti, Pergolese, Fenicia, Ricci, Rocchi, Rousseau, Handel, Dussek, Hoffmann, Glück, Petrella.[27] Musical creation is the most subjective manifestation of thought, the one most intimately connected with the affective emotions, and having less relation to the external world than any other, which causes it to stand more in need of the fervent but exhausting emotions of inspiration.

Perhaps the study of these peculiarities of art in the insane, besides showing us a new phase in this mysterious disease, might be useful in æsthetics, or at any rate in art-criticism, by showing that an exaggerated predilection for symbols, and for minuteness of detail (however accurate), the complication of inscriptions, the excessive prominence given to any one colour (it is well known that some of our foremost painters are great sinners in this respect), the choice of licentious subjects, and even

27 My attention was called many years ago to the frequent occurrence of insanity among great musicians by Dr. Arnaldo Bargoni, and afterwards by Mastriani, of Naples, in an excellent article in Roma, 1881.

an exaggerated degree of originality, are points which belong to the pathology of art.

Chapter III

Literary and Artistic Mattoids

Definition — Physical and psychical characteristics — Their literary activity — Examples — Lawsuit mania — Mattoids of genius — Bosisio — The décadent poets — Verlaine — Mattoids in art

We have just been considering, in madmen, the substantial character of genius under the appearance of insanity. There is, however, a variety of these, which permits the appearance of genius and the substantial character of the average man; and this variety forms the link between madmen of genius, the sane, and the insane properly so called. These are what I call semi-insane persons or mattoids.

This variety constitutes, in the world of mental pathology, a particular species of a genus distinguished by Maudsley as "odd, queer, strange" persons of insane temperament, and previously by Morel. Legrand du Saulle, and Schüle

(*Geisteskrunkheit*, ii., 1880) regard them as *hereditary neurotics*, Raggi as neuropathics, and now many as *paranoiacs*—a terminology which produces a hopeless confusion.

The graphomaniac, representing the commonest variety, has true negative characteristics that is to say, the features and cranial form are nearly always normal (Bosisio, Cianchettini, F——, P——, &c.). His characteristics are not the result of heredity; at most, he is the son of a man of genius (Flourens, Broussais, Spandri, Knester, &c.). This form of aberration is most frequently found in men; I only know of one exception in Europe—Louise Michel— and it appears more especially in great cities, worn out with civilization. The mattoid shows far fewer signs of degeneracy than the insane properly so called:—Of 33 mattoids only 21 showed degenerative characters, and of these last 12 had 2, 2 were found to have 3, there were 2 with 4, and only 1 with 6.

Another negative characteristic is the survival of family affection, and even of that for the human race in general, sometimes reaching such a point as to become exaggerated altruism; though, in many cases, vanity enters largely into the composition of this virtue. Thus Bosisio thinks of and provides for the well-being of posterity, and even of the dead. Thus D—— loves his wife and grandchildren, and constantly works for his family; Cianchettini supported a deaf and dumb sister; Sbarbaro, Lazzaretti, Coccapieller, adored their wives.

In prison, a few days ago, I had occasion to perform the operation of blood-transfusion, and wasted much time in trying to find a healthy individual from whom to take the blood. All refused; but a consumptive mattoid, as soon as he heard of the matter, volunteered for the operation, and was overwhelmed with shame when I would not make use of him.

They have an exaggerated conviction of their own personal merit and importance, with the peculiar characteristic that this opinion shows itself rather in writing than in words or actions, so that they do not show irritation at the contradictions and evils of practical life.

Cianchettini compares himself to Galileo and to Jesus Christ; but sweeps the barrack-stairs. Passanante proclaims himself President of the Political Society while working as a cook. Mangione classified himself as a martyr to Italy and to his own genius; yet he condescended to act as a broker. Caissant claimed to be a cardinal, but, in the meantime, he was a clever parasite, and made large profits through his very insanity. The shepherd Bluet[1] believed himself to be an apostle and count of Permission, and, like the author of *Scottatinge*, deigned to address himself to none but royal personages. Yet he did not refuse to carry on the trade of a horse-breaker.

1 Bernard de Bluet d'Arbères (1566 – 1607). *See* Bertrand Guégan, *La vie extravagante du Comte de Permission: bouffon de Henri IV* (Paris: La Renaissance du Livre, 1924). —Ed.

Stewart, the eccentric author of the *New System of Physical Philosophy,* who travelled all over the world to discover the polarity of truth, asserted that all the kings of the earth had entered into an alliance to destroy his works. He therefore gave the latter to his friends, with the request to wrap them up well, and bury them in remote localities,—never revealing the latter, except on their death-beds. Martin Williams—brother of that Jonathan Williams, who, in an attack of insanity, set fire to York Minster, and of John Williams, who struck out a new line in painting—published many works to prove the theory of perpetual motion. After having convinced himself by means of thirty-six experiments of the impossibility of demonstrating it scientifically, it was revealed to him in a dream that God had chosen him to discover the great cause of all things, and perpetual motion; and this he made the subject of many works.[2]

These persons would not come under the heading of mattoids, if, in their writings, the earnestness and persistence in one idea which make them resemble the monomaniac and the man of genius, were not often associated with the pursuit of absurdity, continual contradictions, and the prolixity and utility of insanity. One tendency overpowers all others—one which we find predominant in insane genius: *viz.,* personal vanity. Thus, out of 215 mattoids, we find forty-four prophets.

2 Jasnot, *Vérités positives* (1854).

Filopanti, in the *Dio Liberale*, places his father Berillo, a carpenter, and his mother Berilla among the demigods. He discovered three Adams, and gives a minute narrative, year by year, of the actions of each. Cordigliani prepared to insult the Chamber of Deputies in order to obtain an annuity from the Government, and thought this action much to his own credit. Guiteau thought he was saving the Republic by the murder of the President, and had himself called a great lawyer and philosopher. In the same way Passanante, after having preached the abolition of capital punishment, condemns the guilty members of the Assembly to death; and, after having given orders to a respect the forms of government," insults the monarchy, makes an attempt at regicide, and proposes to "abolish all misers and hypocrites."

A physician, S——, prints a statement that blood-letting exposes to an excess of light, another announces in two thick volumes, that *diseases are elliptical.*

Critics have said, referring to the works of Démons, that his Dialectic Quintessence and sextessence are a true quintessence of absurdity.[3] Gleizes affirms that flesh is atheistical. Fuzi (a theologian) asserts that the menstrual blood has the property of quenching conflagrations.

Hannequin, who used to write in the air with his fingers, and had an *aromal trumpet*, by means of which he communicated with the spirits dispersed

3 *Les fous littéraires* 51.

through the air, declares that in the future age many men shall become women and demigods.

Henrion, at the Académie des Inscriptions, advanced the theory that Adam was forty feet in height, Noah twenty-nine, Moses twenty-five, &c.

Leroux, the celebrated Paris Deputy, who believed in metempsychosis and the cabbala, defined love as "the ideality of the reality of a part of the totality of the Infinite Being," &c., and wished to insert the principle of the *triad* in the preamble of his Constitution.

Asgill maintained that men might live for ever, if only they had faith.

It is true that, here and there, some new and vigorous notion emerges from the chaos of such minds, because the only symptom of genius developed in them by psychosis is a less degree of aversion to novelty, or, to employ my own terminology, of misoneism.[4] Thus, for example, amid the most absurd opinions, Cianchettini has some very fine passages:

> All animals have the instinct of self-preservation, with the minimum of fatigue, of escaping from troublesome thoughts, and of enjoying the delights of life; and to obtain these things, liberty is indispensable to them.
>
> All animals, except man, gratify and always have gratified these instincts, and perhaps will always continue to do so. Mankind alone, constituted as a society, find themselves fettered,

4 See *Tre Tribuni* (1887).

> and in such a way that no one has ever succeeded, not merely in bringing them into a state of peace and liberty, but even in snowing how they may attain this end.
>
> Well—I propose to demonstrate this proposition, And, as a locked door cannot be opened without breaking it, save by means of a key or a picklock; so, as man has lost his liberty by means of the tongue, nothing but the tongue, or its equivalents, can set him free without injury to his nature.

Amid the doggerel jargon of the *Scottatinge*, I find this beautiful line on Italy—

> *Padrona e schiava sempre, ai figli tuoi nemica.*[5]

We shall see, in Passanante's biography, that sometimes, in his writings and still more in his speeches, he struck out vigorous and original ideas which, in fact, led many persons into error as to the nature and reality of his disease. I may mention the sentence, "Where the learned lose themselves, the ignorant man may triumph,"—and another, "History learnt from the people is more instructive than that which is studied in books." Bluet distinguishes "the maid from the virgin, in that the first has the will for evil without the power, and the second has neither the power nor the will."

It is natural that mattoids should repeat in their conceptions the ideas of stronger politicians and

5 "Always mistress or slave a foe to thine own children."

thinkers, but always in their own way, and always exaggerated. Thus Bosisio exaggerates the delicate consideration of our lovers of animals, and anticipates the ideas of Mlle. Clémence Royer and Comte on the necessity for the application of the Malthusian theory. In the same way, Detomasi, a dishonest broker, discovered a practical application (except for the morbid eroticism which he added to it) of the Darwinian system of natural selection. Cianchettini wishes to put Socialism into practice.

But the stamp of insanity is evident, not so much in the exaggeration of their ideas, as in the disproportion of the latter among themselves; so that, from some well-expressed and even sublime conception, we pass suddenly to one which is more than mediocre and paradoxical, nearly always opposed to the received ideas of the majority, and at variance with the position and education of the author. In short, we have that by means of which Don Quixote, instead of extorting our admiration, makes us smile. Yet his actions, in another age, and even in a different man, would have been admirable and heroic. In any case, among mattoids, traits of genius are rather the exception than the rule.[6]

6 *"Il se trouvait là des philosophes plus forts que Leibnitz, mais sourdsmuets de naissance, ne pouvant produire que les gestes de leurs idées et pousser des arguments inarticulés; des peintres tourmentés de faire grand, mais qui posaient si singulièrement un homme sur ses pieds, un arbre sur ses racines, que tous leurs tableaux ressemblaient à des vues de tremblements de terre ou à des intérieurs de paquebots un*

Most of them show a deficiency rather than an exuberance of inspiration; they fill entire volumes, without sense or savour; they eke out the commonplaceness of their ideas and the poverty of their style with a multitude of points of interrogation and exclamation, with repeated signatures, with special words coined by themselves, as is the habit of monomaniacs; thus Menke already observed that some mattoids contemporary with himself had invented the words *derapti felisan*. Berbiguier created the word *farfiderism*. A monomaniac, Le Bardier, wrote a work entitled *Dominatmosfheri*, intended to show farmers how to obtain double harvests, and sailors to avoid storms. He entitled himself *Dominatmosfherifateur*[7] Cianchettini invented the *travaso* of the idea; Pari invented *cafungaia*, and *morbozoo*, and we owe to Wahltuch, *alitrologia* and *anthropomognotologia*, and to G—— *lepidermocrinia* and *glossostomopatica*.

We often find an eccentric handwriting, with vertical lines cut by horizontal ones and tranverse furrows, even with unusually formed letters, as in Cianchettini.

They frequently introduce drawings into their sentences, as if to heighten their force, thus re-

---

jour de tempête. Des musiciens inventeurs de claviers intermédiaires, des savants à la façon du docteur Hitisch, de ces cervelles bric-à-brac, où il y a de tout mais où l'on ne trouve rien, à cause du désordre, de la poussière, et aussi parceque tous les objets sont cassés, incomplets, incapables du moindre service" (Daudet, Jack).

7 Delepierre, *Littérateur des fous*.

turning (as we have already seen to be the case with megalomaniacs) to the ideographic writing of the ancients, in which the figure served as a determining symbol.

Wahltuch published two books on Psychography, a new kind of philosophic system which, however, has found a serious commentator in a sane philosopher—which speaks volumes for the seriousness of some philosophers. According to this system, ideas are represented by so many images impressed on each of the cerebral convolutions. Thus the symbol of Physics is a lighted candle; that of alitrology, or the faculty of judgment, is the nose (or the sense of smell); of ethics, a ring; and of motion, a fishing-hook. The author, despairing (and with good reason) of making himself understood in words, philosophises with his pencil, and has crammed his book with diagrams of brains covered with such figurative signs.

In order to prove the applicability of these principles to literature, he has presented us with a tragedy—*Job*— in which the characters have their heads covered with similar signs, and chant verses worthy of the system, *e.g.*, "O that I could separate the two united conceptions of myself and impiety. I am just. Satan is impious."[8]

The Jesuit missionary, Paoletti, wrote a book against St. Thomas, and illustrated it with a drawing of the vessels used in the Tabernacle, so as

8 *Staccar potessi i due concetti uniti*
Di me ed empio. Io giusto. Empio è Satana.

to determine the future condition of the sons of Adam with regard to predestination. The Divine and human wills are figured as two balls revolving in opposite directions, and finally meeting at a common centre.

The titles of all their works show an exuberance which is really singular. I possess one of eighteen lines, not counting a note included in the title-page itself, and intended to explain it. A socialistic work published in Australia, by an Italian, and in pure Italian, has a title arranged in the shape of a triumphal arch.

It is precisely in the title-page that nearly all of them at once betray the taint of madness. This example—from the work of the mattoid Démons—will suffice:

> The demonstration of the fourth part of nothing is something; everything is the quintessence extracted from the quarter of nothing and that which depends on it, containing the precepts of the holy, magic, and devout invocations of Démons, to discover the origin of the evils which afflict France.

Many have the crotchet of mixing up with their sentences accumulated series of numbers, which is also sometimes done by paralytics. In a mad production of Sovbira's, entitled "666," all the verses are accompanied by the number 666. The strange thing is that, at the same time, a certain Porter, in England, had published a work on the number 666, declaring it the most exquisite and perfect of numbers.[9] Lazzaretti, too, had a singular partiality for this number. Spandri, Levron, and C—— have a similar preference for the number 3. A special characteristic found in mattoids, and also, as we have already seen, in the insane, is that of repeating some words or phrases hundreds of times in the same page. Thus, in one of Passanante's chapters, the word *riprovate* occurs about 143 times.

Some have had special paper manufactured for their works, like Wirgman, who had it made with different colours on the same sheet, at an enormous increase of expense, so that a volume of four hundred pages cost him over £2,200 sterling. Filon had every page of his book of a different colour.

Another characteristic is that of employing an orthography and calligraphy peculiar to themselves, with words in large type or underlined. They will sometimes write even private letters in double column, or with vertical lines traversed by horizontal and sometimes by diagonal ones. They sometimes underline one letter in preference to others in the same word (Passanante), or they write in detached verses like those of the Bible, or introduce points after every two or three words, as in the MS. (in my possession) of a certain Bellone, or parentheses, even one within the other, as Madrolle used to do, or notes upon notes, even in the title-page, as in the case of Cas—— and of La——. The latter (a

9 Delepierre, *op. cit.*

University professor) in a work of twelve pages has nine consisting of notes alone.

Hepain invented a *physiological* language, which consists in the main of our own letters reversed, and of numbers used in their places.

Many have a calligraphy quite peculiar to themselves, close, continuous, with lengthened letters, and always extremely legible.

Many (like some of the insane, whom they surpass in this point) continually intersperse their conversation with puns and plays on words. A certain Jassio wished to prove the analogy of the *hand* and the *week* in which God created the world, by means of a pun on the words *main* and *semaine*. Hécart, who had himself said that it is the peculiarity of the insane to occupy themselves with useless trifles, wrote the biography of the madmen of Valenciennes, and the strange book entitled *Anagrammata, poëme en VII. chants, XCVe édition* (as a matter of fact, it was the first), *rev. corr. et augmentée; à Anagrammatopolis, l'an XIV. de l'ère anagrammatique* (Valenciennes, 1821, 16°). The book is almost entirely composed of inversions of words. The following is an example:

Lecteur, il sied *que je vous* dise
Que le sbire *fera la* brise;
Que le dupeur *sans* pudeur,
Qu' on pent maculer *sans* clameur. . . .

La nomade *a mis la* madonne
À la paterne *de* Pétronne

Quand le grand Dacier *était* diacre
Le caffier *cultivé du* fiacre.

And so on for twelve thousand lines, concluding with this:

Moi je vais poser mon repos.

Here it is as well to note that, on the margin of a copy of the *Anagrammata* belonging to the Bibliothèque Nationale of Paris is the following confession, in the author's handwriting, "Anagrams are one of the greatest inanities of which the human mind is capable; one must be a fool to amuse one's self with them, and worse than a fool to make them." This is a correct diagnosis of his case.

Filopanti, in the *Dio Liberale*, explains Luther's propaganda by a caprice on the part of the Deity, who caused Mars to become a monk. The latter thus became Martin, and then Martin Luther.

The origin of Gleizes' vegetarian mania was a dream, in which he heard a voice crying in his ears, "*Gleizes* means *église*." He thus thought himself suddenly appointed by God to preach his doctrine to mankind. Du Monin has the plague decapitated, "Take away this head from hence; I fear that this head will deprive my people of their heads by a new mischief."[10]

10 *"Lève ce chef d'ici, je crains que ce chef prive de chef les miens par un nouveau méchef."*

But a still more prevalent characteristic is the singular copiousness of their writings. Bluet left behind no less than 180 books, each more foolish than the other. We shall see how Mangione, who, in addition, was crippled in one hand and could not write, deprived himself of food to defray the cost of printing, and sometimes spent more than one hundred scudi per month to enable him to gratify his taste for authorship. We know how many reams of paper Passanante covered, and how he attached more importance to the publication of a foolish letter of his than to his own life. Guiteau used so much paper as to incur a considerable debt which he was unable to pay. The list of George Fox's works is so long that the bibliographer Lowndes does not venture to give it. Howerlandt's *Essay on Tournay* consists of 117 volumes.

Sometimes they content themselves with writing and printing their vagaries, and make no attempt to diffuse them among the public, though they assume that the latter must be acquainted with them.

In these writings, apart from their morbid prolixity, let it be noted that the aim is either futile, or absurd, or in complete contradiction with their social position and previous culture. Thus two physicians write on hypothetic geometry and astrology; a surgeon, a veterinary surgeon and an obstetric practitioner, on ærial navigation; a captain on rural economy; a sergeant on therapeutics; and a cook on high political questions. A theologian writes a treatise on menstrua, a carter on theology. Two porters are the authors of tragedies, and a customhouse officer of a work on sociology.

As to the subjects chosen, an examination of 186 insane books in my collection gives the following result:

51	deal with Personal Topics
36	are works on Medicine
27	are works on Philosophy
25	contain Lamentations
7	are Dramatic
6	are Religious
6	are Poetry
4	are on Astronomy
4	are on Physics
4	are on Politics
4	are on Political Economy
3	are on Rural
2	are on Veterinary Medicine
2	are on Literature
2	are on Mathematics
1	are on Grammar
1	is a Dictionary

186	

I do not count miscellaneous works, such as controversial treatises, essays on mechanics, studies in magnetism, funeral orations, eccentric theological works, researches in literary history, proclamations, matrimonial advertisements, &c.

Some statistics compiled by Philomneste give a list of such books known in Europe, which are thus classified:

Theology	82
Prophecy (esoteric mysticism)	44
Philosophy	36
Politics	28
Poetry and Drama	9
Languages and Grammar	8
Erotic Literature	5
Hieroglyphics	3
Astronomy	2
Aeronautics	2
Chemistry	1
Physics	1
Zoology	1
Strategy	1
Chronology	1
Hygiene	1
Pedagogy	1
Archæology	1

While poetry prevails among the insane, theology and prophecy predominate in the mattoids, and so on in diminishing proportions for the more abstract, uncertain and incomplete sciences, as we see by the scarcity of the naturalists and mathematicians. It is well to note the small number of atheists—three only, amid such a swarm of theologians and philosophers (162). Spiritualism, on the other hand, is so much in favour, that

Philomneste gave up the task of cataloguing the works which treated of it.

All topics are welcome to mattoids, even those most foreign to their profession or occupation; but they are found to choose by preference the most grotesque and uncertain subjects, or questions which it is impossible to solve. Such are the quadrature of the circle, hieroglyphics, exposition of the Apocalypse, air-balloons, and spiritualism. They are also fond of treating the subjects most talked of—what one might call the questions of the day. Speaking of Démons, who has already been mentioned, Nodier said,

> He was not a monomaniac—very much the contrary; he was a many-sided madman, always ready to repeat any strange thing that came to his ears, a chameleon-like dreamer, who insanely reflected the colours of the moment.[11]

Thus, at the time of our great national deficits, projectors appeared by the dozen, with proposals to restore the Italian finances, either by means of assignats, or by the spoliation of the Jews or the clergy, by forced loans, &c. Later on, came the social and religious problem (Passanante, Lazzaretti, Bosisio, Cianchettini); at the present moment the question most under discussion is that of the *pellagra.*

---

11 Philomneste, Junior, *Les fous littéraires: essai bibliographique sur la littérature excentrique, les illuminés, visionnaires*, etc. (Brussels: Gay et Doucé, 1880).

Thus we have, among others, Pari, who has discovered the cause of the disease in certain fungi, which fall from the roofs of dirty huts into the peasants' food, and make them ill. The proof is evident: photograph the section of a hut, and place it under the microscope, and you will find, on comparison, that fungi are more numerous than in town houses where *pellagra* is unknown.

But why do these fungi produce the *pellagra*? The reason is very simple. These fungi contain the substance *fungina*, which burns at 47° (sic). Now, when the outside temperature is at 13° and the body at 32° (sic) the two quantities of caloric are added together, and we burn! This is why sufferers from the *pellagra* appear scorched by the sun!

It is noteworthy that in nearly all—Bosisio, Cianchettini, Passanante, Mangione, De Tommasi, B——, the convictions set forth in their written works are exceedingly deep and firmly fixed. They show as much absurdity and prolixity in their writings as they do common sense and prudence in their verbal answers—even rebutting objections with a single monosyllable, and explaining their own eccentricities with so much good sense and sometimes acuteness that the unlearned may well take their fancies for wisdom; while, later on, they relieve their insane impulses by covering reams of paper.

"The guardian is the true sentinel of the people and government, liberty, the circulation of the press"—was a sentence of Passanante's, which at first seems a mere play on words, but he explained it to experts in these terms: "The liberty of the press, the free circulation of journals constitute a surveillance over the rights of the people." When I asked Bosisio why he was so eccentric as to wear sandals and walk about bare-headed and half-naked in the heat of July, he replied, "To imitate the Romans, and to keep the head healthy, and, lastly, to call public attention to my theories by some visible sign. Would you have stopped to speak to me if I had not been dressed like this?"

Moreover, mattoids—the reverse being the case both with genius and with insanity are united by common interest and sympathy, and, above all, by hatred to the common enemy, the man of genius. They form a kind of freemasonry,—all the more powerful that it is irregular—founded on the common need of resisting the ridicule which inexorably attacks them on every side, on the need of extirpating, or at least opposing, their natural antithesis, genius. Though hating one another, they are firmly united; and though they do not enjoy one another's triumphs, they rejoice in common over the victims who never fail to fall to the lot of one or the other. For, as we have seen, the vulgar, called upon to choose between the mattoid and the man of genius, never hesitate to sacrifice the latter. Even at the present day, many practitioners who take the dosimetricians seriously, laugh at homœopathy; and the academic multitudes who laugh at homœopathy; and the academic multitudes who laugh at Schliemmann and Ardigo never treated the archæological discoveries of Father Secchi in the same way. This is also shown by the emphatic and senseless addresses presented to Coccapieller and Sbarbaro by many individuals who were still more insane than their idols.[12]

This explains why, in spite of the fact that universal suffrage was introduced under the Roman Republic of 1849, the populace never thought of electing Ciceruacchio to the parliament. Ciceruacchio was a rough workingman, but he was sane.

One characteristic which further distinguishes mattoids from criminals and from many of the actually insane is an extreme abstemiousness, which sometimes equals the excesses of the early Cenobites. Bosisio lived on polenta without salt; Passanante on bread only; Lazzaretti often on nothing but a few potatoes; Mangione on peas, beans, rice, &c., at thirteen sous a day. This may be explained by their finding sufficient support and comfort in their own grotesque lucubrations,[13] as is the case

---

12 "Have you ever noticed," writes Daudet (Jack, 2:58), speaking of mattoids, whom he called *les ratés*, "how these people seek each other in Paris, how they are attracted to each other, how they group themselves with their grievances, their demands, their idle and barren vanities? While, in reality, full of mutual contempt, they form a Mutual Admiration Society, outside which the world is a blank to them."

13 "*Mais parmi ces groupes tapageurs qui s'en allaient fredonnant, déclamant, discutant encore, personne ne prenait garde au froid sinistre de la nuit ni au brouillard humide qui tombait. A l'entrée de l'avenue, on s'aperçut que l'heure des omnibus était passée. Tous ces pauvres diables en prirent*

with ascetics and great thinkers; and besides, being usually poor, they prefer to spend their small means in securing the triumph of their ideas rather than in satisfying their stomachs; all the more so, as nearly all of them (Cianchettini, Bosisio, F——, for instance) were scrupulously honest, and almost excessively methodical, keeping account even of scraps of waste-paper, which they catalogued with singular order.

In short, such men, certainly insane in their writings, and sometimes as much so as any patient in an asylum, are scarcely so in the ordinary acts of life, in which they show themselves full of good sense, shrewdness, and even of a sense of order; so that they are quite the reverse of men of real genius—especially those inspired by madness, whose ability in literature is nearly always in inverse proportion to their aptitude for practical life. This is how it happens that many authors of medical eccentricities are practitioners of great repute. Three

---

bravement leur parti. La chimére aux écailles d'or éclairait et abrégeait leur route, l'illusion leur tenait chaud, et répandus dans Paris désert, ils se tournaient courageusement aux misères obscures de la vie.

"*L'art est un si grand magician! Il crée un soleil qui luit pour tons comme l'autre, et ceux qui s'en approchent, même les pauvres, même les laides, même les grotesques, emportent un peu de sa chaleur et de son rayonnement. Ce feu du del imprudemment ravi, que les ratés gardent au fond de leurs prunelles, les rend quelquefois redoutables, le phis souvent ridicules, mais leur existence en reçoit une sérénité grandiose, un mépris du mal, une grâce à souffrir que les autres misères ne connaissent pas*" (Daudet, Jack, 1:3).

such are directors of hospitals. The author of the *Scottatinge* is a captain and commissariat officer. Another, the inventor of almost prehistoric machines, and author of works which are more than humorous, fills an office which exposes him to continual contact with cultivated men who have never suspected him of madness. Five are professors, two of whom are attached to a university; three are deputies, two senators, one is a counsellor of state, one counsellor of prefecture, and another counsellor of the Court of Cassation. Three are provincial counsellors, and five, priests; and nearly all of them are of advanced age and respected in their vocations. Frécot was mayor of Hesloup, Leroux and Asgill were members of parliament. Mattoid theologians—Simon Morin, Lebreton, Geoffroi Vallée, Vanini—have unfortunately been taken so seriously as to be burned alive or hanged. Joris's bones were burned with his writings under the gallows at Bale. Kehler was beheaded for the sole offence of having corrected Joris's proofs. We shall see, in the following chapter, how many others—Smith, Fourier, Kleinov, Fox—found fanatical followers.

That calmness, in spite of obstinate persistence in a delusion, which distinguishes them from more ordinary insane patients, may also be observed in monomaniacs—is even their most prominent characteristic—and is not rarely found in some of the stages of inebriety.

But, precisely as in the ordinary insane, so also in mattoids, the calm sometimes suddenly ceases, and gives place to impulsive forms of mania and delusion, especially under the stimulus of hunger or irritated passion, or during the return of the various neuroses which accompany and often generate the disease, as in the cases of Cordigliani and Mangione.

This is why it is important to note that many are subject to symptoms which indicate the pre-existence of disturbance at the nervous centres. Giraud and Spandri have convulsive movements of the face, lowering of the right eyebrow, and ptosis on the right side. Anæsthesia was found in Lazzaretti, Mangione, and De Tommasi; delusions of short duration in Cordigliani. P——, a young man of distinguished abilities, became mattoid only after an attack of typhus fever. Kuhlmann became a prophet at eighteen, after suffering from disease of the brain. These impulsive outbursts make such cases extremely important to alienist physicians who, finding no similar cases in any of the better-known forms of mental disease, often erroneously infer imposture, or soundness of mind—and still more to politicians who, by not at once placing such men (at first, it is true, far more ridiculous than dangerous) in asylums, expose themselves to perils perhaps greater than those threatened by actual madmen, who betray themselves at once, thus making it possible to take measures for rendering them harmless.

There is a much more dangerous variety of these graphomaniacs—those whose disease was formerly known as "lawsuit mania." These individuals feel a continual craving to go to law against others, while considering themselves the injured party. They display an extraordinary activity, and a minute knowledge of the law, which they always try to interpret to their own advantage, heaping up petition on petition, memorial on memorial, in such quantities as is difficult to imagine. Many attach themselves to some person, to obtain whose influence they are continually scheming; then they apply to the King or the Parliament. They are apt to succeed at first, especially with members of Parliament, or at least to be considered merely as over-zealous suitors. At last, however, when their persistence has wearied every one out, they convert their forensic and literary violence into deeds, certain that everything will be pardoned them in consideration of the justice of their cause—nay, that their action will have the effect of deciding the suit in their favour. This result, to tell the truth, sometimes ensues, thanks to the institution of the jury. Thus G——, having lost his cause, shot at and wounded Count Colli, but was acquitted through the singular eloquence he displayed before the jury. Ten years later, he forced his way, armed, into an apartment which he had already sold, and which, nevertheless, he insisted on having back.

As the erotomaniac falls in love with an ideal person, and imagines himself loved by one who has never even seen him, so they can see no aspect of the case but their own; and the lawyers and judges who do not support them become enemies on whom they concentrate the fiercest hatred, and whom they look on as the cause of every misfortune that may befall them. It is not rare to find them constituting themselves judges in their own cause, pronouncing sentence, on their own responsibility, on their adversaries, and sometimes going the length of executing the same. A certain B——, from whom the parish priest had taken a field by a perfectly legal and regular contract, took it into his head that he had the right to assault all the priests of his village, "because," he said, "Catholicism is in opposition to the Government." For the same reason he tried to burn down the church; and all this, after a series of lawsuits and proclamations, very just, it may be conceded, in principle, but certainly not in application.

These persons have, too, a similar kind of handwriting, with very much lengthened letters; and they likewise abuse the alphabet. Their theme, however, is confined to their immediate circle, and they show more violence in dealing with it; they, only touch by rebound, as it were, on social and religious questions.

Yet the personal litigations of many of these suitors are mixed up with political differences; and this is the kind from which most danger is to be expected in our day. These are usually individuals whose scant education and extreme poverty do not allow them to air their ideas in print, so that they have to relieve their feelings by deeds of violence.

Such was Sandon, who caused such annoyance to Napoleon and to Billault, and was a genuine political mattoid; such, too, were Cordigliani, Passanante, Mangione, and Guiteau. Krafft-Ebing speaks of a man who had founded a Club of the Oppressed, for the assistance of those who could get no justice from the Courts, and forwarded its rules to the king.

Mattoids of Genius.—Not only is there an imperceptible gradation between sane and insane, between madmen and mattoids, but also between these last (who are the very negation of genius) and men of real genius. So much so, that among my collection there are certain individuals I find a difficulty in classifying. Such, for instance, is Bosisio, of Lodi.

L. Bosisio, of Lodi, fifty-three years of age, has one cousin, a *crétin*. His mother is sane and intelligent; his father intelligent, but given to drink. He had two brothers who died of meningitis. As a young man he became a revenue officer; left his native town in 1848, and when nearly dying of hunger at Turin, threw himself from a balcony and broke his legs. Having obtained promotion in 1859, he fulfilled his duties in a satisfactory manner up to the year 1866, when—though still showing intelligence and accuracy in the duties of his office—he began to perform eccentric actions, especially inexplicable in a member of the bureaucracy. Thus, one day, he bought all the birds for sale in the village of Bussolengo, and then opened their cages and set them at liberty. He took to reading newspapers all day long, and began to send energetic protests to the Government, petitioning them to put a stop to the disforesting of the country, the massacre of birds, &c. Being dismissed from his post, with a meagre pension, he suddenly gave up all the luxuries of life, and took no food but polenta without salt. He left off, one at a time, all his clothes except shirt and drawers, and spent all his scanty means in the purchase of books and papers, and in publishing works on the regeneration of posterity, which he distributed gratuitously—*Criticism on My Times, The Cry of Nature*, "§ 113 of the *Cry of Nature*".

To any one who studies these books, and, still more, to one who hears him talk, it is evident that he has worked out in his own head a system not entirely illogical. We suffer loss, he says, through the grape disease, through the diseases among the silkworms and crabs, through floods. All these things are caused by injury done to the globe through the destruction of forests and the extermination of birds, and (this is where we first perceive his madness) the torture inflicted on it by the railways which pass over its surface. In economical matters, we are doing equally ill; by raising ruinous loans we are compromising the future of that posterity whose champion he has appointed himself.

"Add to this," he continues,

> that the ancient Romans took much exercise, had not the luxury that we have, and did not take coffee. All these things compromise posterity, because they ruin the germs of humanity. And what ruins them far more is the ill-treatment of women, marriages for the sake of money, and certain forms of ill-judged charity. Unhappy children, crippled or consumptive, are kept alive, who, if killed in time, would not reproduce themselves; and, in the same way, if, instead of keeping sickly individuals alive in hospitals, at great trouble and expense, people were to help the strong and healthy when they fall ill, the race would be improved. And thieves and murderers are they, too, not sick men who ought to be exterminated, if the race is not to be ruined? How deadly and bestial is human greed! Everything is neglected for the sake of satisfying the appetites, without a thought for the fate of the generations who are to succeed us. . . . The ill-omened mania for procreation, which is inexorably precipitating all nations into an abyss whence one can see no outlet, and which arrested the attention of Malthus, reminds me of the story of Midas, who asked of a god that everything which he touched might turn to gold. The divinity consented; but his first transports of joy were followed by grief and despair, and his very food being changed into gold, he saw himself condemned by himself to die of hunger.

I think there could be no better example than this to prove the existence of an active and powerful mind, unsound on a single given point. Any one who knows the writings of Clémence Royer and Comte will, in fact, find nothing insane in these ideas of Bosisio's, except his refusal to eat salt (which he scarcely justifies by adducing the example of savages who are strong and healthy without it), his notion of railways ruining the globe, and his very airy fashion of dress. For this last whim, however, he gives a tolerably good reason, by alleging the example of Roman simplicity, and by the assertion (not altogether without foundation) that the wearing of a hat tends to promote baldness. Moreover, he observed, very justly, that without those eccentric habits he would be unable to gain a hearing and promulgate his ideas.

A truly morbid symptom, however, is to be found in the fact that he based all his conclusions on the information gained from political journals—poor material, indeed, for study. However, he justified himself thus: "What can I do? They are modern studies, and I cannot do without them, much as I dislike them, as I have no other means of gaining information about mankind." But the point where his insanity comes out most clearly is in the importance attached by him to the slightest fact gathered up in these sweepings of the political world. If a child falls into the water at Lisbon, or a lady sets her skirts on fire, he immediately infers from these facts the degeneracy of the race. The student of hygiene must be astonished at seeing a man retain robust health (and Bosisio walks his twenty miles a day) on unsalted polenta. The psychologist cannot refuse to recognize in this case that madness acts like leaven on the intellectual powers, and excites the psychic functions so as almost to reach the level of genius, though not without traces of disease. It is certain that if Bosisio had been a student of law or medicine, instead of a poor exciseman, and had been grounded in the culture which he only gained at haphazard, and under the influence of mental disease, he might have become a Clémence Royer or a Comte, or at least another Fourier; for his philosophic system is, in the main, similar to that of the latter, except for the peculiarities engrafted on it by mental aberration.

But, when we think of the integrity of his life, the method and order to be perceived in all his affairs, can we dismiss him merely as a man of unsound mind? And, when we remember the relative novelty of his ideas, can we confuse him with the many absurd mattoids already described? Certainly not.

Let us suppose that Giuseppe Ferrari, instead of a superior culture, had only received Bosisio's education; we should certainly have had, in place of a savant justly admired by the world, something similar to Bosisio. Certainly, indeed, those systems of historical arithmetic, with kings and republics dying on a fixed day, at the will of the author, can only belong to the world of mental alienation.

The same thing might be said of Michelet, if one thinks of his fancy natural history, his academic obscenities, his incredible vanity,[14] and the later

14 "*Toute une littérature est née de mon Insecte et de mon*

volumes of his *History of France* which are nothing but a tangled thicket of scandalous anecdotes and grotesque paradoxes.[15] So, too, of Fourier and

---

Oiseau.—L'Amour et la Femme restent et resteront, comme ayant deux bases, l'une scientifique, la nature même,—l'autre morale, le cœur des citoyens. . . .

«J'ai défini l'histoire une résurrection.—C'est le titre le plus approprié à mon 4 volume. . . .

"*En 1870, dans le silence universel, seul, je parlai. Mon livre fait en 40 jours fut la seule défense de la patrie. . . .*" [The above text is inaccurate; the original source is an article by Othenin D'Heussonville, published in two parts in *Revue des deux mondes*, in May 1876 and June 1876, memorialising the life and works of Jules Michelet. The text reads (and this is D'Heussonville's voice, not Michelet's, except when quoting): "*Toute une littérature est née de l'Oiseau et de l'Insecte. L'Amour et la Femme «restent et resteront comme ayant deux fortes bases, la base scientifique, la nature elle-même, et la base morale, le cœur d'un citoyen.» . . . «J'ai défini l'histoire: résurrection. Si cela fut jamais, c'est au quatrième volume (le volume de Charles VI) . . . »*" The paragraph beginning "En 1870 . . ." does not appear in the text. —Ed.]

15 He studies, as an important document, the journal of Louis XIV.'s digestion, and divides his reign into two periods before and after the fistula. In the same way Francis I.'s reign is divided into the periods before and after the abscess. Conclusions of the following kind abound:

"*De toute l'ancienne monarchie, il ne reste à la France qu'un nom, Henri IV.; et deux chansons Gabrielle et Marlborough.*" [This is taken from the D'Heussonville's article mentioned in the previous footnote and is not quite right; the first chapter of the third volume of Jules Michelet's *Histoire de France* (Paris: Libraire Internationale A. Lacroix & Cie, 1877) actually reads: "*De toute l'ancienne monarchie, il reste à la France un nom, Henri IV, plus, deux chansons. La première est Gabrielle, ce doux rayon de la paix après les horreurs de la Ligue. La seconde chanson, c'est Marlborough, une dérision de la guerre, une ironie innocente par laquelle le pauvre peu-*

his disciples, who predict with mathematical exactness that, 80,000 years hence, man will attain to the age of 144; that in those days we shall have 37 millions of poets (unhappy world!); likewise 37 millions of mathematicians equal to Newton; of Lemercier, who, along with some very fine dramas, wrote some in which speeches are assigned to ants, seals, and the Mediterranean; and of Burchiello, who asks painters to depict for him an earthquake in the air, and describes a mountain giving a pair of spectacles to a bell-tower! The same is true of the heir of Confucius, the astronomer who created the *Dio Liberate*; of the pseudo-geologist who has discovered a secret of embalming bodies which might be known to any assistant demonstrator of anatomy, and who believes that the world can be purified by cremation.

In Italy, a man has for many years been a professor in one of the great universities who, in his treatises, created the nation of the *cagots*, and suggested a certain instrument for resuscitating the apparently drowned, which would have been enough to suffocate a healthy person. Another talked of baths at a temperature of—20°, and the advantages of sea-water owing to the exhalations of the fish! Yet his volumes contain some very fine things, and have reached a second edition, and none of his colleagues ever suspected that his mind was not perfectly sound. How is he to be classified? He occupies a middle place between the

ple de Louis XIV se revengeait de ses revers." —Ed.]

madman, the man of genius, and the graphomaniac, with which last he has in common the sterility of his aims, and his calm and persistent search after paradoxes.

Italy, for the rest, as I have shown in *Tre Tribuni*,[16] has had, and idolized, for a brief quarter of an hour, two mattoids of considerable gifts, Coccapieller and Sbarbaro, who, in the midst of immoralities, trivialities, contradictions, and paradoxes, had a few traits of genius,[17] explicable by a less degree of misoneism, and a greater facility in adopting new ideas.

Décadent Poets.—Some acquaintance with this new variety of literary madmen will explain to us the existence, in the seventeenth century, of the French *précieux*, and, at the present day, that of the *Parnassiens*, *Symbolistes*, and *Décadents*.

"I have read their verses," says Lemaitre,

> and not even seen as much as the turkey in the fable, who, if he did not distinguish very well, at

16 119, 120, 121.

17 Sbarbaro, *e.g.*, in the midst of numberless absurdities, wrote; "The man who feels no hatred for the foul and unjust things which cumber our social life is the false phantom of a citizen, a eunuch in heart and mind" Forche, 21).

"Parliamentary systems do not work well, since they do not allow of the best being at the top, and nonentities at the bottom" (Forche, 3). This, however, is borrowed from Machiavelli's Decades.

"If you call me a malcontent," he said to the Council of Public Instruction, "you do me honour: progress is due to rebels and malcontents. Christ Himself was a rebel and an agitator."

least saw something. I have been able to make nothing of these series of words, which—being connected together according to the laws of syntax—might be supposed to have some sense, and have none, and which spitefully keep your mind on the stretch in a vacuum, like a conundrum without an answer. . . .

En ta dentelle où n'est notoire
Mon doux évanouisseinent,
Taisons pour l'âtre sans histoire
Tel vœu de lèvres résumant.

Toute ombre hors d'un territoire
Se teinte itérativement
À la lueur exhalatoire
Des pétales de remuenient.

One of them, however, has explained to us what they intended doing, in a pamphlet modestly entitled, *Traité du Verbe*, by Stéphane Mallarmé. By this it appears that they have invented two things—the symbol, and "poetic instrumentation."

The invention of the symbolists seems to consist in *not saying* what feelings, thoughts, or states of mind they express by images. But even this is not new. A SYMBOL is, in short, an enlarged comparison of which only the second term is given—a connected series of metaphors. Briefly, the symbol is the old "allegory" of our fathers.[18]

Now, here is the second discovery made by our wild-eyed symbolists. Men have suspected, ever since Homer's time, that there are re-

18 We have seen that a love of symbolism is one of the characteristics of monomaniacs.

lations, correspondences, affinities, between certain sounds, forms, and colours, and certain states of mind. For instance, it was felt that the repeated sound of *a* had something to do with the impression of freshness and peace produced by this line of Virgil—

Pascitur in silva magna formosa juvenca.

It was known that sounds may, like colours, be striking or subdued; like feelings, sad or joyful. But it was thought that these resemblances and relations are somewhat fugitive, having nothing constant or sharply-defined, and that they are, at least, hinted at by the sense of the words which compose the musical phrase.

Now, attend to this! For these gentlemen, *a* = black, *e* = white, *i* = blue, *o* = red, *u* = yellow.

Again, black = the organ, white = the harp, blue = the violin, red = the trumpet, yellow = the flute.

Again, the organ expresses monotony, doubt, and simplicity; the harp, serenity; the violin, passion and prayer; the trumpet, glory and ovation; the flute, smiles and ingenuousness.

It is difficult to make out to what degree the young *symbolards* still take account of the sense of words. That degree, however, is, in any case, very slight, and, for my part, I cannot well distinguish the passages where they are obscure from those where they are only unintelligible.

In short, a poetry without thoughts, at once primitive and subtle, which does not (like classic poetry) express a connected series of ideas, nor (like the poetry of the *Parnassiens*) the physical world in its exact outlines, but states

> of mind in which we can scarcely distinguish ourselves from surrounding objects, where sensation is so closely united to sentiment; where the latter grows so rapidly and naturally out of the former, that it is quite sufficient for us to note down our sensations at random just as they present themselves, to express *ipso facto* the emotions which they successively give rise to in the mind.
>
> Do you understand? . . . Neither do I. One would have to be drunk in order to understand this.[19]

I can only conceive that the poetry, an attempt to define which has here been made, could be that of a solitary, a nerve-sufferer, and almost a madman. This poetry thus flourishes on the borderland between reason and madness.

Yet these mattoids have their man of genius—Verlaine. Let us hear Lemaitre on this subject:—

> I imagine he must be almost illiterate. He has a strange head the profile of Socrates, an enormous forehead, a skull knobbed like a battered basin of thin copper. He is not civilized, he ignores all received codes of morality.
>
> One day he disappears. What has become of him? It would be in character for him to have been publicly cast out from regular society. I see him behind the grate of a prison, like François

19 Julies Lemaitre, "M. Paul Verlaine et les poètes «symbolistes» & «decadents»", *Revue politique et littéraire* XLI.1 (7 January 1888) 2-14.

Villon—not for having, like him, become an accomplice of thieves and rogues, for the love of a free life, but rather for an error of over-sensitiveness—for having avenged (by an involuntary stab, given, as it were, in a dream) a love reprobated by the laws and customs of the modern and Western world. But, though socially degraded, he remains innocent. He repents as simply as he sinned with a Catholic repentance, all terror and tenderness, without reasoning, without pride of intellect. In his conversion, as in his sin, he remains a purely emotional being. . . .

Then, it may be, a woman took pity on him, and he let himself be led like a little child. He reappears, but continues to live apart. No one has ever seen him on the Boulevards, or in a theatre, or at the Salon. He is somewhere at the other end of Paris, in the back-room of a wine-merchant's shop, drinking blue wine. He is as far from us as if he were an innocent satyr in the great forests. When he is ill, or at the end of his resources, some doctor, whom he knew formerly, when in jail, gets him into the hospital; he stays there as long as he can and writes verses; he hears queer, sad songs whispered to him out of the folds of the cold white calico curtains. He is not a *déclassé*, for he never had a class. His case is rare and peculiar. He finds means to live, in a civilized society, as he could live in a state of the freest nature.

It may be that he has sometimes felt for an instant the influence of some contemporary poets, but these have done nothing for him, save to awaken and reveal to him the extreme and painful sensibility which is his whole being. In the main, he is without a master. He moulds language at his will, not, like a great writer because he knows it, but, like a child, because he is ignorant of it. He gives wrong senses to words in his simplicity. Little as we might expect it, this poet, whom his disciples regard as such a consummate artist, writes on occasion (if we may dare to speak out), like a pupil of the technical schools, or a second-rate chemist subject to lyric outbursts. After this, it is amusing to see him while posing as the impeccable artist, the sculptor of strophes, the gentleman who distrusts imagination, write, with the keenest sense of enjoyment:—

À nous qui ciselons les mots comme des coupes
Et qui faisons des vers émus très froidement. . . .
Ce qu'il nous faut, à nous, c'est, aux hieurs des lampes,
La science conquise et le sommeil dompté.

Yet this writer, so wanting in ordinary technical skill, has yet written—I cannot tell how—verses of a penetrating sweetness, a languid charm which is peculiarly his own, and which perhaps arises from a union of these things charm of sound, clearness of feeling, and partial obscurity in the words. Thus, when he tells us that he is dreaming of an unknown woman, who loves him, who understands him, and weeps with him, he adds:—

Son nom? Je me souviens qu'il est doux et sonore,
Comme ceux des aimés que la vie exila.

Son regard est pareil au regard des statues,
Et pour sa voix lointaine, et calme, et grave, elle a

L'inflexion des voix chères qui se sont tues.'

I am also very fond of the *Chanson d'Automne*, though certain words (*blême* and *suffocant*) are not perhaps used with entire accuracy, and scarcely correspond with the "languor" described just before.

Les sanglots longs
Des violons
De l'automne
Blessent mon cœur
D'une langueur
Monotone.

Tout suffocant
Et blême, quand
Sonne l'heure,
Je me souviens
Des jours anciens,
Et je pleure.

Et je m'en vais
Au vent mauvais
Qui m'emporte
De ça, de là,
Pareil à la
Feuille morte.

He celebrates the Virgin in an exceedingly fine hymn:—

Je ne veux plus aimer qne ma mère Marie.

. . . . . .

Et, comme j'etais faible et bien médiant encore,
Aux mains lâches, les yeux éblouis des chemins,
Elle baissa vies yeux, et me joignit les mains
Et m'enseigna les mots par lesquels on adore.

. .

. .
Et tous ces bons efforts vers les croix et les claies,
Comme je l'invoquais, Elle en ceignit mes reins.

His piety inspires him with some very sweet lines:—

Écoutez la chanson bien douce
Qui ne pleure que pour vous plaire.
Elle est discrète, elle est legère:
Un frisson d'eau sur de la mousse! . . .

Elle dit, la voix reconnue,
Que la bonté c'est notre vie,
Que de la haine et de l'envie
Rien ne reste, la mort venue. . . .

Accueillez la voix qui persiste
Dans son naïf épithalame.
Allez, rien n'est meilleur à l'âme
Que de faire une âme mains triste! . . .

Je ne me souviens plus que du mal que j'ai fait.

Dans tons les mouvements bizarres de ma vie,
De mes "malheurs" selon le moment et le lieu,
Des auttres et de moi, de la route suivie,
Je n'ai rien retenu que la grace de Dieu.

But, even in the *Poëmes Saturmens*, we already meet with pieces of an oddity difficult to define—pieces which seem to belong to a poet who is slightly mad, or perhaps to one who is only half awake, and whose brain is darkened by the fumes of his dreams, or of drink; so that external objects only appear to him through a mist, and the indolence of his memory prevents him from getting hold of the right words. Take this for an example:—

La lune plaquait ses teintes de zinc
Par angles obtus;

Des bouts de fumée en forme de cinq
Sortaient drus et noirs des hauts toils pointus.

Le ciel était gris. La bise pleurait
Ainsi qu'un basson.
An loin un matou frileux et discret
Miaulait d'étrange et grêle façon.

Moi, j'allal's révant du divin Platon
Et de Phidias,
Et de Salamine et de Marathon,
Sous l'œil clignotant des bleus becs de gaz.

That is all. What is it? It is an impression—the impression of a gentleman who walks about the streets of Paris at night, and thinks about Plato and Salamis, and thinks it funny to think of Plato and Salamis "*sous l'œil des becs de gaz.*" Why should it be funny? I cannot tell.

Aimez donc la raison: que toujours vos écrits
Empruntent d'elle seule et leur lustre et leur prix.

One might almost say that Paul Verlaine is the only poet who has never expressed anything but sentiment and sensation, and has expressed them for himself, and for no one else,[20] which dispenses him from the obligation of showing the connection between his ideas, since he knows it. This poet has never asked himself whether he should be understood, and he has never wished to prove anything. This is why (*Sagesse* excepted) it is almost impossible to give a *résumé* of his collections, or to state their main idea in a succinct form. One can only characterise them by means of the state of mind of which they are most frequently the rendering—

20 M. Jules Tellier has not inaptly called him, in Victor Hugo's style, "*l'homine-frisson.*"

semi-intoxication, hallucination which distorts objects, and makes them resemble an incoherent dream; uneasiness of the soul which, in the terror of this mystery, complains like a child; then languor, mystic sweetness, and a lulling of the mind to rest, in the Catholic conception of the universe accepted in all simplicity.

There is something profoundly involuntary and illogical in the poetry of M. Paul Verlaine. He scarcely ever expresses movements of full consciousness or entire sanity. It is on this account, very often, that the meaning of his song is clear—if it is so at all—to himself alone. In the same way, his rhythms are sometimes perceptible by no one but himself. I do not refer here to the interlaced feminine rhymes, alliterations, assonances within the line itself, of which none has made use more frequently or more successfully than he.

But there are two sides to him. On one, he looks very artificial. He has an *Ars Poetica* of his own, which is entirely subtle and mysterious, and which, I think, he was very late in discovering:—

De la musique avant toute chose,
Et pour cela préfère l'impair
Phis vague et plus soluble dans l'air,
Sans rien en lui qui pèse ou qui pose.

Il faut aussi que tit n'ailles point
Choisir tes mots sans quelque méprise:
Rien de plus cher que la chanson grise
Où l'indécis au précis se joint. . . .

Car nous vonlons la nuance encor,
Pas la couleur, rien que la nuance!
Oh! la nuance seule fiance
Le rêve an rêve, et la flute au cor. . . .

On the other side, he is quite simple:—

Je suis venu, calnie orphelin,
Riche de mes seuls yeux tranquilles,
Vers les hommes des grandes villes:
Ils ne m'ont pas trouve malin.

Or, elsewhere:—

J'ai peur d'un baiser
Conime d'une abeille.
Je souffre et je veille
Sans me reposer
J'ai peur d'un baiser.

Thus far Lemaitre.

It will be seen that the *décadents* correspond exactly to the diagnosis of literary mattoids, in all their old vacuity, but with the appearance of novelty. At the same time, there are among them, real men of genius who—amid the (frequently atavistic) oddities of mattoidism—have struck an original note.

All these cases show us that the gradations and transitions between sanity and insanity are far from being as hypothetical as Livi asserts them to be. Moreover, all this is in perfect harmony with the eternal evolution which we see going on in the ample realm of nature, which, as has been well said, never proceeds by leaps, but by successive and gradual transformations.

Now, it is natural that, as these gradations exist in this very strange form of literary insanity, they should also be found in the forms of criminal insanity, and that, in consequence, many of those asserted to be guilty or mad, are only half responsible, although no human thought can trace the limits with entire certainty.

It is well to observe here, what a different appearance madness assumes, according to the age in which it occurs. Had Bosisio lived in the Middle Ages, or in Spain or Mexico at a later period, the kind-hearted liberator of birds, the martyr for posterity, would have become a St. Ignatius or a Torquemada—the Positivist atheist an ultra-Catholic, commanded by a cruel Deity to immolate human victims; but Bosisio was an Italian, living in 1870.

This case affords an excellent explanation of the occurrence, in remote times, and among savage or slightly civilized nations, of numerous outbreaks of epidemic insanity; and shows that many historical events may have been the result of mania on the part of one or more persons. Cases in point are those of the Anabaptists, the Flagellants, the witch-mania, the Taeping revolution.

Mental aberration gives rise in some men to ideas which, though bizarre, are sometimes gigantic and rendered more efficacious by a singular force of conviction, so as to sweep along the feeble-minded multitude, who are all the more attracted by any singularity in dress, attitudes or abstinence (which such disease alone can suggest and render possible), that these phenomena are made inexplicable to them (and therefore worthy of veneration) by their ignorance and barbarism. The ignorant man always adores what he cannot understand.

Our poor sufferer from hallucinations wanted nothing but a favourable epoch to impress his ideas on the multitude—neither muscular strength, nor a certain vigour of thought, nor extraordinary endurance under privations, nor disinterestedness, nor conviction. At another epoch, Italy would have found her Mahomet in Bosisio.

Mattoids in Art.—At the competition opened at Rome for designs for a proposed monument to Victor Emmanuel—the subject being an international one—mattoids came forward in crowds. In fact, we find, in Dossi's curious book,[21] not less than 39 out of 296 (13 per cent.), a number which would be raised to 25 per cent, if we add 38 more, who, in addition to their eccentricity, gave tokens of being imbecile.

The most general characteristic of these productions is their stupidity. One of them proposes a square stone box without a roof (similar to the "magnaneries" or roofless stone buildings used in the South of France for silkworms), which he calls a "Right Quadrangular Tower"—destined to receive the late king's remains, and protect them against the inundations of the Tiber. Tr——'s monument "destined to live for centuries" consists of a column surrounded by obelisks, by four flights of steps, and four triangles, each surrounded by twelve small spires. Each of the latter is to sup-

21 Carlo Dossi, *I mattoidi al primo concorso pel monument in Roma a Vittorio Emanuele II* (Rome: A. Sommaruga E. C., 1884).

port a bust, each of the columns a statue of some great Italian; with regard to six statues, the artist reserves the right of changing them at the death of our illustrious men—Sella, Mamiani, &c. This is a case for saying, "Perish the astrologer!" Another competitor—two, in fact—have projected rooms to serve as public lavatories at the base of their columns. There is a curious coincidence and emulation of hatred in nearly all; most of them make use of celebrated monuments, whose destruction is, of course, a *sine qua non* to the erection of theirs.

But, if wanting in every sign of genius, these designs are not deficient in allegorical symbols of the most grotesque type, or in inscriptions. Some of them, indeed, are nothing but a mass of irrelevant inscriptions, relating to everything in the world, except the poor *Re Galantuomo* himself—but more particularly to the supposed genius of the artist.

Here we find that the main characteristic of such minds—vanity, heightened to the point of disease—makes each of them think his own production a masterpiece. Cànfora declares that he is "neither engineer nor architect, but *inspired by God alone*." A. B. does not send in his design to the Committee, because it is too grand; and another ends by saying, "How mighty is the thought of the artist!"

Nearly all are absolutely ignorant of the art in which they claim to excel. Thus Dossi found among the projectors, teachers of mathematics and of grammar, doctors in medicine and in law, military men, accountants, and others who themselves asserted that they had never before handled pencil or compasses. At the same time, their far from humble social position bears out what I consider to be one of the principal points: *viz.*, that we have before us (as might be suspected) idiots, or persons actually insane, but men quite respectable outside their special artistic mania. Such should be M——, a member of the Russian Archæological Society, of the Hellenic Syllage, Architect-in-chief of Roumelia and the palaces of the Sultan, Knight and Commander of various Orders, &c., &c.

When we compare these stupid abortions with the pictures inspired by insanity (I am not now speaking of those painters who, like various poets and musicians, in losing their reason, lost artistically more than they gained—especially in right proportion and the harmony of colour), we shall often find the absurd and disproportionate; but also, at the same time, a true, even excessive originality, mingled with a savage beauty *sui generis*, which, up to a certain point, recalls the masterpieces of mediæval, and, still more, of Chinese and Japanese, art, so extraordinarily rich in symbols. We shall see, in short, that art suffers here, not from a defect, but from an excess of genius, which ends by crushing itself.

In conclusion, it is very evident that the insane artist is as superior to the mattoid in the practice of his art, as he is inferior to him in practical life; that, in short, in the region of art, the mattoid approaches nearest to the imbecile, and the lunatic to the man of genius.

CHAPTER IV

Political and Religious Lunatics and Mattoids

Part played by the insane in the progressive movements of humanity — Examples — Probable causes — Religious epidemics of the Middle Ages — Francis of Assisi — Luther — Savonarola — Cola da Rienzi —Campanella — San Juan de Dios — Prosper — Enfantin — Lazzaretti — Passanante — Guiteau — South Americans

All this helps us to understand why the great progressive movements of nations, in politics and religion, have so often been brought about, or at least determined, by insane or half-insane persons. The reason is that in these alone is to be found, coupled with originality (which is the special characteristic of the genius and the lunatic, and still more of those who partake of the character of both), the exaltation capable of generating a sufficient amount of altruism to sacrifice their own interests, and their lives, for the sake of making known the new truths, and, often, of getting them accepted by a public to which innovations are always unwelcome, and which frequently takes a bloody revenge on the innovator.

"Such persons," says Maudsley,

> are apt to seize on and pursue the bypaths of thought, which have been overlooked by more stable intellects, and so, by throwing a side-light on things, to discover unthought-of relations. One observes this tendency of mind even in those of them who have no particular genius or talent; for they have a novel way of looking at things, do not run in the common groove of action, or follow the ordinary routine of thought and feeling, but discover in their remarks a certain originality and perhaps singularity, sometimes at a very early period of life.
>
> Notable, again, is the emancipated way in which some of them discuss, as if they were problems of mechanics, objects or events round which the associations of ideas and feelings have thrown a glamour of conventional sentiment. In regard to most beliefs, they are usually more or less heterodox or heretical, though not often constant, being apt to swing round suddenly from one point to a quite opposite point of the compass of belief. . . . Inspired with strong faith in the opinions which they adopt, they exhibit much zeal and energy in the propagation of them.[1]

They are careless of every obstacle, and untroubled by the doubts which arise in the minds of calm and

---

1 Henry Maudsley, *Responsibility in Mental Disease* (New York: D. Appleton and Co., 1896) 47.

sceptical thinkers. Thus they are frequently social or religious reformers.

It should be understood that they do not *create* anything, but only give a direction to the latest movements prepared by time and circumstances, as also—thanks to their passion for novelty and originality—they are nearly always inspired by the latest discoveries or innovations, and use these as their starting-point in guessing at the future.

Thus Schopenhauer wrote at an epoch in which pessimism was beginning to be fashionable, together with mysticism, and only fused the whole into one philosophic system. Cæsar found the ground prepared for him by the Tribunes.

When, says Taine, a new civilization produces a new art, there are ten men of talent who express the idea of the public and group themselves round one man of genius who gives it actuality; thus De Castro, Moreto, Lopez de la Vega, round Calderón; Van Dyck, Jordaens, De Vos, and Snyders round Rubens.

Luther summed up in himself the ideas of many of his contemporaries and predecessors; it is sufficient to mention Savonarola.

The spherical shape of the earth had already been maintained by St. Thomas Aquinas, and by Dante, before the discoveries of Columbus, which are also antedated by those of the Canary Islands, Iceland, and Cape Verde.

If the new ideas are too divergent from prevalent popular opinion, or too self-evidently absurd, they die out with their author, if, indeed, they do not involve him in their fall.

Arnold of Brescia, Knutzen,[2] Campanella, tried to shake off the dominion of the clergy, and take away the temporal power of the Pope; they were persecuted and crushed.

"The insane person," says Maudsley,

> is in a minority of one in his opinion, and so, at first, is the reformer, the difference being that the reformer's belief is an advance on the received system of thought, and so, in time, gets acceptance, while the belief of the former, being opposed to the common sense of mankind, gains no acceptance, but dies out with its possessor, or with the few foolish persons whom it has infected.[3]

Of late years there has arisen in India, owing to the efforts of Keshub Chunder Sen, a new religion which deifies modern rationalism and scepticism; but here, also, the madness of Keshub evidently outran the march of the times; for the triumph of

2 Knutzen, of Schleswig, in 1674, preached that there was neither God nor devil, that priests and magistrates were useless and pernicious, that marriage was unnecessary, that man ended with death, and that every one ought to be guided by his own inner consciousness of right. For this reason he gave to his disciples the name of the Conscientarii, garnishing his discourses with grotesque quotations. He went about begging and preaching in strange garments. It is not known what became of him after 1674. His writings are Epistola amici ad amicum, Schediasma de lacrimis Christi, &c.

3 Maudsley 53.

a similar religion is not probable, even among us, with our much greater progress in knowledge. Thus, too, Buddhism, finding the ground contested by the caste system in India, took no firm hold there, while it extended itself in China and Tibet. Keshub was induced to take up this line of action by a form of madness analogous to that which we shall also see in B—— of Modena. In fact, this strange rationalist believes in revelation, and in 1879 he declaimed, "I am the inspired prophet," &c.[4]

The same thing may be said of politics. Historical revolutions are never lasting, unless the way has been prepared for them by a long series of events. But the crisis is often precipitated—sometimes many years before its time—by the unbalanced geniuses who outrun the course of events, foresee the development of intermediate facts which escape the common eye, and rush, without a thought of themselves, on the opposition of their contemporaries, acting like those insects which, in flying from one flower to another, transport the pollen which would otherwise have required violent winds, or a long space of time to render it available for fertilization.

Now, if we add the immovable, fanatical conviction of the madman to the calculating sagacity of genius, we shall have a force capable, in any age, of

4 Eugène Goblet d'Alviella, "La Cinquantième anniversaire du Brahma Somaj: Une tentative de religion naturelle dans l'Inde contemporaine", *Revue des Deux Mondes* XLI (1880) 413-445.

acting as a lever on the torpid masses, struck dumb before this phenomenon, which appears strange and rare even to calm thinkers and spectators at a distance. Add further, the influence which madness, in itself, already has over barbarous peoples at early periods, and we may well call the force an irresistible one.

The importance of the madman among savages, and the semi-barbarous peoples of ancient times, is rather historical than pathological. He is feared and adored by the masses, and often rules them. In India, some madmen are held in high esteem, and consulted by the Brahmins—a custom of which many sects bear traces. In ancient India the eight kinds of *demonomania* bore the names of the eight principal Indian divinities; the Yakshia-graha have deep intelligence; the Deva-graha are strong, intelligent, and esteemed and consulted by the Brahmins; the Gandharva-graha serve as choristers to the gods. But, in order to know what a point the veneration of the insane may reach, and how little modern India has changed in this respect, it is quite sufficient to observe that there exist at present in that country 43 sects which show particular zeal towards their divinity, sometimes by drinking urine, sometimes by walking on the points of sharp stones, sometimes by remaining motionless for years exposed to the rays of the sun, or by representing to their own imagination the corporeal image of the god, and offering up to him, also in imagination, prayers, flowers, or food.

The existence of endemic insanity among the ancient Hebrews (and, by parity of reasoning, among their congeners, the Phœnicians, Carthaginians, &c.—the same words being used for *prophet*, *madman*, and *wicked man*) is proved by history and language. The Bible relates that David, fearing that he would be killed, feigned madness,[5] and that Achish said, "Have I need of madmen that ye have brought this fellow to play the madman in my presence?" This passage is evidence of their abundance, and also of their inviolability, which was certainly owing to the belief, still common among the Arabs, which causes the word *nabi* (prophet) to be constantly used in the Bible in the sense of *madman*, and *vice versa*. Saul, even before his coronation, was suddenly seized with the prophetic spirit, so much to the surprise of the bystanders that the event was made the occasion of a proverb—"Is Saul also among the prophets?" One day, after he had become king, the spirit of an evil deity weighed upon him, and he prophesied (here *raged*) in the house, and attempted to transfix David with a lance.[6] In Jeremiah xxix. 26, we read "The Lord hath made thee priest, . . . for every man that is mad and maketh himself a prophet, that thou shouldst put him in prison and in the stocks." In 1 Kings xviii. we see the prophets of the groves, and of Baal crying out like madmen, and cutting their flesh. In the First Book of Samuel

5 I Samuel xxi. 14, 15.

6 Ibid., xix. 9, 10, 23.

we find Saul as a prophet rushing naked through the fields.[7] Elsewhere we see prophets publicly approaching places of ill-fame, cutting their hands, eating filth, &c. The Medjdub of the Arab, and the Persian Davana are the modern analogues.[8]

"*Medjdubim*" says Berbrugger,

> is the name given to these individuals who, under the influence of special circumstances fall into a state which exactly recalls that of the Convulsionnaires of St. Medard. They are numerous in Algeria, where they are better known under the names of Aissawah or Ammarim.

Mula Ahmed, in the narrative of his journey (translated by Berbrugger) speaks of

> Sidi Abdullah, the Medjdub, who brought the best influence to bear on the Hammis, his thievish and vicious fellow-citizens. He would remain for three or five days like a log, without eating, drinking, or praying. He could do without sleep for forty days at the end of which, he was seized with violent convulsions (p. 278).

Further on, he speaks of one Sidi Abdel-Kadr, who wandered from place to place, forgetful of himself and his family—an indifference probably due to

7 Ibid., xix. 24.

8 Louis-Adrien Berbrugger, *Exploration scientifique de l'Algérie pendant les années 1840, 1841, 1842: Par ordre du gouvernement et avec le concours d'une commission académique* (Paris: Librairie de Firmin Didot frères, 1844-1867).

his sainthood. Drummond Hay shows us how far respect for the insane is carried in Morocco, and among the neighbouring nomadic tribes:

> The Moor tells us that God has retained their reason in heaven, whilst their body is upon earth; and that when madmen or idiots speak, their reason is, for the time, permitted to return to them, and that their words should be treasured up as those of inspired persons.

The author himself and an English consul were in danger of being killed by one of these novel saints, who, naked, and often armed, insist on acting out the strangest caprices which enter their heads; and those who oppose them do so at their peril.

In Barbary, says Pananti,[9] the caravans are in the habit of consulting the mad santons (Vasli), to whom nothing is forbidden. One of them strangled every person who came to the mosque; another at the public baths violated a newly married bride,

9 *Travels*, p. 133. [I was unable to find a book by this or similar title by Filippo Pananti. The most likely source seems to be Filippo Pananti, *Avventure o osservazioni di Filippo Pananti sopra le coste di Barberia* (Florence: Firenze, Presso L. Ciardetti, 1817), but the information referred to is not contained in the page given. An English language text recounting Pananti's travels exists with the title *Narrative of a residence in Algiers: comprising a geographical and historical account of the regency; biographical sketches of the dey and his ministers; anecdotes of the late war; observations on the relations of the Barbary States with the Christian powers* (London: H. Colburn, 1818). —Ed.]

and her companions congratulated the fortunate husband on the occurrence.

The Ottomans[10] extend to the insane the veneration which they have for dervishes, and believe that they stand in a special relation to the Deity. Even the ministers of religion receive them into their own houses with great respect. They are called *Eulya, Ullah Deli*—"divine ones," "sons of God"—or, more accurately, "madmen of God." And the various sects of Dervishes present phenomena analogous to those of madness. Every monastery[11] has its own species of prayer or dance—or rather its own peculiar kind of convulsion. Some move their bodies from side to side, others backwards and forwards, and gradually quicken the motion as they go on with their prayer. These movements are called *Mukabdi* (heightening of the divine glory), or *Ovres Tewhid* (praise of the unity of God). The Kufais are distinguished above all other orders by exaggerated sanctity. They sleep little, lying, when they do, with their feet in water, and fast for weeks together. They begin the chant of Allah, advancing the left foot and executing a rotatory movement with the right, while holding each other by the forearm. Then they march forward, raising their voices more and more, quickening the motion of the dance, and throwing their arms over each other's shoulders, till, worn out and perspiring, with

10 Christian Daniel Beck, *Allgemeine Schilderung des Othomanischen Reichs*, 2 vols. (Leipzig: Weidmann, 1788) 177.

11 *Ibid.* 529.

glazing eyes and pale faces, they fall into the sacred convulsion (*haluk*). In this state of religious mania (says our author) they submit to the ordeal of hot iron, and, when the fire has burnt out, cut their flesh with swords and knives.

In Batacki, when a man is possessed by an evil spirit, he is greatly respected; what he says is looked on as the utterance of an oracle, and immediately obeyed.[12]

In Madagascar, the insane are objects of veneration. In 1863 many people were seized with tremors, and impelled to strike those who came near them. They were also subject to hallucinations and saw the dead queen coming out of her grave. The king ordered these persons to be respected, and for a space of at least two months, soldiers were seen beating their officers, and officials their superiors.

In China the only well defined traits of insanity are to be found in the only Chinese sect which was ever conspicuous, in that sceptical nation, for religious fanaticism. The followers of Tao[13] believe in

12 In the original footnote, Lombroso give's as his source 'Ida Pfeiffer, *Voyage*, vols. v., vi.', suggesting he is using the French translation—*Voyage à Madagascar, traduit de l'allemand avec l'autorisation de la famille de l'auteur, par W. de Suckau et précédé d'une notice historique sur Madagascar, par Francis Riaux* (Paris: Hachette, 1881). However, the latter is a single volume of around 400 pages. The German-language edition—*Reise nach Madagaskar: nebst einer Biographie der Verfasserin, nach ihren eigenen Aufzeichnungen* (Vienna: Carl Gerold's Sohn, 1861)—has only four volumes. —Ed.

13 Walter Henry Medhurst, *China, its state and prospects: with especial reference to the spread of the Gospel containing allu-*

demoniacal possession, and endeavour to gather the future from the utterances of madmen, thinking that the possessed person declares in words the thought of the spirit.

In Oceania, at Tahiti, a species of prophet was called *Eu-toa*—*i.e.*, possessed of the divine spirit. The chief of the island said that he was a bad man (*toato-eno*). Omai, the interpreter, said that these prophets were a kind of madmen, some of whom, in their attacks, were not conscious of what they were doing, nor could they afterwards remember what they had done.[14]

With regard to America, Schoolcraft, in that enormous medley entitled *Historical and Statistical Information of the Indian Tribes*[15] (1854), says that the regard for madmen is a characteristic trait of the Indian tribes of the north, and especially of Oregon, who are considered the most savage. Among these latter, he mentions a woman who showed every symptom of insanity—sang in a grotesque manner, gave away to others all the trifles she possessed, and

---

sions to the antiquity, extent, population, civilization, literature, and religion of the Chinese (London: John Snow, 1838) 75.

14 Cook, *Voyages*, 2:19. [No edititon specified. —Ed.]

15 Henry Rowe Schoolcraft, *Historical and Statistical Information Respecting the History, Condition, and Prospects of the Indian Tribes of the United States: Collected and Prepared under the Direction of the Bureau of Indian Affairs, Per Act of Congress of March 3d, 1847*, 6 vols. (Philadelphia: Lippincott, Gambo & Company, 1851, 1852, 1854; J. B. Lippincot & Co., 1855, 1857) 4:49.

cut her flesh when they refused to accept them. The Indians treated her with great respect.

The Patagonians[16] have women-doctors and magicians who prophesy amid convulsive attacks. Men may also be elected to the priesthood, but they must then dress as women, and cannot be admitted unless they have, from their childhood, shown special qualifications. What these are is shown by the fact that epileptics are appointed as a matter of course, as possessing the divine spirit.

In Peru, besides the priests, there were prophets who uttered their improvisations amid terrible contortions and convulsions. They were venerated by the people, but despised by the higher classes.[17]

All revolutions in Algeria and in the Soudan[18] are due to lunatics or neurotics who make, of their own neurosis and the religious societies to which they attach themselves, instruments for invigorating religious fanaticism and getting themselves accepted as inspired messengers of God. Such were the Mahdi, Omar, and a madman who headed the great revolt of the Taepings in China.[19]

---

16 Alcide Dessalines Orbigny, *L'homme américain (de l'Amérique Méridionale): considéré sous ses rapports physiologiques et moraux*, 2 vols. (Paris: Pitois-Levrault et C., 1839) 2:92.

17 Johann Georg Müller, *Geschichte der amerikanischen Urreligionen* (Basel: Schweighauser, 1855).

18 *Revue Scientifique*, 1887. [Prossibly Gustave Le Bon, "L'Algerie et les idées régnantes en France en matière de Colonisation", *Revue Scientifique* 15 (8 Octobre 1887) 449- 457. —Ed.]

19 See my *Tre Tribuni* (1887).

Phenomena which present such complete uniformity must arise from like causes. These seem to me to be reducible to the following:

1. The mass of the people, accustomed to the few sensations habitual to them, cannot experience new ones without wonder, or strange ones without adoration. Adoration is, I should say, the necessary effect of the reflex movement produced in them by the overwhelming shock of the new impression. The Peruvians applied the word *Huacha* (divine) to the sacred victim, the temple, a high tower, a great mountain, a ferocious animal, a man with seven fingers, a shining stone, &c. In the same way the Semitic *El* (divine) is synonymous with *great*, *light*, *new*, and is applied to a strong man, as well as to a tree, a mountain, or an animal. After all, it is quite natural that men should be struck by the phenomenon of one of their fellow-creatures completely changing his voice and gestures, and associating together the strangest ideas—when we ourselves, with all the advantages of science, are often puzzled to understand the reasons for his actions.

2. Some of these madmen possess (as we have seen, and shall see again, in the Middle Ages and among the Indians) extraordinary muscular strength. The people venerate strength.

3. They often show an extraordinary insensibility to cold, to fire, to wounds (as among the Arab Santons, and among our own lunatics), and to hunger.

4. Some, affected either by theomania or ambitious mania, having first declared themselves inspired by the gods, or chiefs and leaders of the nation, &c., drew after them the current of popular opinion, already disposed in their favour.

5. The following is the principal reason. Many of these madmen must have shown a force of intellect, or at any rate of will, very much superior to those of the masses whom they swayed by their extravagances. If the passions redouble the force of the intellect, certain forms of madness (which are nothing but a morbid exaltation of the passions) may be said to increase it a hundred-fold. Their conviction of the truth of their own hallucinations, the fluent and vigorous eloquence with which they give utterance to them—and which is precisely the effect of their real conviction—and the contrast between their obscure or ignoble past, and their present position of power or splendour, give to this form of insanity, in the mind of the people, a natural preponderance over sane but quiet habits of mind. Lazzaretti, Briand, Loyola, Molinos, Joan of Arc, the Anabaptists, &c., are proofs of this assertion. And it is a fact that, in epidemics of prophecy—such as those which prevailed in the Cevennes, and, recently, at Stockholm—ignorant persons, servant-maids, and even children, excited by enthusiasm, are fired to deliver discourses which are often full of spirit and eloquence.

A maid-servant said, "Can you put a piece of

wood in the fire without thinking of hell?—the more wood, the greater the flames." Another prophetess, a cook, cried out, "God pronounces curses on this wine of wrath (*i.e.*, brandy), and the sinners who drink of it shall be punished according to their sin, and torrents of this wine of wrath shall flow in hell to burn them. "A child of four said, "May God in heaven call sinners to repentance! Go to Golgotha—there are the festal robes!"[20]

6. Mania, among barbarous people, often takes the epidemic form, as among the savage negroes of Juidah, among the Abipones and among the Abyssinians in those affections analogous to the tarantula which are called *tigretier*. Thus, in Greece, an instance is recorded of an epidemic madness among the people of Abdera, who had been deeply moved by the recital of a tragedy; and those Thyades who appeared at Athens and Rome—worshippers of Bacchus, thirsting for luxury and blood, and seized with sacred fury—were affected by erotico-religious insanity. But this is more especially seen in the Middle Ages, when mental epidemics were continually succeeding one another.

The strangest forms of madness were thus communicated, like a true contagion, from whole villages to whole nations, from children to old men,

---

20 Karl Wilhelm Ideler, *Versuch einer Theorie des religiöser Wahnsinns*, 2 vols(Halle: Schwetschke und Sohn, 1848) 236. [The original footnote gives 1842 as the publication year. —Ed.]

from the credulous to the most resolute sceptics. Demonomania, more or less associated with nymphomania and convulsions, &c., produced sometimes witches, sometimes persons possessed with devils, according as it was boasted of and displayed, or suffered with horror, by its victims. It showed itself in the most obscene hallucinations (especially of commerce with evil spirits, or the animals which represented them), in an antipathy to sacred things, or those believed to be such (*e.g.*, the bones said to be relics), or in an extraordinary development, sometimes of muscular, sometimes of intellectual, power, so that they spoke languages of which they had previously only the slightest knowledge, or recalled and connected the most remote and complicated reminiscences. This form of insanity was sometimes associated with erotic ecstasies, or partial anæsthesia, and often with a tendency to biting, to murder, or to suicide. Sometimes there was a shuddering horror, oftener gloomy hallucinations; but always a profound conviction of their truth.

When the prophetic enthusiasm became epidemic in the Cevennes, women, and even children, were reached by this contagion, and saw Divine commands in the sun and in the clouds. Thousands of women persisted in singing psalms and prophesying, though they were hanged wholesale. Whole cities, says Villani, seemed to be possessed of the devil.

At Aix-la-Chapelle, in 1374, there spread, from

epileptics and choreics to the people in general—affecting even decrepit old men and pregnant women—a mania for dancing in the public squares, crying, "*Here Sant Johan, so so, vrisch und vro!*" This was accompanied by religious hallucinations, in which they saw heaven opened, and within it, the assembly of the blessed. The subjects also had an antipathy to anything red, unlike tarantula subjects who are madly attracted to red. The mania extended to Cologne, where 500 persons were seized with it; thence to Metz, where there were 1,100 dancers,[21] Strasburg, and other places. Nor did it cease speedily, for it recurred periodically in subsequent years; and on the day of St. Vitus (probably chosen as a patron on account of the Celtic etymology of his name) thousands of dances took places near his relics. In 1623 these pilgrimages still continued.

Most curious is that epidemic mania for pilgrimages, developed among children in the Middle Ages. When men's minds were cast down with grief for the loss of the Holy Land, in 1212, a shepherd-boy of Cloes, in Vendôme, thought himself sent by God, who had appeared to him in the

21 Here there is an orphaned footnote in the English text, providing a source in German. I have located the English-language equivalent and replaced the source accordingly: Justus Hecker, *The Black Death and the Dancing Mania* (London: Cassell & Company, Limited: 1888) 106-110. The original German was titled *Tanzmania* and was published in 1834, with page 120 given as the source. Lombroso adds 'Traces exist even today, as at Echternach, in Luxembourg'. —Ed.

shape of an unknown man, accepted bread from him, and entrusted him with a letter for the king. All the sons of the neighbouring shepherds flocked to him; 30,000 men became his followers. Soon there arose other prophets of eight years old, who preached, worked miracles, and led hosts of delirious children to the new saint at Cloes. They made their way to Marseilles, where the sea was to withdraw its waves in order to let them pass over dryshod to Jerusalem. In spite of the opposition of the king and their parents, and the hardships of the journey, they reached the sea, were put on board ship by two unscrupulous merchants, and sold as slaves in the East.

The first impulse towards the epidemic form caused by mania was the veneration for individuals affected by it, which rendered them liable to be taken as models; but the principal cause is just that isolation, that ignorance, which is the accompaniment of barbarism. It is, above all, the advance of civilization, the greater contact of a greater number of persons, which gives definite form to the sense of individuality, sharpening it by means of interest, diffidence, ambition, emulation, ridicule; but, above all, by the continual variety of sensations and consequent variety of ideas. Thus it seldom happens that great masses of people are equally predisposed towards, and impressed by, the same movement. In fact, though epidemics of mental alienation have shown themselves, even in the most recent times, it has always been among the most ignorant classes of the population, and in districts remote from the great centres of communication; always, moreover, in mountainous countries (certainly through atmospheric influences, as well as on account of greater isolation)[22]—as in Cornwall, Wales, Norway, Brittany (the barking women of Josselin), in the remotest colonies of America, in the distant valley of Morzines in France, and the Alpine gorge of Verzegnis in Italy, where Franzolini has so well described it. Thus, at Monte Amiata (where, later on, we shall find Lazzaretti), the chroniclers record that one Audiberti lived in an extraordinary state of filth, and was for this reason venerated as a saint. Not far from this place, Bartolomeo Brandano, a tenant of the Olivetan monks, who lived towards the end of the sixteenth century—perhaps overcome by the sufferings of his country during the occupation by the Spanish army—was seized by religious monomania, and believed himself to be John the Baptist. He assumed the dress of the saint, and, covered with a hair-shirt reaching to his knees, with bare feet, a crucifix in his hand, and a skull under his arm, he travelled through the district of Siena, preaching, prophesying, working miracles, and finding proselytes. He then went to Rome, and, on the square

22 Cesare Lombroso, *Pensiero e meteore; studii di un alienista; seguite dall'osservazioni psichiatrico-meteorologiche del prof. A. Tamburini e dalle note sugli abitanti dei paesi in grandi altezze del prof. G. Marinelli* (Milano, Dumolard, 1878) 129.

of St. Peter's, preached against the Pope and the Cardinals. But Clement VII., instead of having him hanged, sent him to the Tordinona prison, where it was usual at that time to seclude the insane, when they were not burnt at the stake as being possessed of demons. When he came out of prison he returned to Siena, and several times insulted Don Diego Mendoza, commander of the Spanish army; but Don Diego, unable to tell whether he were a saint, a prophet, or a madman, had him seized and taken to the prison of Talamone, so that the governor might decide the question. The Siennese governor would have nothing to do with him, and said, "If he is a saint, saints are not sent to the galleys; if he is a prophet, prophets are not punished; and if he is mad, madmen are exempt from the laws." Brandano was thus liberated in a short time, and, after having preached a sermon to the prisoners, he went away, and returned to his prophecies and his exorcisms.

Even recently, in the remote village of Busca, in Piedmont, two saints have arisen, one of whom had been a convict for twenty years,[23] and the other already had a congregation of over 300 members. Not far from there, in the Alpine village of Montenero, there appeared, in 1887, the epidemic delirium of the second coming of Christ, in expectation of which event more than 3,000 inhabitants

23 *Archivio di psichiatria, antropologia criminale e scienze penali per servire allo studio dell' uomo alienato e delinquent* 1.2 (1880).

assembled, in spite of the snow. About the same time a vagabond Messiah was arrested at Vezzola, in the Abruzzi.

The retrograde metamorphosis of the intellectual faculties passes through slighter gradations in the barbarian than in the civilized man. The former is much less able to distinguish illusions from realities, hallucinations from desires, and the possible from the supernatural, and also to keep his imagination in check.

The Norwegian preaching epidemic of 1842 was termed *Magdkrankheit*—the maid-servants' disease—because it attacked servants, hysterical women in general, and children of the lower classes. The Redruth epidemic was diffused entirely among persons "whose intellect is of the very lowest class";[24] whereas when, in recent years, the craze of magnetism, and the still more foolish one of table-rapping, appeared, they never presented any other characteristic than that of widely diffused errors, and mental alienation in this direction could only boast of isolated victims.

It is not long since the Haytian negroes looked on certain trees which had been hung with cloths as images of saints; and the Nubians see their gods in the grotesque forms of splintered rocks. The

24 Friedrich Christian Nasse, *Zeitschrift für Psychiatrie Ätzte* 1 (1818) 255. [The original footnote says only *Zeitschrift* and gives 1814 as the publication year. However, the earliest of the journals associated with Nasse, the *Zeitschrift für Psychiatrie Ätzte*, was not founded until 1818. —Ed.]

slightest cause predisposes the barbarian to terror; and from terror to superstition is but a short step. This last, which disappears before the logic and the sarcasm of civilized people, is the most important factor in the development of insanity. Ideler,[25] speaking of the Stockholm epidemic of 1842, mentions it as a historical fact that, in the places where the disease first appeared, people's minds had for a long time past been disturbed and excited by sermons and devotional exercises; and that, in these places, the number of those affected had perceptibly increased.

This is the explanation of ancient and modern prophets, and their sudden power which has left traces on the history of nations.

Many unhappy persons affected by ambitious mania, or theomania, are looked upon as prophets, and their delusions taken for revelations; and this is the origin of a number of sects which have intensified the struggle between religion and liberty both in the Middle Ages and in modern times.

Picard, for example, imagined himself to be a son of God, sent on earth as a new Adam, to re-establish the natural laws, which consisted, according to him, in going naked, and in the community of women. He met with believers and imitators, and founded the sect of the Adamites, who were exterminated by the Hussites in 1347, but were afterwards revived under the name of Turlupins.

In the same way, the Anabaptists, at Münster,

25 *Versuch* 1:274.

at Appenzell, and in Poland, believed that they saw luminous forms of angels and dragons fighting in the sky, that they received orders to kill their brothers or their best-beloved children (homicidal mania), or to abstain from food for months together, and that they could paralyze whole armies by their breath or by a look. Later on, those sects of Calvinists and Jansenists, which caused the shedding of so much blood, had—as Calmeil has demonstrated—an analogous origin. This is also the origin of the belief in wizards and demoniacs.

If we glance over the lists of literary madmen and *illuminati* given by Delepierre, Philomneste, and Adelung, the number of followers found by many of them makes us laugh and sigh in the same breath at the extent of human folly. Let us mention, for example, Kleinov, who, in the middle of the eighteenth century, claimed to represent the King of Zion, whose sons his followers asserted themselves to be; and Joachim of Calabria, who declared that the Christian era was to end in 1200, when a new Messiah was to appear with a new gospel. Swedenborg, who believed that he had spoken with the spirits of the various planets for whole days, and even for months together, who had seen the inhabitants of Jupiter walking partly on their hands and partly on their feet, those of Mars speaking with their eyes, and those of the Moon with their stomachs, incredible as it may seem, has believers and followers even up to the present time.[26]

---

26 Edouard Ferdinand de la Bonninière, vicomte de Beau-

Irving, in 1830, asserted that he had received, by divine inspiration, the gift of unknown tongues, and founded the sect of the Irvingites.

John Humphrey Noyes, of the United States, believed himself to have the gift of prophecy, and founded the sect of "Perfectionists" established at Oneida, who considered marriage and property as theft, did not recognize human laws, and believed every action, even the commonest, to be inspired by God.

At the beginning of the century that prophetess of monarchy, Julie de Krüdener, possessed great influence. She was hysterical, and so far erotic as to throw herself on her knees in public before a tenor; afterwards, impelled by disappointment in love towards the ancient faith, she believed herself chosen to redeem humanity, and found in this belief the vigour of a burning eloquence. She went to Bale and turned the city upside down by preaching the speedy coming of the Messiah. Twenty thousand pilgrims responded to her call; the Senate became alarmed and banished her. She hastened to Baden, where four thousand people were waiting on the square to kiss her hands and her dress. A woman offered her ten thousand florins to build a new church; she distributed them to the poor "whose reign was at hand." She was exiled from Baden, and returned to Switzerland, followed by crowds.

mont-Vassy, *Swedenborg ou Stockholm en 1756* (Paris: Charles Gosselin, 1842); Jacques Matter, *Emmanuel de Swedenborg: sa vie, ses écrits et sa doctrine* (Paris: Didier, 1863).

Though persecuted by the police, she passed from town to town, followed by acclamations and blessings. She said that her works were dictated to her by angels. Napoleon, who had treated her with contempt, became, for her, the "dark angel," Alexander of Russia, the angel of light. Her influence became the inspiration of the latter; so much so, that the idea of the Holy Alliance seems to be due to her alone.[27]

Loyola, when wounded, turned his thoughts to religious subjects, and, terrified by the Lutheran revolt, planned and founded the great Company. He believed that he received the personal assistance of the Virgin Mary in his projects, and heard heavenly voices encouraging him to persevere in them.

Analogous phenomena may be observed in the lives of George Fox and the early Quakers.[28]

Francis of Assisi.[29]—The son of a religious woman, Francis of Assisi was forced to devote himself to business after receiving only the elements of education from the priests of S. Giorgio. Being rich, and able to spend money as he pleased, he became the life and soul of the joyous companies of young men, whose custom it was to go about the city by

---

27 Mayor, *Madame de Krüdener* (Turin: 1884).

28 See Thomas Babbington Macaulay, *The History of England from the Accession of James the Second*, 5 vols. (Philadelphia: Porter & Coates, 1848) vol. 2.

29 Ruggero Bonghi, *Francesco d'Assisi: studio* (Città di Castello: S. Lapi, 1884).

day and night, singing and diverting themselves. He seemed to be the son of a great prince rather than of a merchant. The citizens of Assisi called him "the flower of youths," and his companions deferred to him as to their leader. He excelled in singing, his biographers praise his sweet and powerful voice; and he was also dexterous in feats of arms. When taken prisoner, in a skirmish between the burghers of Perugia and those of Assisi, he encouraged his companions in prison, and exhorted them to cheerfulness both by word and example. His naturally refined and noble disposition was shown both in his person and manners, and in a liberality which delighted in giving to the poor.

It is said that, in his twenty-fourth year, a severe illness confined him for a long time to his bed. At the beginning of his convalescence, he left the house, leaning on a stick, and stood still to gaze at the beautiful country which surrounds Assisi, but could find no pleasure in it, as he had once done. From that day forward, he was sad and thoughtful. He often left his companions, and retired to a cave, where he spent hours in meditation.

In order to relieve his sufferings, he had recourse to prayer, and prayed so fervently that one day he thought he saw before him Christ nailed to the cross, and felt "the passion of Christ impressed even upon his bowels, upon the very marrow of his bones, so that he could not keep his thoughts fixed upon it without being overflowed with grief." He was then seen wandering about the fields with his face bathed in tears; and when asked whether he felt ill, he replied, "I am weeping for the passion of my Lord Jesus." His friends said to him, "Think of choosing a wife," and he replied, "Yes, I am thinking of a lady—of the noblest, the richest, the most beautiful, that was ever seen!" Who was the lady of his thoughts, he revealed on the day when, laying aside the dress of his rank, he threw a beggar's mantle over his shoulders, to the unbounded anger of his father, who in vain tried to imprison him, and to the great scandal of every one. By many, we read in the *Fioretti*, he was thought a fool; and as a madman he was mocked and driven away with stones, by his relations and by strangers; and he suffered patiently all mockery and harsh treatment, as though he had been deaf and dumb.

Francis of Assisi, however, was original and great, not through those qualities which he had in common with the vulgar herd of ascetics—abstinences, mortifications, prayers, ecstasies, visions—but on account of something which was, without his knowing it, the very negation of asceticism—the affirmation and the triumph of the gentlest and sweetest feelings of humanity. The ascetic abhorred, condemned, and fled from nature, life, all human affections, in order to steep himself in solitary contemplation: Francis, by example and precept, preached the love of nature, concord, mutual affection between human beings, and work. The ascetic called everything beautiful in the world the work of Satan: Francis brought about a true revolution by calling it the work of God, praising and thanking God for it. It was a new kind of loving and passionate Pantheism which inspired him with the *Song of the Sun*, in which all creatures, animate and inanimate, are joined in fraternal embrace, in which the beautiful and radiant sun, the bright and precious moon and stars, the wind, the clouds, the clear sky—water, "useful, humble, precious, and chaste,"—fire, shining, joyous, "hardy and strong," Mother Earth, who sustains and feeds us, together with man, who up to that time had been taught to despise everything that might distract him from the selfish thought of his fate in the next world—all these are called upon to sing the glory of the Lord *who is good*, to bless Him for having made the universe so rich, varied, and beautiful, so worthy to be loved.[30]

If we think of this bold and far-reaching change, we shall no longer smile in reading the *Song*; remembering, too, that it was the first attempt made by the Italian people to express their religious feelings in the vulgar tongue.

For such a song to burst from the impassioned heart of Francis, the germs of universal love which he cherished there must already have come to perfect growth. He must have freed himself entirely from the ancient terror, which, in the common superstitious belief, peopled woods, mountains, air and water, with hidden enemies. As also, in order to bring men back to mutual love, in an age when

30 Bonghi.

"those whom one wall and one ditch confined, gnawed one another," he had, through the natural tendency to extremes, to include, not only Brother Sun and Sister Moon, but even Brother Wolf.

Having composed the *Song*, Francis was so well pleased with it that he adapted to it a musical melody, taught it to his disciples, and thought of choosing among his followers some who should go about the world singing the praises of God, and "asking, as their only recompense that their listeners should repent, should call themselves just 'God's jesters'—*Joculatores Domini*." Thus he gave the first and most vigorous impulse to religious poetry in the vulgar tongue.

Luther.—Luther[31] attributed his physical pains and his dreams to the arts of the devil, though all those of which he has left us a description are clearly due to nervous phenomena. He often suffered, *e.g.*, from an anguish which nothing could lighten, caused, according to him, by the anger of an offended God. At 27, he began to be seized with attacks of giddiness, accompanied by headaches and noises in the ears, which returned at the ages of 32, 38, 40, and 52, especially when he was on a journey. At thirty-eight, moreover, he had a real hallucination, perhaps favoured by excessive solitude. "When, in 1521," he writes,

31 Oswald Berkhan, *Die nervösen Beschwerden des Dr. Martin Luther Archiv für Psychiatrie und Nervenkrankheiten* 11.3 (1881) 798-803.

> I was in my Patmos, in a room which was entered by no one except two pages who brought me my food, I heard, one evening, after I was in bed, nuts moving inside a sack, and flying of themselves against the ceiling and all round my bed. Scarcely had I gone to sleep, when I heard a tremendous noise, as if many berries were being thrown over; I rose, and cried, 'Who art thou?' commended myself to Christ,"

&c.

In the church at Wittenberg, he had just begun explaining the Epistle to the Romans, and had reached the words, "The just shall live by faith," when he felt these ideas penetrate his mind, and heard that sentence repeated aloud several times in his ear. In 1507, he heard the same words when on his journey to Rome, and again in a voice of thunder, as he was dragging himself up the steps of the Scala Santa. "Not seldom," he confesses, "has it happened to me to awake about midnight, and dispute with Satan concerning the Mass," and he details the many arguments adduced by the Devil.

Savonarola.—But the illustration in every respect most apposite (if it did not seem almost a national blasphemy to say so) is that offered us by Savonarola. Under the influence of a vision, he believed himself, even from his youth, sent by Christ to redeem the country from its corruption. One day, while speaking to a nun, it seemed to him that heaven suddenly opened; and he saw in a vision the calamities of the Church, and heard a voice commanding him to announce them to the people.

The visions of the Apocalypse and of the Old Testament prophets passed in review before him. In 1491 he wished to leave off treating of politics in his sermons. "I watched all Saturday, and the whole night, but at daybreak, while I was praying, I heard a voice say, 'Fool, dost thou not see that God will have thee go on in the same way?'"

In 1492, while preaching during Advent, he had a vision of a sword, on which was written, "*Gladius Domini super terram.*" Suddenly, the sword turned towards the earth, the air was darkened, there was a rain of swords, arrows, and fire, and the earth became a prey to famine and pestilence. From this moment, he began to predict the pestilence which, in fact, afterwards came to pass.

In another vision, becoming ambassador to Christ, he makes a long journey to Paradise, and there holds discourse with many saints and with the Virgin, whose throne he describes, not forgetting the number of the precious stones with which it is adorned.[32]

We shall see how a similar scene was described by Lazzaretti. Savonarola was continually meditating on his dreams; and he tried to distinguish which among his visions were produced by angels, and which were the work of demons. Scarcely ever is he touched by a misgiving that he may possibly be in error. In one of his dialogues he declares that

32 Pasquale Villari, *La Storia di Girolamo Savonarola e de'suoi tempi*, 2 vols. (Florence: Felice Le Monnier, 1859-1861) 2:304.

"to feign one's self a prophet in order to persuade others, would be like making God Himself an impostor. Might it not be," continues the objector, "that you were deceiving yourself? No," is the reply, "I worship God—I seek to follow in His footsteps; it cannot be that God should deceive me."[33]

Yet, with the contradiction peculiar to unhinged minds, he had written a short time before, "I am not a prophet, neither the son of a prophet; it is your sins that make me a prophet perforce." Moreover, in one page he says that his prophetic illumination is independent of grace, whereas, a few pages back, he had declared that the two were one and the same thing.

Villari justly remarks that "this is the singularity of his character, that a man who had given to Florence the best form of republic, who dominated an entire people, who filled the world with his eloquence and had been the greatest of philosophers should make it his boast that he heard voices in the air, and saw the sword of the Lord!"

"But," as the same author well concludes,

> the very puerility of his visions proves that he was the victim of hallucinations; and a still stronger proof is their uselessness, even hurtfulness, as far as he himself was concerned. What need was there, if he wished to cheat the masses, to write treatises on his visions, to speak of them to his mother, to write reflections

33 Girolamo Savonarola, *De Veritate Prophetica Dialogus* (Florence: 1497).

> on them on the margins of his Bible? Those things which his admirers would have been most eager to hide, those which the simplest intelligence would never have allowed to get into print, these very productions he continued to publish and republish. The truth is that, as he often confessed, he felt an inward fire burning in his bones, and forcing him to speak; and as he was himself swept away by the force of that ecstatic delirium, so he succeeded in carrying with him his audience, who were moved by his words in a way we find it hard to understand when we compare the impression produced with the text of the sermons themselves.

This helps us to understand how—exactly in the same manner as Lazzaretti—he propagated his divine madness among the people, not only epidemically, by the contagion of ideas, but producing actual insanity in persons, who, being nearly or quite without education, preached and wrote extempore in consequence of their madness. Thus Domenico Cecchi[34] was the author of a work entitled *Sacred Reform*,[35] which contains the very just suggestions of relieving the Great Council from minor business, taxing church property, imposing a single tax, and creating a militia, also that of fixing the amount of girls' dowries. In his preface, he writes:

34 Villari [2:]406.

35 Domenico Cecchi (1449 - ?)'s book was *Riformasancta et pretiosa per conservatione della città di Firenze et pel ben commune* (Florence: Francesco di Dino, 1497). —Ed.

> I set myself with my fancy to make such a work, and I can make no other, and by day and night methinks I have made such efforts that I might call them miraculous; but it has come to pass that I myself stand amazed thereat.

A certain Giovanni, a Florentine tailor, seized with morbid enthusiasm, wrote *terzine* in which he extolled the future glories of Florence, and produced verses worthy of Lazzaretti,[36] and prophecies like the following, "Yet it must needs be that the Pisan shall descend, with irons on his feet, into the sewer, since he has been the cause of so much woe."

If I were asked whether, in our asylums, we often meet with types analogous to these, I should reply that there is, perhaps, not an asylum in Italy which has not received one of these strange lunatics.

Cola da Rienzi.—In 1330, Rome was sinking into chaos. Historians have left us an appalling picture of the disorders of the time, the absence of any regular government, and the lawless tyranny of the robber barons.

The general conditions of the age were favourable to popular movements. King Robert, the protector of the barons was dead; and Todi (1337), Genoa (under Adorno, in 1367), and Florence (1363), had initiated a democratic *régime*, which ushered in the terrible Ciompi revolution of 1378. A premature thrill of revolt ran through Europe, and was

36 Villari 2:408.

felt even in feudal and monarchical France, where the movement was organized, for a short time, at Paris, under Marcel.[37]

Under these circumstances, Cola—a young man, born in the Tiber district, in 1313, the son of an innkeeper and a washerwoman, or water-seller, who though at first little better than a field-labourer, had studied as a notary, and acquired a considerable knowledge of the history and antiquities of his country—saw his brother murdered by the wretches who formed the government, or rather the misgovernment of Rome.

Then he—who, as the anonymous historian tells us, always had "a fantastic smile" on his lips, and already, when meditating on ancient books and the ruins of Rome, had often wept, exclaiming, "Where are the good Romans of the old time? Where is their justice?"—was seized, as he afterwards acknowledged,[38] by an irresistible impulse to put into action the ideas which he had acquired from books.

In his capacity of notary, he devoted himself to the protection of minors and widows, and assumed the curious title of their Consul, just as there were, in his time, consuls of the carpenters, cloth-workers, and other guilds.

---

37 See François-Tommy Perrens, *Étienne Marcel et le gouvernement de la bourgeoisie au quatorzième siècle: 1356-1358* (Paris: L. Hachette, 1880); and *Democratie en France dans le Moyen Age* (Paris: Didier et Cie, 1875).

38 Letter to Charles IV. Document 33 in Papencordt.

In 1343, in one of the numerous small revolutions of the period, the people had attempted to overthrow the Senate, creating the government of the Thirteen, under the papal authority. On that occasion, Cola was sent as spokesman of the people, to Avignon, where he vividly depicted the evils prevalent in Rome, and, by his bold and powerful eloquence, amazed and won over the cool headed prelates, from whom he attained the appointment of notary to the Urban Chamber, in 1344.

On his return to Rome, he continued to exercise this office with exaggerated zeal, and got himself called Consul no longer *of the widows*, but *of Rome*. He excelled others in courtesy, was also inflexible in the administration of justice, and never failed to involve himself in long harangues against those whom he called the dogs of the Capitol.

One day, in a moment of exaggerated fanaticism, he cried to the barons, in full assembly, "Ye are evil citizens—ye who suck the blood of the people." And, turning to the officials and governors, he warned them that it was their place to provide for the good of the State. The result of this was a tremendous buffet dealt him by a chamberlain of the House of Colonna. He then took matters more calmly, and began to depict the former glories and present miseries of Rome, by means of paintings, in which the homicides, adulterers, and other criminals were represented by apes and cats, the corrupt judges and notaries by foxes, and the senators and nobles by wolves and bears.

On another day, he exhibited the famous table of Vespasian, and invited the public, including the nobles, to a dramatic explanation of it. He appeared, arrayed in a German cloak with a white hood, and a hat also white and surrounded by many crowns, one of which was divided in the midst by a small silver sword. The interpretation of these grotesque symbols, which already indicate his madness (the continual use of such being, as already stated, characteristic of monomaniacs, till they end by sacrificing to their passion for symbols the very evidence of the things which they wish to represent), is unknown. Thus, applying—somewhat after his own fashion—the decree of the Senate which granted to Vespasian the right of making laws at his pleasure, of increasing or diminishing *the gardens of Rome and of Italy* (if he had been a scholar, he would have said the area of the Roman district), and of making and unmaking kings, he called on them to consider into what a state they had fallen. "Remember that the jubilee is approaching, and that you have made no provision of food or other necessaries. Put an end to your quarrels," &c.

But along with these, he delivered other discourses which were, to say the least, eccentric; *e.g.*, "I know that men wish to find a crime in my speeches, and that out of envy; but, thanks to heaven, three things consume my enemies—luxury, envy, and fire."[39] These two last words were great-

39 "*Invidia e fuoco.*" Thus the anonymous historian, and Zeffiri-

ly applauded; I do not understand them, however, especially the last. I believe that they were applauded, precisely because the audience did not understand them, as happens to many street orators, with whom resonant and meaningless words supply the place of ideas, and are even greeted with greater enthusiasm.

The fact is, that, among the upper classes, he passed for one of those persons of unsound mind who were then in great request for the amusement of society.[40] The nobles, especially the Colonna, disputed the pleasure of his company with each other, and he would tell them of the glories of his future government. "And when I am king or emperor, I will make war on all of you. I will have such an one hanged, and such another beheaded." He spared none of them, and mentioned them by name, one by one, to their faces; and, all the time, both to nobles and commons, he continued to speak of the good state, and of how he was going to restore it.

Here I insert a parenthesis. It has been said (by Petrarch in particular) that he feigned madness, and was a second Brutus; but when we see his love for pomp, luxury, strange symbols, and garments,

---

no Re. Muratori reads juoco, "gaming," but not even thus can the sentence be explained; for it was certainly other vices than envy and gambling that were consuming the nobility of those days.

40 Even after the first *plébiscite*, Stefano Colonna, in opposing him, said, "If this madman makes me angry, I will have him thrown from the Capitol" (349).

gradually increasing as he advanced in his political career, and after his rise to power, we no longer have any doubt as to the reality of his madness.

He continued to put forth new symbolical pictures, among others one with this inscription: "*The day of justice is coming—Await this moment.*" Be it noted that this picture represented a dove bringing a crown of myrtle to a little bird. The dove stood for the Holy Spirit (as we shall see, one of the favourite objects of his delirium) and the bird was himself, who was to crown Rome with glory. At last, on the first day of Lent, 1347, he affixed to the door of San Giorgio another placard: "*Before long, the good State of Rome shall be restored.*"

Not being feared by the nobles, who thought him mad, he was able to conspire secretly, or rather to keep up the ferment of public opinion, by taking apart, gradually, one by one, the men who seemed to him best adapted for the purpose, and assigning them their posts on Mount Aventine, towards the end of April, on a day when the governor was to be absent.

In this assembly, the only one which, up to that time, had been held in secret, the mode of bringing about the Good State was deliberated on. Here he showed the eloquence of a man who speaks from conviction, and of things which are too true not to produce a deep impression. He described the discord of the great, the debasement of the poor, the armed men roaming about in quest of plunder, wives dragged from their marriage-beds, pilgrims murdered at the gates, priests drowned in sensual orgies, no strength or wisdom among those who held the reigns of power. From the nobles there was everything to fear and nothing to hope. Where were they, in the midst of all these disorders? They were leaving Rome, to enjoy a holiday on their estates, while everything was going to wreck and ruin in the city.

As the members of the popular party were hesitating for want of funds, he gave them a hint that these might be obtained from the revenues of the Apostolic Chamber, reckoning 10,000 florins for the tax on salt alone, 100,000 for the hearth-tax, figures which Sismondi (chapter xxxviii.) declares to be absolutely erroneous. He also gave them to understand that he was acting in accordance with the wishes of the Pope (*which was false*), and that he was able with the consent of the latter, to seize upon the revenues of the Holy See.

On May 18, 1347, in Colonna's absence, he had proclamation made through the streets, by sound of trumpet, that all citizens were to assemble in the night of the day following, in the church of Sant' Angelo, to take measures for the establishment of the Good State. On the 19th, Rienzi was present at the meeting, in armour, guarded by a hundred armed men, and accompanied by the Papal Vicar, and by three standards covered with the most extraordinary symbols—one of them representing Liberty, one Justice, and one Peace.

Among the measures which he caused to be adopted by this improvised assembly were some which would be well suited to our own times; the following, for instance:—

All lawsuits were to be terminated within fifteen days.

The Apostolic Chamber was to provide for the support of widows and orphans.

Every district of Rome was to have a public granary.

If a Roman were killed in the service of his country, his heirs to receive a hundred *lire* if he were a foot soldier, and a hundred *florins* if a horseman.

The garrisons of cities and fortresses to be formed of men chosen from among the Roman people.

Every accuser who could not make good his accusation, to be subject to the penalty which his victim would have incurred.

The houses of the condemned not to be destroyed (as was then the case in all communities), but to become the property of the municipality.

Cola received from this popular assembly entire lordship over the city; he associated the Papal Vicar with himself as a harmless assistant, entitled himself Tribune, and performed an actual miracle in restoring peace where there had been chaos. He saw the proud barons—even the rebellious and powerful prefect of Vico—prostrate at his feet. He executed severe justice upon the most powerful nobles as well as the populace. Members of the

Orsini, Savelli, and Gaetani families were hanged by him, for violation of the laws; and, what is more, even priests, such as the monk of St. Anastasius who was accused of several murders.

By means of the so-called Tribunal of Peace, he reconciled with each other 1800 citizens, who had previously been mortal enemies. He abolished, or, more accurately speaking, tried to abolish, the servile use of the title *Don*, which is still rampant among us in the south; he prohibited dicing, concubinage, and fraud in the sale of provisions—which last was the measure which conduced most to his popularity. Finally, he created a true citizen militia, a real national guard.

He caused the escutcheons of the nobles to be erased from all palaces, equipages, and banners, saying that there was to be in Rome no other lordship than the Pope's and his own.

He re-established a tax on every hearth, in all the towns and villages of the Roman district, and was obeyed even by the Tuscan communities, who might have claimed exemption. The collectors were not sufficient for the work. All the governors, except two, submitted; and he finally appointed a kind of justice of the peace, to decide even criminal cases.

He did even more. He was the first to conceive, what even Dante had not thought of, an Italy neither Guelf nor Ghibelline, under the headship of the Roman municipality, in which like Marcel of Paris, he attempted to assemble a true national

Parliament.[41] He was the first man in Italy to think of this, and was only understood by thirty-five communes.

At Avignon, finally, he was able to achieve what I consider his greatest enterprise: to get himself pardoned, after a course of speech and action so hostile to the Papal Court, by those who never pardon—the clergy of that ferocious and implacable age; and not only pardoned, but sent back, though for a short period and in an inferior capacity, to a position fraught with the greatest dangers to that order.

But all these miracles, alas! lasted for a few days only. The man who in his political ideas surpassed not only his contemporaries, but many modern thinkers, and preceded Mazzini and Cavour in the idea of unity, was in fact a monomaniac, as is recorded by the historians, Re and Papencordt; if he was great in conception, he was uncertain and incapable in practical matters. This was fully shown, *e.g.*, when, though he had his greatest enemy, the prefect of Vico, in his hands, he let him go, keeping his son as a hostage; and when he failed to profit by his unexpected victory over the barons.

Always incapable of taking any resolution which was not merely theoretical, he believed that everything he did was done by the grace of the

41 See Felice Papencordt, *Cola di Rienzi e il suo tempo (Turin: Giuseppe Pomba e Comp.*, 1844); Ferdinand Gregorovius, *Geschichte der Stadt Rom im Mittelalter*, 8 vols. (Stuttgard: Cotta, 1859–1872) 4:267.

Holy Spirit,[42] under whose auspices we have seen that he began his enterprize.

He was still further confirmed in his delusion by a heresy which had then recently sprung up, according to which the Holy Spirit was to regenerate the world, and especially by the fact, very insignificant in itself, that a dove alighted near him while he was showing the people one of his allegorical pictures. To this dove he attributed his successful beginning, as he ascribed to his prophetic inspiration the victory over the Colonna and that over the Prefect.[43]

In the most important affairs, he believed that he heard in himself, through the medium of a dream or other sign, the voice of God, with whom he took counsel, and to whom he referred everything.

Sustained by the *prestige* of this inspiration, he furthermore enacted religious laws, *e.g.*, one compelling confession once a year, under pain of confiscation to the extent of one-third of a man's property.

He did not fail to exhibit the usual contradictions peculiar to the insane. Very religious himself, he had no hesitation in comparing himself to Christ, only on account of the coincidence implied in his having gained a victory at the age of thirty-three. After his defeat, he again compared himself to him, in a play upon numbers such as is common among the insane, because he was for thirty-three months an

42 Papencordt.

43 *Ibid.* 1:17.

exile in the Majella, in a wild and lonely hermitage, surrounded by several persons subject to hallucinations, followers of the Holy Spirit, who prophesied that he would once more be victorious, and even rule over the whole world. The megalomaniac delirium which usually prevailed in his case, explains the greater part of these contradictions. He believed that in his own person were centred all the hopes of a Messiah of Italy, who was to restore the Roman Empire, nay, even redeem the world.

At a moment when he must have thought himself near death, in the prison at Prague,[44] he thought himself the victim of diabolical imaginations, or believed that he was obeying the will of heaven. Thus he wrote, "I kiss the key of the prison, as it were the gift of God."

One day he arose from the throne and, advancing towards his faithful followers, said in a loud voice,

> We command Pope Clement to present himself before our tribunal, and to live at Rome; and we give the same command to the College of Cardinals. We cite to appear before us the two claimants, Charles of Bohemia and Ludwig of Bavaria, who take upon themselves the title of Emperors. We command all the electors of Germany to inform us on what pretext they have usurped the inalienable right of the Roman people—the ancient and legitimate sovereign of the empire.

44 See letter to Fra Michele.

Then he drew his sword, waved it three times towards the three divisions of the known world, and said, three times, in a transport of ecstasy, "This, too, belongs to me!"

All this because he had bathed in the porphyry basin of Constantine—to the great scandal of his followers—and believed that he had thus succeeded to the power of that emperor.

While he was going on this course the Papal Legate, by whose concurrence alone all these eccentricities could, up to a certain point, be justified, protested with all the force his slight degree of energy would allow. It would be pretty much as if the Consul of San Marino were to take it into his head, on the strength of a majority of votes, or because he had worn a hat belonging to Napoleon I., that he could summon before his tribunal the emperors of Austria, Germany, and Russia, with a few dukes into the bargain. And if this would appear ridiculous in our own times, when, in theory at least, right is esteemed above might, what must it have seemed in that age?

Nor was this a mere momentary aberration. We still possess the diplomatic communication (dated Aug. 12th), destined for the emperors, after that mad theatrical ceremony. I extract some passages:[45]

> In virtue of the same authority, and of the favour of God, the Holy Spirit, and the Roman

45 Ionanne Hoxemio, *De actis pontif.*, vols. 2. and 3.

> people, we say, protest, and declare that the Roman Empire, the election, jurisdiction, and monarchy of the Sacred Empire belong, by full right, to the city of Rome, and to all Italy, for many good reasons which we shall mention at the proper place and time, and after having summoned the dukes, kings, &c., to appear between this day and that or Pentecost next following, before us in St. John Lateran, with their titles and claims; failing which, on the expiry of the term, *they will be proceeded against* according to the forms of law, and the inspiration of the Holy Spirit.

Moreover, he adds, as though he had not yet expressed himself clearly enough,

> Besides what has been heretofore said, in general and in particular, we cite in person the illustrious princes, Louis, Duke of Bavaria, and Charles, Duke of Bohemia, *calling themselves* emperors, or elected to the empire; and, besides these, the Duke of Saxony, the Marquis of Brandenburg, &c., that they may appear in the said place before us in person, and before other magistrates, failing which we shall proceed against them, as contumacious,

&c.

This was too much. The mutual animosity of the Colonna and the Orsini was momentarily suspended. They united their forces to combat him openly and conspire against him in secret.

An assassin, sent by them to attempt the tribune's life, was arrested, and, when put to the torture, accused the nobles. From that instant Rienzi incurred the fate of a tyrant, and adopted a tyrant's suspicions and rules of conduct. Shortly afterwards, under various pretexts, he invited to the capital his principal enemies, among whom were many of the Orsini and three of the Colonna. They arrived, believing themselves called to a council or banquet; and Rienzi, after inviting them to take their places at table, had them arrested; innocent and guilty had to undergo this terror alike. After the people had been summoned to the spot, by the sound of the great bell, they were accused of a conspiracy to assassinate Rienzi, and not a single voice or hand was raised to defend the heads of the nobility.

They passed the night in separate rooms; and Stefano Colonna, battering at his prison door, several times entreated that he might be freed by a swift death from so humiliating a position. The arrival of a confessor, and the sound of the funeral bell, showed them what was awaiting them.

The great hall of the Capitol, where the trial was to take place, was hung with white and red, as was usual when a death-sentence was about to be pronounced. All seemed ready for their condemnation, when the tribune, touched by fear or pity, after a long speech to the people, *in their defence*, caused them to be acquitted, and even granted them some offices (such as the Prefecture of arms), which could not fail to be formidable weapons against him. It was not the sort of thing which was done in those days; and even Petrarch thought he had been too lenient, while the lower classes expressed their sense of his folly in a coarser and more energetic fashion.

Such was his madness, says the anonymous historian, that he allowed his enemies to entrench themselves afresh, and then sent a messenger to summon them to his presence. The messenger was wounded, whereupon he summoned them a second time, and then had two of them painted, hanging head downward. They, in their turn, took the town of Nepi from him, for which he could devise no other retribution than the drowning of two dogs, supposed to represent them. After some bloodless and useless marches, he returned to Rome, and, having put on the *dalmatica* (*!*) of the emperors, had himself crowned for the third time. Worse still, he at the same time expelled the Papal legate, Bertrando,[46] thus throwing away his last anchor of safety at the moment when he needed it most.

Besides the eccentricity of his consecration as Knight of the Holy Spirit, preceded by the bath in the vase of Constantine (which, though it can readily be explained by the ideas of the period, did him serious injury in the estimation of the majority, and especially the religious, as being an act of profanation), he was guilty of the egregious politi-

46 *Cronaca Estense*, Ed. Ludovico Antonio Muratori (n.d.) 18:409.

cal folly of declaring that, after that ceremony, the Roman people had returned to the full possession of their jurisdiction over the world; that Rome was the head of the world, that the monarchy of the empire and the election of the emperor were privileges of the city, of the Roman people, and of Italy. This was clearly a declaration of war against both pope and emperor. Later on, on August 15th, with his usual monomaniac tendency to symbolism, he crowned himself with six wreaths of different plants—ivy, because he loved religion; myrtle, because he honoured learning; parsley, because of its resistance to poison (as the emperor was supposed to resist the malevolence of his enemies). To these he added, for no discoverable reason, the mitre of the Trojan king, and a silver crown!

All this proves, says Gregorovius, that it was his intention to get himself crowned emperor.

And, as it was the custom of the Roman emperors to promulgate edicts after their coronation, so he, immediately after this ceremony, by political decrees confirmed to the whole of Italy the right of Roman citizenship. Alberto Argentaro[47] adds that he threatened Pope Clement with deposition, if he did not return to Rome within the year, and that he would have elected another pope. Villani says,[48] that he wished to reform the whole of Italy in the ancient manner, and subject it to the dominion of Rome. To understand how truly insane was this

47 Cronaca 140.

48 Book 10.

project, it must be remembered that his sacred militia—that which he believed most faithful—numbered no more than 1600 men, and that the whole army, counting both horse and foot, did not, on an outside calculation, exceed 2000.

After defeating the nobles, without any merit on his part, he, who had formerly been so generous, forbade the widows to weep for the dead; and was guilty of words and actions which, even in that ferocious age, struck his *Sacred Knights* (as he called them) as so barbarous and foolish, that they refused to bear arms for him any longer. From this moment date, on the one hand, his undoubted insanity, on the other, the contempt of all honourable men, vigorously expressed by Petrarch himself in a well-known letter.

It can now be understood why he was, even from the time of his first exploits, so fond of pompous titles. After calling himself "Consul of the Widows," and "Consul of Rome," he adopted the title of Tribune, which afterwards became "Clement and Severe Tribune," the contradiction being nothing to him, so long as he could suggest the name of Severinus Boethius, whose arms he had also adopted; and, not long after this (referring, with that kind of play upon words so dear to the insane and to idiots, to his nomination in August), "August Tribune."[49] We can also comprehend that, stripped of all his power, an exile and a prisoner, he should have turned to the prosaic Emperor Charles IV.,

49 Gregorovius, 6:294.

telling him his dreams, as we shall see, with complete confidence in their reality.

At Rome, after his first fall (which was, perhaps, one cause of the indulgence with which he was treated by the pope), there had been a new outburst of disorder, which a tribune who has remained almost unknown—one Baroncelli—in vain endeavoured to stem. Nor did Rienzi himself meet with any better success on his return, shorn of his ancient *prestige*, and without that youthful audacity which, united to a maniacal erethism, had increased the strength of the poor scholar a hundredfold; and he was overthrown by the populace themselves. For men, whether madmen of genius or complete geniuses, have no power against the natural force of things. Marcel had no success at Paris, though he had far greater forces at his disposal, and was allied with the Jacquerie of the country districts.

But Rienzi could not even succeed in realizing the prodigies of insane genius, since he had by this time fallen into true dementia.

It appears that in the early stages of his government he was a sober and temperate man, so much so that he had to make an effort to find time to eat. From this he passed to the opposite extreme of continued orgies and actual dipsomania, which he excused by alleging the effects of a poison which he believed to have been administered to him in prison.[50] I believe, on the contrary, that this phenome-

50 "He said that they had bewitched him in prison" (Anonimo).

non was occasioned by the progress of his malady, since we see that it began in the early months of his first tribunate,[51] and since slow poisons produce emaciation, not obesity, in their victims.

> At every hour he was eating dainties and drinking; he observed neither time nor order; he mixed Greek with Flavian wine; he drank new wine at any hour. He used to drink too much.
>
> Moreover he had now become enormously stout, he had a face like a friar, round and jovial as that of a bonze, a ruddy complexion, and a long beard. His eyes were white, and suddenly he would turn red as blood, and his eyes would become inflamed.

In short, as is usually the case with persons inclining to dementia, his body became enormous, and his eyes were often bloodshot, while his face acquired an entirely brutal cast of expression. His mind was much less active, and his temper fundamentally changed, while the fickleness, restlessness, and oddity, which had served to excite great admiration for him in the mind of the populace, now had so degenerated as to redound to his injury. Those who saw most of him said that he changed his mind, as well as his expression of face, from one minute to the next, and was never

51 Even within a few months from his first assumption of the tribunate he became "addicted to rich food, and began to multiply suppers, banquets, and revels of divers meats and wines. About the end of December he began to grow stout and ruddy, and eat with a better appetite" (Anonimo 92).

constant to the same thought for a quarter of an hour together. Thus he began the siege of Palestrina, and then abandoned it; he would appoint a skilful commander, and then cashier him.

In later times, when he was forced to impose taxes on wine and salt, even for the poor, he restrained his luxurious tendencies, and became apparently temperate; but his other evil propensities did not change. To the intermittent generosity of which he had given proofs in his early period succeeded a cold selfishness, which excited horror even in that cruel age—when, for instance, he had Fra Monreale beheaded, for not repaying a sum of money which Rienzi had lent him. His friend Pandolfo Pandolfini, respected by all Rome as the model of an honourable man, was beheaded by him, without the shadow of a reason, merely from envy of his reputation. Thus he sacrificed, or despoiled of their property, the best men in the country, and passed from the extreme of timidity to that of ferocity.

He was seen to laugh and weep almost at the same time, and in both cases without sufficient cause; his paroxysms of joy were followed by sighs and tears.

But it is chiefly in his letters that the whole of his genius and of his madness is revealed.

The letters of Cola da Rienzi were sought for and collected with singular curiosity, as though (Petrarch several times writes to him) "they had fallen from the Antipodes, or the sphere of the moon."

Four collections of his letters are extant—at Mantua, at Turin (twenty-two closely written pages), at Paris, and at Florence (the last-named being autographs). They have been published and republished by Gaye, De Sade, Hobhouse, Hoxemio, Pelzel, and Papencordt,[52] and would by themselves be sufficient material on which to base a diagnosis.

In fact, there is not one of them which does not bear the impress, either of a morbid vanity, or of those trivial repetitions and plays upon words especially characteristic of the insane.

The first point to note is their great abundance, in an age when very little was written.

When his residence in the Capitol was sacked, after his first flight, what most surprised those who entered his private office was the mass of letters which had been drafted and never sent. It was well

52 Giovanni Gaye, *Carteggio inedito d'artisti dei secoli XIV, XV, XVI*, 3 vols. (Florence: Giuseppe Molini, 1839-40); Jean Chapeauville, *Qui gesta pontificum tungrensium, trajectensium et leodiensium scripserunt auctores præcipui*, 3 vols. (Leodii [Liège]: Christiani Ouwerx iunioris, 1612, 1613, 1616) 2:272-514 [The original footnote appears to be an error, for it attributes Qui Gesta Pontificum to Hoxemio and gives a publication date of 1822. —Ed.]; Felix Papencordt, *Cola di Rienzo und seine Zeit* (Hamburg: F. und A. Perthes, 1841) [Corrected publication date from 1847. —Ed.]; John Hobhouse, *Historical illustrations of the fourth canto of Childe Harold: containing dissertations on the ruins of Rome; and an essay on Italian literature* (New York: Kirk and Mercein, 1818); Laure de Sade, *Mémoires pour la vie de François Pétrarque, tirés de ses œuvres et des auteurs contemporains avec les notes ou dissertations et les pièces justificatives*, 3 vols. (Amsterdam-Avignon, 1764-1767) vol 3.

known that the numerous staff of clerks employed by him could not keep pace with the amount of matter he dictated, and that he was continually sending couriers not only to friendly republics, but to indifferent or hostile potentates, like the King of France, who sent a jesting reply by an archer—a functionary somewhat analogous to a modern policeman. Thus, too, the lords of Ferrara, Mantua, and Padua returned him his letters.

Add to this their style, their exaggerated length, the addition of postscripts longer than the letter itself, and the singular signature, richer in laudatory titles than was ever used except by Oriental princes.

These letters have, indeed, a flavour of their own, a vivacity breaking loose from the restraints of the classical writers who served as his models, an exuberant self-confidence which, at first sight, obliged the reader to put faith in the falsehoods with which they swarmed. Nay, it seems that—as happens with some lunatics, and some incorrigible liars—he ended by himself believing in his own fictions.

Leaving aside many strange blunders, surprising in a Latin scholar,[53] and the prolixity already

53 Even in the autograph MSS. we find *cotidie* for *quotidie*; *Capitalo* for *Capitolis*; *patrabantur* for *perpetrabantur*; *speraverim* for *spreverim*; *michi* for *mi hi*. I have already noted the strange blunder of explaining the Pomcerium the district between the inner and outer walls of Rome by "the garden of Italy." All this indicates a scholarship which was neither very full nor very accurate. As to his caligraphy, there is nothing

mentioned, without dwelling on the very undiplomatic want of delicacy, present to a morbid extent, and all the more surprising in a statesman of that age, when reserve was more general than at present, one fact particularly strikes me—an inveterate habit of punning, a symptom of extreme frivolity, which was certainly not a characteristic of mediæval diplomacy.

What man in his senses would, even in the depths of the Dark Ages, have written as he did to Pope Clement, in the letter dated August 5, 1347?—

> The grace of the Holy Spirit having freed the Republic under my rule, and my humble person having been, at the beginning of *August*, promoted to the militia, there is attributed to me, as in the signature, the name and title of August.
>
> Given as above on the 5th of *August*,
> HUMBLE CREATURE,
>
> Candidate of the Holy Spirit, Nicolò the Severe and Clement, Liberator of the City, Zealous for Italy, Lover of the World, who kisses the feet of the blessed.

Note that, after all this signature, the letter goes on for three pages more, on much more serious topics, which he had postponed to the pun on "August."

In this respect, a clear proof of his insanity is to be found in the letter which he wrote in the ela-

---

particular to remark.

tion of his victory over the barons. Not to dwell on the strange familiarity with the Deity which he shows, when he writes "that God formed to war those fingers which had been trained to the use of the pen" (whereas, as a matter of fact, he had no knowledge whatever of the art of war), it is well to note that, among his gravest charges against the Colonna was that of their having sacked a church where *he had deposited his golden crown*. Still more strange is the following claim to prophecy, addressed to the clergy—who, as dealing in such matters, are likely to be most sceptical concerning them:

> We should not forget to tell you that, two days before these occurrences, we had a vision of Pope Boniface, who foretold our triumph over those tyrants. We made a report thereof in full season, and in the presence of the assembled Romans, and going into St. Peter's, to the altar of St. Boniface, we presented to him a chalice and a veil.
>
> The vision, at last, thanks to Heaven, was fulfilled, thanks to the help of the Blessed Martin, His tribune.

(Here he forgets that, two pages previously, in the same letter, he had attributed his victories to St. Laurence and St. Stephen.) "As those traitors," he continues,

> had plundered the pilgrims on the day of his festival, that Saint took vengeance on them, by

> the hand of a *tribune*, *three* days afterwards, that is to say, on the day of *St. Columba*, who glorified the dove (*colomba*) of our flag.

Note the puns in the above.

He concludes with some of those postscripts which are so frequent in the letters of monomaniacs, and are found in nearly all of his:

> Given at the Capitol, on the very day of the victory—the 3rd of November, on which day there perished six tyrants of the house of Colonna, and none remained but the unhappy old man Stefano Colonna, who is half dead. He is the seventh, and this is how Heaven was willing to make the number of the slain Colonna equal the crowns [*sic*] of our coronation,[54] and to the branches of the fruit-bearing tree which recall the seven gifts of the Holy Spirit.

Absolute insanity is here shown, both in the idea and the word, in which he makes the Deity intervene to extinguish a family of heroes for the sake of a sinister freak of language, in honour of the man who, a few pages previously—with a hypocrisy soon belied by facts—had written, "Consistently with our character, we were not willing to employ the severity of the sword—however just—against those whom we might bring back

54 Among his vagaries, we have already noted that of crowning himself with seven crowns. In his seals there were seven stars and seven rays, which, under the second Tribunate, became eight.

to grace without injury to freedom, justice, and peace."

Both comic and insane is the way in which, in another letter to Rinaldo Orsini (Sept. 22, 1347), he tries to disguise, by a number of useless fictions, the enormous error of which he had been guilty in setting at liberty the nobles arrested shortly before. "We wish that Your Paternity should know how, having judged certain nobles, lawfully suspected by the people and by us, it pleased God that they should fall into our hands" (We see, on the contrary, that he had expressly invited them).

> We caused them to be shut up in the dungeons of the Capitol; but, finally (our scruples and suspicions having been removed), we made use of an innocent artifice [*sic*] to reconcile them not only with ourselves, but with God, wherefore we procured them the happy opportunity of making a devout confession. It was on the 15th of September that we sent confessors to each one of them, in prison, and as the latter were ignorant of our good intentions, and believed that we were going to be severe, they said to the nobles, 'The Lord Tribune will condemn you to death.' Meanwhile the great bell of the Capitol tolled without ceasing for the assembly, and thus the terrified nobles gave themselves up for lost; and, in the expectation of death, confessed devoutly and with tears, . . . I then made a speech in praise of them,

&c.

Let the reader judge of the condition of the moral sense in a man who could write thus. It should be noted, besides, that, diplomatically, an excuse of this sort (especially in dealing with priests, who, being in the trade, so to speak, would know its exact value), would not only be useless, but even constitute a serious accusation. Nor is his conclusion less strange,

> Withal their hearts are so united to ours and to those of the people, that this union must last for the good of our country; because thus they see that we are impartial, and do not wish to be as severe as we might be.

But his useless hypocrisies did not end there; the confusion of the patricians probably suggested the order, already mentioned, that all citizens were to confess and receive the communion at least once a year, under pain of losing a third of their goods—half the forfeited property to go to the parish church of the defendant, the other to the city. And the notaries were obliged to act as spies for every testator. Now, Rienzi, in a postscript to the above letter (and I repeat that I have frequently observed in monomaniacs this fad of postscripts occurring at the end of letters), gives notice of his new edict, adding, "It seemed to us fitting that, as a second Augustus provides for the temporal profit of the Republic, he should also seek to favour and promote its spiritual welfare." This, if one thinks about it, was a usurpation of the special rights and duties of the pontiff, even according to the most modern view of them, as also when he prescribed to the clergy special ceremonies and ecclesiastical processions of his own invention, and enacted decrees against the members of religious orders who should fail to return to Rome. This, in fact, was one of the principal accusations—and a just one—levelled against him at Prague and at Avignon, and one which he only rebutted by false statements.

Elsewhere he speaks of being inspired by the Holy Spirit, with a confidence which would be altogether unintelligible except in a man who was perfectly sincere, and therefore under the influence of hallucination.

A glance at other letters explains at once that the bath in the vase of Constantine was for him what the tattooed marks on his forehead were to Lazzaretti—one of those symbolic freaks to which the insane attach a peculiar significance; in fact, a kind of imperial investiture.

A long letter to Charles IV., written from prison in July, 1350, dwelling on a supposed intrigue of his mother with the Emperor Henry VII., bears, in subject-matter and style, the unmistakable impress of insanity.[55]

---

55 Monomaniacs while remaining constant to a fixed erroneous idea, vary, to a degree which amounts to contradiction, in the accessory details. It is thus that I explain the fact that, in his second tribunate he claimed to be the son, not of the emperor, but of a bastard of his. There has been found, near the Ponte Senatorio, in excavating the ruins of a building, restored apparently by Rienzi, this inscription dictated by him according

A little later (Aug. 15, 1350), we find him writing to the emperor another letter full of senseless puns, in which he tells him, with doubly absurd freaks of thought and language, how, in the idea that the mother of Severinus Boethius was descended from the kings of Bohemia (!) he had called Boethius the younger and himself, the *Severe*; and how he had adopted from them the device of the seven stars—matters which could neither interest the emperor nor be of advantage to himself, but have all the characteristics of insanity.

So also, when he wrote that he was persuaded by the prophecies of the Majella hermits already mentioned, that his second exaltation should be much more glorious than the first, as the sun long hidden by the clouds appears more beautiful to the eye of the beholder: Perhaps the Lord, justly indignant at the wicked and unheard-of murder of Rienzi's illustrious grandfather, Henry VII., and the losses in souls and bodies suffered by the world during the Interregnum, had raised up Cola for the advantage of Charles, chosen him to re-establish the empire, and ordained that he should be *baptized in the Lateran*, in the Church of the Baptist, and in the *bath of Constantine*, that he might be the forerunner of the emperor, as John the Baptist was of Christ. Charles, it is true, had said that

---

to Gabrini in order to publish to the world his disgraceful delusion: "Nicolaus, Tribunus, Severus, Clemens, Laurentii, Teutonici filius, Gabrinius, Romæ Senator," with a timid allusion to a German, who was not Henry, but an illegitimate son of his (Tomasso Gabrini, *Osservazioni storico-critiche sulla Vita di Rienzi Rome: Fulgoni* (1806) 96).

the empire could only be restored by a miracle; but was not this a miracle, that one poor man should be able to succour the falling empire, as St. Francis had succoured the Church? Let him awake, and gird on his sword—let him not count for anything the revelation of the friars, since the whole Old and New Testaments were full of revelations: he alone could become master of Rome. If he did not do so at once, Charles would lose at least one hundred thousand gold florins from the tax on salt and the other revenues of the city which had been increased by the approach of the Jubilee. . . . Within a year and a half, the pope should die, and many cardinals be slain. . . . In fifteen years there should be but one shepherd and one faith, and the new pope, the Emperor Charles, and Cola should be, as it were, a symbol of the Trinity on Earth. Charles should reign in the west, the Tribune in the east. For the present, he was content with supporting the emperor in his journey to Rome—he was willing to open the way for him with the Romans and the other peoples of Italy, who would otherwise be averse to the empire; so that Charles might come among them peaceably and without bloodshed, and his arrival should not be the signal for mourning to the city and the whole nation, as had that of former emperors.

So far did he go, that the Archbishop of Prague wrote to him,

> that he wondered how the Tribune, who had done things which at first appeared to come

> from God, could be so far from exercising the virtue of humility as to consider his own elevation the work of the Holy Spirit, and to call himself the candidate of the latter

—words which may well be noted by those who see in his madness only the effect of the superstitions of the period.

The emperor replied, with much common sense, advising him to

> cease from ignorant hermits, who think themselves to be walking in the spirit of humility, without being able even to resist their sins and save their own souls, and who speak fantastically of knowing hidden things and governing in the spirit all that is under heaven . . .

and telling him that, out of love to God and his neighbours, he has "caused thee to be imprisoned as a sower of tares, and, withal, out of love for thine own soul, to cure it."

Later on, he counsels him to "lay aside all these vagaries, and, whatever his origin may have been, to remember that we are all God's creatures, sons of Adam, made out of the earth," &c. A curious lesson in democracy, given by a king of Bohemia to the extribune of an Italian republic!

But all was useless, and when, after many vicissitudes, he once more acquired a shadow of his former power by the aid of money obtained by sheer trickery—he announced the fact at Florence, in a pompous proclamation, adding that "women, men, boys, priests, and lay-folk had gone to meet him with palms and olive-branches, and trumpets, and cries of welcome."

These speeches seemed so very extravagant that their genuineness has been doubted by Zeffirino Re, on the ground of the extreme improbability of Petrarch's having defended him, or the emperor regarded him with favour for a single moment, had he really entertained ideas so eccentric and heretical.

But that, however improbable, such is the fact is already evident *à priori* to any one who—even without examining these strange letters and still stranger circulars—has observed the progressive development of insanity in Cola's career, and knows that it was just through his unheard-of audacity that he triumphed, and that the Bohemians were not so much scandalized as struck dumb by his eloquence,[56] and afterwards astonished and deeply moved by his recantations.

Moreover, these writings were refuted by the Bohemian bishops, in a document which is still extant, and afterwards retracted by himself. With a delicacy of which historians have not taken sufficient account, they were not consigned in their entirety to the Papal Court along with the person of the Tribune, whose condemnation, indeed, could bring neither pleasure nor profit to the host who had been already forced by political

56 Anonimo 92.

considerations to betray the confidence reposed in him.

He remained, meanwhile, an isolated phenomenon, an enigma to historians, since it was not so much history as the science of mental pathology which could succeed in completely explaining him. That science has pointed out to us in Rienzi all the characteristics of the monomaniac: regular features and handwriting, exaggerated tendency to symbolism and plays upon words—an activity disproportioned to his social position, and original even to absurdity, which entirely exhausted itself in writing—an exaggerated consciousness of his own personality, which at first aided him with the populace, and supplied the want of tact and practical ability, but afterwards led him into absurdities—a defective moral sense—a calm marking the approach of dementia, which was only disturbed by the abuse of alcohol, or by a spirited opposition.[57]

Campanella.—If Cola da Rienzi was a strange problem for historians until resolved by the modern psychiatric studies on monomania, not less strange has been the problem presented by Campanella, who, from being a humble and disdained monk in a forgotten district of Calabria, claimed to be a monarch and, as it were, a demigod against the power of Spain and of the Pope, and then suddenly became and died a zealot for both, contradicting himself, even against his own advantage, certainly against that of his fame.

57 Anonimo 92.

At last, it seems to me, the problem is approaching solution, after the classical works of Baldacchino, of Spaventa, of Fiorentino, but, above all, of Amabile, especially since Carlo Falletti[58] has passed those powerful works through the alembic of his synthetic criticism and removed from this strange medal the stains deposited by legends and historical prejudices.

"Campanella," remarks Falletti, "with his badly formed skull, surmounted by seven inequalities—hills, as he himself called them—possessed most sensitive nerves, an acute intellect, and easily exalted emotions." The mystical education of the order to which he belonged completed the work of nature; having entered a Dominican monastery at the age of fourteen, he always lived outside the real world. He spent eight years in the schools of Calabria amid disputes with his masters and fellow-pupils, and then departed, almost fled, from Cosenza and went to Naples. But no good fortune met him there. Soon after his arrival he chanced to speak slightingly of excommunication. He was

58 Pio Carlo Falletti, *Del carattere di Fra Tommaso Campanella* (Turin: Bocca, 1889); Rivista Storica Italiana 6.2 (1889); Luigi Amabile, *Fra Tommaso Campanella, la sua congiura, i suoi processi e la sua pazzia*, 3 vols. (Naples: Morano, 1882); *Fra Tommaso Campanella ne' castelli di Napoli, in Roma e in Parigi* (Naples: Morano, 1887) vol. 2; Fra T. Pignatelli e la sua congiura e la sua morte (Naples: Morano, 1887); Domenico Berti, *Lettere inedite di T. Campanella e catalogo dei suoi scritti* (Rome: Salviucci, 1878); *Nuovi documenti su Campanella* (Rome: Tipografia Bodoniana, 1881).

at once denounced, imprisoned, taken to Rome, tried, and condemned. On leaving prison he decided to go to Padua; on the way he was robbed of his manuscripts; three days after reaching Padua he was accused of using violence against the General of the Dominicans; hence a fresh imprisonment and fresh trial. Discharged and set at liberty, he took part in public discussions, but the doctrines he openly professed led to another trial arid imprisonment. He was only twenty-six, and had already spent three years in prison.

At the age of twenty, in the monastery at Cosenza, Campanella had associated with a certain Abramo, from whom he received lessons in necromancy, and who predicted that he would one day be a king. This was the starting point of his wild and ambitious imaginations. It should be added that when studying astrology, especially in 1597, he talked with many astrologers, mathematicians, and prelates who all held that the end of the world was approaching. Excited by their arguments, he gave himself to the study of prophecy, seeking it in the Bible, the Fathers, and the poets of antiquity; and in the symbol of the white horses and the white-robed elders of the New Zion he saw the brothers of Saint Dominic. Convinced that the prediction of the Holy Republic referred to the Dominicans, he retired to Stilo. All the political and social disorders of his time were for Campanella manifest signs; and to these were added earthquakes, famines, floods, and comets. Evidently the prophecies were being fulfilled. No doubt 1600 was the fatal year which would indicate the beginning of great changes and revolutions. Campanella spread the prophecies, and prepared the ground for the Holy Republic. There can be no question that these predictions and preparations led to a real rebellion, because they fitted in with the miserable condition of Calabria. Such prophecies pleased many who cherished desires of revenge. In the ears of these exasperated people Campanella's words sounded like a call to rebellion. Maurizio di Rinaldi, the leader of a band, so understood it, as did other bandits. Rinaldi cared little for religious reforms, and knew nothing of what the seven seals of the Apocalypse signified. He understood, however, that his arm was needed, and persuaded that it was not possible to fight against Spain with writings and words and the weapons of brigands, he sought the aid of the Turks. He was the real rebel, the real martyr in the liberation of Calabria from subjection to Spain. Of all the chief persons concerned in this disturbance he alone confessed himself a rebel; the others either denied the existence of a rebellion or professed their innocence. Seeing the old world doubled by the discovery of new lands, and Europe turned upside down by wars, Campanella thought of a universal monarchy with the Pope and himself for king and pastor.

Turn to his Utopia of the City of the Sun, in which all are educated in common. All the Solarians call each other brother; they are all sons of the great

Father adored on the summit of the mountain on which the city is built. There is not, and cannot be, among them any selfishness. All consider the common good, and, under the guidance of the priest and head, live happily together; since all are instructed, and knowledge is the foundation of every honour, there is a noble strife of intelligence. The Solarian citizens have made wonderful progress in the arts and sciences. They have ships that plough the seas without sails and without oars; and cars that are propelled by the force of the wind; they have discovered how to fly, and they are inventing instruments which will reveal new stars. They know that the world is a great animal in whose body we live, that the sea is produced by the sweat of the earth, and that all the stars move. They practise perpetual adoration, offer up bloodless sacrifices, and reverence, but do not worship, the sun and the stars.

All this simplicity, happiness, and prosperity are due in the first place to education and to communism, and in the second place to the magistrates who are all priests. The spiritual and temporal head is Hoch, who is assisted by Pom, Sim, and Mor. Pom has charge of all that refers to war; Sim presides over the arts, industries, and instruction; Mor directs human generation and the education of children; he regulates the sexual relationships in order to produce healthy and robust offspring, only permitting the strong to procreate; the rest are allowed to sacrifice to the terrestrial Venus after fecundation has been ascertained.

The City of the Sun is not in favour of war, but does not refuse to fight; in battle her citizens are invincible, because they fight in defence of their country, natural law, justice, and religion.

The felicity of the City of the Sun rested, therefore, on a community of goods, of women, of pleasures, and of knowledge; on wholesome generation, on sacerdotal government, and on simplicity in religion. Campanella aimed at founding in Calabria a *fac-simile* of the City of the Sun. The whole of his trial for heresy showed that he wished to reform religion and to render it more in harmony with human nature; by his own confession it is proved that he wished to establish a sacerdotal government. Nauder affirms, in fact, that he aimed at becoming King of Calabria in order to extend his authority thence over the whole world. Campanella's mind was in such a condition that it may be held, with Amabile, that he saw the possibility of founding a republic similar to that described in the City of the Sun. Naturally the head of this little Holy Republic, the Hoch of the City of the Sun, would be a philosopher, and, therefore, himself. All nations, observing the felicity enjoyed by the citizens of the New Sion, would accept the new law, and thus Campanella would become the monarch and guide of the world.

Only a lunatic would consider it possible to undertake the reorganization of society at a stroke, *ab imis fundamentis*, changing the form of government, and overturning the most ancient customs, institutions, laws, and traditions. But the madness diminishes if this reorganization is the consequence of a profound and general upheaval, like that proclaimed by the prophets for the end of the world. In his writings, certainly, we find puerilities which go to prove his insanity; if he had been an ordinary man they would not be remarkable; they would harmonize with the common prejudices of the day; but he had broken with theology, and had undertaken to examine its *ratio*; he had caught a glimpse of the modern state, and he proposed reforms which for his time were most liberal and remarkable. Thus he writes: "Law is the consent of all, written and promulgated for the common good" (*A. pol*, 32). "The laws should establish equality" (*Ibid.* 40). "The laws should be such that the people can obey them with love and fear" (*Mon. di Spagna*, c. xi.). "Heavy taxes should be levied on articles that are not necessary and are of luxury, and light ones on necessaries" (B. ii. doc. 197, p. 91). "There should be unity of government" (*Mon. di Spagna*, c. xii.). "The barons should be deprived of the *jus carcerandi*" (*Ibid.* c. xiv.). "They should be deprived of fortresses" (*Ibid.*); a national army should be established; education should be free (*Ibid.*); medical aid should be gratuitous (B. ii. doc. 97, p. 82). In fact, Campanella proposed what Sully, Richelieu, Colbert, and Louis XIV. did for the French nation.

Now when a man who reasons so profoundly fails to see the absurdity and impossibility of becoming, with a few followers in a remote country-side, the monarch and reformer of the whole world, he can only be insane. And so he was judged by the more sagacious among his contemporaries. Thus Father Giacinto, the confidant of Richelieu, wrote: "No one believes so easily any story that is told him, and examines things that he believes to be *de facto* with less judgment." And again: "I shall always hold him for a man wilder than a fly, and less sensible in worldly affairs than a child." Peirescio called him "*bon homme.*"

Following human intellect, Campanella reached Pantheism, the soul of things, the transformation of animate and inanimate beings, veneration of the sun, that "beneficent star, living temple, statue and venerable face of the true God." Stricken by adversity, not assisted by his god, he returned to Catholicism, to the angels and miracles, to the future life which promises enjoyments which cannot be had on earth, and the restoration of the beloved lost.

Like all madmen, incapable of moderation he became furiously intolerant; hence his ferocious suggestions for oppressing the Protestants, and the title which he took of emissary of Christ or of the Most High. He imagined that his works would serve to confute the Protestants, wrote and disputed against Lutherans and Calvinists, wished to found colleges of priests for the diffusion of Catholicism, gave advice to those who would none of it for overthrowing heresy and propagating the true faith. In short, he ended as he had begun, in a delirious dream of religious ambition, which only varied in subject, going from one pole to the opposite.

But, I repeat, this phenomenon of contradiction, and of the passage from opposite excesses of feeling, is one of the most marked characters of monomania, and especially of religious monomania. I remember nuns of whom I had charge at the asylum at Pesaro, who on first becoming insane were violent and blasphemous, and later on in the course of their madness, apostles of Christianity; and thus it is easy to see that the miserly may, under the influence of insanity, develop extraordinary prodigality. We have seen Lazzaretti, a drunkard and a blasphemer, become austere and pious under the influence of insanity; and then from being a fanatical Papist becoming and dying an Anti-Papist, when he found himself repulsed by the Vatican. Recently De Nino, in his book *Il Messia degli Abruzzi*, has described a certain priest, become a Messiah, who, while insane, attempted reforms, at all events in rites, and who, during the last months of his life, like Campanella, starved himself in penitence for his revolutionary sins, and in spite of fasts and penances believed that he was damned.

San Juan de Dios.—Juan Ciudad was born on March 8, 1495, in the town of Montemor-o-Novo, in Portugal.[59] He seems to have been tormented by

59 Abbe Saglier, *Vie de Saint Jean de Dieu* (Paris: Plon, 1877);

the spirit of adventure from his childhood, as he left his father's house at the age of eight. A priest took him as far as Oropesa, where he entered the service of a Frenchman in the capacity of shepherd. After some years he became tired of this work, and, being tall and strong, enlisted as a soldier.

The life he led in the army cannot be described; the officers set the example, and plundered as greedily as the privates. One of the former entrusted his share of the booty to Juan, who either lost or stole it. He was condemned to death, and was just going to be hanged, when a superior officer, passing by, granted him his life, but dismissed him from the army. He then returned to Oropesa, and resumed his former position. Towards 1528, he enlisted a second time, and marched under the orders of the Count of Oropesa. When the war was over, he returned to Montemor-o-Novo, to see his parents; but he lost his memory, and forgot his father's name. He then left the place, and went to Ayamonte in Andalusia, where he became a shepherd. It was there that he believed himself to have been called, and, later on, to have had a dream in which he dedicated himself to God and to the poor.

Those were the days when the Barbary pirates nourished, making descents on ill-defended countries, and kidnapping their inhabitants, whom they sold at Fez, Algiers, and Tunis. Two religious orders had made it their special task to collect

Maxime du Camp, *La charité privée à Paris* (Paris: Hachette, 1885).

alms for the ransom of the Catholics who were being sold in the slave-market.

It seems that Juan Ciudad had the intention of consecrating himself to this sacred duty. He embarked for Ceuta, where he entered the service of an exiled and ruined Portuguese family, whom, it is said, he supported by his labour as an artizan. After a time, he grew weary of this life; he left his master and sailed for Gibraltar, where he established a small trade in relics and other sacred objects.

The sale of these having brought him some money, he left Gibraltar and settled at Granada, where he opened a shop. He was then aged 43, and was just about to undergo that mental convulsion which determined his vocation.

On the 20th of January, 1539, after hearing a sermon by Juan d'Avila, he was seized with a fit of frantic devotion. He confessed his sins in a loud voice, rolled in the dust, pulled out the hair of his head, tore his clothes, and rushed through the streets of Granada, imploring the mercy of God, and followed by boys shouting after him as a madman. He entered his library, destroyed all the secular books in his possession, gave away the sacred ones, distributed his furniture and clothes to any one who was willing to have them, and remained in his shirt, beating his breast and calling on every one to pray for him. The crowd followed him noisily as far as the cathedral, where, half-naked, he again began his vociferations and bursts of despair. The preacher, Juan d'Avila, having been informed of the conversion occasioned by his words, listened to the poor man's confession, consoled him, and gave him advice, which does not appear to have had much effect, since, on leaving him, Ciudad rolled himself on a dung-heap, proclaiming his sins in a loud voice. The crowd amused themselves by hissing him, throwing stones and mud, and otherwise maltreating him. Some, however, took pity on him, and conducted him to the place set apart for the insane in the Royal Hospital. He was subjected to the treatment then in vogue, that is, he was bound and scourged, in order to deliver him from the evil spirit supposed to possess him.

This attack of mania appears to have been one of great violence. In general, with regard to mental maladies, the more excessive the alienation, the more easily it ceases. It is said that, in the midst of the blows inflicted on him, he took avow "to receive poor madmen, and treat them as is fitting."

When the nervous exacerbation was calmed, he employed himself in attending on the sick, and, later on, obtained his liberty, and a certificate attesting his sanity. Having made a vow to go on pilgrimage to the shrine of the Virgin of Guadalupe, he started barefoot, without a farthing, in the middle of winter. On his way through the forests and across the moors, he picked up dry sticks and made them into a faggot, which, when he reached an inhabited place, he gave in exchange for a little food and a night's lodging.

It is said that, when he reached Guadalupe, he had a vision which exercised a decisive influence on him. The Virgin appeared to him, and gave him the Child Jesus, naked, with clothes to cover him. This was to show him that he ought to have pity on the weak, shelter the destitute, and clothe the poor—at least such was his interpretation. His mission dates from that day, and he executed it with so much the more zeal, as he believed it to have been laid upon him by the Virgin whom he adored.

Dressed in a white garment, which an Hieronymite monk had given him, with a wallet on his back, and a pilgrim's staff in his hand, he returned to Oropesa, and went to lodge in the poor-house.

The misery of the inmates so touched him, that he went outside the city, begged alms for them, and gave them all that he received. Later on, he took to selling faggots in the public square, gave to the poor and sick all that he gained, and slept in stables, through the charity of their owners.

One day, having seen a notice posted up in the square, "House to let for the poor," he conceived the idea of making it into an asylum. Having begged money from the rich, with which he bought mats, blankets, and utensils, he received and sheltered forty-six sick and crippled paupers. In order to maintain them, he went about the streets at the dinner hour, to collect from the rich the remnants of their meals, crying, "Do good, my brethren; it will return in blessing to yourselves,"

Juan de Dios' example provoked emulation; several men offered themselves to help him. He instructed them in their new duties, and thus became the head of a group, which, by multiplying, has become the great congregation now in existence.

The resources now put at his disposal permitted him to treat the sick, "as is fitting."

It is worthy of attention that Juan de Dios was a reformer in the manner of treating the sick, only placing one patient in each bed. He was the first to divide the sick into classes—he was, in short, the creator of the modern hospital, and the founder of casual wards; for he opened, in connection with his hospital, a house where the homeless poor and travellers without money could sleep.

It was at this period that he took the name of Juan de Dios. The good done by him did not remain unknown, and the name of Juan de Dios, father of the poor, was spread abroad through Spain. Profiting by this, he made a journey as far as Granada, and returned with abundant contributions.

He was exhausted by hard work and exposure rather than by years. He treated himself with exaggerated austerity—always travelling on foot without shoes, hat, or linen—only covered with a single grey garment; he fasted with extreme frequency, and imposed on himself the most trying exertions. He would rush through a burning house to save the sick, he often threw himself into the water to save children; he may be said to have died of the hardships he endured.

During his last days, he sent for Antonio Martin, his earliest disciple, and recommended the work to his care. Feeling the approach of death, he left his bed to pray, and died on his knees.

He was born on March 8, 1495, and died on Saturday, March 8, 1550.

He had a splendid funeral; sick men touched the bier in the hope of being healed; the sheet which covered the corpse was torn to pieces, and each rag became a relic. He was canonised on September 21, 1630, by Urban VIII., and is now known as San Juan de Dios.[60]

Prosper Enfantin.—Prosper Enfantin, though an engineer, a railway director, and otherwise connected with such rational and prosaic subjects as mathematics, nevertheless, in 1850, believed himself to be, and in fact was, the head of a new religion, a variation of that of Saint Simon. He had a handsome face and large forehead of an Olympian cast; he was very kind-hearted, but profoundly convinced of his own infallibility on all subjects—on industrial and philosophical questions—on painting as well as on cooking. He had what, in the peculiar language of monomaniacs, he called *circumferential* ideas, in which every new fact found, in its pre-established place, the proper solution. The new religion was to equalize men and women, and to make the language of finance and industry poetical. He himself represented the Father, and

60 It is a curious point, that all these saints (Lazzaretti, Loyola, &c.) began by leading a wild life.

was always hoping to find the Mother, the free woman, the Eve,—a woman, reasoning like man, who, knowing the needs and capabilities of women, would make the confession of her sex without restriction, so as to furnish the elements for a declaration of the rights and duties of women. But the right woman was never found, for Madame de Staël and George Sand, to whom he and his friends first turned, laughed at them; they sought her in the East, at Constantinople, and found, instead, a prison! But for all that, he never lost his illusion. He used to say that only great men could found a new religion.

His goodness was exquisite; he constantly sacrificed himself for his followers—his sons, as he called them. These wore at one time, like certain monomaniacs, a symbolical uniform—white trousers to represent *love*, red waistcoat for work, and blue coat for *faith*. This signified that his religion was founded on love, strengthened the heart with *work*, and was wholly encompassed by *faith*. Every one was to have his name written on his shirt-front, and to wear, in addition, a collar adorned with triangles, and a semi-circle which was to become a circle as soon as the Mother, the Eve aforesaid, had been found.

These are the symbols usual with the monomaniac and the mattoid.

This is seen in their programmes, in which they announced—in type of various sizes—that: "Man recalls the Past, Woman represents the Future,—

the two united see the present." Yet, in spite of all this, he foresaw—and even tried to undertake—the Suez Canal, and counted among his followers such men as Chevalier, Lambert, and Jourdan.[61]

Lazzaretti.—An example the more curious as well as authentic, as it has manifested itself in recent years, under the eyes of all, and has arrived at the dignity of an historic event, is the case of David Lazzaretti.[62]

61 Maxime Du Camp, *Souvenirs littéraires*, 2 vols (Paris: Hachette et Cie, 1882–3). (2nd ed.)

62 See the paper on David Lazzaretti, by Nocito and Lombroso, in the *Archivio di psichiatria, antropologia criminale e scienze penali per servire allo studio dell'uomo alienato e delinquente* 1.2-3 (1881); Andrea Verga, *David Lazzaretti e la pazzia sensoria* (Milan: Rechiedei, 1880); Edoardo Caravaggio, "Inchiesta e Relazione su Arcidosso", *Gazzetta Ufficiale del Regno d'Italia* 321 (1 October 1878).

This man was born at Arcidosso, in 1834. His father, a carter, appears to have been given to drink, but was of great strength. He had some relatives who were suicidal, and others insane; one, in particular, died a religious maniac, and believed himself to be the Eternal Father. Lazzaretti's six brothers were all strong men, of gigantic stature, ranging from 1·90 to 1·95 m. in height (which, however, is not uncommon in that part of the country), of quick wits and tenacious memory.

David was distinguished from the rest by his superior stature, by the distinction and regularity of his features, by greater intelligence, by the large size of his head, which was dolichocephalic in form, and by his eyes, which some found fascinating, though to many (says the advocate Pugno) they seemed to have the character of possession and of insanity. It is asserted that he was hypospadic and perhaps impotent in his youth—anomalies of no slight importance, if we remember that Morel and, especially, Legrand du Saulle have often discovered them in hereditary madmen.

Even from his childhood, he showed those contradictions, those tendencies to extremes in character, which are frequent precursors of insanity. Thus, when a boy he wished to become a monk; later on, after he had taken to his father's trade, he began to lead an irregular life, and gave himself up to alcoholic intemperance. In the meantime, however, he cultivated his mind by a course of reading which was singular for a man in his position, including Dante and Tasso; and at fifteen he was called "Thousand Ideas" from the strange songs he invented,[63] though he could never succeed in learning the rules of grammar. He was quarrelsome, used the foulest language, and was dreaded by all, so much so that, one day, on the occasion of a festival, unarmed and followed only by his brothers, he put to flight the entire population of Castel del Piano. Yet he was easily excited by a speech, a poem, a sermon, a play—anything that appeared noble and great. He had an extreme veneration for Christ and Mahomet, whom he used to call the two greatest men that had ever appeared in the world.

According to his own confessions, he had, at

63 Andrea Verga, *David Lazzaretti e la pazzia sensoria* (Milan: Rechiedei, 1880).

the age of fourteen, various hallucinations of the same kind as those which proved so fatal to him in 1878. It is certain, besides, that, at one time in his youth, he had a strong sympathy for a Jewess of Pittigliano, awakened by the eloquence with which she defended her religion. Yet at that time he was accustomed to say that there were three things he abhorred—women, churches, and dancing.

In 1859, at twenty-five, he enlisted as a volunteer in the cavalry; and in 1860, he took part in Cialdini's campaign,[64] but rather as an officer's servant than as a soldier. Before starting, he wrote a patriotic hymn, which was sent to Brofferio, and surprised him by the novelty of its thoughts and the beauty of some of the verses, contrasting strangely with the roughness of the phraseology, and the numerous grammatical errors.

After this, he again returned to his trade as a carter, and at the same time to his habits of debauchery and foul language. He also rejoined his wife, whom he had married three years previously, and for whom he felt a poetic affection which he carried so far as to write love-songs to her. Here, again, his ambitious ideas reappeared, and induced him anew, though so uncultivated, to seek fame through his verses and tragedies, which read like burlesques.

64 The Battle of Castelfidardo, led by Enrico Cialdini on 18 September 1860. The battle was fought between the Sardinian army—acting as the driving force in the war for Italian unification, against the Papal States. —Ed.

Gradually, his fantastic delusions took another direction. In 1867, at thirty-three, he had—whether as an effect of drink, or of political excitement—a return of the religious hallucinations of 1848, in a more marked form than previously. One day he disappeared, in consequence of a vision of the Madonna, who had commanded him to go to Rome, and remind the Pope (who at first refused to receive him, but afterwards treated him with courtesy, though, it is said, not without advising him to try the remedy of a good shower-bath) of his divine mission. He then went to the hermitage of Montorio Romano, in the Sabine mountains, inhabited by a Prussian monk named Ignazio Micus. The latter kept him with him for three months in the "Grotto of the Blessed Amadeus," directing him in his theological studies.

It is very probable—though on this point we can only conjecture, as all direct evidence is wanting—that this monk assisted him to make the tattoo-marks on his forehead, which he claimed to have received from the hand of St. Peter, and which he hid under a lock of hair from the gaze of the profane, showing them only to true believers.

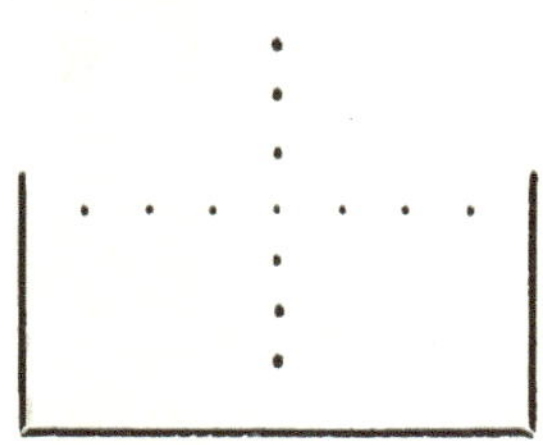

This tattooing, according to the testimony of medical men, consists of an irregular parallelogram, on the upper side of which are thirteen dots, disposed in the form of a cross. To this mark, and to two others which he afterwards produced on himself, on the deltoid muscle and the inside of the leg, he attributed—through a tendency common among the insane—a strange and mysterious significance, as seals of a special covenant with God.

From that moment a complete change took place in him, such as is often observed in the insane.[65] From being quarrelsome, blasphemous, and intemperate, he became tractable, gentle, and abstemious to the point of living on bread and water in Sabina, and, in the *tempora* on the mountains, on herbs with salt and vinegar. At other times he had no other food but polenta, or *soupe-maigre*, or bread with onions or garlic. On the island of Monte Cristo, in 1870, he lived for over a month on six loaves, garnished with a few herbs;[66] and in the French monastery, he got through several days on two potatoes a day. What must have appeared still more strange, and surprised even cultured minds, was the fact that the chaotic and burlesque writer became sometimes elegant, always effective—full

65 At Pesaro I had under my care several nuns from Roman convents, whose language I never heard surpassed in obscene blasphemy. I have also attended exceedingly devout Jews, whose first symptom was the wish to be baptised, and who, immediately after their recovery, became more orthodox than before.

66 Deposition of the witness Vichi.

of vigorous images supplied by a piety comparable alone to that of the early Christians.

This, in fact, struck the clergy of the district, who, rightly seeing in him a repetition of the ancient prophets, took him seriously, all the more that, according to their usual custom, they perceived the means of making a profit out of him and getting a church rebuilt.

The people, already justly astonished at his changed ways of life, no less than by his tattooings, his inspired speech, his long neglected beard and grave bearing, rushed in masses to hear him, encouraged by the priests.

A procession was then organized, in which Lazzaretti, accompanied by priests and by some of the most influential among the laity, marched to Arcidosso, Roccalbegna, Castel del Piano, Pian Castagnaio, Cinigiano, and Santafiora. In all these places he was received with rejoicings by the people on their knees; and the parish priests kissed his face and his hands and even his feet. The construction of the church was begun, and contributions to the building fund flowed in abundantly. But though numerous, the amounts were small, the mountaineers being unable to give much. The notion was then suggested of employing the labour of their arms.

The site of the church had been selected not far from Arcidosso—about a hundred paces from the village, at the spot called *La Croce dei Canzacchi*, where, by a strange fatality, he was to receive his death-shot.

The faithful assembled by thousands to begin the building. Men, women and children were employed in carrying fascines, beams of wood, and stones. But, unfortunately, architecture, like grammar, has rules; and in carrying them out prophetic inspiration is of little use without training. Thus, as Lazzaretti's verses remained lame, so the materials collected with so much labour remained a useless heap, like the tower which was to reach to heaven, and never became more than a pile of stones.

In January, 1870, he founded the "Society of the Holy League," a mutual assistance society which he called the symbol of charity. In March of the same year, after having assembled his followers at a Last Supper, he set out, accompanied by Rafifaello and Giuseppe Vichi, for the island of Monte Cristo, where he remained for some months, writing epistles, prophecies, and sermons. He then returned to Montelabro, where he wrote down the visions or prophetic inspirations which he had, and where he was arrested for sedition (April 27th). After his liberation,[67] he founded a society to which he gave the name of "Christian Families." This was considered, very erroneously, as a proof of continued fraud; and he was arrested, but discharged, through the efforts of the advocate Salvi, after seven months' imprisonment.

67 His first arrest took place in the island of Monte Cristo, for preaching sedition among the fishermen. Thence, he was transferred to Orbetello (see Andrea Verga, *David Lazzaretti e la pazzia sensoria* (Milan: Rechiedei, 1880)).

In 1873, Lazzaretti, in obedience to other divine commands, started on a journey, passing through Rome, Naples, and Turin, whence he proceeded to the Chartreuse at Grenoble. Here he wrote the Rules and Discipline of the Order of Penitent Hermits, invented a system of cipher, with a numerical alphabet, and dictated the *Book of the Heavenly Flowers*,[68] in which it is written that "The great man shall descend from the mountains, followed by a little band of mountain burghers." To which are added the visions, dreams, and divine commands which he believed himself to have received in that place.

On his return to Montelabro he found an immense crowd, attracted both by devotion and curiosity, encamped on the summit of the mountain, to whom he addressed a sermon on the text, "God sees us, judges us, condemns us." For this he was denounced to the authorities as tending to overthrow the government and promote civil war.

In the night of Nov. 19, 1874, ne was arrested a second time, and brought before the court at Rieti. This time the authorities were desirous of obtaining the opinion of non-specialist experts, who, with inexplicable want of perception, pronounced him to be of sound mind and a cunning knave.[69] Thus,

68 *Le livre des fleurs célestes* (Lyon: Pitrat Aîné, 1876).

69 Pietro Nocito and Cesare Lombroso, "Davide Lazzaretti", *Archivio di psichiatria, antropologia criminale e scienze penali* 2 (1880). In this article are detailed the causes of the error into which the experts fell—an error, which cost the country an

in spite of his strange publications and his tattoo marks, he was condemned to fifteen months' imprisonment, and one year of police supervision, for fraud and vagabondage.

The sentence, however, was referred to the Court of Appeal at Perugia; and on the 2nd of August, 1875, he was allowed to return to Montelabro, where he reconstituted his society, and placed the priest Imperiuzzi at the head of it. His health had suffered in prison, and for this reason—perhaps, also, to avoid new arrests, and to enjoy the glory of easy martyrdom among the Legitimist fanatics—he went to France in October. Being mysteriously carried, as he expresses it, by the Divine power, into the environs of a town in Burgundy, he produced a book, which with good reason he calls "mysterious," entitled *My Wrestling with God, or The Book of the Seven Seals, with the description and nature of the Seven Eternal Cities*[70]—a mixture of Genesis and Revelation, with sentences and rhapsodies entirely of an insane character. He also wrote a manifesto addressed to all the princes of Christendom, in which he calls himself the great Monarch, and invites them to make alliance with him, for, "at an unexpected time the end of the world shall be manifested to the Latin nation in a way quite opposed to human pride." In the same document he declares himself Leader, Master,

enormous expenditure and several human lives.

70 *La mia lotta con Dio ossia Il libro dei Sette Sigilli* (Bourg: Villefranche, 1877).

Judge, and Prince over all the potentates of earth. These writings were copied for him by the priest Imperiuzzi, who corrected the most conspicuous mistakes; and many of them attained not only the undeserved honour of appearing in print, but also that of being translated into French, by the aid of M. Lon du Vachat, and various Italian and foreign reactionaries, who had taken Lazzaretti seriously.

However, a short time after, he was so far carried away by delirium as to begin inveighing against the corruptions of the priesthood and the practice of auricular confession, for which he wished to substitute a public one. Thereupon the Holy See declared his doctrines false and his writings subversive, and the same man who had formerly written a work[71] in favour of the Pope, now wrote, and despatched on May 14, 1878, an exhortation addressed to his brethren of the Order of Hermits, against Papal idolatry, and the beast of the seven heads. After all this, with the usual contradictoriness of the insane, he went to Rome to lay aside his symbolic seal and his rod, and retracted before the Holy Office; yet, afterwards, returning to Montelabro, he continued to deliver addresses against the Catholic Church, which, he said, had become a shopkeeping church, and against the *priests, true atheists in practice, who, not believing themselves, profit by the belief of others.* Preaching the Holy Reformation, and declaring himself the Man of Mystery, the New Christ, Leader and Avenger,

71 *Lo Statute Civile del Regno Pontificio in Italia.*

he exhorted believers to separate themselves from the world, and prove their separation by abstaining from food and from sexual intercourse, even in the case of married persons, who, however, if they indulged, were required to pray for at least two hours, naked, outside their bed, before the act. He issued paper money for considerable sums, in proportion to the means at the disposal of the community, *i.e.*, up to 104,000 francs; but it should be noted that this was absolutely useless, being kept shut up in a closed vase. This idea savours unmistakably of insanity.

After announcing a great miracle, he caused to be prepared, with a part of the money collected, banners and garments for the members, embroidered with the animals which had appeared to him in his hallucinations—all of strange and grotesque shapes. He had a richer one made for himself, and, for the rank and file, a square piece of stuff to wear on the breast, which showed a cross, with two C's reversed, † C, the usual emblem of the association.

In August, 1878, he assembled a larger number than ever, and, having prescribed prayers and fasts for three days and three nights, delivered addresses, some of which were public, others private and reserved for believers (who were divided into the various classes of Priest-Hermits, Penitentiary Hermits, Penitent Hermits, and simple associations of the Holy League and Christian Brotherhood) and caused the so-called Confession of Amendment to be made on the 14th, 15th, and

16th August. On the 17th, the great banner with the inscription, "The Republic is the Kingdom of God," was raised on the tower. Then, having assembled all the members at the foot of a cross, erected for the purpose, the Prophet administered the solemn oath of fidelity and obedience. At this point, one of David's brothers tried to persuade him to renounce his perilous enterprise, but in vain; for, on the contrary, he replied to those who pointed out the possibility of a conflict,

> He would, on the following day, show them a miracle to prove that he was sent from God in the form of Christ, a judge and leader, and therefore invulnerable, and that every power on earth must yield to his will; a sign from his rod of command was enough to annihilate all the forces of those who dared oppose him.

A member having remarked on the opposition of the government, he added that "he would ward off the balls with his hands, and render harmless the weapons directed against himself and his faithful followers; and the Government Carbineers themselves would act as a guard of honour to them." More and more intoxicated with his delirium, he wrote in all seriousness to the Delegate of Public Safety—to whom he had already shown the preparations, and, later on, given a half-promise to countermand the procession—"That he was no longer able to do so, having received superior orders to the contrary from God Himself." He threatened unbelievers with the Divine wrath, if, through want of faith, they rebelled against his will.

With such intentions, on the morning of August 18th, he set out from Montelabro at the head of an immense crowd, going down towards Arcidosso. He was dressed in a royal cloak of purple embroidered with gold ornaments, and crowned with a kind of tiara surmounted by a crest adorned with plumes; and he held in his hand the staff which he called his rod of command. His principal associates were dressed, less richly than himself, in strangely-fashioned robes of various colours, according to their position in the hierarchy of the Holy League. The ordinary members were dressed in their everyday clothes, without other mark of distinction than the emblematic breastplate previously described. Seven of the graduates of the Brotherhood carried as many banners with the motto, "The Republic is the Kingdom of God." They sang the Davidian hymn, each stanza of which ended with the refrain, "Eternal is the Republic," &c. It is needless to relate what took place in those last hours. The man who had shortly before called himself the King of kings, and believed himself invulnerable, fell, struck by a shot fired by the orders, perhaps by the hand, of a delegate who had many a time been his guest. It appears that he exclaimed as he fell, under the influence of a last delusion, "The victory is ours!"

It is certain that the procession he had arranged was not only unarmed, but appeared to be in every way calculated to turn out perfectly harmless.

Nocito has well remarked that an examination of the strange emblematic properties of the League proved beyond all doubt that the Government had mistaken a monomaniac for a rebel.

He took his stand on that passage of the Nicene Creed, which states that Christ rose from the dead, and ascended to the right hand of the Father, "Whence He shall come to judge the quick and the dead." Having waited in vain for the appearance of Christ, he came to believe that this part must be reserved for him. Christ had twelve apostles, therefore he wished to have twelve. Christ had included St. Peter among the number, and Lazzaretti also determined to have a St. Peter, who was distinguished by the badge of a pair of crossed keys on his breast. In imitation of the forty days' fast, Lazzaretti fasted in mid-winter, in the island of Monte Cristo, and there received communications from God amid the noise of the tempest, the crash of thunders, and the shaking of the whole island. There, too, he held a sort of Last Supper with his disciples, on January 15, 1870, in the course of which he said, "Thus it has pleased Him who directs me in all my works. Know that this supper carries with it the greatest of mysteries; think that you are in a place which God has chosen for His dwelling—or, to speak more correctly, for His adoration. Here, here, not far from us, on this soil, shall be raised marvellous pyramids in honour of His most Holy Name, and the said pyramids shall be an oracle of the Divine Majesty."

To say the truth, he did not, at this supper, institute any sacrament. But that nothing might be wanting in his mad idea of imitating Jesus Christ, he evolved a sacrament of his own—that of the Confession of Amendment—at bottom a slight variation of auricular confession.

All this, however, was not sufficient. David Lazzaretti was determined to have his *transfiguration* and his *earthquake*, and promised them for August 18, 1878.

When the surgeon was hesitating to operate on one of his sons for calculus, he took the knife out of his hand, and performed the operation. The boy died under it, but Lazzaretti, quite undisturbed, kept on repeating, "The son of David cannot die."

At the *post-mortem* examination, a second tattoo mark was discovered on his body. This was the usual cross, placed inside a reversed tiara. His brothers, questioned on the subject, replied that he had had a golden seal made in France, which he called the *imperial* seal, and that after immersing it in boiling oil, he had branded, first his own flesh, and then that of his sons and his wife. With this impression (which is, in fact, a convincing proof of the insensibility to pain peculiar to the insane, and of their tendency to express their eccentric ideas by means of figures and symbols) he claimed to leave a visible sign of the descent which, in common with all his family, he boasted from the Emperor Constantine.

However, not satisfied with descent from a royal race, he also wanted to rule the world in his own person, though afterwards he was willing to content himself with the creation of a prince whom he would invest with it. In a manifesto addressed "to all Christian princes," he makes the following proclamation:—

> I address myself to all the princes of Christendom—Catholics, schismatics, or heretics—provided only they have been baptized. It matters little whether or not they have been invested with power or the government of nations, so long as they are sprung from royal blood. I call them all, and the first one who shall present himself to me, who is not under twenty years of age, or over fifty, and has no bodily imperfection, I constitute him king in my stead.

The strange thing is, that he was taken at his word by the Comte de Chambord, who sent an embassy to him.

"I have need," he continued,

> of a Christian alliance. I am decided, to-day, to hasten this great enterprise; and if they (the Christian princes) do not come to me within the fixed time of three years, from the date of publication of this programme, I will leave Europe and go to the unbelieving nations to do with them what I have not been able to do with Christians.
>
> But in that case, woe to all of you, princes of Christendom. Ye shall be punished by the seven

> heads of the great Antichrist, which shall arise in the midst of Europe, and, above all, by a youth, who, after my departure, shall advance from the regions of the north towards Central France, and shall pretend to be that which *I myself* am.

From henceforward, there appears in David Lazzaretti, the fixed idea of being the King of kings and Prince of all princes. To the head of the municipal body of Arcidosso, who would not obey him, he said, "I am the King of kings, the Monarch of all monarchs, I bear on my shoulders all the princes of the world. All the carbineers and soldiers there are, are mine, and dependent on me, and there are no ropes that can bind me." To Minucci, who was trying to escape unnoticed, he said, "You do not know that I am the Prince of princes, the King of all the earth, and if you try to run away, I will have you stoned alive."

The witness G. B. Rossi was present at the sermon on the 17th, and heard David say that he was the King of kings, Christ the Judge; that the Pope was no longer to reside at Rome, but that he (Lazzaretti), on certain conditions, would provide him with another residence, and that the king of Italy, too, would be his subject.

The witness Mariotti also deposed that he had heard David say in his sermon, "that he had no fear of force, and that, even with a million of soldiers, it was impossible for a subject to arrest his monarch."

Lastly—not to lengthen the series of proofs—the witness Giuseppe Tonini heard him assert, in the sermon, that he was "the King of kings, and commanded the whole world;" while the witness Valentino Mazzetti says that Lazzaretti was determined to hold the procession of Aug. 18th at any cost, and said, "Do you think they are going to arrest us? No, no, it is not possible for subjects to arrest their monarch."

The emblematic device he adopted is worth noting: the double C, to which he attached so much importance, representing the first and second Christ, *i.e.*, Christ, the son of St. Joseph of Nazareth, and Christ, the son of the late Joseph Lazzaretti of Arcidosso. In truth, it is not in any way comprehensible what relation Christ could hold to Constantine, the latter to David, and all these to Lazzaretti. But the relation exists precisely in those strange contradictions and absurdities, which—amid the persistence of the *Prince* idea—constantly come to the surface in monomaniacs, so that some have wished to class their disease as dementia. In fact, although they keep up the character, so to speak, far better than general paralytics, and try to give a plausible appearance to their delirium, yet, oftentimes, when overpowered with the necessity of finding a vent for their persistent ambitious idea, they pay no attention to the contradictions they fall into. A Pavia embroideress, believing herself a descendant of the Bonaparte family, modelled her dress, language, and aspect with great success on those of the members of the reigning families. Yet, while she asserted herself to be the daughter of

Marie Louise, she at the same time claimed Victor Emmanuel as her father; as, on other occasions, she tried to persuade us that she had found the poison of vipers in the eggs she was eating.

Thus, though at first calling on the Pope to liberate Italy, Lazzaretti, when excommunicated, or merely treated with contempt by the Pope, wrote against Papal idolatry. Though he wished to die a member of the Catholic Apostolic Church, he inveighed against auricular confession, which is the very pivot of Catholicism; and, while he called himself the son of David, he also wished to be thought the son of Constantine.

Passanante.—Passanante, the would-be regicide of Naples, has no morbid hereditary antecedents.[72] At the age of 29, his height was 1·63 m., and his weight 51½ kilogrammes, *i.e.*, 14 kilogrammes less than the Neapolitan average. His head may be described as almost submicrocephalic—cephalic index 82, probable capacity 1513. His features show the characteristics of the Mongol and the *cretin*—small and deeply-set eyes abnormally far apart, zygomatic bones highly developed, beard scanty. The pupils show a low degree of mobility; and the genitals are atrophied—a fact connected with that of almost complete anaphrodisia. On the other hand, the liver and spleen are hypertrophied, which partly explains the increase of the tempera-

72 See Cesare Lombroso, *Considerazioni al processo Passannante* (Naples: Enrico Detken, 1879) 16, 17. [Corrected publication date from 1876 to 1879. —Ed.]

ture (varying from 38° to 37·8° at the arm-pits) the weakness of the pulse (88), and the very slight degree of strength, which, moreover, is less on the right side (60 kil.) than on the left (78 kil.). This last fact—which perhaps arises from an old burn on the hand—is most important, because rendering the complete carrying out of the crime improbable, especially taking into account the clumsy weapon with which he was armed, and the unfavourable position which was the only one he could take. The sensibility was perverted—the tactile presenting 5 mm. on the back of the hand (where the normal sensitiveness is from 16 to 20), and 7 on the forehead, where it is usually from 20 to 22 (that on the palm of the hand was not registered). On the contrary, the sensitiveness of the skin to puncture was much weakened. In prison he had attacks of delirium accompanied by hallucinations.

All these characteristics are clear indications of disease, both in the abdominal viscera, and in the nervous centres. This result is even more evident from the psychological study of the case. A merely superficial examination might have induced the belief that his affections and moral sentiments were normal. He showed, indeed, a horror of crime, lived a most frugal and abstemious life; and, while sometimes over-religious, sometimes exaggeratedly patriotic, always appeared to prefer the advantage of others to his own. He thus presented to those unversed in the study of mental pathology, the appearance, as it were, of a martyr to an idea which had been maturing for years, the mouthpiece and tool of a powerful sect, who might call for execration politically, but as an individual commanded respect.

This view, however, is at once seen to be fallacious, (even leaving aside the delirium, which might have been the effect of imprisonment), if we remember that, as has already been said, frugality and unselfishness are special characteristics of the mattoid, and, not seldom, also of the insane, some of whom seem to have more affection for their country, and for humanity in general, than for their families and themselves, and if we notice the indifference or even pleasure with which, in his writings, he refers to the murders committed by his countrymen, when, "to the sound of axes, they make foreigners give them money," above all, the enjoyment with which he records the cruel practical joke played on a poor man who was very fond of his cherry tree, by digging up the latter, bringing it back stripped of its fruit, and leaving it at his front door. This morbid apathy is especially revealed in the want of emotion shown after the crime, in the face of the anger of the populace which was let loose against him. Yet even the greatest fanatics among political assassins, such as Orsini, Sand, and Nobiling, have been overwhelmed by emotion after the deed, and have often attempted suicide.

The true motive of the act is quite sufficient to prove this: being dismissed from his situation on account of his political vagaries, arrested as a vagabond, and, in addition, ill-used by the police, he thought—with a vanity as boundless as his impotence to gratify it, or even to live—of imitating the heroes he had heard talked of in the clubs (and against whom he had himself declaimed), so as to find a way of ending his life by the hand of another.

"As I found myself ill-used by my employers, and felt a horror of life, I formed the design of assassinating the king, so as not to have to kill myself," he said to the magistrate, immediately after his arrest. To the judge Azzaritti, "I attempted the king's life in the certainty that I should be killed." In fact, two days previously, he had been much more occupied with his dismissal from his place than with projects of regicide; and at his arrest he did all he could to make his situation more serious, reminding the delegate that he had forgotten his revolutionary card on which was written, "Death to the King! long live the Republic!" It was a case of *indirect* suicide, such as Maudsley, Crichton, Esquirol,[73] and Krafft-Ebing have recorded in great numbers. These, however, are only committed by the insane, or by cowardly and immoral men; and I insist upon this motive all the more that he formed at the same time the means of satisfying that incoherent vanity which in him predominated over the love of life. It is well known that many vain suicidal maniacs enjoy the sight of their own

73 Esquirol mentions a madwoman who said to him, "I have not the courage to kill myself; I must kill some one else, so that I can die." She attempted the life of her daughter.

death surrounded by pomp, like the Englishman who had a mass composed and executed in public, and shot himself while the *Requiescat* was being chanted.

If, therefore, we find in him any fanaticism, it is not for politics, but for his own ridiculous and ungrammatical effusions. When he lost his temper and shed tears at the trial, the outburst was not provoked by any insult to his party, but by a refusal to permit the reading of one of his letters, and when his reputation as a scullion was attacked by the assertion that he was continually reading instead of washing up the dishes, which he flatly denied, though the implied proof of unsoundness of mind would have been entirely in his favour.

His intelligence might be called unusual and original rather than superior to the average; and appeared much more brilliant in his conversation than in his writings—in which it is difficult to find a vigorous expression, such as we so frequently meet with in the works of the insane, as distinguished from mattoids.

However, searching here and there amid the enormous mass of his writings, and piecing out their gaps, we meet with some few fragments which are both original and curious. For example, though grotesque enough, his idea of having deputies and officials chosen by lot, like soldiers for the conscription, "that they may not be so proud," is not without originality. Equally striking is the idea of forcing the convicts, who pass their time in enforced idleness, to cultivate waste lands, of calling out the young men for conscription before they have chosen a trade, and of crying after the Emperor William who "wants five milliards from France": "He who sows thorns should be made to walk barefoot." Good, too, in its way, though somewhat Turkish, is that of establishing a free inn for travellers in every village.

Still more remarkable is this, which, if it had not been written some time previously, might be taken as referring to his own case:

> It is blamable that the authorities should exercise severity of punishment towards a man whose only idea is to change the form of government and attack the head of the State. The country is the mother of all without distinction; to all, without distinction, the law should be sister of death, which has no respect for any, but cuts them down when their time has come.

His contrast between man isolated and man in association with his fellows is worthy of Giusti. "When you see him alone he is weak as a glass tumbler—if you see a glass, think of the strength of man, there is no great difference; but, united, men become hard and have the strength of a thousand Samsons."

Where he really appeared superior to the average was in his *viva-voce* answers. Thus: "History studied practically among the people is more instructive than the history studied in books. The people is the best teacher of history," &c. To justify the literary pretensions which seemed so inconsistent with his position as a poor cook, he replied, "Where the learned man goes astray, the ignorant often triumphs."

When asked what takes place in the conscience when one is about to commit a bad action, he replied, "In us there are, as it were, two wills—one pushing us on, the other holding us back,—and the one that proves strongest determines the action."

But it is precisely in his intermittent flashes of political insight, so strange in his position, that a morbid abnormality becomes evident. For it must be remarked that they constitute rather the exception than the rule. What we find, as a rule, is the commonplace and the absurd. In the same code he proposes to hang coiners and burn thieves, and abolish the death penalty! He wishes to kill the king, yet in another article he demands for him a pension of two-and-a-half millions![74]

Guiteau.—The same thing may be said of Guiteau, who presented an enormous number of degenerative characteristics. His handwriting is quite that of the mattoid; and he was descended from a family which counted among its members many lunatics and fanatics. Advocate, theologian, politician, and swindler, he had tried all trades, and claimed to have made a great discovery about

74 In spite of all this, six Italian mental specialists have declared Passanante free from all suspicion of insanity; and he is still confined in a convict prison.

the birth of Christ. The fact is that he had spoilt a great deal of paper, and issued one or two journals and ridiculous works on *The Existence of Hell* and on *Truth* which he believed to be written under Divine dictation. He thought that God would pay his debts as a reward for his eccentric preachings; it was in obedience to a Divine command that he killed Garfield—yet it was only done in revenge for his failure to appoint him U.S. consul at Liverpool, ambassador to Austria, &c.—which showed great ingratitude on Garfield's part, considering the trouble Guiteau had taken, in his own belief, to secure his election as President.[75]

South Americans.—The number of great men in the Argentine Republic suffering from cerebral affections is so considerable that it has enabled Mejia to compose on this subject a work which is among the most curious and valuable produced in the New World.

Thus, according to Mejia, Rivadura was a hypochondriac, and died of softening of the brain. Manuel Garcia also suffered from hypochondria, and finally succumbed to a brain affection. Admiral Brown was subject to the delusion that he was persecuted. Varela was epileptic, Francia was a melancholiac, Rosas was morally insane, and Monteagudo was hysterical.

75 See, for further details, *Archivio di psichiatria, antropologia criminale e scienze penali per servire allo studio dell'uomo alienato e delinquente* 4 (1883).

PART IV

SYNTHESIS. THE DEGENERATE PSYCHOSIS OF GENIUS

CHAPTER I

Characteristics of Insane Men of Genius

Characterlessness — Vanity — Precocity — Alcoholism — Vagabondage — Versatility — Originality — Style — Religious doubts — Sexual abnormalities — Egoism — Eccentricity — Inspiration

The conception of the morbid and degenerative character of genius is confirmed and completed more and more when its isolated phenomena are subjected to a more rigorous examination, and, as in chemical reactions, to mutual contact. If, in fact, we analyze the lives and works of those great diseased minds which have become famous in history, we find that they can at once be distinguished by many characteristic traits from the average man, and also, in part, from other geniuses, who have completed their life's orbit without trace of madness.

I. These insane geniuses have scarcely any character. The full, complete character, "which bends not for any winds that blow," is the distinctive mark of honest and sound-minded men.

Tasso, on the contrary, declaims against courts, and yet, even to his last hour, we find him perpetually coming back to beg their grudging favours. Cardan accuses himself of lying, evil-speaking, and gambling. Rousseau, though so sensitive, abandons to want the tenderest and kindest of friends, casts off his children, calumniates others and himself, and apostatizes three times over—from Catholicism, from Protestantism, and, what is worse, from the religion of philosophy.

Swift, though an ecclesiastic, wrote the obscene poem of the loves of Strephon and Chloe, and belittled the church of which he was a dignitary, though his pride reached the proportions of delirium.

Lenau, religious to fanaticism in *Savonarola*, shows himself in the *Albigenses* even cynically sceptical; he knows it, confesses it, and laughs at it.

Schopenhauer denounced women, and at the same time was too warm an admirer of the sex; he professed to believe in the happiness of Nirvana, and then predicted for himself more than a hundred years of life.

II. Genius is conscious of itself, appreciates itself, and, certainly, has no monkish humility. Yet the conceit seething in diseased brains passes the limits of all truth and probability. Tasso and Cardan covertly, and Mahomet openly, declared themselves inspired by God, and the slightest criticism, therefore, appeared to them as deadly persecution. Cardan wrote of himself, "My nature is placed on the very limits of human substance and conditions, and within the confines of the immortals."[1] Rousseau believed that all men, and sometimes even the elements, were in a conspiracy against him. Perhaps it is on this very account that we have seen almost all these unhappy great spirits fly from association with other men. Swift humiliated and insulted cabinet ministers, and wrote to a duchess desirous of making his acquaintance that the greater men were, the lower must they bow before him. Lenau had inherited the pride of rank from his mother, and in his delirium believed himself king of Hungary.

III. Some of these unfortunate men have given strangely precocious proofs of their genius. Tasso could speak when six months old, and knew Latin at the age of seven. Lenau, at a very early age, composed most touching sermons, and played the bagpipes and the violin with astonishing skill. Cardan at eight had apparitions and revelations of genius. Ampère was a mathematician at thirteen. Pascal, at ten, inspired by the noise made by a plate struck with a knife, worked out a theory of sound, and at fifteen composed his celebrated treatise on Conic Sections. Haller preached at four, and devoured books at five.

IV. Many of them have been excessive in their abuse of narcotics, or of stimulants and intoxicants. Haller was in the habit of taking enormous

1 *De Vita Propria.*

doses of opium, and Rousseau was excessive in his use of coffee. Tasso was renowned as a drinker, as also the modern poets Kleist, Gérard de Nerval, Musset, Murger, Majláth, Praga, and Rovani, as well as the very original Chinese writer Li-Tai-Po, who was inspired by alcohol, and died of it. Lenau also, in his latter years, was an immoderate consumer of wine, coffee, and tobacco. Baudelaire abused opium, tobacco, and wine. Cardan confessed himself an indefatigable drinker. Poe was a dipsomaniac; so was Hoffmann.

V. Nearly all of these great men, moreover, showed anomalies of the reproductive functions. Tasso, who was guilty of exaggerated licentiousness in his youth, was rigidly chaste after his thirty-eighth year. On the other hand, Cardan, impotent in his youth, gave himself up to excess at thirty-five. Pascal, sensual in his early youth, afterwards believed even a mother's kiss to be a crime. Rousseau was affected by hypospadias and spermatorrhœa, and, like Baudelaire, was subject to a sexual perversion. Newton and Charles XII., so far as is known, were absolutely continent. Lenau wrote, "I have the painful conviction that I am unsuitable for marriage."[2]

VI. Instead of preferring the quiet seclusion of the study, they cannot rest in any place, and have to be continually travelling. Lenau removed from Vienna to Stokerau, and then to Gmünden, and fi-

2 Anton Schurz, *Lenau's leben: Grossentheils aus des dichters eigenen briefen*, 2 vols. (Stuttgard and Augsburg: 1855) vol. 2.

nally emigrated to America. "I need," he said, "a change of climate every now and then to stir up my blood."[3] Tasso was continually travelling from Ferrara to Urbino, Mantua, Naples, Paris, Bergamo, Rome, and Turin. Poe was the despair of his editors, because he was continually wandering about between Boston, New York, Richmond, Philadelphia, and Baltimore. Giordano Bruno wandered to Padua, Oxford, Wittenberg, Magdeburg, Helmstadt, Prague, and Geneva.

Rousseau, Cardan, Cellini were constantly staying now at Turin, now at Paris, now at Florence, Rome, Bologna, or Lausanne. "Change of place," says Rousseau,[4] "is a necessity for me. In the fine season, I find it impossible to remain for more than two or three days in one place without suffering."

VII. Sometimes they change their career and course of study several times in succession, as though the mighty intellect could not find rest and relief in a single science.[5] Swift, in addition to his satiric poems, wrote on the manufactures of Ireland, on theology, on politics, and on the history of the reign of Queen Anne. Cardan was at the same time a mathematician, physician, theologian, and

3 *Ibid.* 283.

4 January, 1765.

5 Of 45 insane writers referred to by Philomneste (*op. cit.*) there were 15 who devoted themselves to poetry, 12 to theology, 5 to prophecy, 3 to autobiography, 2 to mathematics, 2 to mental pathology, 2 to politics. Poetry predominates for the reason above given, while, on the other hand, theology, philosophy, and the like are more prominent in the mattoids.

literary man. Rousseau was painter, music-master, charlatan, philosopher, botanist, and poet; and Hoffmann, magistrate, caricaturist, musician, romance-writer, and dramatist.

Tasso—as did Gogol after him—attempted all varieties of poetry, epic, dramatic, and didactic, in all metres. Newton and Pascal, in moments of aberration, abandoned physics for theology. Lenau cultivated medicine, agriculture, law, poetry, and theology.

VIII. These energetic and terrible intellects are the true pioneers of science; they rush forward regardless of danger, facing with eagerness the greatest difficulties—perhaps because it is these which best satisfy their morbid energy. They seize the strangest connections, the newest and most salient points; and here I may mention that originality, carried to the point of absurdity, is the principal characteristic of insane poets and artists. Ampère always sought out the most difficult problems in mathematics—the abysses—as Arago has noted.

Rousseau, in the *Devin du Village*, had attempted the music of the future, afterwards tried again by another insane genius, Schumann. Swift used to say that he only felt at his ease when treating the most difficult subjects, and those most out of the line of his habitual occupations. In fact, in his *Directions to Servants*, he seems, not a theologian or a politician, but a servant himself. His *Confession of a Thief* was believed to have been really written by a well-known criminal, so that the latter's accomplices, thinking that they were discovered, gave themselves up to justice. In the prophecies of Bickerstaff, he assumed the character of a Catholic, and succeeded in deceiving the Roman Inquisition.

Walt Whitman is the creator of a rhymeless poetry, which the Anglo-Saxons regard as the poetry of the future, and which certainly bears the imprint of strange and wild originality.

Poe's compositions (says Baudelaire, one of his greatest admirers) seem to have been produced in order to show that strangeness may enter into the elements of the beautiful; and he collected them under the title of *Arabesques and Grotesques*, because these exclude the human countenance, and his literature was *extra-human*. Here, too, we note the predilection of insane artists for arabesques, and, moreover, for arabesques which suggest the human figure.[6]

Baudelaire himself created the prose poem, and carried to the highest point the adoration of artificial beauty. He was the first to find new poetic associations in the olfactory sense.[7]

IX. These morbid geniuses have a style peculiar to themselves—passionate, palpitating, vividly coloured—which distinguishes them from all other writers, perhaps because it could only arise

---

6 Page 200.

7 He declares that musk reminds him of scarlet and gold, and describes "perfumes which have the smell of infants' flesh, or of the dawn," &c., &c.

under maniacal influences. So much so that all of them confess their inability to compose, or even to think, outside the moments of inspiration. Tasso wrote, in one of his letters, "I am unsuccessful, and find difficulty in everything, especially in composition."[8] "My ideas," Rousseau confesses, "are confused, slow in arising and developing themselves, nor can I express myself well except in moments of passion." The eloquent and vivid exordiums of Cardan's works, so different from the rest of his tedious books, show what a difference there was between the first and last moments of his inspiration. Haller, though a successful poet himself, used to say that the whole art of poetry consisted in its difficulty. Pascal began his 18th *Provincial Letter* thirteen times.

Perhaps it was this analogy in character and style that was the cause of Swift's and Rousseau's predilection for Tasso, and drew the severe Haller towards Swift; while Ampère was inspired by Rousseau's eccentricities, and Baudelaire by those of Poe (whose works he translated) and of Hoffmann, whom he idolized.[9]

X. Nearly all these great men were painfully preoccupied by religious doubts, raised by the intellect, and combated, as a crime, by the timid conscience and morbid emotions. Tasso was tormented by the fear of being a heretic. Ampère often said

8 Giovanni Battista Manso, *Vita di Torquato Tasso* (Venice: Tipografia di Alvisopoli, 1825) 249.

9 *Du Vin* (1880) vol. 1.

that doubts are the worst torture of man. Haller wrote in his journal, "My God! give me—oh! give me one drop of faith: my mind believes in Thee, but my heart refuses—this is my crime." Lenau used to repeat, towards the end of his life, "In those hours when my heart is suffering, the idea of God passes away from me." In fact, the real hero of his *Savonarola* is Doubt,[10] as is now admitted by all critics.

XI. All insane men of genius, moreover, are much preoccupied with their own *Ego*. They sometimes know and proclaim their own disease, and seem as though they wished, by confessing it, to get relief from its inexorable attacks.

It is quite natural that, being men of great intellect and therefore acute observers, they should at last notice their own cruel anomalies and be struck by the spectacle of the Ego which obtruded itself so painfully on their notice. Men in general, but more particularly the insane, love to speak of themselves, and on this theme they even become eloquent. All the more should we expect it in those whose genius is accompanied and quickened by mania. It is thus we get those wonderful records of passion and grief, monuments of phrenopathic poetry, which reveal the great and unhappy personality of the writer. Cardan wrote, not only his autobiography, but also poems on his misfortunes, and the work *De Somniis*, entirely composed of his dreams and hallucinations. The poems of Whitman are the glorification of the Ego. Rousseau, in

10 Schurz 1:328.

his *Confessions*, *Dialogues*, *Rêveries*. like De Musset in his *Confessions*, and Hoffmann in *Kreisler*, [11]only give a minute description of themselves and their own madness.

Thus also Poe, as Baudelaire has well remarked, took as his text the exceptions of human life, the hallucination which, at first doubtful, afterwards becomes a reasoned conviction; absurdity enthroned in the region of intellect and governing it with a terrible logic; hysteria occupying the place of the will; the contradiction between the nerves and the mind carried so far that grief is driven to utter itself in laughter.

Pascal, who was driven by delirium into exaggerated humility, who said that Christianity suppressed the *Ego*, has not written his autobiography; yet he, too, showed traces of his hallucinations in the celebrated *Amulet*, and, in his *Pensées*, subtly described himself when speaking of others. It is certain that he was alluding to himself when he wrote that "extreme genius is close to extreme folly, and men are so mad that he who should not be so would be a madman of a new kind;" and when he observed that "maladies influence our judgment and sense; and while great ones perceptibly alter them, even slight ones cannot but influence them in proportion;" and that "men of genius have their heads higher, but their feet lower than the rest of us; they are all on the

11 Kreisler is, like himself, full of strange ideals, always at war with reality, and ends by becoming insane.

same level, and stand on the same clay as ourselves, children, and brutes."

Haller, in his diary, gives detailed notes of his own religious delusions, and often confesses to having completely changed his character in the course of twenty-four hours, and being "giddy, mad, persecuted by God, and scorned and despised by men."

Lessmann who, at a later time, hanged himself, wrote the humorous *Diary of a Melancholiac* (1834). Tasso, in his letter to the Duke of Urbino, and in the stanza already quoted, clearly depicted his own insanity. "Francesco," he says elsewhere, "O Francesco, within my infirm limbs I have an infirm soul."[12] It is a curious fact that, shortly before his first attack of mania, he wrote these words, "As I do not deny that I am mad, I must believe that my madness has been caused by drunkenness or love, since I know well that I drink to excess," &c.[13]

Dostoyevsky continually introduces semi-insane characters, and especially epileptics, in *Besi* and *The Idiot*, and moral lunatics in *Crime and Punishment*.

Gérard de Nerval was the author of *Aurelia*, which has been well called the "Song of Songs of Fever," and is a mixture of poetry and gibberish. Barbara wrote *Les Détraqués*. Buston described his own hallucinations. Allix, though not a medical man, wrote on the treatment of the insane. Lenau,

12 *"Francesco, inferma, entro le membra infertile Ho l'anima."*

13 Epistolario 3:1

twelve years before he actually succumbed to the attacks of insanity, had foreseen and described it. All his poems depict, in colours painfully vivid, suicidal and melancholic tendencies. The reader may judge of this from the mere titles of some of his lyrics, "To a Hypochrondriac," "The Madman," "The Diseased in Soul," "The Violence of a Dream," "The Moon of Melancholy."

I do not think that it is possible to find, in the most doleful pages of J. Ortis so accurate and vividly coloured a description of suicidal tendencies as in the following extract from the *Seelenkranke*,

> I carry a deep wound in my heart, and will carry it in silence to the grave; my life is broken from hour to hour. One alone could comfort me, . . . but she lies in the grave. . . . O my mother! let thyself be moved by my entreaties, if thy love still survives death, if it is still permitted thee to care for thy child. . . . Oh! let me soon escape from life! I long for the night of death! Oh! only help thy crazy son to lay aside his grief.

His *Traumgewalten* is, as I have already observed, a terribly truthful picture of that hallucination which preceded or accompanied the first attack of suicidal mania; and here the reader can easily trace in the phrases and ideas that disconnected and fragmentary character which is the mark of the delirious paralytic.

Here is a specimen—

> The dream was so terrible, so wild, so frightful, that I wish I could tell myself it was nothing but a dream; . . . yet I continue to weep, and to feel that my heart beats; I awaken, and find the sheets and the pillow wet. . . . Did I seize them in my dream and wipe my face? I do not know. . . . While I was sleeping, my hostile guests have been holding an orgy here. . . . Now they are gone, those savages, they are gone, but I find their traces in my tears. They have fled, and left the wine on the table,

&c.

He had previously, in the *Albigenses*, dropped some allusions to the terrible impression made on him by his dreams: "Terrible, often, is the might of dreams; it shakes, pains, presses, threatens, and if the sleeper does not awaken in time, in the twinkling of an eye, he is a corpse."[14]

XII. The principal trace of the delusions of great

---

14 "Mad Nat Lee," who was for a long time an inmate of Bedlam, minutely describes the insanity of genius in his poems; *e.g.*, in *Cæsar Borgia*:

> "Like a poor lunatic that makes his moan,
> And, for a while, beguiles his lookers-on,
> He reasons well. His eyes their wildness lose,
> He vows his keepers his wronged sense abuse,
> But if you hit the cause that hurts his brain,
> Then his teeth gnash, he foams, he shakes his chain."

See Forbes Winslow, *On Obscure Diseases of the Brain and Disorders of the Mind* (London: Churchill, 1860) 210. See also the chapter "On the Art of Insanity," for proofs of a like tendency on the part of insane painters.

minds is found in the very construction of their works and speeches, in their illogical deductions, absurd contradictions, and grotesque and inhuman fantasies. Thus Socrates was clearly of unsound mind when, after having all but arrived, intuitively, at Christian morality and Judaic monotheism, he directed his steps in accordance with a sneeze, or the voice and signs of his imaginary genius. Thus Cardan, who had anticipated Newton in discovering the laws of gravitation, and Dupuis in theology—who, in his book *De Subtilitate*, explains as hallucinations the strange and portentous symptoms of the possessed, and also of some of those hermits who were accounted saints, comparing them to the delirium of quartan fever—Cardan was insane, when he attributed to the influence of a genius, not only his scientific inspirations, but the creaking of the table and the vibration of the pen, when he declared that he had been several times bewitched, and when he produced his book *On Dreams*, which speaks to the mental pathologist as a pseudo-membrane would to the physical. In this, at first, he puts on record the most accurate and curious observations on the phenomena of dreams—*e.g.*, how severe physical pains act with less energy, slight ones with greater—a fact recently confirmed by psychiatrists; that the insane are much given to dreaming; that in a dream, as on the stage, a long series of ideas passes in a very short space of time; and finally (and this is a remark of much justice) that men have dreams either entirely analogous to, or entirely at variance with, their own habits. But, after these clear and undoubted proofs of genius, he re-affirms one of the most absurd and contemptible theories ever held by the populace of ancient times, namely, that the slightest accidental circumstance of a dream must be the revelation of a more or less distant future. Thus he draws up, with the sincerest conviction, a dictionary, identical in form and origin (which last is undoubtedly pathological) with Cabalistic productions. Every object, every word, which may find a place in a dream, is there attached to a series of allusions which serve to interpret each other. *Father* may signify author, husband, son, commander. *Feet*, foundation of a house, arts, workmen, &c. A horse, appearing in a dream, may signify flight, riches, or a wife. *Shoemaker* and *physician* are interchangeable in meaning. In short, it is not actual analogies which prevail, but analogies in words, in sounds, even in terminations. *Orior* and *morior* have an equal prophetic value, because "since they differ from each other only by a single letter, the one passes over to the other." We are seized with compassion for human nature and for ourselves, when we find him relating that a knight who suffered from the stone always, if he dreamed of food, had an attack on the following day, and adding *cibos enim et dolores degustare dicimus*—as though nature were in the habit of amusing herself by making puns in Latin. Yet this was the man who had intuitively divined the admirable theory of painful sensations in sleep already alluded to, and who, a physician, and one of no mean distinction, had clearly conceived the sympathetic action of the solar plexus.

Newton himself can scarcely be said to have been sane when he demeaned his intellect to the interpretation of the Apocalypse, or the horns of Daniel; nor, again, when he wrote to Bentley,

> By means of the law of attraction, one can very well understand the elongated orbits of comets; but as to the nearly circular orbits of planets, I see no possibility of obtaining their lateral difference, and this can only be accomplished by God.

Yet in his *Optics*, Newton had inveighed against those who, after the manner of the Aristotelians admit occult properties in matter, thus arresting the researches of natural philosophers, without leading to any conclusion. In fact, a century later, the true cause, which had escaped Newton's observations, was discovered by La Place.

Ampère believed, in all sincerity, that he had found the method of squaring the circle.

Pascal, though he had been the first to study the laws of probability, believed that the touch of a relic had power to cure a lachrymal fistula—a statement which he printed in one of his works.

Rousseau makes of his own maniacal savagery the ideal type of man, and believes that every natural production, if agreeable to the sight or taste, must be innocuous, so that arsenic, according to him, could not be harmful. His life is made up of contradictions: he prefers the country, and lives in the Rue Platonière; he writes a treatise on education, and sends his children to the foundling hospital; he adjudicates on the claims of the various religions with the acuteness of an unbiassed sceptic, and throws stones at trees in order to divine the future and decide the question of his own salvation; nay, he writes to the Deity, and lays his letters on the altars of churches, as though they were His exclusive abode.

Baudelaire finds the sublime in the artificial—"like the rouge which enhances the beauty of a handsome woman." He carries out an insane idea by describing a metallic landscape, with neither water nor vegetation. "All is rigid, polished, shining; without heat and without sun; in the midst of the eternal silence the blue water is enclosed, like the ancient mirrors, in a golden basin." He finds his ideal in the Latin of the Decadence, "the only tongue which can thoroughly render the language of passion," and adores cats to such a degree as to address three poems to them.

Lenau, in his "Moon of the Hypochondriac," sees, contrary to the usual practice of poets, in the cold moon, without water and without atmosphere, "the sexton of the planets, who, with a silver thread entwined, enchains the sleepers and draws them to death; she beckons with her finger, leads sleep-walkers astray, and counsels the thief."

Though, as a young man, he had frequently expressed his opinion that "mysticism is a symptom of insanity," he often showed mystical tendencies, especially in his later poems.

In the Koran, there is not a single chapter which has any connection with another; on the contrary, it often happens that, in the course of a single *sura*, the ideas are interrupted, and follow each other almost at random. "On Mahomet," writes Morkos,

> the most contradictory verdicts may be pronounced, for it is impossible to deny his great excellence, while at the same time there is no disguising the fact that we find in him the most signal artifices of imposture, the grossest ignorance, and the greatest imprudence.

It appears to me, moreover, that the great writers who have been under the dominion of alcohol, have a style peculiar to themselves, whose characteristics are a deliberate eroticism, and an inequality which is rather grotesque than beautiful, owing to too unrestrained fancy, frequent imprecations and abrupt transitions from the deepest melancholy to obscene gaiety, and a marked preference for such subjects as madness, drink, and the gloomiest scenes of death. "Poe," says Baudelaire,

> likes to place his figures against greenish or violet backgrounds, surrounded by the phosphorescence of decay, and the atmosphere of

> storms and orgies. He throws himself into grotesquery for the love of the grotesque, into horror for the love of the horrible.

The same thing is done by Baudelaire himself, who loves to describe the effects of alcohol or opium.

"There are days when my heart faints in me, and the mud overwhelms me,"[15] sang poor Praga, who killed himself with alcohol, and who, singing the praises of wine, blasphemed thus:

"Let it come—the reproach of the sober man; come—the contempt of the human race,—come, the hell of the Eternal Father: I will go down into it with my glass in hand."[16]

Steen, the drunken painter, usually painted drinking scenes. Hoffmann's drawings ended in caricatures, his tales in extra-human extravagancies, his music in a senseless succession of sounds.

Alfred de Musset saw in the ladies of Madrid,

sous un col de cigne
Un sein vierge et dort comme la jeune vigne.

Murger admired women with green lips and yellow cheeks—no doubt through a species of col-

15 *"Vi son del giorni che il mio cor vien meno*
E il fango mi conquista."

16 *"Venga l'obbrobrio dell'uomo sobrio;*
Venga il disprezzo del gen ere umano;
Venga l'inferno del Padre Eterno;
Vi scenderò col mio bicchiere in mano."

our-blindness, such as we have already met with among painters.

XIII. Nearly all of these great men—for instance, Cardan, Lenau, Tasso, Socrates, Pascal—attached great importance to their dreams, which, no doubt, assumed a more vivid and powerful colouring than those of sane persons.

XIV. Many presented voluminous but very irregular skulls; and, like madmen, have ended by serious alterations of the nervous centres. Pascal's cerebral substance was harder than is normally the case, and the left lobe had suppurated. The brain of Rousseau revealed dropsy in the ventricles. Byron and Foscolo, great but eccentric geniuses, both showed premature ossification of the sutures. Schumann died of chronic meningitis and cerebral atrophy.

XV. The insane characters of men of genius are scarcely ever found alone. Thus melancholia was associated and alternated with exaggerated self-esteem in Chopin, Comte, Tasso, Cardan, Schopenhauer; with alcoholic mania, impulsive insanity, or sexual perversion in Baudelaire and Rousseau; with erratic and alcoholic mania and that of self-esteem, in Gérard de Nerval. In Coleridge, the mania of morphia was associated with *folie du doute*.

XVI. But the most special characteristic of this form of insanity appears to reduce itself to an extreme exaggeration of two alternating phases, *viz.*, erethism and atony, inspiration and exhaustion, which we see physiologically manifested in nearly all great intellects, even the sanest—phases to which they, all alike, give a wrong interpretation, according as their pride is gratified or offended. "An indolent soul, afraid of every kind of business, a bilious temperament, which suffers easily and is sensitive to every discomfort, seem as though they could not be combined in one character—yet they form the groundwork of mine." Such is Rousseau's confession in Letter II. Therefore, as the ignorant man explains the modifications of his own *ego* by means of material and external objects, they often attribute to a devil, a genius, or a God, the happy inspiration of their exalted moments. Tasso, speaking of his familiar spirit, genius, or messenger, says, "It cannot be a devil, since it does not inspire me with a horror for sacred things; nor yet a natural creature, for it causes to arise in me ideas which I never had before." A genius inspires Cardan with his written works, his knowledge of spiritual matters, his medical opinions; Tartini with his Sonata, Mahomet with the pages of the Koran. Van Helmont asserted that he had seen a genius appear before him at all the most important moments of his life; and, in 1633, he discovered his own soul under the form of a shining crystal. William Blake often retired to the sea-shore to converse with Moses, Homer, Virgil, and Milton, with whom he believed himself to have been previously acquainted. When questioned as to their appearance, he replied, "They are shades full of majesty—grey, but luminous, and much taller than the generality of men." Socrates was counselled in his actions by a genius who, as he expressed it, was better than ten thousand teachers; and he often advised his friends as to what they ought, or ought not to do, according as he had received instructions from his *δαιμονιον*.

It is certain that the vivid and richly-coloured style of all these great men—the clearness with which they describe their most grotesque eccentricities, such as the Liliputian Academies, or the horrors of Tartarus, denote that they saw and touched, as it were, with the certainty of hallucination, all that they describe; that, in short, in them inspiration and insanity became fused, and resulted in a single product.

It may be said, indeed, of some—as of Luther, Mahomet, Savonarola, Molinos, and, in modern times, the chief of the Taeping rebels—that this false explanation of the *afflatus* was of great service to them, giving to their speeches and prophecies that air of truth only resulting from a profound conviction, which alone can shake the popular ignorance and carry it in the wake of a new doctrine. This characteristic is common to the insanity of genius and the most trivial aberrations of eccentricity.

When inspiration and high spirits fail together, and depression of mind prevails, then these great unfortunate ones, interpreting their own condition still more strangely, believe themselves to have been poisoned, like Cardan; or to be condemned to eternal fire, like Haller and Ampère; or persecuted by inveterate enemies, like Newton, Swift, Barthez, Cardan, and Rousseau.

Moreover, in all these cases, religious doubt, raised by the intellect in despite of the heart, appears to the subject himself as a crime, and becomes both cause and instrument of new and real misfortunes.

XVII. Yet the temper of these men is so different from that of average people that it gives a special character to the different psychoses (melancholia, monomania, &c.) from which they suffer, so as to constitute a special psychosis, which might be called the psychosis of genius.

CHAPTER II

Analogy of Sane to Insane Genius

Want of character — Pride — Precocity — Alcoholism — Degenerative signs — Obsession — Men of genius in revolutions

But these characteristics are not confined to insane genius; they are also met with, though far less conspicuously among the great men freest from any suspicion of insanity, those of whom the insane geniuses just mentioned are but the exaggeration and caricature. It is thus that the complete and perfect character, while conspicuously seen in Socrates, Columbus, Cavour, Christ, Galileo, Spinoza, is not to be found in Napoleon, Bacon, Cicero, Seneca, Alcibiades, Alexander, Julius Cæsar, Machiavelli, Carlyle, Frederick II., Dumas, Byron, Comte, Bulwer Lytton, Petrarch, Aretino, Gibbon.

Self-esteem, carried to an almost incredible point, has been noticed in Napoleon, Hegel, Dante,

Victor Hugo, Lassalle, Balzac, and Comte; and, as we have already seen, even in men of talent, but not of genius, as Cagnoli, Lucius, Porta, &c.

Precocity, moreover, does not fail to appear in normal men of genius, such as Mozart, Raphael, Michelangelo, Charles XII., Stuart Mill, D'Alembert, Lulli, Cowley, Otway, Prior, Pope, Addison, Burns, Keats, Sheffield, Hugo.

Among these we also find the abuse of alcohol, sexual deficiencies, or excesses followed by sterility, the tendency to vagrancy, and impulsive acts of violence, alternating, or associated, with convulsive movements. Bismarck once said to Beust, "Do you ever feel the wish to break anything as an amusement?" Like Gladstone and the Belgian Malon, he often takes exercise by cutting down trees like a woodman.

We have also found, in some of them, numerous anomalies in the shape of the skull and conformation of the brain. Degenerative symptoms, such as stammering, left-handedness, precocity, sterility, abound in both, as well as divergences from ancestral character.

There is also seen in them that invasion, or rather possession, by their subject which transforms the creature of the imagination into a true hallucination, or an auto-suggestion. Flaubert says that his characters seized upon him, and pursued him, or that, more correctly speaking, he lived through them. When he described the poisoning of Madame Bovary, he felt the taste of arsenic on his tongue, and showed symptoms of actual poisoning so far as to vomit. Dickens, too, was affected by sorrow and compassion for his characters, as if they had been his own children.[1]

"To my mind," writes Edmond de Goncourt,

> my brother died of over-work, and more especially the elaboration of literary form, the chiselling of phrases, the labour of style. I can still see him taking up again pieces which we had written together, and which, at first, had satisfied us, working at them for hours, for half a day at a time, with an almost angry persistency. . . .
>
> You must remember, in short, that all our work—and in this, perhaps, consists its originality, an originality dearly bought—has its root in nervous illness; that we drew our pictures of disease from our own experience, and that, by dint of analyzing, studying, dissecting ourselves, we at last attained a kind of super-acute sensitiveness, which was wounded on all sides by the infinite littlenesses of life. I say we, for, when we wrote *Charles Demailly*, I was more diseased than he. Alas! he took the first place, later on. *Charles Demailly*!—it is a strange thing to write one's own history fifteen years in advance.[2]

The obsession of genius sometimes attains such a point as actually to create a double personality,

---

1 *See* Wilhelm Dilthey, *Einbildungskraft und Wahnsinn* (Leipzig: Duncker & Humblot, 1886).

2 Letter from Edmond de Goncourt to Emile Zola (*Lettres de Jules de Gonconrt* (Paris: Charpentier, 1885)).

and transform a philanthropist into an overbearing tyrant, a melancholy man into a jovial reveller.

Finally, we have found, even in the sanest and most complete genius, the incomplete and rudimentary forms of mania—as melancholy, megalomania, hallucinations, &c.—a fact which helps to explain the convictions of certain prophets and founders of dynasties, convictions so deeply rooted as to serve the purpose of inspiration, as far as the mass of the people were concerned. Maudsley says that one of the conditions essential to the originality of genius is a disposition to be dissatisfied with the existing state of things.

We have also met with the use of peculiar words which is so frequent a characteristic of monomania, and also those uncertainties which reach their extreme point in the madness of doubt.

The whole difference resolves itself, at bottom, into this: that in sane genius the symptoms are less exaggerated, the double personality is less conspicuous, the choice of subjects connected with madness less frequent (Shakespeare, Goncourt, and Daudet being exceptions), and the note of absurdity less emphasized. This, however, is scarcely ever wanting, inasmuch as nothing is closer to the ridiculous than the sublime.

It is also not without importance to note that, whenever genius appears in a race, the number of the insane also increases. Of this fact we have found remarkable proofs among the Italian, German, and English Jews. So much is this the case, that it is the custom, in German lunatic asylums, to reckon genius in the parents among the etiological elements of insanity. Both genius and insanity are influenced by violent passions at the time of conception, by advanced age, or alcoholism in the parents; and as, in all degenerate natures, genius is only exceptionally transmitted, it almost always assumes the form of more and more aggravated neurosis, and rapidly disappears, thanks to that beneficent sterility through which nature provides for the elimination of monsters. Though all the proofs we have given should have been forgotten, the fact would be quite sufficiently demonstrated by the pedigrees of Peter the Great, the Cæsars, and Charles V., in which epileptics, men of genius, and criminals, alternate with ever greater frequency, till the line ends in idiocy and sterility.[3]

In all these three types (insanity, insane genius, and sane genius), we see at work, with nearly equal intensity, the influence of race,[4] of hot climates, of diminutions (unless greatly exaggerated), in the

---

3 Joseph J. Déjerine, *L'hérédité dans les maladies du système nerveux* (Paris: Asselin-Houzeau, 1886); Théodule Ribot, *L'hérédité psychologique* (Paris: Ballière, 1873); William W. Ireland, *The Blot upon the Brain* (London: Bell and Bradfute, 1885).

4 See Part II, pp. 230-238. I must rectify a mistake I have made in not assigning sufficient importance to the influence of race in France. In fact, in revising my studies on a large scale, I find that the departments peopled by the Belgio-Germanic race yield the maximum proportion of geniuses as 40 per cent., while the Celtic departments yielded only 13.5 per cent., and the Iberian 20 per cent.

degree of atmospheric pressure, and, in frequent cases, of maladies accompanied by a high temperature.

But the most convincing proof of all is offered by the insane who, though not possessed of genius, apparently acquire it, for a time, while under treatment. These cases prove that geniality, originality, artistic and æsthetic creation may show themselves in the least predisposed natures, as a consequence of mental alienation. Finally, not the least important proof is contained in the singular phenomenon of the mattoid, who, as distinguished from the really insane, has all the appearances, without the reality, of genius.

Taking all this into consideration, we may confidently affirm that genius is a true degenerative psychosis belonging to the group of moral insanity, and may temporarily spring out of other psychoses, assuming their forms, though keeping its own special peculiarities, which distinguish it from all others.

The identity of genius with moral insanity is seen in that general alteration of the affective instincts, which shows itself, more or less disguised, in all,[5] even in those rare altruistic persons with a

---

5 T. Gautier, according to the Goncourts, often declared that he could not on account of his youth convince himself that he was really the father of his daughter (*Journal des Goncourt—Mémoires de la vie littéraire*, 6 vols. (Paris: Charpentier, 1888-92)). "La Fontaine was not far removed from a bad man," says Bourget. "What are we to think of a husband who deserts his young wife and his child, with out any motive what-

genius for goodness to whom the name of saints has been given. This also explains their longevity.

There is, beyond all doubt, some connection between all these observations, and the fact, established by Tamburini and myself, that the best artists of the asylums were all morally insane.

It should be remembered here, that the Klephts were brigands, and that the moral character of many great conquerors has been so far subject to alteration as to make of them true brigands on a large scale. Arved Barine, in noticing the beauty of countenance of certain brigands figured in my work in *L'uomo Delinquente*, has very justly observed[6] that

> such a profession requires high intellectual endowments, and precisely the same as those needed by conquerors, who certainly have had no superabundance of moral sense. History proves that the moral sense is in no degree a function of the intellect. Great men have been so often devoid of it, that the world has been forced to invent for them a special morality which may be summed up in five words, frequently uttered by such—from Napoleon down

ever?" Stendhal (Beyle) hated his father and was hated by him; he always declared his invincible repugnance towards compulsory family affection (Paul Bourget, *Essais de psychologie contemporaine* (Paris: Alphonse Lemerre, 1881-1883) 310). "I consecrated myself to grief for her," wrote Chateaubriand of Pauline de Baumont. ". . . She had not been dead six months, when her place was filled in my heart." (*Ibid.*).

6 *Revue Littéraire* 3 (15 August 1887).

to Benvenuto Cellini: *Everything is permitted to genius.*

Men of genius are among the principal factors in true revolutions.[7] History records the saying of Tarquin that for the preservation of despotism it was necessary to cut down the tallest heads. Carlyle believed that the whole of history is that of great men. Emerson wrote that every new institution might be regarded as the prolonged shadow of some man of genius, Islamism of Mahomet, Protestantism of Calvin, Quakerism of Fox, Methodism of Wesley, Abolitionism of Clarkson, &c. Men of genius, wrote Flaubert,[8] summarise in a single type many separate personalities, and bring new persons to consciousness in the human race. This is one of the causes of their immense influence. And not only are they not misoneistic; they are haters of old things and ardent lovers of the new and the unknown. Garibaldi, when he pushed on into almost unknown regions of America, said, "I love the unknown."[9] And Christ carried his idea of the new world, that was about to appear, as far as complete communism. Many men of genius rule beyond the tomb: Cæsar was never so powerful

---

7 Cesare Lombroso and R. Laschi, *Il Delitto politico e le rivoluzioni* (Turn: Bocca, 1890).

8 Gustave Flaubert, Correspondance, 4 vols. (Paris: Bibliotheque-Charpentier, 1887-93) [1889, no volume indicated]: 538.

9 Enrico Ferri, "Garibaldi nelle sua 'memorie'", *Nuova Antologia* 104 (1889) 430-461.

(wrote Michelet) as when he was a corpse; and so William the Silent. Max Nordau even claims that all human progress is owing to despots of genius. "Every revolution is the work of a minority whose individuality cannot conform to conditions which were neither calculated nor created for them." The only real innovators known to history are tyrants endowed with ability and knowledge. "No revolution succeeds without a leader," wrote Machiavelli; and elsewhere, "A multitude without a head is useless." This is natural, because the man of genius, being essentially original and a lover of originality, is the natural enemy of traditions and conservatism: he is the born revolutionary, the precursor and the most active pioneer of revolutions.

CHAPTER III

The Epileptoid Nature of Genius

Etiology — Symptoms — Confessions of men of genius — The life of a great epileptic — Napoleon — Saint Paul — The saints — Philanthropic hysteria

We may, however, enter more deeply into the study of the phenomena of genius by the light of modern theories on epilepsy. According to the entirely harmonious researches of clinical and experimental observers, this malady resolves itself into localised irritation of the cerebral cortex, manifesting itself in attacks which are sometimes instantaneous, sometimes of longer duration, but always intermittent and always resting on a degenerative basis—either hereditary or predisposed to irritation by alcoholic influence, by lesions of the skull, &c.[1] In this way we catch a glimpse of another

1 See *Archivio di psichiatria, antropologia criminale e scienze penali per servire allo studio dell'uomo alienato e delinquente*

conclusion, *viz.*, that the creative power of genius may be a form of degenerative psychosis belonging to the family of epileptic affections.

The fact that genius is frequently derived from parents either addicted to drink, of advanced age, or insane, certainly points to this conclusion, as also does the appearance of genius subsequently to lesions of the head. It is also indicated by frequent anomalies, especially of cranial asymmetry; the capacity of the skull being sometimes excessive, sometimes abnormally small; by the frequency of moral insanity, and of hallucinations; by sexual and intellectual precocity, and not rarely by somnambulism. To these we may add the prevalence of suicide, which is, on the other hand, very common among epileptic patients; the intermittence of bodily and mental functions, more particularly the occurrence of amnesia and analgesia; the frequent tendency to vagabondage; religious feeling, manifesting itself even in the case of atheists, as with Comte; the strange terrors by which they are often seized (W. Scott, Byron, Haller); the double personality, the multiplicity of simultaneous delusions, so common in epileptic cases;[2] the frequent recurrence of delusions produced by the most trifling caus-

2.1-2 (1881); *L'Uomo Delinquente* [no edition indicated], part III.

2 *L'Encephale Journal des Maladies Mentales et Nerveuses et de Physiologie Cérébrale* 5 (1885). [Publication year corrected from 1887. —Ed.]

es; the same misoneism; and the same relation to criminality, which finds its point of union in moral insanity. Add to this the origin and ancestry of criminals and imbeciles, which constantly show traces both of genius and epilepsy, as may be seen in the genealogical charts given of the families of the Cæsars and Charles V.;[3] and the strange passion for wandering, and for animals, which I have also often found in degenerated, and especially in epileptic, subjects.[4]

The distractions of mind for which great men are so famous, are often, writes Tonnini, nothing else but epileptic absences.[5]

The greatest proof of all, however, is that affective insensibility, that loss of moral sense, common to all men of genius, whether sane or insane, which makes of great conquerors, even in the most recent times, nothing else than brigands on a large scale.

Such conclusions may seem strange to persons unacquainted with the way in which the region of epilepsy has been extended in modern times, so that many cases of headache (hemicrania) or sim-

3 See the table in Déjerine, op. cit.

4 Mahomet had a strange fondness for his monkey; Richelieu for his squirrel; Crebillon, Helvetius, Bentham, Erskine, for cats the latter also for a leech. Schopenhauer was very fond of dogs, and named them his heirs; and Byron had a regular menagerie of ten horses, eight dogs, three monkeys, five cats, five peacocks, an eagle, and a bear. Alfieri had a passion for horses. (Smiles, *op. cit.*).

5 Silvio Tonnini, *Le Epilessie* (Turin: Bocca, 1886) 19. [Corrected year of publication from 1880. —Ed.]

ple loss of memory, are now recognized as forms of epilepsy, though in disguise; their manifestation—as Savage has observed—causing the disappearance of every trace of the pre-existing epilepsy. It is sufficient, however, to recall to the reader the numerous men of genius of the first order who have been seized by motory epilepsy, or by that kind of morbid irritability which is well known to supply its place. Among these we find such names as Napoleon, Molière, Julius Cæsar, Petrarch, Peter the Great, Mahomet, Handel, Swift, Richelieu, Charles V., Flaubert, Dostoieffsky, and St. Paul.[6]

To those acquainted with the so-called binomial or serial law, according to which no phenomenon occurs singly—each one being, on the contrary, the expression of a series of less well-defined but analogous facts—such frequent occurrence of epilepsy among the most distinguished of distinguished men can but indicate a greater prevalence of this disease among men of genius than was previously thought possible, and suggests the hypothesis of the epileptoid nature of genius itself.

In this connection, it is important to note how, in these men, the convulsion made its appearance but rarely in the course of their lives. Now it is well known that, in such cases, the psychic equivalent (here the exercise of creative power) is more frequent and intense.[7]

---

6 Shenstone, Darwin, Swift, and Walter Scott were subject to giddiness (Smiles).

7 See *L'Uomo Delinquente*, part III: 623.

But, above all, the identity is proved to us by the analogy of the epileptic seizure with the moment of inspiration. This active and violent unconsciousness in the one case manifests itself by creation, and in the other by motory agitation.

The demonstration is completed when we come to analyse this creative inspiration or cestrus which has often suggested epilepsy, even to those ignorant of the recent discoveries with regard to its nature. And this, not only on account of its frequent association with insensibility to pain, with irregularity of the pulse, and with an unconsciousness which is often that of a somnambulist, of its instantaneous occurrence and intermittent character; but also because it is not seldom accompanied by convulsive movements of the limbs, followed by amnesia, and provoked by substances or conditions which cause or increase the excessive flow of blood to the brain; or by powerful sensations; and also because it may succeed or pass into hallucinations.

This resemblance between inspiration and the epileptic seizure, moreover, is demonstrated by an even directer and more cogent—proof the confessions of eminent men of genius, which show how completely the one may be confounded with the other. Such confessions are those of Goncourt [8]and Buffon, and

8 "There is a fatality," says Goncourt, "in the first chance which suggests your idea. Then there is an *unknown force, a superior will*, a sort of necessity of writing which command your work and guide your pen; so much so, that sometimes the book which leaves your hands does not seem to have come out of yourself; it astonishes you, like something which was in

especially of Mahomet and Dostoyevsky.

"There are moments," writes the latter (in *Besi*)—

> and it is only a matter of five or six seconds—when you suddenly feel the presence of the eternal harmony. This phenomenon is neither terrestial nor celestial, but it is an indescribable something, which man, in his mortal body, can scarcely endure—he must either undergo a physical transformation or die. It is a clear and indisputable feeling: all at once, you feel as though you were placed in contact with the whole of nature, and you say, "Yes! this is true." When God created the world, He said, at the end of every day of creation, "Yes! this is true! this is good!" . . . And it is not tenderness, nor yet joy. You do not forgive anything, because there is nothing to forgive. Neither do you love—oh! this feeling is higher than love! The terrible thing is the frightful clearness with which it manifests itself, and the rapture with which it fills you. If this state were to last more than five seconds, the soul could not endure it, and would have to disappear. During those five seconds, I live a whole human existence, and for that I would give my whole life and not think I was paying it too dearly.

---

you, and of which you were unconscious, That is the impression which *Sœur Philomene* gives me" (*Journal des Goncourt* ((1888)). Even Buffon, who had said that invention depends on patience, adds, "One must look at one's subject for a long time; then it gradually unfolds and develops itself; you feel a slight electric shock strike your head and at the same lime seize you at the heart; that is the moment of genius."

"You are not epileptic?"

"No."

"You will become so. I have heard that it begins just in that way. A man subject to this malady[9] has minutely described to me the sensation which precedes the attack; and in listening to you, I thought I heard him speaking. He, too, spoke of a period of five seconds, and said it was impossible to endure this condition longer. Remember Mahomet's water-jar; for the space of time it took to empty it, the prophet was rapt into Paradise. Your five seconds are the jar—Paradise is your harmony—and Mahomet was epileptic! Take care you do not become so also, Kiriloff!"[10]

And in *The Idiot* (vol. i. p. 296):—

. . . I remember, among other things, a phenomenon which used to precede his epileptic attacks, when they came on in a waking state. In the midst of the dejection, the mental marasmus, the anxiety, which the madman experienced, there were moments in which, all of a sudden, his brain became inflamed, and all his vital forces suddenly rose to a prodigious degree of intensity. The sensation of life, of conscious existence, was multiplied almost tenfold in these swiftly-passing moments.

A strange light illuminated his heart and mind. All agitation was calmed, all doubt and perplexity resolved itself into a superior harmony, a serene and tranquil gaiety, which yet

9 Evidently the author himself.

10 Fyodor Dostoyevsky, *Bésy*.

was completely rational. But these radiant moments were only a prelude to the last instant—that immediately succeeded by the attack. That instant was, in truth, ineffable. When, at a later time, after his recovery, the prince reflected on this subject, he said to himself, "Those fleeting moments, in which our highest consciousness of ourselves—and therefore our highest life—is manifested, are due only to disease, to the suspension of normal conditions; and, if so, it is not a higher life, but, on the contrary, one of a lower order." This, however, did not prevent his reaching a most paradoxical conclusion. "What matter, after all, though it be a disease—an abnormal tension—if the result, as I with recovered health remember and analyze it, includes the very highest degree of harmony and beauty; if at this moment I have an unspeakable, hitherto unsuspected feeling of harmony, of peace, of my whole nature being fused in the impetus of a prayer, with the highest synthesis of life?"

This farrago of nonsense seemed to the prince perfectly comprehensible; and the only fault it had in his eyes was that of being too feeble a rendering of his thoughts. He could not doubt, or even admit the possibility of a doubt, of the real existence of this condition of "beauty and prayer," or of its constituting "the highest synthesis of life."

But did he not in these moments experience visions analogous to the fantastic and debasing dreams produced by the intoxication of opium, haschisch, or wine? He was able to form a sane judgment on this point when the morbid condition had ceased. These moments were only distinguished to define them in a word—by the

> extraordinary heightening of the inward sense. If in that instant—that is to say, in the last moment of consciousness which precedes the attack the patient was able to say clearly, and with full consciousness of the import of his words, "Yes, for this moment one would give a whole lifetime," there is no doubt that, as far as he alone was concerned, that moment was worth a lifetime.
>
> No doubt, too, it is to this same instant that the epileptic Mahomet alluded, when he said that he used to visit all the abodes of Allah in less time than it would take to empty his water-jar.

I will add here some lines from the *Correspondence* of Flaubert:—

> If sensitive nerves are enough to make a poet, I should be worth more than Shakespeare and Homer. . . . I who have heard through closed doors people talking in low tones thirty paces away, across whose abdomen one may see all the viscera throbbing, and who have sometimes felt in the space of a minute a million thoughts, images, and combinations of all kinds throwing themselves into my brain at once, as it were the lighted squibs of fireworks.

Let us now compare these descriptions of an attack, which might be called one of *psychic epilepsy* (and which corresponds exactly to the physiological idea of epilepsy—*i.e.*, cortical irritation), with all the descriptions given us by authors themselves of the inspiration of genius. We shall then see how perfect is the correspondence between the two sets of phenomena.

In order the better to illustrate these strange displacements of function in epileptic subjects, I should call attention to an example, cited by Dr. Frigerio, of an epileptic patient who, at the moment of seizure, felt the venereal desire awaken, not in the generative organs, but in the epigastrium, accompanied by ejaculation.[11]

Let me add that, in certain cases, it is not only isolated paroxysms which recall the psychic phenomenology of the epileptic, but the whole life. Bourget remarks that, "for the Goncourts, life reduces itself to a series of epileptic attacks, preceded and followed by a blank." And what the Goncourts wrote has always been autobiography. Zola in his *Romanciers Naturalistes* gives us this confession by Balzac:

> He works under the influence of circumstances, of which the union is a mystery; he does not belong to himself; he is the plaything of a force which is eminently capricious; on some days he would not touch his brush, he would not write a line for an empire. In the evening when dreaming, in the morning when rising, in the midst of some joyous feast, it happens that a burning coal suddenly touches this brain, these

11 *Archivio di psichiatria, antropologia criminale e scienze penali per servire allo studio dell'uomo alienato e delinquente* 9.1 (1888) 89.

> hands, this tongue: a word awakens ideas that are born, grow, ferment. Such is the artist, the humble instrument of a despotic will; he obeys a master.

Let us glance at the pictures which Taine has given us of the greatest of modern conquerors, and Renan of the greatest of the apostles:—

"The principal characteristics of Napoleon's genius," says Taine,

> are its originality and comprehensiveness. No detail escapes him. The quantity of facts which his mind stores up and retains, the number of ideas which he elaborates and utters, seem to surpass human capacity.
>
> In the art of ruling men his genius was supreme. His method of procedure—which is that of the experimental sciences—consisted in controlling every theory by a precise application observed under definite conditions. All his sayings are fire-flashes. "Adultery," said he to the Conseil d'État, when the question of divorce was under discussion, "is not exceptional; it is very common—*c'est une affaire de canapé.*" "Liberty," he exclaimed, on another occasion (and he remained faithful all his life to the spirit of this exclamation), "is the necessity of a small and privileged class, endowed by nature with faculties higher than those of the mass of mankind; *it may therefore be abridged with impunity*. Equality, on the contrary, pleases the multitude."
>
> He possesses a faculty which carries us back to the Middle Ages—an astounding *construc-*

tive imagination. What he accomplished is surprising; but he undertook far more, and dreamed much more even than that. However vigorous his practical faculties may have been, his poetic faculty was still stronger; it was even greater than it ought to have been in a statesman. We see greatness in him exaggerated into immensity, and immensity degenerating into madness. What aspiring, monstrous conceptions revolved, accumulated, superseded each other in that marvellous brain! "Europe," he said, "is a mole-hill; there have never been great empires or great revolutions save in the East, where there are six hundred millions of men.

In Egypt, he was thinking of conquering Syria, re-establishing the Eastern Empire at Constantinople, and returning to Paris by way of Adrianople and Vienna. The East allured him with the mirage of omnipotence; in the East he caught a glimpse of the possibility that, a new Mahomet, he might found a new religion. Confined to Europe, his dream was to re-create the empire of Charlemagne; to make Paris the physical, intellectual, and religious capital of Europe, and assemble within its precincts the princes, kings, and popes, who should have become his vassals. By way of Russia, he would then advance towards the Ganges, and the supremacy of India.

The artist enclosed within the politician has issued from his sheath; he creates in the region of the ideal and the impossible. We know him for what he is a posthumous brother of Dante and Michelangelo; only these two worked on paper and in marble; it was living man, sensitive and suffering flesh, that formed his material.

Napoleon differs from modern men in character as much as do the contemporaries of Dante and Michelangelo. The sentiments, habits, and morality professed by him are the sentiments, habits, and morality of the fifteenth century. "I am not a man like other men," he exclaimed: "the laws of morality and decorum were not made for me."

Mme. de Stäel and Stendhal compare Napoleon psychologically to the lesser tyrants of the fourteenth century—Sforza and Castruccio Castracani. Such, in fact, he was.

On the evening of the 12th Vendemiaire, being present at the preparations made by the Sections, he said to Junot, "Ah! if the Sections would only place me at their head, I would answer for it that they should be in the Tuileries within two hours, and all these wretched Conventionnels out of it!" Five hours later, being called to the assistance of Barras and the Convention, he opened fire on the Parisians, like a good *condottiere*, who does not give but lends himself to the first who offers, to the highest bidder, reserving for himself full liberty of action, and the power of seizing everything, should the occasion present itself. . . .

Never, even among the Borgias and Malatestas, was there a more sensitive and impulsive brain, capable of such electric accumulations and discharges. . . . In him, no idea remained purely speculative; each one, as it occurred, had a tendency to embody itself in action, and would have done so, if not prevented by force. . . . Sometimes the outburst was so sudden that restraint did not come in time. One day, in Egypt, he upset a decanter of water over a lady's dress, and, taking her into his own room, under the pretext of remedying the accident, remained there with her for some time—too long—while the other guests, seated around the table, waited, gazing at each other. On another occasion he threw Prince Louis violently out of the room; on yet another, he kicked Senator Volney in the stomach.

At Campo-Formio, he threw down and broke a china ornament, to put an end to the resistance of the Austrian plenipotentiary. At Dresden, in 1813, when Prince Metternich was most necessary to him, he asked him, brutally, how much he received from England for defending her interests.

Never was there a more impatient sensibility. He throws garments that do not fit him into the fire. His writing—when he tries to write—is a collection of disconnected and indecipherable characters. He dictates so quickly that his secretaries can scarcely follow him—if the pen is behindhand, so much the worse for it; if a volley of oaths and exclamations give it time to catch up, so much the better. His heart and intellect are full to overflowing; under pressure like this, the extempore orator and the excited controversialist take the place of the statesman.

"My nerves are irritable," he said of himself; and, in fact, the tension of accumulated impressions sometimes produced a physical convulsion; he was not seldom seen to shed tears under strong emotion. Napoleon wept, not on account of true and deep feeling, but because "a word—an idea by itself is a stimulus which reaches the inmost depth of his nature." Hence, certain distractions, consequent upon vomitings or fainting fits, which caused, it is said, the loss of General Vandamme's corps, after the battle of Dresden. Though the regulator is so powerful, the balance of the works is, from time to time, in danger of being deranged.

An enormous degree of strength was necessary, to co-ordinate, to guide and to dominate passions of such vitality. In Napoleon, this strength is an instinct of extraordinary force and harshness—an egoism, not inert, but active and aggressive, and so far developed as to set up in the midst of human society a colossal *I*, which can tolerate no life that is not an appendix, or instrument of its own. Even as a child, he showed the germs of this personality; he was impatient of all restraint, and had no trace of conscience; he could brook no rivals, beat those who refused to render homage to him, and then accused his victims of having beaten him.

He looks upon the world as a great banquet, open to every comer, but where, to be well served, it is necessary for a man to have long arms, help himself first, and let others take what he leaves.

"One has a hold over man through his selfish passions—fear, greed, sensuality, self-esteem, emulation. If there are some hard particles in the heap, all one has to do is to crush them." Such was the final conception arrived at by Napoleon; and nothing could induce him to change it, because this conception is conditioned by his character; he saw man as he needed to see him. His egoism is reflected in his ambition—"sc much a part of his inmost nature that he cannot distinguish it from himself; it makes his head swim. France is a mistress who is his to enjoy." In the exercise of his power he acknowledges neither intermediaries, nor rivals, nor limits, nor hindrances.

To fill his office with zeal and success is not enough for him; above and beyond the functionary, he vindicates the rights of the man. All who serve him must extinguish the critical sense in themselves; their scarcely audible whispers are a conspiracy, or an attack on his majesty. He requires of them anything and everything—from the manufacture of false Austrian and Russian banknotes in 1809 and 1812, to the preparation of an infernal machine, to blow up the Bourbons in 1814. He knows nothing of gratitude; when a man is of no further use to him as a tool, he throws him away. . . .

During a dance, he would walk about among the ladies, in order to shock them with unpleasant witticisms; he was always prying into their private life, and related to the empress herself the favours which, more or less spontaneously, they granted him.

What is still stranger, he carried the same methods of proceeding into his relations with sovereigns and ambassadors of foreign states. In his correspondence, in his proclamations, in his audiences, he provoked, threatened, challenged, offended; he divulged their real or supposed amorous intrigues (the bulletins 9, 17, 18, 19, after the battle of Jena, evidently accuse the Queen of Prussia of having had an intrigue with the Emperor Alexander), and reproaches them with a personal insult to himself, in the

> employment of such or such a man. He requires of them, in short, to modify their fundamental laws: he has but a poor opinion of a government without the power of prohibiting things which may displease foreign governments.[12]

This is the completest view of Napoleon ever given by any historian. To any one acquainted with the psychological constitution of the epileptic, it becomes clear that Taine has here given us the subtlest and precisest pathological diagnosis of a case of psychic epilepsy, with its gigantic megalomaniacal illusions, its impulses, and complete absence of moral sense.

It is not, therefore, only in moments of inspiration that genius approaches epilepsy; and the same thing may be said of St. Paul.

St. Paul[13] was of low stature, but stoutly made. His health was always poor, on account of a strange infirmity which he calls "a thorn in the flesh," and which was probably a serious neurosis.

His moral character was anomalous; naturally kind and courteous, he became ferocious when excited by passion. In the school of Gamaliel, a moderate Pharisee, he did not learn moderation; as the enthusiastic leader of the younger Pharisees, he was among the fiercest persecutors of the Christians. . . . Hearing that there was a certain

12 Hypolite Taine, "Napoleon Bonaparte", *Revue des Deux Mondes* 79 (15 February 1887) 721-752 and *Revue des Deux Mondes* 80 (1 March 1887) 5-48.

13 Ernest Renan, *Les Apôtres* (Paris: Michel Lévy Frères, 1866)

number of disciples at Damascus, he demanded of the high priest a warrant for arresting them, and left Jerusalem in a disturbed state of mind. On approaching the plain of Damascus at noon, he had a seizure, evidently of an epileptic nature, in which he fell to the ground unconscious. Soon after this, he experienced a hallucination, and saw Jesus himself, who said to him in Hebrew, "Paul, Paul, why persecutest thou me?" For three days, seized with fever, he neither ate nor drank, and saw the phantom of Ananias, whom, as head of the Christian community, he had come to arrest, making signs to him. The latter was summoned to his bed, and calm immediately returned to the spirit of Paul, who from that day forward became one of the most fervid Christians. Without desiring any more special instruction—as having received a direct revelation from Christ himself—he regarded himself as one of the apostles, and acted as such, to the enormous advantage of the Christians. The immense dangers occasioned by his haughty and arrogant spirit were compensated a thousand times over by his boldness and originality, which would not allow the Christian idea to remain within the bounds of a small association of people "poor in spirit," who would have let it die out like Hellenism, but, so to speak, steered boldly out to sea with it. At Antioch he had a hallucination similar to that of Mahomet at a later period; he felt himself rapt into the third heaven, where he heard unspeakable words, which it is not lawful for a man to utter.

Anomalies are also observable in his writings.

> He lets himself be guided by words rather than ideas; some one word which he has in his mind overpowers him and draws him off into a series of ideas very far removed from his main subject. His digressions are abrupt, the development of his ideas is suddenly cut short, his sentences are often unfinished. No writer was ever so unequal; no literature in the world presents a sublime passage like 1 Corinthians xiii., side by side with futile arguments and wearisome detail.[14]

Epilepsy in men of genius, therefore, is not an accidental phenomenon, but a true morbus totius *substantive*, to express it in medical language. Hence we gather a fresh indication of the epileptoid nature of genius.

If, as seems certain, Dostoieffsky described himself in *The Idiot*, we have another example of an epileptic genius, whose whole course of life is determined by the psychology peculiar to the epileptic—impulsivity, double personality, childishness, which goes back even to the earliest periods of human life, and alternates with a prophetic penetration, and with morbid altruism and the exaggerated affectivity of the saint. This last fact is most important, as bearing on the objection that the usual immorality of the epileptic would forbid us to connect this type with that of the saintly character. This objection, however, has been part-

14 Renan.

ly eliminated by the researches of Bianchi, Tonnini, Filippi, according to whom there are cases, though rare (16 per cent.), of epileptic patients of good character, who even manifest an exaggerated altruism, though accompanied by excessive emotionalism.[15]

Hysteria, which is closely related to epilepsy, and similarly connected with the loss of affectivity, often shows us, side by side with an exaggerated egoism, certain bursts of excessive altruism, which, at the same time, have their source in, and depend on, a degree of moral insanity, and show us the morbid phenomenon in excessive charity.

"There are some ladies," justly observes Legrand du Saulle,[16]

> who, though remaining in the world, take an ostentatious part in all the good works going on in their parish; they collect for the poor, work for the orphans, visit the sick, give alms, watch by the dead, ardently solicit the benevolence of others, and do a great deal of really helpful work, while at the same time neglecting their husbands, children, and household affairs.
>
> These women ostentatiously and noisily proclaim their benevolence. They set on foot a work of charity with as much ardour as bogus com-

15 Silvio Tonnini, *Le Epilessie* (Turin: Bocca, 1886); *Archivio di psichiatria, antropologia criminale e scienze penali per servire allo studio dell'uomo alienato e delinquente* 7 (1886).

16 Henri Legrand du Saulle, *Les hystériques: état physique et état mental, actes insolites, délictueux et criminels* (Paris: J.-B. Ballière, 1883).

pany-promoters launch a financial enterprise which is to result in hyperbolical dividends.

They go and come, in constantly increasing numbers; they instinctively act with a charming tact and delicacy, think of everything necessary to be done, whether in the midst of private mourning or public catastrophe, and affect to blush on receiving tributes of admiration from grateful sufferers, or deeply moved spectators. . . . Their ready tact and sympathy are surprising, and the greater the trouble, the more admirably do they seem to rise to the occasion—while the paroxysm lasts. When their feelings are calmed, the benevolent impulse passes away; being essentially mobile and spasmodic, they cannot do good deliberately and on reflection.

The "charitable hysteric" is capable of achieving feats of courage which have been quoted and repeated, and even become legendary.

They have been known to show extraordinary presence of mind, resource, and courage in saving the inmates of a burning house, or in facing an armed mob during a riot. If questioned on the following day, these heroines will be found in a state of complete prostration; and some of them candidly avow that they do not know what they have done, and were at the time unconscious of danger.

At a time of cholera epidemic, when fear causes such ill-advised and reprehensible derelictions of duty, hysterical women have been known to show an extraordinary devotion; nothing is repugnant to them, nothing revolts their modesty or wearies out their endurance. . . .

For such persons, devotion to others has be-

> come a need, a necessary expenditure of energy, and, without knowing it, they pathologically play the part of virtue. People in general are taken in by it, and, for the sake of example, it is just as well. It was this consideration which induced me to ask and obtain a public acknowledgment of the services of a hysterical patient—at one time an inmate of a lunatic asylum—whose deeds of charity in the district where she lives are truly touching. While constantly active in attendance on the sick, and spending liberally on their behalf, she confines her personal expenditure to what is strictly necessary, her dress being the same at all seasons of the year. Now this lady shows a great variety of hysterical symptoms, becomes intensely excited on the slightest occasion, sleeps very badly, and is a serious invalid.
>
> Lastly, in private sorrows, the hysteric patient often departs from the normal manifestations of grief. At the loss of her children, she remains calm, serene, resigned; does not shed a tear, thinks of everything that ought to be done, gives numerous orders, forgets none of the most painful details, imposes on all around her the most dignified attitude, and attends the funeral without breaking down. People think that this mother is exceptionally gifted, and has a courage superior to others. This is a mistake; she is weaker than they—she is "suffering from disease."

In order fully to grasp the seeming paradoxes contained in these conclusions, we must remember that many philanthropists love their neighbours, but only at a distance, and nearly always at the expense of the more physiological, more general, affections love for their family, their country, &c. We must remember Dostoyevsky's remark (in *The Brothers Karamanzov*, i. p. 325) that "What one can love in one's fellow is a hidden and invisible man; as soon as he shows his face, love disappears. One can love one's fellow-men in spirit, but only at a distance; never close at hand." One also recalls Sterne, who was overcome with emotion at the sight of a dead ass, and deserted his wife and his mother.

The greatest philanthropists—such men as Beccaria and Howard—have been harsh fathers and masters; even the Divine Philanthropist was, as we have seen, hard towards his own family.[17]

St. Paul, before his conversion, distinguished himself by his vehement and cruel persecution of the Christians.

It is well known how, only too often, the man of real and fervent religion has to forget his family and make a duty of celibacy and hatred to the other sex. Thus St. Liberata was angry with her husband for weeping at parting from their children; and, according to the legend, the mother of Baruch replied to her son when, during his martyrdom, he implored her for water in his anguish, "Thou shouldst desire no water now save that of heaven."[18]

17 Julien Vinson, *Les religions actuelles* (Paris: Adrien Delahaye et Émile Lecrosnier, 1888) [Corrected year of publication from 1884. —Ed.]; Luke ii.49; Matt. xii.48; Mark iii.33.

18 Anfosso, *La légende religieuse au moyen-âge* (1887).

These cases, moreover, show that, very often, exaggerated altruism is itself only a pathological phenomenon, a hypertrophy of sentiment accompanied—as always happens in cases of hypertrophy—by loss and atrophy in other directions.[19]

We have seen in Juan de Dios, in Lazzaretti, Loyola, and St. Francis, of Assisi, saintliness showing itself, in true psychic polarization, as a perfect contrast to their former life in which the tendency to evil was strongly pronounced.

If we add to these phenomena, so frequent in epileptic and hysteric patients, all those others, of clairvoyance, thought-transference, transposition of the senses, fakirism, mental vision, temporary manifestations of genius, and monoideism, so frequently observed in these maladies, phenomena so strange that many scientists, unable to explain, endeavour to deny them, we can demonstrate the hysterical character of saintliness, even in its least explicable manifestations—those of miracles.[20]

---

19 On altruism in moral insanity and epilepsy, see *L'Uomo Delinquente*, pp. 556, 557. We have seen St. Francis love even the stars, the water, tne fire, &c., and—abandon his family!

20 Cesare Lombroso, *Studi sull'ipnotismo, con ricerche oftalmoscopiche del prof. Reymond e dei professori Bianchi e Sommer sulla polarizzazione psichica*, 3d ed. (Torino, Fratelli Bocca, 1887); Étiene Eugène Azam, *Hypnotisme, double conscience et altérations de la personnalité: le cas Félida X* (Paris: J.-B. Ballière, 1887); Henry Beaunis, *Le somnambulisme provoqué: études physiologiques et psychologiques* (Paris: J.-B. Ballière et fils, 1887); "Un fait de suggestion mentale", *Revue philosophique de la France et de l'étranger* 21 (1886) 204; Drs. H. Bourru and F. Burot, Dugay, Richet, Janet, *Re-*

vue Philosophique (1884-89); Krafft-Ebing, *Ueber den Hypnotismus*, 1889; Ernő Jendrassik, "Einiges über Suggestion", *Neurologisches Zentralblatt* 7 (1888) 321–330.; Alfred Binet and Charles Féré, "La polarisation psychique", *Revue Philosophique de la France et de l'Etranger* 19 (April 1885) 369-402; Alfred Binet and Charles Féré, *Le magnetisme animal* (Paris: Alcan, 1887); George M. Beard, *Nature and Phenomena of Trance* (New York, W. Wood & Company, 1880); Cesare Lombroso and Salvatore Ottolenghi, *Nuovi studi sull'ipnotismo e sulla credulità* (Turin: Stamperia dell'unione tipografico-editrice, 1889); and A. Grimaldi e R. Fronda, *Trasmissione del pensiero e suggestione mentale: studio sperimentale e critico di seguito da alcune indagini fatte sullo stesso soggetto a richiesta del prof. Cesare Lombroso* (Napoli: Luigi Pierro, 1891). [The original footnote has as the title 'Sulla transmission del pensiero', but that does not match any source I found find. This, though by another author, seems the closest match. A source by Lombroso would be Cesare Lombroso on the topic would be, "Pickman e la trasmissione del pensiero", *Gazzetta letteraria* (22 e 29 March 1890). —Ed.]

CHAPTER IV

Sane Men of Genius

Their unperceived defects — Richelieu — Sesostris — Foscolo — Michelangelo — Darwin

But a graver objection is that afforded by those few men of genius who have completed their intellectual orbit without aberration, neither depressed by misfortune nor thrown out of their course by madness.

Such have been Galileo, Leonardo da Vinci, Voltaire, Machiavelli, Michelangelo, Darwin. Each one of these showed, by the ample volume and at the same time the symmetrical proportion of the skull, force of intellect restrained by the calm of the desires. Not one of them allowed his great passion for truth and beauty to stifle the love of family and country. They never changed their faith or character, never swerved from their aim, never left their work half completed. What assurance, what faith, what ability they showed in their undertakings; and, above all, what moderation and unity of character they preserved in their lives! Though they, too, had to experience—after undergoing the sublime paroxysm of inspiration—the torture inflicted by ignorant hatred, and the discomfort of uncertainty and exhaustion, they never, on that account, deviated from the straight road. They carried out to the end the one cherished idea which formed the aim and purpose of their lives, calm and serene, never complaining of obstacles, and falling into but a few mistakes—mistakes which, in lesser men, might even have passed for discoveries.

But I have already answered, in the opening pages of this book, the objection furnished by these rare exceptions, pointing out that epilepsy and moral insanity (which is its first variety) often pass unobserved, not only in distinguished men, the prestige of whose name and work dazzles our judgment, and prevents our discerning them, but in those criminals to whom such researches might at least restore self-respect, by depriving them of all responsibility.

Who, but for the revelations of some of his intimate friends, would have suspected that Cavour was repeatedly subject to attacks of suicidal mania, or thought that Richelieu was epileptic? No one would have paid any attention to the morbid impulsiveness of Foscolo, or recorded it as a symptom, if Davis had not examined his skull after death. Who could make any assertion with regard to the moral sense of Sesostris? Yet, as Arvède Barine justly remarks,[1] his skull completely corresponds to the criminal type. The low and narrow forehead, prominent superciliary arch, thick eyebrows, eyes set close together, long, narrow, aquiline nose, hollow temples, projecting cheek-bones, strong jaws; the expression not intelligent, but animal, fierce, proud, and majestic; the head small in proportion to the body, are all so many indications of the most complete absence of moral sense.

In all the biographies of Michelangelo we do not discover one spot on that gentle and yet robust soul, who trembled for the sorrows of his country as at the expression of beauty. But the publication of his letters,[2] and the keen researches of Parlagreco,[3] have revealed physical anomalies never before suspected.

One of the most important is his complete indifference to women. This may be observed in his works, and his masterpieces were all masculine—Moses, Lorenzo, Giuliano de' Medici, &c. He never used, it appears, the living female model, though he made use of corpses; his Bacchante is a virago with masculine muscles, unformed breasts and no

1 *Revue Lettéraire* (1887).

2 Gaetano Milanesi, *Le lettere di Michelangelo Buonarroti : pubblicate coi ricordi ed i contratti artistici* (Florence: Coi tipi dei successori le Monnier, 1875).

3 Carlo Parlagreco, *Michelangelo Buonarotti* (Naples: Fratelli Orfeo, 1888).

feminine touch. In his many love sonnets, written rather to follow the prevailing fashion than from any true inspiration of passion, none bear the mark of being addressed to real women; only fourteen times, it is said, does the word "donna" occur. On the other hand, in the Barbera Collection, Sonnets xviii. and xii. show a very marked admiration for the male, and Varchi considers that these are addressed to Cavalieri who was of great physical beauty. There are in existence two of his letters addressed to Cavalieri (July 28, 1523, and July 28, 1532), which seem to be written to a mistress, and in which, humiliating himself, he swears that, if banished from the other's heart, he will die. There is a similar letter written to Angelini.

This moral anomaly, which he would share with many artists, Cellini, Sodoma, &c., is not the only one met with. "In his letters," writes Parlagreco,

> may be seen constant contradictions between ideas that are great and generous, and others that are puerile; between will and speech; between thought and action; extreme irritability, inconstant affection, great activity in doing good, sudden sympathies, great outbursts of enthusiasm, great fears, sometimes unconsciousness of his own actions, marvellous modesty in the field of art, unreasonable vanity in the appearances of life—these are the various psychical manifestations in the life of Buonarroti which lead me to believe that the great artist was affected by a neuropathic condition bordering on hysteria.

Every day in his old age he discovered some sin in his past life, and he sent money to Florence for masses to be said and for alms to the poor, and to enable poor girls to be married, and, which is stranger, to be made nuns. All this was to gain Paradise (Lett. 187, 214, 240, 330), to save his soul—he who had said: "It is not strange that the monks should spoil a chapel [at the Vatican], since they have known how to spoil the whole world."

At some moments he feels that his conscience is clean and then he desires to die, so that he may not fall back into evil; but then his discouragement returns, and he believes (strange blasphemy), that it was a sin to have been born an artist.

> *Conosco di quant' era d'error carca*
> *L'aflettuosa fantasia*
> *Che* l'arte *mi fece idolo e monarca. . .*
> *Le parole del mondo mi hanno tolto*
> *II tempo dato a contemplar Iddio.*

And he believes himself destined by God to a long life simply that he may complete the fabric of St. Peter's.

In old age he who had shown so little vanity where his work was concerned, and so much modesty in speaking of it, went about studying how he could best exhibit the nobility of his descent, claiming to trace it in a direct line from the Counts of Canossa, a claim which, even if valid, would not be worth a finger of his Moses.

Michelangelo tenderly loved his father and

brother and nephews, and enabled them to live in easy circumstances; yet in his letters to them he frequently shows himself suspicious and treats them unjustly. In 1544, he fell seriously ill at Rome. His nephew naturally hastened to his bedside. Michelangelo became very angry and wrote: "You are come to kill me and to see what I leave behind. . . . Know that I have made my will and that there is nothing here for you to think about. Therefore, go in peace and do not write to me more." Three months after he changed his tone. "I will not fail in what I have often thought about, that is, in helping you." He has himself left a confession of his almost morbid melancholy in a letter (97), to Sebastiano del Piombo: "Yesterday evening I was happy because I escaped from my mad and melancholy humour."

Without the recent biographical and autobiographical notes published by his son,[4] no one could have imagined that Darwin, a model father and citizen, so self-controlled and even so free from vanity, was a neuropath. His son tells us that for forty years he never enjoyed twenty-four hours of health like other men. Of the eight years devoted to the study of the cirripedes, two, as he himself writes, were lost through illness. Like all neuropaths he could bear neither heat nor cold; half an hour of conversation beyond his habitual time was suffi-

4 Francis Darwin, *The Life and Letters of Charles Darwin, Including an Autobiographical Chapter* (London: John Murray, 1887).

cient to cause insomnia and hinder his work on the following day. He suffered also from dyspepsia, from spinal anæmia and giddiness (which last is known to be frequently the equivalent of epilepsy); and he could not work more than three hours a day. He had curious crotchets. Finding that eating sweets made him ill, he resolved not to touch them again, but was unable to keep his resolution, unless he had repeated it aloud. He had a strange passion for paper—writing the rough drafts of his correspondence on the back of proof-sheets, and of the most important MSS. which were thus rendered difficult to decipher. He often instituted what he himself called "fool's experiments"—*e.g.*, having a bassoon played close to the cotyledons of a plant.[5] When about to make an experiment, he seemed to be urged on by some inward force. From a morbid dislike to novelty, he used the millimetric tables of an old book which he knew to be inaccurate, but to which he was accustomed. He would not change his old chemical balance though aware that it was untrustworthy; he refused to believe in hypnotism, and also, at first, in the discovery of prehistoric stone weapons.[6] He frequently, says his daughter, inverted his sentences, both in speaking and writing, and had a difficulty in pronouncing some letters, especially *w*. Like Skoda,

5 Francis Darwin, *The Life and Letters of Charles Darwin, Including an Autobiographical Chapter* (London: John Murray, 1887) 1:149.

6 Ibid., vol. 1.

Rockitanski, and Socrates, he had a short snub nose, and his ears were large and long. Nor were degenerative characteristics wanting among his ancestors. It is true that he reckoned among them several men of intellect and almost of genius, such as Robert (1682), a botanist and intelligent observer; and Edward, author of a *Gamekeeper's Manual*, full of acute observations on animals. His father had great powers of observation; but his paternal grandfather, Erasmus—poet and naturalist at the same time—had a passionate temper and an impediment in his speech. One of his sons, Charles, a poet and collector, resembled him in this respect. Finally, another uncle, Erasmus, a man of some intellect, a numismatist and statistician, ended by madness and suicide.

It might be objected that the fact of such different forms of psychosis—melancholy, moral insanity, monomania—being found either complete or undeveloped in men of genius, excludes the special psychosis of genius, and still more that of epilepsy. But it may be answered that recent research, which has enlarged the domain of epilepsy, has also demonstrated that, apart from impulsive and hallucinatory delusions, epilepsy may be superadded to any form of mental alienation, especially megalomania and moral insanity. And, as is the case in nearly all degenerative psychoses, undeveloped forms of mental disease, and recurring multiform delusions brought on by the most trivial causes, especially predominate in epilepsy.

CHAPTER V

Conclusions

Between the physiology of the man of genius, therefore, and the pathology of the insane, there are many points of coincidence; there is even actual continuity. This fact explains the frequent occurrence of madmen of genius, and men of genius who have become insane, having, it is true, characteristics special to themselves, but capable of being resolved into exaggerations of those of genius pure and simple. The frequency of delusions in their multiform characters of degenerative characteristics, of the loss of affectivity, of heredity, more particularly in the children of inebriate, imbecile, idiotic, or epileptic parents, and, above all, the peculiar character of inspiration, show that genius is a degenerative psychosis of the epileptoid group. This supposition is confirmed by the frequency of a temporary manifestation of genius in the insane, and by the new group of mattoids to whom disease gives all the semblance of genius, without its substance.

What I have hitherto written may, I hope (while remaining within the limits of psychological observation), afford an experimental starting-point for a criticism of artistic and literary, sometimes also of scientific, creations.

Thus, in the fine arts, exaggerated minuteness of detail, the abuse of symbols, inscriptions, or accessories, a preference for some one particular colour, an unrestrained passion for mere novelty, may approach the morbid symptoms of mattoidism. Just so, in literature and science, a tendency to puns and plays upon words, an excessive fondness for systems, a tendency to speak of one's self, and substitute epigram for logic, an extreme predilection for the rhythm and assonances of verse in prose writing, even an exaggerated degree of originality may be considered as morbid phenomena. So also is the mania of writing in Biblical form, in detached verses, and with special favourite words, which are underlined, or repeated many times, and a certain graphic symbolism. Here I must acknowledge that, when I see how many of the organs which claim to direct public opinion are infected with this tendency, and how often young writers undertake to discuss grave social problems in the capricious phraseology of the lunatic asylum, and the disjointed periods of Biblical times, as though our robust lungs were unable to cope with the vigorous and manly inspirations of the Latin construction, I feel grave apprehensions for the future of the rising generation.

On the other hand, the analogy of mattoids with genius, whose morbid phenomena only are inherited by them, and with sane persons, with whom they have shrewdness and practical sense in common, ought to put students on their guard against certain systems, springing up by hundreds, more particularly in the abstract or inexact sciences, and due to the efforts of men incompetent, from a lack either of capacity or knowledge of the subject, to deal with them. In these systems declamation, assonances, paradoxes, and conceptions often original, but always incomplete and contradictory, take the place of calm reasoning based on a minute and unprejudiced study of facts. Such books are nearly always the work of those true though involuntary charlatans, the mattoids, who are more widely diffused in the literary world than is commonly" supposed.

Nor is it only students who should be on their guard against them, but especially politicians. Not that, in an age of free criticism like our own, there is any danger that these pretended reformers, who are stimulated and guided solely by mental disease, should be taken seriously; but the obstacles justly opposed to them may, by irritating, sharpen and complete their insanity, transforming a harmless delusion—whether ideological, as in the case of most mattoids, or sensorial, as in monomaniacs—into active madness, in which their greater intellectual power, the depth and tenacity of their convictions, and that very excess of altruism which compels them to occupy themselves with public affairs, render them more dangerous, and more inclined to rebellion and regicide, than other insane persons.

When we reflect that, on the other hand, a genuine lunatic may give proof of temporary genius, a phenomenon calculated to inspire the populace with an astonishment which soon produces veneration, we find a solid argument against those jurists and judges who, from the soundness and activity of the intellect, infer complete moral responsibility, to the total exclusion of the possibility of insanity. We also see our way to an interpretation of the mystery of genius, its contradictions, and those of its mistakes which any ordinary man would have avoided. And we can explain to ourselves how it is that madmen or mattoids, even with little or no genius (Passanante, Lazzaretti, Drabicius, Fourier, Fox), have been able to excite the populace, and sometimes even to bring about serious political revolutions. Better still shall we understand how those who were at once men of genius and insane (Mahomet, Luther, Savonarola, Schopenhauer), could—despising and overcoming obstacles which would have dismayed any cool and deliberate mind—hasten by whole centuries the unfolding of truth; and how such men have originated nearly all the religions, and certainly all the sects, which have agitated the world.

The frequency of genius among lunatics and of madmen among men of genius, explains the fact that the destiny of nations has often been in the hands of the insane; and shows how the latter have been able to contribute so much to the progress of mankind.

In short, by these analogies, and coincidences between the phenomena of genius and mental aberration, it seems as though nature had intended to teach us respect for the supreme misfortunes of insanity; and also to preserve us from being dazzled by the brilliancy of those men of genius who might well be compared, not to the planets which keep their appointed orbits, but to falling stars, lost and dispersed over the crust of the earth.

Appendix

The following letter was written by a druggist confined in the Asylum of Sainte-Anne:—

Sainte-Anne, le 26 février 1880.

MADAME,

Veuillez agréer l'hommage
De ce modeste sonnet
Et le tenir comme un gage
De mon sincère respect.

SONNET.

Souvenez-vous, reine des dieux,

Vierge des vierges, notre mère,
Que vous êtes sur cette terre
L'ange gardien mysterieux.

The same man addressed to M. Magnan a long poem on a dramatic representation accompanied by the following graceful envoi:—

VÉNÉRÉ DOCTEUR,

L'estime et la reconnaissance
Sont la seule monnaie du cœur
Dont votre pauvre serviteur
Dispose pour la récompense
Qu'il doit a vos soins pleins d'honneur.
Recevez done cet humble hommage,
Docteur admiré, révéré,
Et j'ajouterai bien-aime',
Si vous vouliez tenir pour gage
Qu'en cela du moins J'AI PAYE.

The following lines are from a long satirical poem by a writer who appears to have cherished much less respect for his physician. He believed that he had been changed into a beast, and recognised a colleague in every horse or donkey he met. He wished to browse in every field, and only refrained from doing so out of consideration for his friends:—

Les medicastres sans vergogne
Qui changent en sale besogne
Le plus sublime des mandats,
Ces infâmes aliénistes,

Oui, reconnus pour moralistes,
Sont les pires des scélérats!
Ils detruisent les écritures
Pour maintenir les impostures
Des ennemis du bien public.
Ils prostituent leur justice
Pour se gorger du bénéfice
De leur satanique trafic.

The author of the following lines on the same day made an attempt at suicide, and then a homicidal attack on his mother.

À MONSIEUR LE DOCTEUR C.

ÉPITRE (13 mat 1887).

Un docteur éminent sollicite ma muse.
Certes l'honneur est grand; mais le docteur s'amuse,
Car, dans ce noir séjour, le poète attristé
Par le souffle divin n'est guere visité. . . .
Faire des vers ici, quelle rude besogne!
On pourra m'objecter que jadis, en Gascogne,
Les rayons eclatants d'un soleil du Midi
Réveillaient quelquefois mon esprit engourdi;
II est vrai: dans Bordeaux, cité fière et polie,
J'ai fêté le bon vin, j'ai chanté la folie,
Celle bien entendu qui porte des grelots.
Mais depuis, un destin fatal à mon repos
M'exile loin des bords de la belle Gironde,
Qu'enrichissent les vins les plus fameux du monde!
Aussi plus de chansons, de madrigaux coquets!
Plus de sonnets savants, de bacchiques couplets!
Ma muse tout en pleurs a replié ses ailes,
Comme un ange banni des sphères éternelles!

Dans sa cage enfermé l'oiseau n'a plus de voix. . . .
Hélas! je ne suis point le rossignol des bois,
Pas même le pinson, pas même la fauvette;
Vous me flattez, docteur, en m'appelant poète. . . .
Je ne suis qu'un méchant rimeur, et je ne sais
Si ces alexandrins auront un grand succès. . . .
Cependant mon désir est de vous satisfaire;
Votre estime m'honore et je voudrais vous plaire,
Mais Pégase est rétif quand il est enchainé;
D'un captif en naissant le vers meurt condamné.
Si vous voulez, docteur, que ma muse renaisse,
Je ne vous dirai pas: renclez-moi ma jeunesse.
Non, mais puisque vos soins m'ont rendu la santé,
Ne pourriez-vous me rendre aussi la liberté?
Des vers! Pour que le ciel au poète en envoie
Que faut-il? le grand air, le soleil et la joie!
Accordez-moi ces biens: mon luth reconnaissant,
Pour vous remercier comme un Dieu bienfaisant,
Peut-être trouvera, de mon cœur interprète,
Des chants dignes de vous, et dignes d'un poète!

The following lines well express the solitary sadness of the melancholiac:—

A SE STESSO.

E con chi l'hai?
Con tutti e con nessuno,
L'ho con il cielo, che si tinge a bruno,
L'ho con il metro, che non rende i lai,
Che mi rodono il petto.
Nell'odio altrui, nel mal comun mi godo.

And these are of marvellous delicacy and truth:—

TIPO FISICO-MORALE DI P. L.

QUI RECOVERATO.

Al primo aspetto
Chi ti vede, saria
Costretto a dir che a te manca l'affetto;
E male s'apporria;
Che invece spesse fiate,
Sotto ruvido vel, palpitan lene
L'anime innamorate
Che s'accendon, riscaldansi nel bene.
Così rosa dal petalo
Invisibile quasi
Mette l'effluvio dai raccolti vasi,
Come dal gelsomino,
E i delicati odor dell'amorino;
Nemico a tutti i giuochi,
Di Venere, di Bacco indarno i fuochi
Ti soffiano; la cute
E di tal forza che sembrano mute
Le vezzose lusinghe. . . Sei di pietra,
E invano a darti il fiato spira l'etra.

M.S.

The following little piece is a masterpiece of insane poetry:—

A UN UCCELLO DEL CORTILE.

Da un virgulto ad uno scoglio
Da uno scoglio a una collina,
L'ala tua va pellegrina

Voli o posi a notte e dì.

Noi confitti al nostro orgoglio,
Come ruote in ferrei perni,
Ci stanchiamo in giri eterni,
Sempre errand e sempre qui!

CAVALIERE Y.

Index

Æ

A

B

C

G

H

I

J

K

L

M

N

O

P

S

U

V

W

Z

www.ingramcontent.com/pod-product-compliance
Lightning Source LLC
LaVergne TN
LVHW091513200926
848483LV00007B/456/J
* 9 7 8 1 9 9 9 3 5 7 3 9 9 *